WOODY ALLEN ON LOCATION

Books by Thierry de Navacelle

Tay Garnett's UN SIÈCLE DE CINÉMA

SUBLIME MARLENE

VINCENTE MINNELLI

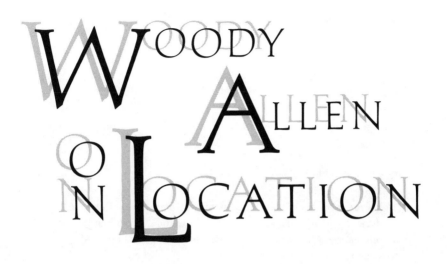

Woody Allen on Location

Thierry de Navacelle

WILLIAM MORROW AND COMPANY, INC.

NEW YORK

Library of Congress Cataloging-in-Publication Data

Navacelle, Thierry de.
   Woody Allen on location.

   Includes index.
   1. Radio days.   2. Allen, Woody.   I. Title.
PN1997.R2183   1987   791.43'72   86-31138
ISBN 0-688-06643-7

Printed in the United States of America

First Edition

1 2 3 4 5 6 7 8 9 10

BOOK DESIGN BY MARIA EPES

To *François Truffaut*

ACKNOWLEDGMENTS

I FIRST WANT to thank Woody Allen. Needless to say, this project could not have existed without him. Credit for the good things in the book should go to him; responsibility for its weaknesses is mine. Throughout the nine months I worked on this book, one of the things that made me hang on was my growing respect for him as an individual—in addition to the respect I already had for his work.

Another person without whom this would have been difficult is Carter Crocker. He not only cleaned and dressed my poor English but got involved in the project, giving me needed feedback.

My special gratitude goes to photographer Brian Hamill for his superb pictures, which appear throughout the book and on the front and back of the jacket.

The Gramont family, Laure and Guy, have also been very helpful, especially Laure, who was the first one to believe in the project. Thanks, too, to Amy Vardala.

I am extremely grateful as well to all the cast and crew of *Radio Days*; they made me feel part of it. And a special thanks to Jane Read Martin, who always handled her role of go-between very nicely, even in the most delicate situations.

The encouragement of Lisa Drew, my editor, and of Ken Sherman, my agent, were also essential.

CONTENTS

INTRODUCTION

THIS IS THE STORY of the shooting of Woody Allen's *Radio Days*. It is also the story of a unique and wonderful experience, observing, over a four-month period, the work of one of the most private and talented directors in the world.

The first days of shooting, I was overwhelmed. How should I proceed? Where should I start? What would people like to know? What is important? I was forever living with the fear of not being equal to the situation, with a man who, as Grandpa says, "is always thinking!"* Why didn't I choose Sylvester Stallone?

Quickly I decided to take notes on everything, even the smallest details, always mechanically, without thinking too much. As Roger says, "The trick is not to panic." ** Day after day, as I was more and more taken by the atmosphere of the shooting, the story, and Woody Allen's complexity, the book took shape and built itself. I became totally entranced by the humor and the richness of the story and by the warmth of its characters. I was so involved it became difficult to make the distinction between what was happening in the film and what was happening around it. I started to dream about Miss Gordon, to be shocked by the Communist's lack of respect, to be jealous of Bea's dates, and to "explode

*See page 293, 4:15 P.M.
**See page 273, 7:30 P.M., Shot 68A.

with desire" for Sally. To keep track of reality, I made daily notes from the newspapers about what was happening in Manhattan and in the world. This book is the result of my unique journey.

For each of his films, Woody Allen proceeds the same way: a first shooting of about two to four months; a first editing period of approximately one and a half months, from which he obtains a rough cut; then a reshoot for three to four weeks, depending on what he needs. About a month after that, he has a final cut.

This book tells the story as it was in the script, how Woody Allen filmed it, and how he molded it into the final film. It also contains a day-by-day diary of the two shootings, from November 5, 1985, to February 19, 1986, and the reshoot from April 25 to May 9, 1986.

Finally, I want to make an announcement that should please Woody's fans: Woody Allen is going to live forever. It happened the other evening at Michael's Pub, where he goes to play clarinet every Monday. A biologist from Massachusetts approached him with a proposition. All Woody had to do was send him a piece of his skin, the man said, and through the miracles of modern science he could guarantee Woody immortality.

Woody, just to be on the safe side, took his address.

—Los Angeles, July 1986

"At least a hundred times during the shooting I was asked, 'But aren't you afraid of "demystifying" (demythifying, one might almost say!) a craft you love so much?' I answer each time with a question of my own: An aviator can easily explain all he knows about piloting a plane—and will he ever succeed in 'demystifying' the intoxicating rapture of flying? Moviemaking is a marvelous business, a wonderful craft. If anyone still needs proof of that, let him consider how of all those who have the good fortune to work in films not one ever wishes to do anything else! You may have heard of the great circus impresario who, having gone bankrupt, ended up taking care of an acrobatic elephant who continually kicked him in the ass and who daily pissed in his face. One of the impresario's old friends, shocked at seeing the man fallen so low, berated him: 'You have a university degree and there's nothing you don't know about accounting! Why don't you get yourself a wonderful position in business administration?' To which the impresario answered: 'What? And leave show business?' "

—FRANÇOIS TRUFFAUT in *Day for Night*
The Complete Script of the Film by François Truffaut
New York: Grove Press, Inc., 1975
Paris: Editions Seguers, 1974.

CAST OF PRINCIPAL CHARACTERS

(in alphabetical order)

CAST

BELOW ARE THE MAIN CHARACTERS from the cast, those with recurring roles in the drama. A more complete listing of credits may be found in the Appendix.

ABE (Josh Mostel): Little Joe's uncle, Ceil's husband, and Ruthie's father. His favorite radio show is *Bill Kern's Favorite Sports Legends* (sequence 84). Josh is Zero Mostel's son.

ABERCROMBIE, THOMAS (Martin Sherman): Radio personality, host of *The Court of Human Emotions* (sequence 97), Mom and Pop's favorite show.

ANDREW (Fletcher Previn): One of Little Joe's gang. Fletcher is the son of Mia Farrow and André Previn.

BAXTER, BIFF (Jeff Daniels): Radio personality, star of *Biff Baxter, G-Man* (sequence 121), and one of Little Joe's heroes.

BEA (Dianne Wiest): Little Joe's aunt, Mom's sister.

BIG MAN (Dennis Vestunis): Nick Norris's huge "Oriental" assistant (sequence 42).

BIGOT, THE (George Hamlin): One of the people interviewed on the street after the declaration of war (sequence 111).

BROADWAY STAR, THE: *see* SINGER 2.

MR. BROOKS (Mark Hammond): Another man interviewed on the street after the declaration of war (sequence 111).

BURGLARS, THE (Mike Starr and Paul Herman): The two burglars who win *Guess that Tune* while robbing the Needlemans' house (sequence 74).

BURT (Sal Tuminello): One of Little Joe's gang.

CEIL (Renee Lippin): Little Joe's aunt, Mom's sister, Abe's wife, Ruthie's mother. Her favorite radio show is *The Famous Ventriloquist* (sequence 96).

CHARLES, MONICA (Diane Keaton): Sings "You'd Be So Nice to Come Home to" in the King Cole Room on New Year's Eve (sequence 175).

CHESTER (Jimmy Sabat): Bea's date, the one who takes her and Little Joe to Radio City Music Hall (sequence F102). Sabat is also sound mixer on the film.

COMMUNIST NEIGHBOR, THE (Larry David): Lives in the house next door to Little Joe's. Doris's father. He creates an uproar when he plays his radio on Yom Kippur (sequence 76).

COMMUNIST'S DAUGHTER, THE: *see* Doris.

COMMUNIST'S SON, THE (Louis T. Granirer): A sometimes member of Little Joe's gang.

COOPER FAMILY, THE: Mrs. Cooper (Alice Beardsley), Mr. Cooper, and Eunice (Joanne Dillon) have their own amateur radio show (sequence 41).

CROONER, THE (Todd Field): Makes Ruthie swoon when he sings "All or Nothing At All" (sequence 12).

DAVE (Maurice Toueg); A member of Little Joe's gang.

MR. DAVIS (Peter Castellotti): Owner of the El Morocco, killed by Rocco.

DORIS (Rebecca Schaeffer): The Communist's daughter, believes in free love. She is responsible for Mrs. Silverman's stroke, and for Abe's interest in Marxism.

DORIS, THE SPONSOR'S WIFE (Hannah Rabinowitz): Wife

of the sponsor of the "Get Regular with Re-Lax." commercial (sequence 142). She doesn't like Sally.

DRAGONETTE, JESSICA (Molly Regan): Radio personality. She sings "Italian Street Song" (sequence 43).

EFFECTS ACTOR (John Rothman): The actor in *The Sound Effects Studio Show* (sequence 45). During the reshoot, Rothman was replaced by Steve Mittelman (Herbie Hanson). He became one of the actors in the Chekhov radio show.

EFFECTS ACTRESS (Wendy Coates): Actress in *The Sound Effects Studio Show* (sequence 45). She survived all the reshoots but the entire sequence was cut in the end.

EUNICE: *see* COOPER FAMILY, THE.

FIREMAN REILLY (Frank O'Brien): The fireman who tries to save Polly Phelps (sequence 163).

FOXX, CARLETON (Michael Murray): The newsman covering the Tonino episode.

FRED (Robert Joy): One of Bea's dates, the "effeminate" one, on whom Bea has a crush (sequence 113).

GAIL (Victoria Kennedy): A friend of Roger and Irene, joins their table in the King Cole Room (sequence 60).

MR. GLOBUS (Martin Chatinover): One of the men interviewed on the street after the declaration of war (sequence 111).

MRS. GLOBUS (Armellia McQueen): Wife of Mr. Globus, also interviewed on the street.

GORDON, MISS (Sydney A. Blake): The woman who Little Joe and his pals see naked through the window (sequence 124), also their substitute teacher (sequence 134).

GRANDMA (Leah Carrey): Little Joe's grandmother, mother of the three sisters: Mom, Ceil, and Bea.

GRANDPA (William Magerman): Little Joe's grandfather, father of the three sisters: Mom, Ceil, and Bea.

HANSON, HERBIE (Steve Mittelman): Radio personality, star of *The Herbie Hanson Show* (sequence 106), a sequence that was cut. During the reshoot Mittelman was cast as the new Effects Actor, but that sequence was also cut.

HARRIS, MAX (Marc Goodson): Part of the Jackhammers' dream; they meet him at a party for the beautiful people (sequence 19).

IRENE (Julie Kurnitz): Roger's wife, co-host of *Breakfast with Irene and Roger.*

MR. AND MRS. JACKHAMMER (Irving Selbst and Hope Sacharoff): They listen to *Breakfast with Irene and Roger* over their morning meal (sequence 18).

JESSICA (Janet Frank): Tom's wife. She's at Roger and Irene's table in the King Cole Room (sequence 63).

KERN, BILL (Guy Le Bow): Radio personality, host of *Bill Kern's Favorite Sports Legends* (sequence 84), Abe's favorite show.

KITTY (Kitty Carlisle Hart): After trying two other singers, Woody chose her to sing "I'll Be Seeing You" and "They're Either Too Young or Too Old." An actress and singer of the period, she might well have sung the songs.

KYLE, KIRBY (Brian Mannain): The baseball player who had heart, his story is told on *Bill Kern's Favorite Sports Legends* (sequence 86). Mannain is also a production assistant on the film.

LITTLE ARNOLD (David Mosberg): He brings the contraceptive he found in his parents' room to Show and Tell (sequence 35).

LITTLE EVELYN (Rebecca Nickels): The girl Little Joe liked but who didn't like Little Joe (sequence B102).

LITTLE JOE (Seth Green).

LITTLE LINDA (Natane Adcock): The "pretty girl" who liked Little Joe but whom Little Joe didn't like (sequence B102).

LITTLE PHIL (Josh Saviano): He has his shirt burned by Little Joe in Hebrew class (sequence 22).

LITTLE ROSS (Ross Morgenstern): Shows his Masked Avenger secret-compartment ring to class during Show and Tell (sequence 35).

MAMA (Gina DeAngelis): Rocco's mother.

MANULIS, SIDNEY (Andrew Clark): One of Bea's dates (sequence 50).

MARTIN: Pop's first name.

MASKED AVENGER (Wallace Shawn): Radio personality, one of Little Joe's heroes.

MAX (Tony Roberts): Radio personality, emcee of *The Silver Dollar Jackpot* (sequence 160). Since working together on *Annie Hall*, Tony Roberts and Woody call each other "Max."

MOM (Julie Kavner): Little Joe's mother.

NATHAN: Grandpa's first name.

MR. AND MRS. NEEDLEMAN (Martin Rosenblatt and Helen Miller): They are robbed while at the movies, but get a truckful of gifts that the burglars won for them on *Guess That Tune* (sequence 70).

NICK (Oliver Block): One of Little Joe's gang.

NORRIS, NICK (Ronald Leir): Radio personality, star of *Nick Norris—Private Detective* (sequence 42). Nick Norris became the new Reba Man during the reshoot (sequence 48), but both sequences were cut. Also Called the Tiny Man or "little fellow."

POLLY PHELPS MAN (John Doumanian): He is interviewed by the Newsman about the well that should have been boarded up (sequence 164).

POLLY PHELPS NEWSMAN (Ivan Kronenfeld): Does the broadcast in the Pennsylvania field (sequence 163).

POP (Michael Tucker): Little Joe's father.

PORFIRIO (Dimitri Vassilopoulos): The Playboy of the Western World. He takes Irene to the King Cole roof "for an experience" (sequence 68).

PRETTY GIRL (Shelly Delaney): On the *Nick Norris* show, she asks the detective for help (sequence 42). In the reshoot, she reappeared as Olga in the Chekhov radio show.

PRINCIPAL PETERS (Henry Cowen): He introduces the substitute teacher, Miss Gordon (sequence 134).

RABBI BAUMEL (Kenneth Mars): Little Joe's Hebrew teacher (sequences 22 and 38).

REBA MAN (Jerry Sroka): Radio personality, star of *Reba, the Maid*. Ronald Leir (Nick Norris) played the part in the reshoot, but the whole sequence was eventually cut.

MR. RIENZI (Alfred De La Fuente): He is an inventor of such things as the electric razor for horses, and the lighter that works underwater (but not yet) (sequence 133). The kids think he is a Nazi spy. All his scenes were cut.

ROCCO (Danny Aiello): The gangster who kills Mr. Davis, and plans to bump Sally off. Sequence added during the reshoot (number 106).

ROGER (David Warrilow): Radio personality, Irene's husband (*Breakfast with Irene and Roger*). He explodes with desire each time he sees Sally (sequence 64).

RUTHIE (Joy Newman): Little Joe's cousin, Abe and Ceil's daughter. Her favorite pastime is to listen to the Waldbaums' party line, and keep the family informed.

MR. RYDELL (Everett Quinton): Promoter of the Tonino event. Quinton appeared as the producer's assistant in the Chekhov radio show during the reshoot, but both sequences were dropped.

SALLY (Mia Farrow): The cigarette girl who became a radio star.

SANFORD (Marc Colner): Radio personality, one of the Whiz Kids.

MRS. SILVERMAN (Belle Berger): Little Joe's neighbor, who had a stroke after seeing Doris, the Communist's daughter, kiss a black man. She was taken, mummified, to the hospital (sequence 82).

SINGER 1 (Catherine Hayes): She was supposed to sing "I'll Be Seeing You" and "They're Either Too Young or Too Old," but, while she had a great look, she couldn't sing.

SINGER 2 (Maureen Sadusk): She sang the two songs very well, and was a very good actress, but Woody finally decided she didn't have exactly the right look. During the reshoot, she became

The Broadway Star who had mike fright (sequence X104), but that scene was eventually cut. She is on the King Cole roof for New Year's Eve (sequence 180).

SINGER 3 (Kitty Carlisle Hart): *see* KITTY.

SOUND-EFFECTS MAN (Max Alexander): The technician who did the effects for *The Sound Effects Studio Show* (sequence 45). The sequence was cut.

SPIDER WOMAN (Denise Dummont): The Latin singer who sings "Tico Tico" in the King Cole Room (sequence 62). She was also the singer in *The Kiss of the Spider Woman*.

SY (Richard Portnow): One of Bea's dates, he's married and has children. He takes her and Little Joe for a tour of Manhattan in his new car after Mom has her baby (sequence 156).

TESS: Mom's first name.

TINY MAN: *see* NORRIS, NICK.

TOM (Ed Silk): Jessica's husband, author of *The Christmas in the Congo*. A friend of Roger and Irene, he sits at their table in the King Cole Room (sequence 63).

TONINO, THE ASTONISHING (Verne G. Williams): The World's Greatest Escape Artist.

TONINO, CARMELLA (Camille Saviola): Tonino's wife.

UNCLE WALT (Richard Shull): Radio personality (sequence 69).

MR. AND MRS. WALDBAUM (Hy Anzell and Judith Malina): Little Joe's neighbors, always complaining about Ruthie listening to their party line.

MR. ZIPSKY (Joel Eidelsberg): One of Little Joe's neighbors, has a nervous breakdown and runs in the street in his underwear wielding a meat cleaver (sequence E102).

CREW

Here is a list of the members of the crew and the real characters who appear in the diary. A more complete list can be found in the Appendix.

ADRIANA: Carlo Di Palma's wife.

ANGELA: *see* SALGADO, ANGELA.

BABY DYLAN: *see* FARROW, DYLAN.

BARATTA, RICHIE: Location department.

BARBARA: *see* GREEN, BARBARA.

BARBARA: *see* HELLER, BARBARA.

BERNSTEIN, NICK: Location department. Son of the writer of *The Front*. Has been working on Woody's films since he was fifteen.

BILL: *see* CHRISTIANS, BILL.

BOURNE, TIM: Location manager. Son of Mel Bourne, who worked with Woody as a production designer. At seventeen, he went to Lyon as a cook (he loves France but hates the French). Then he spent four years as Jack Nicholson's cook.

BRIAN: *see* HAMILL, BRIAN.

BURKE, RON: Dolly grip. Nicknamed "Red" because of his hair.

CARLO: *see* DI PALMA, CARLO.

CHAPIN, KAY: Script supervisor. She started with Woody on *Annie Hall* (1977), and hasn't missed one of his movies since.

CHRISTIANS, BILL: Men's wardrobe supervisor.

CLIFF: *see* SCHORR, CLIFF.

DAISY: *see* FARROW, DAISY.

DANNY: Teamster.

DAVIS, JIM: Location department.

DENNIS: *see* KEAR, DENNIS.

DICKIE: *see* MINGALONE, DICK.

DI PALMA, CARLO: Director of photography, started as focus operator on *Ossessione* (1942), Luchino Visconti's adaptation of James M. Cain's novel *The Postman Always Rings Twice*, then worked on Roberto Rossellini's *Open City* (1945), and Vittorio De Sica's *The Bicycle Thief* (1948).

His films as director of photography include Michelangelo Antonioni's *Red Desert* (1964) and *Blow Up* (1966), Sidney Lumet's *The Appointment* (1969), Bernardo Bertolucci's *Tragedia di un Uomo Ridicolo* (1981), Antonioni's *Identificazione di una Donna* (1982), Woody Allen's *Hannah and Her Sisters* (1986), and Michael Dinner's *Offbeat* (1986).

DOUG: *see* ORNSTEIN, DOUG.

DREW: *see* ROSENBERG, DREW.

DUBELMAN, LIZ: Camera trainee.

DYNAMITE KID: *see* TYSON, MIKE.

EIBEN, PATRICIA: Women's wardrobe supervisor.

EZRA: *see* SWERDLOW, EZRA.

FARROW, DYLAN: Mia Farrow's daughter. She plays Little Joe's sister in the New Year's Eve scene (number 182).

FARROW, MOSES: Mia Farrow's son.

FERN: *see* SALAD SISTERS.

FORD, ROMANIA: Makeup artist.

FRANKIE: Jimmy Mazzola's friend, follows the shooting during the first three weeks in Rockaway.

FRANKIE: *see* GRAZIADEI, FRANK.

FREDERICK, JIMMY: Prop department.

GAMBLING DEPARTMENT: The sound department—Jimmy and Louis Sabat, and Frankie Graziadei. They organize the gambling, card games, and Super Bowl pool.

GIL: *see* WILLIAMS, GIL.

GRADISCA: A woman who follows the shooting in Rockaway for a few days. She looks very much like the character of Gradisca (Magali Noel) in Fellini's *Amarcord* (1973).

GRAZIADEI, FRANK: Sound recorder.

GREEN, BARBARA: Seth Green's (Little Joe) mother.

GREEN, MICHAEL: First assistant cameraman.

GREEN, ROMAINE: *see* SALAD SISTERS.

GREENHUT, BOB: The producer, started working with Woody on *Play It Again, Sam* (1972), and has produced all his films since *Annie Hall.*

HAMILL, BRIAN: Still photographer, has known Mike Tyson since Mike was thirteen.

HAMMER: *see* MANZIONE, JIM.

HEBREW TUTOR: Tutors Seth Green (Little Joe) on the set. He appears as one of the photographers in the Polly Phelps episode.

HELLER, BARBARA: Location department.

HYMAN, DICK: The musical director. For *Zelig* he composed the music and lyrics of "Leonard the Lizard," "Doin' the Chameleon," "Reptile Eyes," "You May Be Six People, But I Love You," and "Chameleon Days." For this film, he was musical supervisor, and his compositions include "Get Regular with Re-Lax," "Uncle Walt Squirrel Rangers' Club Song," and most of the jingles for the radio shows. He started with Woody on *Everything You Always Wanted to Know About Sex . . .* (1972).

JANE: *see* MARTIN, JANE.

JAY: *see* LEVY, JAY.

JEFFREY: *see* KURLAND, JEFFREY.

JIMMY: *see* DAVIS, JIM.

JIMMY: *see* FREDERICK, JIMMY.

JIMMY: *see* MAZZOLA, JIMMY.

JIMMY: *see* SABAT, JIMMY.

JOFFE, CAROL: Set decorator, began on *Stardust Memories* former wife of Charles Joffe, Woody's manager and producer.

JUDY: *see* MAKOVSKY, JUDIANA.

KAY: *see* CHAPIN, KAY.

KEAR, DENNIS: Stand-in. He has been Woody's stand-in for almost ten years.

KEN: *see* ORNSTEIN, KEN.

KURLAND, JEFFREY: Costume designer. Formerly Santo Loquasto's assistant.

LARK: *see* PREVIN, LARK.

LEVY, JAY: Second assistant cameraman.

LIZ: *see* DUBELMAN, LIZ.

LOQUASTO, SANTO: Production designer. Does costumes for Twyla Tharp. Twice Oscar-nominated for *Zelig* (costume design) and *Desperately Seeking Susan* (production design). Started with Woody on *Stardust Memories* (1980).

LOUIS: *see* SABAT, LOUIS.

MAKOVSKY, JUDIANA: Assistant costume designer.

MANZIONE, JIM (HAMMER): Electrician. Union representative. Nicknamed "Hammer" because of his stocky build.

MARTIN, JANE: Woody's assistant. Has been with Woody since the reshoot of *Broadway Danny Rose* (1984).

MAZZOLA, JEFFREY: Prop department, Jimmy's younger brother.

MAZZOLA, JIMMY: Propmaster, started with Woody on *Interiors* (1978).

MICKEY: *see* GREEN, MICHAEL.

MINGALONE, DICK: Camera operator.

MORSE, SUSAN (SANDY): Editor.

MOSES: *see* FARROW, MOSES.

MYLA: *see* PITT, MYLA.

NICK: *see* BERNSTEIN, NICK.

NICOLE: *see* STERN, NICOLE.

ORNSTEIN, DOUG: Production assistant, Ken's younger brother.

ORNSTEIN, KEN: Second assistant director.

PATRICK, RICHIE: Production assistant.

PATTI: *see* EIBEN, PATRICIA.

PETE: *see* TAVIS, PETE.

PHOTOGRAPHER, THE: Young man who follows the shooting during the first three weeks in Rockaway.

PITT, MYLA: Stand-in, plays Mom's roommate in the hospital scene and a passerby in the snowman scene.

POPEYE: Piano tuner. He looks like the cartoon character.

PREVIN, DAISY: Mia Farrow's daughter.

PREVIN, LARK: Mia Farrow's daughter.

PRODUCER, EXECUTIVE: *see* ROLLINS, JACK, and JOFFE, CHARLES.

PRODUCERS: *see* GREENHUT, BOB, and SWERDLOW, EZRA.

QUINLAN, RAY: Gaffer.

RAY: *see* QUINLAN, RAY.

REBECCA: Young girl who takes care of Baby Dylan on the set when Mia Farrow works. Arthur Miller's daughter.

RED: *see* BURKE, RON.

REILLY, TOM: First assistant director. Solid Irish type, like John Wayne in John Ford's *The Quiet Man*. He has a loud voice and runs the set: "Let's not fall apart!" "Folks, as quick as we can!" "If you're not in the shot, you're in the way!"

RICHIE: *see* PATRICK, RICHIE.

ROLLINS, JACK: Woody's manager and producer.

ROMAINE: *see* SALAD SISTERS.

ROMANIA: *see* FORD, ROMANIA.

ROSENBERG, DREW: Production assistant.

SABAT, JIMMY: Sound mixer. Woody's longest collaborator, he worked on *Bananas* (1971). He also plays the part of Chester, Bea's date at Radio City Music Hall (sequence F102).

SABAT, LOUIS: Boom man, Jimmy's younger brother.

SALAD SISTERS: FERN BUCHNER (makeup) and ROMAINE GREEN (hair). An institution in the film business, they have been working together for almost fifteen years. Legend has it that Joanne Woodward dubbed them the Salad Sisters because of their first names. They have been working with Woody since *Annie Hall.* (1977).

SALGADO, ANGELA: Production assistant.

SANDY: *see* MORSE, SUSAN.

SANTO: *see* LOQUASTO, SANTO.

SCHERER, WERNER: Hairdresser.

SCHORR, CLIFF: Scenic artist.

STERN, NICOLE: Stand-in, half-French, mother from Brittany. She appears twice in the King Cole Room sequence: at the table next to Roger and Irene's (sequence 63), and on New Year's Eve (sequence 181).

SWERDLOW, EZRA: Associate producer.

TANGO TEACHER, THE: Dance teacher for Dianne Wiest (Bea), Richard Portnow (Sy), Julie Kurnitz (Irene), and Dimitri Vassilopoulos (Porfirio)—scenes in the Tango Palace and in the King Cole Room.

TAVIS, PETE: Teamster captain.

TAYLOR, JULIET: Casting director.

TIM: *see* BOURNE, TIM.

TOM: *see* REILLY, TOM.

TYSON, MIKE (DYNAMITE KID): Heavyweight boxer. Brian's friend.

VOGUE MAGAZINE WRITER: Santo's driver. He writes for the cultural section of *Vogue.*

WARD, BOBBY: Key grip, started with Woody on *The Front* (1976). Thirty-two years in the business. His father was a grip and his brother is a gaffer.

WERNER: *see* SCHERER, WERNER.

WILLIAMS, GIL: Location department.

RADIO DAYS

As soon as Mr. and Mrs. Needleman, two of Little Joe's neighbors, leave their home to go to the movies, a couple of burglars break in. They're in the process of robbing the house when the host of radio's *Guess that Tune* calls. The burglars correctly identify the melodies and win the grand prize. Mr. and Mrs. Needleman return to a gutted home that night, only to awaken the next morning to the arrival of a truckload of gifts.

On another popular radio show, a youthful "Future Star" gives her rendition of "Let's All Sing Like the Birdies Sing." And Little Joe's mom cleans her kitchen while listening to the trendy *Breakfast with Irene and Roger* show. Little Joe prefers *The Masked Avenger.*

Little Joe stands before the Rockaway bathhouse, and in his own house, his parents argue about which is "the greater ocean," the Atlantic or the Pacific? Uncle Abe brings fresh fish from his pal in Sheepshead Bay, while upstairs, Grandpa tries to lace Grandma into her corset. Cousin Ruthie listens in on the Waldbaums' party line, and Mr. Waldbaum yells from next door to complain. Little Joe asks for fifteen cents so he can buy a Masked Avenger ring.

Little Joe and his pals walk to school. At Show and Tell, Little Ross shows off his new Masked Avenger secret-compartment ring.

Later, in Hebrew class, Rabbi Baumel lectures the kids about the need for a new state in Palestine, and how they will have to help by collecting funds.

The boys solicit donations on the street, then take what they've gotten to the beach to count; they want to see if they've come up with enough to buy the latest Masked Avenger ring.

But they're found out. Little Joe and his parents are summoned to Rabbi Baumel's office, where Little Joe is taken to task for this misappropriation of funds. Little Joe tries to handle the situation, but the rabbi cuffs him. Then Mom hits him. Then Pop hits him.

Bea has a date with handsome Sidney Manulis. On their way home, the car "runs out of gas" in foggy Breezy Point. The romantic radio music is interrupted by a special announcement: New Jersey has been invaded by Martians. Brave Mr. Manulis panics and abandons Bea in the night.

Another story unfolds. Several of the town's radio stars are gathered in the King Cole Room nightclub. Roger, of the *Breakfast with Irene and Roger* show, is lusting after Sally the cigarette girl, with whom he is having an affair. She takes him to the roof of the club. But after Roger's needs have been satisfied, they find that they're locked out of the building, with no way down and an electrical storm on the way. They're losing control when Porfirio, the Playboy of the Western World, comes onto the roof for a quick tryst with Roger's wife, Irene.

Back in Rockaway, on Yom Kippur, Little Joe's Communist neighbors are playing their radio loudly, on a day where they're supposed to do nothing but atone for their sins. Abe can finally stand no more and goes next door to talk to them. Two hours later, he still hasn't returned and the radio is still blaring. It prompts Mom to tell the others of what happened to Mrs. Silverman, how she saw the Communist's daughter kissing a black man and had a stroke. Abe finally returns, intoxicated.

The radio world. Abe's favorite show is *Bill Kern's Favorite Sports Legends*. Abe listens, enthralled, to the story of baseball player Kirby Kyle. Ceil enjoys *The Famous Ventriloquist*, and Ruthie and her girlfriends sit in the malt shop swooning to a crooner's voice. Thomas Abercrombie holds his *Court of Human*

Emotions, Mom and Pop's favorite show, over the airwaves; Little Joe imagines his parents on the program. And at the zoo one day, Little Joe and his parents meet a radio personality, Sanford, the Whiz Kid.

Little Joe, to this day, associates certain songs with certain events, such as his lesson on relationships with Little Evelyn, or Mom and Pop's anniversary and the fur coat she got; it was the only time he saw his parents kiss. Other memorable events were the day the kids gave a snowman a penis, the way Ruthie used to pantomime songs from the radio, the day Mr. Zipsky had his nervous breakdown and ran down the street in his underwear, and the time Bea and her date Chester took Little Joe to Radio City Music Hall.

After getting stuck on the roof with Roger, Sally finds a new job in Mr. Davis's nightclub, the El Morocco. Unfortunately, she's there to witness Mr. Davis being killed by Rocco the gangster. Rocco decides to do away with her, too, but at his mother's house, where he stops for bullets and a new gun, he's convinced to spare her and ends up helping her fulfill her life's dream, to be on radio.

She gets a part in a radio dramatization of a Chekhov play. But the moment she's about to deliver her first line, to make her radio debut, the program is interrupted by the announcement that Pearl Harbor has been bombed.

So Sally ends up singing at the USO. Little Joe and his pals do their part for the war effort by collecting scrap iron. The malt-shop waitress shows off her new WAC uniform. Mrs. Riley grows vegetables in her Victory garden. Radio's "Biff Baxter, G-Man," though he's been declared 4F for flat feet, does his part, too, beating up Nazis and Japs in a broadcast studio. Little Joe and his gang go to a rooftop to watch for enemy planes. What they see through their binoculars, however, is a neighbor, Miss Gordon, undressing for a shower. The kids go to the beach to discuss the opposite sex. Later, Joe is alone, dreaming of Miss Gordon, when a Nazi submarine breaks through the waves.

Kitty Carlisle sings "They're Either Too Young or Too Old," and Mom and Bea discuss men, love, marriage, and the need to compromise. Bea thinks her upcoming date, Fred, could be the man for her.

Pop, meanwhile, has come up with yet another harebrained money-making scheme. But Mom would rather discuss what name they'll give their expected child. From his bed, Little Joe listens to the bad news about the war coming from the radio downstairs. The local air-raid warden calls for a blackout. Mom and Pop go out to look at the somehow-beautiful searchlights.

Bea brings her date Fred in for a drink. He's depressed because he's recently lost his fiancée in an auto accident—his fiancée, Leonard. Fred, it appears, will not be the one for Bea.

At school, Little Joe and his pals learn that they're getting a substitute teacher—Miss Gordon.

Sally continues to struggle with her career. She sings commercial jingles ("Get Regular with Re-Lax"). She takes elocution classes ("Hark! I hear the cannon roar"). And finally she gets her own show, *The Gay White Way*. Ceil likes to listen to Sally's program, but when the radio gets staticky, Abe hits it so hard he breaks it.

Little Joe goes to the radio-repair shop to retrieve the family radio. When he hails a cab, he finally learns what his father does for a living—he's a hack.

The family gets involved in a slogan-writing contest, and in the middle of it all, Mom goes into labor. After they all go to visit her in the hospital, Bea and her current date, Sy, take Little Joe for a tour of Manhattan—Times Square, the Horn and Hardart Automat, Exhibition Hall. Bea goes on the radio show *The Silver Dollar Jackpot*, and wins! She buys Little Joe a chemistry set with her prize money, and then they go to the Tango Palace.

Back in the house, Bea dances to conga music, Abe brings home live eels, and Little Joe has burned Mom's fur coat with the chemistry set. Pop chases Little Joe, catches him, and starts hitting him. But the chaos quickly ends as the radio music is interrupted by a report about a little girl, Polly Phelps, who is trapped in a well in a Pennsylvania field. The family listens, rapt, as do people of all ages, from all classes, all around the city. Hours and hours later, young Polly is brought out of the well, but she has died.

It's New Year's Eve, 1943. Sally and her date, the Masked Avenger, join other radio stars in the King Cole Room. Little Joe's family spends the evening at home, listening to a broadcast from the club.

At Sally's suggestion, the radio stars go to the roof of the building to welcome the New Year. Midnight arrives. On the roof of the King Cole Room and in Little Joe's house, everyone cheers in 1944. Snow starts falling on the roof of the club, and the radio stars go back downstairs.

FOREWORD TO THE READER

IN THE FOLLOWING DIARY, the actors will go by their characters' names. All the persons mentioned in the diary are listed in alphabetical order starting on page 17. The sequence numbers correspond to those in the Continuity, page 407. A number of the sequences do not appear in the final film; the ones that have been cut are indicated in the Continuity, page 407.

DIARY: FIRST SHOOTING

Tuesday, November 5, 1985   *First Week*

8:00 A.M. Chinatown. In front of the Nom Wah Tea Parlor on Doyers Street. Breakfast is being served—coffee and doughnuts. As the crew moves the equipment inside, Woody chats by the door. Seeing me hanging around, he approaches. I introduce myself. We shake hands. "Welcome," he says. "Have you met Jane? If you need anything, ask her." I thank him, and he goes back to his conversation.

Unshaven and dressed in brown leather shoes, corduroy trousers, a green hunting jacket, and the inevitable hat, Woody looks relaxed.

9:30 A.M. Inside the Nom Wah Tea Parlor. The year is 1943. The lighting is being adjusted by Carlo Di Palma, the director of photography, and his team (the gaffers and grips). There is the inevitable disorder of a movie set. And when the room is not that big, no matter what you do you are in the way. The crew, though, seems totally at ease, moving swiftly between the equipment and the people. To be shot: tea-parlor customers listening to the radio, to the story of Polly Phelps, the eight-year-old Pennsylvania girl who has fallen into a well (sequences 168 and 172).

An old Chinese couple (who must be in their seventies) and a young sailor and his girlfriend are brought in. Woody looks carefully at their costumes and orders a jacket change. They are seated at two tables, and Woody, after checking the scene through the camera, talks to Tom Reilly, the first assistant director, who then transmits the directions to the actors. The elderly Chinese woman is eventually not in the shot. Once the scene is blocked, Woody goes to talk to each of the actors and tells them they should just listen to the radio, to the story of the little girl, the sailor eating and the Chinese man puffing his cigarette.

9:45 A.M. Shot 168: A wide shot of the old Chinese man, the sailor, and his girl, listening to the Polly Phelps drama on the radio. *(5 seconds.)*
(3 takes and 3 prints.)
The extras stay in position and we go directly to the next shot.
Shot 172: The sailor and his girl have stopped eating. The old Chinese man has stopped puffing on his cigarette. All are stunned. They have just learned of Polly's death. *(5 seconds.)*
(4 takes and 2 prints.) Completed at 10:15 A.M.

11:00 A.M. The firehouse of Company No. 18 at Tenth Street in Greenwich Village. We are now in 1926. Cars of the period are parked in front of the station. To be shot: Firemen listening to the radio, to Carleton Foxx telling them, live from the Jersey shore, about a stunt by the man known as "The Cat with Nine Lives," The World's Greatest Escape Artist, The Astonishing Tonino (sequences 2, 4, 6, and 8).

The production assistants (PAs) are trying to block the street, but they are having a hard time of it. Again and again they ask people to either step back or stay outside the camera frame or move away from the crew. Some of the people make it past the PAs, though, and a man gets to Woody to ask him for an autograph. Woody refuses politely but firmly. Tom, always at Woody's side, gently pushes the man away. Another, video camera in hand, wants to shoot Woody and the scene. A PA asks him to move. "Leave me alone!" the man all but screams. "The streets belong to everybody. This is America!"

Jane Martin, Woody's assistant, introduces me to Bob Greenhut, the producer (with Woody since *Play It Again, Sam* [1972]): "We're used to working together," he says of the company. "We all know each other. We all hate each other!" She also introduces me to Brian Hamill, the still photographer, who is from Brooklyn; he seems very friendly with Woody. And I begin to make friends with Jimmy Sabat, the sound mixer, who started with Woody on *Bananas* (1971). Of the shots this morning, none have had sound recording, so Jimmy finds himself with spare time.

Jimmy Mazzola, the property master, takes a Dalmatian to the firemen (the extras) who have taken their positions under the porch. The real firemen (the 1985 ones) watch the scene with us. The passersby (the extras, all in period dress) are in position and waiting. The engines are started.

12:00 noon. Shot 2: A wide shot of the firemen, with another man, listening to Tonino's story. Cars and pedestrians pass through the frame. *(10 seconds.)*

(3 takes and 3 prints.)

We go directly to the next shot.

Shot 2A: Same as 2 but closer. For takes 2 and 4, Woody keeps only the man listening. The firemen have left.

(4 takes and 4 prints.) Completed at 12:30 P.M.

The real firemen ask to be photographed with Woody, and he agrees. In the middle of these tall, smiling men, Woody poses with his usual, Zelig-type face—serious, but with a cowering look. Then he dashes into the station wagon to reach the next location before the rain. The sky is very low.

1:15 P.M. The rain is here, light and persistent, on Fiftieth Street, between Fifth and Sixth avenues, just in front of the RCA building. Woody is with Andrew (Fletcher Previn, Mia Farrow's son). They are standing under an awning, waiting for the crew to bring the equipment and set the shot. We are "back" in the 1940s now, to get an establishing shot of the studio where Sally (Mia Farrow) is singing "Get Regular with Re-Lax," the jingle for the laxative commercial (sequence 141).

Thirties- and forties-era cars are parked on both sides of the street, near the entrance. Posters reading WAR BONDS: TO HAVE AND TO HOLD flank the doorways. A few extras are scattered in the street and the building interior.

2:15 P.M. Shot 141: The camera tilts down the RCA tower to the entrance, where people are going in and out of the building. *(6 seconds.)*

The street is blocked. And for a few seconds, Fiftieth Street goes back almost half a century, here against the noisy background of 1985 Manhattan.

(2 takes and 2 prints.) Completed at 2:45 P.M.

We break for lunch.

4:30 P.M. Inside the Marlboro Cleaners at First Avenue and Thirteenth Street, to shoot others listening to the Great Tonino's adventure. The back rooms of this establishment have not changed since the twenties. The location is tiny and it is, as it was this morning, difficult—with all the equipment and the crew—to find a spot near the director. While Carlo works on the lighting, Woody hangs prop laundry with Jeffrey Kurland, the costume designer. Woody frequently checks the composition through the camera viewfinder.

Because it is a very simple shot, because the place is tiny and overcrowded, because it is the first day and everybody—after the race through Manhattan—is a little tense, I decide to withdraw. Already, in asking Jane for the script this morning, I have moved too fast. Her answer comes this afternoon: "Woody is going to think about it."(!) She also asks me to notify her the night before when I want to be on the set.

Two shots will be done.

Shot 2B: A wide shot of a Chinese couple steam-ironing while listening to Tonino's story on the radio. The man turns the radio up. *(10 seconds.)*

(3 takes and 3 prints.)

Shot 8: The Chinese man jiggling the radio when it gets staticky. *(5 seconds.)*

(3 takes and 3 prints.)

Wednesday, November 6, 1985

Yesterday, Ed Koch won a third term as mayor by a three-to-one margin. He vows to combat inequities, "for all the people in this town without regard to race, religion, national origin or sexual orientation." (New York Times)

In the bus with the extras en route to the baseball field in New Jersey where Kirby Kyle—the lean southpaw from Tennessee who lost one leg, one arm, and went blind, but who had heart—is going to perform.

8:45 A.M. The baseball field. We are in the late 1930s. Huge posters (BUY CHESTERFIELD) hang on the backfield wall. Kirby Kyle (Brian Mannain) is dressed and ready to pitch. In reality, Mannain works in the office of Rollins and Joffe Productions, and plays baseball on the same team as Ezra Swerdlow, the associate producer. Woody is having his breakfast—white bread, like in *Hannah*, but toasted and covered with brown sugar, and a cup of "colorless liquid" (hot water), like in *Manhattan*. I get acquainted with Kay Chapin, the script supervisor, who has not missed a movie with Woody since *Annie Hall* (1977).

9:00 A.M. No sound is to be recorded: There will be a voice over by Bill Kern.
Shot 86: Kirby is on the mound pitching to the camera. *(5 seconds.)*
(3 takes and 3 prints.)
The camera is moved back for a wider angle.
Shot 86A: Kirby pitches and the batter swings. *(3 seconds.)*
(2 takes and 2 prints.)
We go back to the first position.
Shot 88: Kirby is on the mound pitching, with one leg. *(5 seconds.)*
(4 takes and 4 prints.)
Shot 90: Kirby is on the mound pitching, with one leg and one arm. *(5 seconds.)*
(5 takes and 5 prints.)
And finally:
Shot 92: Kirby is on the mound pitching. He has one leg, and one arm, and is blind. *(5 seconds.)*
(6 takes and 5 prints.)
Even with all his heart, it is becoming more and more difficult, physically, for Kirby to pitch the ball in a satisfying way. With his arm tied behind his back, then with his leg bent up to his behind, Kirby has to be carried to the mound by Jimmy Mazzola and his men. But Kirby, as an actor on the set, also has heart. Not pleased with his performance, although Woody is, he asks for another chance and the director gives it to him. For the last shot, Kirby—blind now—misses the ball being thrown back to him. He's good at it. The scene is funny and everybody, with no respect for the disabled, laughs.

11:15 A.M. The sequence is finished. Woody and Carlo go to have lunch somewhere in Jersey City while the crew and cast, including all the extras for this afternoon's scene, are served in a corridor in the stadium building. The extras are now all costumed, with makeup. The catering is very good; the mothers of the young extras seem to appreciate it.

12:15 P.M. Back on the bus with the extras to the next location. At the moment, we're stuck in front of the baseball stadium because we cannot travel during lunch hour—union rules!

1:30 P.M. The Brummers Confectionary on Grand Street in Jersey City. It is an ice cream parlor that also sells all sorts of candies and chocolates, a family-owned store since Grandpa Fred Brummer opened it at the turn of the century. Grandma is still living upstairs. They have their own factory in the basement, where they make chocolates of all shapes and sizes, including that of naked women. The place is ideal—a malt-shop counter, a room in the back, and all of it unchanged since Grandpa built it. Santo Loquasto, the production designer, discovered it while looking for another location.

Woody has already decided the camera setup, and Carlo and the crew are involved in the lengthy preparation of the lighting. The place is loaded with delicate antique display cases, and the walls are covered with mirrors. It will take at least an hour and a half.

3:20 P.M. While final adjustments are made on the lighting, Cousin Ruthie (Joy Newman) and her friends are lined up in front of Woody. As Tom gets the girls laughing with a few jokes, Woody, very serious, looks them over closely. He has Jeffrey change some sweaters, and the first rehearsal begins.

Shot 13: The Crooner is singing "All or Nothing At All" on the radio. The waitress turns up the volume, then goes to take orders. Cousin Ruthie is with her girlfriends, sipping huge ice cream sodas and squealing over the song. (32 seconds.)

It starts slowly. The shot is difficult. There is camera movement to be coordinated with the actions of the extras—the waitress, the counterman, and the customers. The point of the scene is that everyone is nearly hypnotized by the Crooner's voice. Woody rides the camera dolly several times and makes some changes, but is not yet satisfied. Complete silence. Woody seems uncertain. More camera movement and different blocking of the extras is tried. There is a definite tension now. The set becomes noisy. Woody, in a very low voice, complains to Tom, who shouts: "Please, folks. We can't hear!" Finally: "I got it. I think I got it now," Woody says. And the first take is shot.

(16 takes and 10 prints.)

Woody is satisfied—"Thanks a lot, kids," he tells the girls— and he decides on the day's last shot, which takes place after the declaration of World War II. The location has to be dressed a little differently and the costumes changed, updating us to 1942. After choosing the camera setup, Woody goes out, leaving Carlo and his crew to work.

6:30 P.M. Carlo is ready, but there is a problem with the former waitress's WAC uniform. Everybody is waiting. Woody sits on one of the soda-counter stools, head bent toward the floor; he seems tired and thoughtful. Suddenly, he sees me and approaches. "Everything's OK? You're not too bored?" Then, with the waitress's uniform ready, he goes back to work.

Shot 108: Cousin Ruthie and her girlfriends are admiring the waitress in her WAC uniform. *(5 seconds.)*

It's a very short shot, to be edited to the song "I'll Be Seeing You."

(2 takes and 2 prints.)

"It's a wrap" at 7:30 P.M.

Back to Manhattan in the crew van. It has been a long day (the crew call was 7:30 A.M.) and there is a lot of traffic in the Holland Tunnel. Danny, the teamster who is driving us, is getting nervous.

Thursday, November 7, 1985

In Colombia, twenty-five leftist guerrillas have seized the Palace of Justice, holding judges and government workers hostage. Twelve are dead at this point. (New York Times)

Kean wants a ball club in Jersey. (Daily News)

Shultz and McFarlane are back from the Soviet Union. They see a big gap between the two countries and doubt success at Ron

and Gorby's meeting in Geneva in two weeks. (New York Times)
And Edgar Bronfman, the president of the World Jewish Congress, has made a dramatic appeal to John Cardinal O'Connor, urging him to press the Vatican for diplomatic recognition of Israel. (New York Times)

We're in the crew van to Rockaway. Danny likes classical music. He is a former musician (clarinet and saxophone) and has played in different groups, jazz and classical. We cross the Brooklyn Bridge, a beautiful view of Manhattan behind us, with Vivaldi's *Four Seasons.*

7:45 A.M. Rockaway, in front of the Brignati residence, on Beach Ninety-seventh Street. Breakfast is served in an abandoned lot where all the trucks are parked. Coffee with Red, the dolly grip, and a few others. We begin to socialize. The discussion is about Woody. "He is becoming too serious," one says. "His films aren't as funny as they were. And people don't go to see them as often. But I'm sure that later his films will be considered classics, and he will be regarded as a genius. . . ."

8:15 A.M. We are in 1943. The first floor of an abandoned house has been decorated as a radio-repair shop. All the graffiti has been painted over and signposts taken out. There's a little problem with the weather, though; it's sunny and Woody wants overcast.
Woody, wearing the same hat, same shoes, same green jacket, but new corduroy trousers, is inside the repair shop, then on the street, discussing the setting with Carlo. Tom follows.
The sequence inside the radio-repair shop is dropped, and a shot of Little Joe exiting the shop, a huge radio in his arms, is chosen.
Woody takes Little Joe (Seth Green) by the hand and shows him what to do, walking in a childlike way, swaying his shoulders. Then Little Joe waits outside the repair shop while Woody jogs back to the camera.

9:35 A.M. Shot 146: Long shot of Little Joe exiting the repair shop with his oversize radio, struggling with it along the road between pedestrians and fast-moving cars. Little Joe is trying to save himself cab fare. *(25 seconds.)*
The image of this tiny boy struggling with this big radio, try-

(L to R:) Carlo DiPalma; Woody Allen; Tom Reilly

ing to see where he is going, passing close to the speeding cars, is already funny. After each take Jimmy Frederick, Jimmy Mazzola's assistant, helps Little Joe with the radio, and all the cars reverse to their starting positions.

The first take is good. The second is interrupted by a Concorde leaving Kennedy Airport. Woody puts his fingers in his ears.

(5 takes and 4 prints.) Completed at 10:00 A.M.

We move to the next location.

10:30 A.M. The Rockaway Freeway, between Beach Ninety-sixth Street and Beach Ninety-eighth Street. The freeway is in fact a road that runs under the elevated subway tracks, separated in the middle by the pillars of the structure. It's getting cold. To be shot:

the scene following the one outside the repair shop, a sequence with a yellow cab stopping by Little Joe and his big radio. It is then that Little Joe learns, at last, what his father does for a living.

While Carlo finishes setting up the camera, Woody, hands in his trousers (he often sticks his little finger out), whistles.

11:00 A.M. Shot 146A: Long shot of Little Joe with his radio in his arms, walking along the roadway. The yellow cab enters the frame and stops by Little Joe. Getting in, radio first, he doesn't recognize his father initially. *(15 seconds.)*

Once more airplanes interrupt several takes, and there is some problem getting the cab stopped in the proper spot.

(10 takes and 7 prints.) Completed at 11:30 A.M.

The next shot is closer. Carlo needs more time to light it; the two previous scenes have been shot with natural light. Little Joe goes to play with his stand-in, a boy his age, costumed the same.

12:00 noon. Woody checks the framing: "It's good."

Carlo: "Yes?"

Woody: "Are you surprised?"

Shot 147: The cab is stopped. We look over Pop's shoulder at Little Joe struggling to get the radio in, then we see the boy's stunned expression as he recognizes his father. *(6 seconds.)*

(3 takes and 3 prints.) Completed at 12:15 P.M.

And we move to Pop's reaction shot.

12:45 P.M. Shot 147A: Pop, embarrassed, explains that he is helping a friend. *(6 seconds.)*

(2 takes and 2 prints.) Completed at 1:00 P.M.

1:30 P.M. Last shot for this sequence and for the morning.

Shot 148: The rear of the cab. The car pulls away and disappears in a long shot. *(10 seconds.)*

(4 takes and 3 prints.)

We break for lunch at 2:00 P.M.

The meal is served in Murphy's bar at the corner of Beach Ninety-seventh Street and Rockaway Beach Boulevard.

3:15 P.M. Everybody has moved to Beach 115th Street. The location is Little Joe's house. Woody talks with Tom and Carlo; the light is fading quickly. An old lady, who has taken the PAs by surprise, approaches Woody, trembling, for an autograph. He refuses. Tom gently prods her back.

Two elderly women, costumed, are brought to Woody. He examines them to the finest detail and seems to approve. They will be passing by in the next sequence, another shot to be cut to the song "I'll Be Seeing You."

3:30 P.M. Shot 109: Just after the declaration of war. Mrs Riley points to the vegetables growing in her flowerpots and makes the Victory sign, as the elderly women pass by. *(6 seconds.)*
(3 takes and 2 prints.)

And "It's a wrap" at 4:00 P.M.

Back in Manhattan, in one of the station wagons with Pop (Michael Tucker), Little Joe, his tutor, and Barbara Green (Little Joe's mother in the real world). Tucker had a small part in *The Purple Rose of Cairo*, but he gave a very good performance; he was Jeff Daniels's agent. In real life, he's married to Jill Eikenberry.

The Verrazano Bridge is beautiful in the setting sun.

Friday, November 8, 1985

In Colombia, government troops have recaptured the Palace of Justice. The twenty-five rebels are killed. Death toll reported at one hundred. (New York Times)

Gorby doesn't want Ron to appear on Soviet TV, so Ron will speak to the Soviet people on shortwave radio on Saturday. (New York Times)

In New Jersey, having been impregnated by her brother-in-law's sperm, a surrogate mother delivers a girl for her sterile sister. (Daily News)

AIDS appears to be spreading by conventional sexual intercourse among heterosexuals in Africa, and is striking women nearly as often as men, according to researchers. (New York Times)

Feds urge curb on gay baths. (Daily News)

In the van to Rockaway, listening to Mozart's Flute Concerto in G, with the Salad Sisters (Fern Buchner and Romaine Greene), one of their assistants (Romania Ford), and Kay. Fern, who has been with Woody since *Annie Hall* (1977), tells us about the time she worked on Dustin Hoffman's teeth in *Marathon Man*, for the scene with Laurence Olivier. A famous dentist had prepared the teeth (they were made of plastic) and asked eight thousand dollars for them. He had also done Marlon Brando's teeth for *The God-father.* "I wouldn't go to this dentist," concludes Kay.

We have a late call today because of night shots.

2:00 P.M. Rockaway. Beach 115th Street, where Little Joe lives. Rockaway is not very exciting in winter. Located on a peninsula, it is cold, wet, and windy. Most of the houses are from the turn of the century, and most of the inhabitants are, too. Nothing seems to have improved in the years since. For the film, nearly an entire block has been cleaned and dressed; streetlights and signposts have been removed, and some period facades have been built over more recent structures.

Little Joe lives in the middle of 115th Street, in a nice two-story house with a small porch. On the right is the Communist neighbor, on the left, the Waldbaums. On the other side of the street are Mr. and Mrs. Silverman. Mr. Zipsky lives three houses down. Miss Gordon has an apartment over the hardware store (see map).

Most of the newly built facades are on Rockaway Boulevard, at the end of Beach 115th Street. The Nussbaum Chiropractic Center has become Dubbins', a food market. The auto school is now sundries; the realtor, Neptune Bagel. As for the shoe-repair store, the barber shop, and the kosher meat market, only a few details have had to be changed to make them look as they would have in the 1940s. Across the street, the hardware store is still a hardware store, but with more appropriate window displays. Coughlin's Liquor is now both a Chinese restaurant on one side, and a fabric store—IDEA COTTON: GOWN TO ORDER AND READY TO WEAR—on the other. Woolworth's is still Woolworth's. On a huge poster on the side of the liquor store, Walter Winchell proclaims, "LUCKIES ARE KIND TO YOUR THROAT . . . I KNOW . . . I'VE SMOKED THEM FOR ELEVEN YEARS."

All the rebuilt 1940s facades are constructed just in front of the existing buildings, and business continues as usual behind them.

2:30 P.M. Beach 115th Street is blocked. We are going to shoot Little Joe and his pals collecting tin foil for the war. While Carlo adjusts the camera setting, the kids are brought to Woody so he

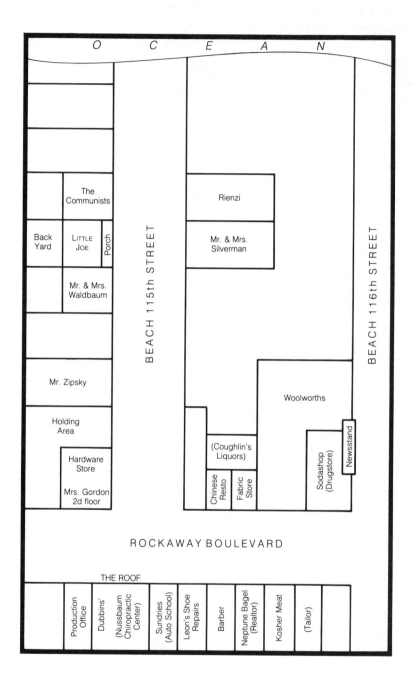

O C E A N

The Communists

Back Yard

LITTLE JOE

Porch

Mr. & Mrs. Waldbaum

Mr. Zipsky

Holding Area

Hardware Store

Mrs. Gordon 2d floor

BEACH 115th STREET

Rienzi

Mr. & Mrs. Silverman

Woolworths

(Coughlin's Liquors)

Chinese Resto

Fabric Store

Sodashop (Drugstore)

Newsstand

BEACH 116th STREET

ROCKAWAY BOULEVARD

THE ROOF

Production Office

Dubbins'

(Nussbaum Chiropractic Center)

Sundries (Auto School)

Leon's Shoe Repairs

Barber

Neptune Bagel (Realtor)

Kosher Meat

(Tailor)

can check their costumes. They are: Dave, the easy-going one (Maurice Toueg); Burt, the tiny one with buck teeth (Sal Tuminello), Nick, the crafty one with glasses (Oliver Block); Andrew the romantic (Fletcher Previn); and, of course, Little Joe (Seth Green). Woody seems genuinely to enjoy their company. Then he's off to inspect Mr. and Mrs. Silverman in their pajamas (great characters and great outfits) for the following scene.

Woody is dressed as always, except with new dark-blue trousers. A police officer asks Woody for an autograph. It's difficult to resist the law!

The first retake is determined. It will be of the Brummers Confectionary. Woody was displeased with the camera movement and the look of a few of the extras.

3:00 P.M. Woody is in a good mood today. He whistles. Then he comes to me. "It's cold and it's going to be a cold night. Are you prepared?" I thank him again and tell him how interesting it is for me. "For us," he answers, "it's a little sloppy."

3:15 P.M. Carlo is ready.

Shot 112: Little Joe and his four friends are being given big balls of tin foil. They thank the housewife, go down the steps with mounds of tin foil in their arms, and run to the next house. (15 seconds.)

(3 takes and 3 prints.) Completed at 3:30 P.M.

We move to the other side of the street to shoot Mrs. Silverman opening her door to see what's happening. "You know Mrs. Silverman. She likes to know what's going on" (sequence 79).

It's getting colder and colder. Woody and Carlo decide to put the camera on the middle of the Silvermans' front stairs. Bobby Ward, the key grip, and his men go into action. (Bobby started with Woody on *The Front* [1976].)

A grip's job is often a challenge and everything must be done ten minutes ago. Hammers hanging on their belts, nails in pockets, pieces of tape stuck on their trousers, clothespins attached everywhere, calling each other "Moe" to speed things up, they have to be able to adapt to any situation—getting a camera into an awkward setup, or laying a smooth dolly track on the roughest of ground. It is satisfying to see them find a new solution to each new problem, working quickly and efficiently in a community of ideas and feelings.

4:30 P.M. Jimmy Sabat tells me about a young man who was shooting a documentary on the making of *The Rain People*, Francis Ford Coppola's fourth movie (1969), on which Jimmy worked. The young man was filming a diary of the film, and his name was George Lucas.

5:15 P.M. It is dark now, and we are ready to shoot.
Shot 79: The light inside the Silvermans' door is switched on. Mrs. Silverman's silhouette appears in the glass door. She opens it, looks out, sipping her cup of cocoa. *(10 seconds.)*
There are little problems because Mrs. Silverman (Belle Berger) has, in the real world, some trouble walking. The timing must be quick and perfect.
(10 takes and 7 prints.) Completed at 6:00 P.M.

6:45 P.M. It is completely dark now, and because it is so cold, it feels like it's midnight. But Woody is still in a good mood, and ready to direct the kissing scene.
Shot 80: Mrs. Silverman's POV (point of view): Doris, the Communist's daughter, who believes in free love, and a black man get out of the car. They go to the front door. And then Doris gives "a big long kiss" to "the shvartza!" *(15 seconds.)*
First, the black musician, guitar in hand, goes to Doris's door and opens it. He takes Doris (Rebecca Schaeffer) to the front door, puts his guitar down, then kisses her. It's a big kiss, long and serious enough to give Mrs. Silverman her stroke. Doris, who has a beautiful chest (Woody had her change into a smaller sweater), is very receptive to the kiss. But the pace is too slow. Woody has the two get out of the car together, but it still doesn't look real. They start the kiss just outside the car, and Woody continues to tighten the shot until the pacing is correct.
(3 takes and 2 prints.) Completed at 7:30 P.M.
We go back to Mrs. Silverman, who has just had her stroke. Jimmy Mazzola brings in the ambulance (a beautiful white Cadillac from the 1940s) and parks it, all doors open and lights flashing, in front of Mrs. Silverman's house. Woody and Carlo decide the camera setup, then the boys start to work.
At 8:00 P.M., we break for dinner. The caterer is waiting for us in the deli next door. Woody sees me, hesitates, then asks Jane to tell me that I can go and have dinner with the crew.

9:45 P.M. We're back on the set. The whole street is lit and blocked. At each end, the PAs have constructed barricades and the onlookers are becoming more numerous. It is Friday night and the local newspaper has announced that Woody is in town. A man arrives and asks for Jimmy Mazzola. A good friend of Jimmy's, he is allowed onto the set.

10:00 P.M. Shot 82: After seeing the kiss, Mrs. Silverman has had a stroke. She is lying on a stretcher, still holding the cup of cocoa and saucer, mummified. The ambulance attendants carry the stretcher to the Cadillac, under the eyes of a very concerned Mr. Silverman. *(15 seconds.)*

The image is very funny. A few rehearsals are done for the camera, and Mrs. Silverman doesn't move an inch. Tom has to tell her to relax after each rehearsal or take, insisting that it is over. *(4 takes and 4 prints.)*

The last shot of the evening is of the ambulance arriving at the house to get Mrs. Silverman.

11:00 P.M. While the crew finishes setting up the shot, a sixteen-year-old girl, dressed and made up for an evening out, succeeds in sneaking past the PAs and stands just next to Woody. She stares at him. Woody, embarrassed, bends to hide behind his cap. But she bends, too, to watch his face. I alert Jimmy Sabat to the scene. "It's normal," he says. "She's from Brooklyn."

Shot 81: The ambulance rounds the corner at full speed, onto Beach 115th Street, sirens going. *(6 seconds.)*

The shot is spectacular (the public is happy) but easy. *(3 takes and 3 prints.)*

At 11:20 P.M., we wrap.

Monday, November 11, 1985   *Second Week*

Two planes collide over New Jersey: three dead. (New York Times)

There is some static on Ron's shortwave radio speech to the Soviets, but on several channels he can be heard clearly. It is not known whether the clear signals are the result of Gorby's decision

*to suspend jamming, as Ron has requested, or are produced by a
technical failure in the jamming system.* (New York Times)

In the van to Rockaway, we listen to Sergio Mendez's "Bossa
Nova" while Drew Rosenberg (one of the production assistants),
who didn't hear her alarm clock, finishes her makeup. She doesn't
need much. She has a very beautiful face, especially with her hair
piled on top the way it is now.

The outskirts of Brooklyn at 7:15 A.M: The different yellows of
the trees; the water; the fog; and the planes of Kennedy Airport
on the left. It's Veterans Day. An older man comes out of his
house to hang an American flag.

8:00 A.M. Beach 115th Street. Because the weather was uncertain, the wardrobe truck went to the cover set (a standby location
should circumstances prevent filming on the scheduled set) instead
of here. It finally returns. Today we are going to shoot the roof
sequence, where Little Joe and his gang go with binoculars to
watch for Nazi planes (sequence 124).

8:15 A.M. Woody and Carlo arrive and go directly to the roof.
It is atop Dubbins', and the crew uses a man lift to transport the
equipment up. People have already started gathering. Jimmy
Mazzola's friend is with us.

From the roof, there is a nice view of all Beach 115th Street,
with the sea at the end. Laundry has been hung on the other side
of the roof to hide the next streets. After discussing the camera
setup with Santo and Carlo, Woody sits and rereads his script.

9:30 A.M. The kids are brought up to the roof. They make a
nice little group, and get along well with each other. They're also
enjoying the shooting. Aside from Little Joe, who is a professional
actor, and Andrew, who had a small part in the Thanksgiving party
in *Hannah,* the three others were found in schools during lunch
time. As soon as they arrive, Woody goes to them, and has them
rehearse their lines.

10:00 A.M. Bob Greenhut and Ezra Swerdlow are beginning to
worry. Nothing has been shot yet. It's sunny (Woody wants overcast), and, though we don't see them, we hear the planes from
Kennedy Airport. The children have been sent back to their tutor,

and it's starting to get cold on the roof. Two more weeks in Rockaway; nobody is really enthusiastic about it.

10:30 A.M. We are ready to shoot. Woody rehearses the kids one last time. He never talks down to them. He explains where the camera is, what its movement is, and when they will be in the frame. He listens to their questions and answers them with precision. When they start to become less attentive—they've begun feeling much more at ease by now—Woody whistles, fingers in his mouth, says, "Listen, folks!" and that serves to make the atmosphere on the increasingly freezing roof a little warmer.

Shot 124: The five kids from the back, looking at the sky through the binoculars. They don't see a lot! Though the Masked

Avenger himself said so, Dave doubts the Germans could get over here so quickly. *(15 seconds.)*

Again, the real planes ruin several takes.

(9 takes and 4 prints.)

The second shot is a reverse angle: The camera is set on the elevated man lift. The man lift is not too stable and has to be attached to the roof. Woody has to check the frame from out on the lift. "Look at him!" Liz Dubelman, the camera trainee, says to me. "He has vertigo." Woody pulls his cap tighter onto his head, makes the face of a man going to the electric chair, and steps out.

Shot 124A: Front shot of the five kids at the edge of the roof. They continue to look at the sky and exchange views on the situation. But there are no Nazi planes. *(20 seconds.)*

(3 takes and 2 prints.)

12:00 noon. Woody eats a couple of crackers and puts on a sleeveless down vest under his green coat. We are going to do a close-up of the children's faces as they spot Miss Gordon in her shower. Woody tells them which direction to look, and explains what they are seeing. "Is she going to be in the window?" Burt asks.

Shot 124B: The camera starts on Nick, then goes to Little Joe, who spots something. It's Miss Gordon undressing. *(10 seconds.)*

There is a problem with light reflecting off Nick's glasses. And it's difficult getting a smooth shot because of the shaky man lift. *(11 takes and 3 prints.)* Completed at 12:30 P.M.

1:00 P.M. Shot 126: The five kids fight to get the binoculars to look at Miss Gordon. But at the end, she disappears, and they go back looking for Nazi planes. *(20 seconds.)*

The kids look anxiously at Woody to see if they are good, unable to make it to the end of the scene. Woody has to shorten the lines.

(14 takes and 5 prints.) Completed at 1:30 P.M.

2:00 P.M. Woody is downstairs to rehearse lines with the kids one more time. We continue to freeze. No break for lunch because it could rain at any minute and we are losing the light. The sky grows darker and darker.

3:00 P.M. Hot soup has been brought to the set.

Shot 128: The five kids look through the binoculars, and discover Rienzi, the inventor, working on his radio. "He must be a Nazi spy." "With a name like that, he must work for Mussolini!" *(33 seconds.)*

(3 takes and 3 prints.) Completed at 3:20 P.M.

The kids are finished for the day. They're brought back downstairs. We are preparing the next shot: The kids' POV of Miss Gordon preparing for her shower.

3:30 P.M. We don't do it; there's not enough light. It's been a difficult day. Woody is exhausted and the producers, by the end, have become a little nervous.

"It's a wrap" at 3:45 P.M.

Tuesday, November 12, 1985

The plane crash over New Jersey is called "unusual." (New York Times)

We listen to Charlie "Bird" Parker and Richard Strauss this morning in the van to Rockaway. Danny gets nervous with all the traffic and keeps changing back and forth, from Strauss to Parker, every ten seconds.

8:15 A.M. Rockaway. Low sky, with a light rain. Two establishing shots are scheduled—Little Joe's house and Rockaway.

Woody has a new black wool hat this morning.

Jane comes over to me. Is this the end of it? What did I do? But she asks me to a screening of *Hannah and Her Sisters*. I had requested that!

An article in the local Rockaway newspaper this morning states that five million dollars have been spent to clean and dress the city for the film(?!).

9:00 A.M. Shot 23: The camera tilts down from a lamppost to the house and the street, where an old man, an old woman, and a mother with two children walk by. *(13 seconds.)*

(6 takes and 3 prints.)

We're ready for the next shot—but a long dolly track has to be set.

(L to R:) Jimmy Mazzola; Woody Allen; Carlo DiPalma; Dickie Mingalone; Tom Reilly

10:00 A.M. Shot A10: The camera moves along the street, passing the different houses and the action in front of them: Two little girls skip rope; a boy throws a ball against the wall as a man comes home from work with his valet; a housewife comes out to get the little boy and takes him inside, hitting his behind. The shot ends on a wide angle of the street with Pop's yellow cab passing by. *(55 seconds.)*

Woody goes to each of the extras to explain what he or she should do. He shows the little boy how to toss the ball. He would like a quicker version, but Carlo doesn't think it will work on-camera. Woody will manage by writing a longer voice over.

(4 takes and 3 prints.) Completed at 10:30 A.M.

11:00 A.M. We are in little Joe's backyard. To be shot: Uncle Abe (Josh Mostel) coming back from Sheepshead Bay, with the fish given to him by his pal at Oscar's dock. Carlo and the boys go to work.

Abe is, in real life, the son of Zero Mostel. Renee Lippin, who plays his wife, Ceil, was Woody's press agent, wearing a neck brace and smoking like a chimney, in *Stardust Memories*.

11:45 A.M. Shot 28: Abe enters the yard. "Ceil, Ceil, I'm home! I've got fish!" He dumps the live fish on the ground. *(14 seconds.)*

A woman screams, "Woody!" from a neighboring yard. Woody looks at her and shows her, with a finger to his lips, that she shouldn't scream. A PA goes to her to explain we are recording sound.

Abe is quite funny dropping his sack of fish to the ground. After each take, Jimmy Mazzola gathers the fish and puts them in an aquarium so they will be in good shape for the next shot.

(4 takes and 3 prints.) Completed at 12:00 noon.

12:15 P.M. It is raining lightly but it won't show up on-camera. The sky is ideally overcast.

Shot 28A: Ceil exits the house, passes in front of Abe, complaining about cleaning the fish, and starts cleaning them. *(20 seconds.)*

The shot requires a little more direction for the blocking. When Ceil passes in front of Abe, the camera holds. Ceil exits on the left to get paper and a knife, while Abe exits on the right for a bench, leaving the screen empty. They return to the frame one after the other.

(12 takes and 3 prints.) Completed at 1:00 P.M.

1:30 P.M. The sky is dark now. Carlo wants to wait awhile before we shoot the next shot: the Waldbaums complaining about Cousin Ruthie listening in on their party line. He hopes that the clouds will part. The shot is set, and everyone stays close in case there is a break.

Dianne Wiest (Bea) comes to visit. She was the "working girl" who took Jeff Daniels to the whorehouse in *The Purple Rose of Cairo.* It's her first time on the set. Woody's behavior changes completely. No longer restrained, he hugs her, takes her by the hand, and talks to her nonstop.

3:15 P.M. There's no hope for any improvement in the light. The shot is all set, though, and will be done first thing tomorrow morning.

"It's a wrap!"

This evening, I see *Hannah and Her Sisters* with twenty people in a small, luxurious screening room on Broadway. Most of the guests are journalists from monthly magazines.

It's peculiar seeing Woody on the screen after having spent the day with him. The movie seems to clarify his behavior this afternoon with Dianne Wiest, who plays Holly in *Hannah.* On-screen, it looks as though he is taking a great deal of pleasure in acting with her. The way he looks at her is affectionate, conniving, and a little ironic, exactly as it was earlier today.

Wednesday, November 13, 1985

"Neighbor held in Queens murders. Suspect arrested after funeral. Called victims Mom and Pop." (Daily News)

Is Solzhenitsyn anti-Semitic? The new version of his novel August 1914 prompts dispute. "Yes," says Professor Richard Pipes of Harvard University. "No," says Professor Adam Ulam of Harvard University. (New York Times)

Rockaway is going Hollywood and Morton Nussbaum and his wife, Ruth, are a little upset; their clients don't recognize the office. "Where have you been? I can't find your office," an old lady told him. But the Nussbaums are not really worried. "It's the movies, after all," they say. "It's exciting!"

Joel Gestel, a restaurant owner, says that it is the best thing to happen to Rockaway in years. "It's putting us on the map!" Leo Ingber, proprietor of Cohen's kosher meat shop, is "quite proud" that Rockaway will be seen by thousands of moviegoers. And Leon Garapolsky, a Russian immigrant and owner of Leon's shoe repairs, says he never heard of Woody Allen but was happy to help his film. "Why not?" he says. (Daily News)

In the van to Rockaway, the radio announces that Jerry Falwell has said that Ferdinand Marcos is a great man.

8:00 A.M. Rockaway. I tell Kay I saw *Hannah* yesterday and that I really laughed when Woody converted to Catholicism. She tells me about a scene in which Woody was confessing to a priest. It looked very funny on the set, but Woody cut it. For each of his films, he cuts a lot of scenes for pace and uses the gags in later films. It is said they are kept on what are called "the black reels"!

The fish have spent the night in Little Joe's backyard in their aquarium. Jimmy Mazzola tells me about the time he had to bring a shark from Florida to New York for a film. It cost $500 for the shark and $1,300 for the transportation, and the director found it expensive! In the end, they ate the shark.

8:35 A.M. To be shot: the Waldbaums complaining about Ruthie listening in on their party line.

Hy Anzell (Mr. Waldbaum) was Joey Nichols in *Annie Hall* (1977), the friend of Little Woody's father who was always doing tricks with nickels. He was also a patient in *Bananas* (1971). Judith Malina (Mrs. Waldbaum) comes from the theater. And Julie Kavner (Mom) was Gail, Woody's assistant in *Hannah* (1986).

While Carlo finishes some adjustments on the lighting, Woody sits in the director's chair, thoughtful. Jimmy Mazzola's friend is back with us today but he is not very happy because the yard is so small that he has to stand in the street with the other onlookers. The atmosphere on the set is relaxed today; even the producers are joking.

9:05 A.M. Shot 30: The Waldbaums scream from their neighboring yard about Ruthie listening in on their party line (Ruthie just announced to the family Mrs. Waldbaum's troubles with her ovaries). "Stop listening to our party line! Stop snooping on us!" screams Waldbaum. Mrs. Waldbaum can hear Ruthie breathing, she says, demonstrating this. Mom and Pop react to them. "Let them take her ovaries out. What's it our business!" Mom yells. Ceil tries to placate the Waldbaums by offering them some of Abe's fish. *(35 seconds.)*

No problem with the action. Once again, the lines and the casting are sufficient to make the scene work. Woody asks Waldbaum to scream louder—"Stop listening to our party line! Stop snooping on us!"—and asks the wife to make her inhaling and exhaling louder, too. But the camera movement between Mom and Pop and the Waldbaums, and then Ceil, is not easily done. Dickie Mingalone, the camera operator, has to adapt his pace to that with which the actors say their lines, and it is changing a little with each take.

Also there are noisy buses on Rockaway Boulevard, and the planes, every one or two minutes sometimes, and often five in a row.

(20 takes and 6 prints.)

10:30 A.M. Shot 31: As Abe offers the Waldbaums "a fresh bluefish," the Communist neighbor (Larry David) races out of his house, chasing his son, who has put a firecracker in the cat's behind. "I'll kill you." Beautiful Doris, who believes in free love, comes out after them. "Dad, we were discussing Trotsky." *(12 seconds.)*

Most of the difficulties are again coming from the outside. There are the planes, always the planes. Then there's a neighbor's radio that Jimmy Sabat is picking up on the sound track, and that has to be hunted down. Woody works to tighten the scene. He has the Communist start before Abe has a chance to finish his sentence. And when at last there is a take that otherwise looks good, Abe says "flesh bluefish." Nobody has noticed except Kay. Abe denies the gaffe, but Kay insists she heard it. We listen to the sound track; Kay is right.

(8 takes and 6 prints.) Completed at 11:00 A.M.

11:30 A.M. It has begun to rain, and there's a race to get the next shot set up while it can still be filmed. It will be of Bea showing her new hat to the family (sequence 29). The scene is in two shots. One is an interior to be filmed later on a soundstage, and the other is an exterior where she appears at the window to show her hat to Abe and Ceil, who are arguing about the fish (sequence 28, done yesterday), just before Waldbaum starts to scream (sequence 30, done this morning).

Shot 29A: Bea appears at the window. Abe and Ceil are in the yard with the fish. She comments on the fish. Abe responds: "If you're not happy, take the gas pipe!" And Waldbaum intervenes out of frame: "Stop listening. . . !" *(15 seconds.)*

No problems with the actors, Bea is very good, and there is no complicated blocking. There are always more planes, though.

(10 takes and 4 prints.) Completed at 12:30 P.M.

A wild track of Waldbaum is made as a backup. There is some difficulty because the actor is a little hard of hearing and misses "cut." "Stop listening to our party line. . . . Stop listening to our party line. . . . Stop . . ."

To be shot next is sequence 76. It is Yom Kippur. As Abe says, "You can't turn on a light switch . . . nothing. . . . You're supposed to just sit, and fast, and pray, and atone for your sins." The Communist neighbor, who is Jewish but has no respect and believes only in Stalin, has his radio on, is eating, and his wife is working. Little Joe's family is in an uproar. The interior scene with the family reacting will be shot on a soundstage. Today, we are only shooting POVs of the Communist's yard.

Woody discusses the camera setting with Carlo. They decide to get two angles of the Communist's yard, one from inside Little

Joe's house, and the second with the camera in the yard.

When Woody discusses the camera setting with Carlo, he speaks very low and it is impossible to hear anything, especially on location, without being on his back. And even when he is concentrating hard on his work, Woody remains aware of everything going on on the set.

1:30 P.M. Shot 76A: Long shot of the Communist, in an undershirt, working with a hammer while his wife hangs the laundry and his kid (Louis T. Granirer) plays with a ball. All this with their radio blaring, and on Yom Kippur! *(5 seconds.)*
(3 takes and 2 prints.)
We move to the other POV. While the boys are setting the dolly track in the Communist's yard, Woody nearly steps in a pile of . . . but Carlo saves him. The yard is full of it. (Abe is right. They have no respect! They're not even clean!) Carlo, laughing, yells, "Jimmy Mazzola!" But Jimmy manages not to hear.

2:15 P.M. Shot 76B: The kid plays ball. The camera moves to the right. Doris brings a sandwich to her father, who starts to eat. The wife continues hanging laundry. *(10 seconds.)*
It's Woody, offscreen, who throws the ball back to the kid. The camera is between the child and the wall. The third time, Woody purposefully doesn't throw the ball well so the boy will miss it and must go after it, and the camera can begin its movement.
(3 takes and 3 prints.) Completed at 2:40 P.M.
We move back next door to Little Joe's yard to shoot Abe, whose nerves are on edge because he hasn't eaten. He decides to act and have a few words with this agnostic next door, "the Communist!"

3:00 P.M. Carlo and his team work against the failing light, "fighting the light." The rain comes and goes, but there is no chance of winning. It is decided that the scene will be done in the morning.
We break for lunch.

4:00 P.M. We're back on the set. To be shot: the Communist family listening to the story of Polly Phelps on the radio. We are, in reality, in Little Joe's house. Woody and Carlo discuss the camera setup. Also in the room are Tom; Jimmy Mazzola, to move the furniture; Ray Quinlan, the gaffer, with Hammer (Jim Manzione), his second, for the lighting; and Bobby Ward, the key grip. The shot is decided. Woody returns to his trailer because Carlo needs at least an hour to light the room, and the boys go to work.

5:00 P.M. Carlo is ready. "Bring the Communists!" screams Tom.

Shot 166: The parents sit at the table while pretty Doris sits at the piano, her brother at her side. They listen to Polly Phelps's story, rapt. *(10 seconds.)*

Woody doesn't like Doris's sweater. Jeffrey gets nervous. Several different ones are brought, and Doris, standing before a very serious, staring Woody, tries them on.

(5 takes and 2 prints.)

We move to the next shot, in which the family learns of Polly's death. Carlo needs to adjust the light.

6:15 P.M. Shot 172A: The camera moves from Doris and her brother to the parents. They're stunned. *(5 seconds.)*

(5 takes and 2 prints.)

At 6:45 P.M., we wrap.

Thursday, November 14, 1985

Homeless in city: Ed announces that a psychiatrist will be dispatched each night to observe homeless people who congregate at major transportation hubs, and to order the hospitalization of those unable to care for themselves. (New York Times)

It's clear and beautiful this morning in Manhattan. The buildings separate themselves sharply from the sky. No fog, no clouds—bad for Woody!

8:15 A.M. Breakfast with Dickie Mingalone. And over the food, we talk about food. He asks me if I know about the good French restaurants in town, then proceeds to recommend two: Pierre au Tunnel on the West Side ("Go on Wednesday. They serve crepes on Wednesday") and Brittany du Soir, at Fifth-third Street ("Ask for Louis, the bartender"). "And if you want to eat good Italian food," he tells me, "go to Brooklyn. Fourth Street. That's where the boys are!"

9:00 A.M. We're back in Little Joe's yard to shoot another sequence where Abe brings back fish. Woody has decided on the camera placement and Carlo has started to work.

The weather is perfect now; the clouds are back. Woody looks elegant in a felt hat. Jimmy Sabat is reading his racing form. "It's better," he says, "than reading news about all the bad that's happening in the world." We hear that Alberto Sordi, the great comic actor from Italy, will be dropping by the set today.

9:30 A.M. Shot 162X: It's 1943 now. Abe has brought eels this time. Ceil can't believe it! Abe tells her, if she is not happy, to "take the gas pipe." Waldbaum appears at his window, ever ready with his leitmotiv: "Stop listening. . . !" *(40 seconds.)*

Jimmy Mazzola brings on the eels, but there is a problem. The eels are wriggling a lot this morning, wrapping themselves around Abe's wrists and arms, and Abe, though he likes fish, isn't really enjoying it. Woody looks fairly disgusted by the sight. Woody hates animals in general; "Pigeons are rats with wings," he says in *Stardust Memories*. Dickie comes to the rescue. When he was a kid in Washington Heights, he used to catch eels in the Hudson River. He shows Abe how to hold them, how to keep them in submission.

Again, it is a little difficult getting the camera movement to perfectly match the actors' lines. The eels, too, are not very cooperative. In one take they look dead; in the next, they're overacting. And finally, Waldbaum, even though he has a PA to cue him, is forever a little too eager with his refrain: "Stop listening . . ."

(10 takes and 5 prints.) Completed at 10:00 A.M.

For the next shot, we're still in the yard, but we've gone back to the thirties and to Yom Kippur. Abe is going to talk to that Communist neighbor. The camera is being set on the roof next door for a high wide shot. Dickie becomes creative; he has a branch cut from a tree, attached to a stand, and placed so the limbs will be in the frame.

10:45 A.M. Everything is set, but there are problems with the light; now there's too much of it. Yesterday, the sky was overcast, and today has to match.

So we wait for clouds.

Jeffrey likes to hug actresses. The other day it was Mom. Today it's Ceil.

11:15 A.M. Woody has earphones on, his hat over them, ready to listen to the dialogue as it is recorded.

Shot 77: Abe comes out the door and goes down the stairs, furious. He crosses the yard, and breaks through the fence around the Communist's yard.

Abe: "Can't you turn your radio off?! We're praying!"

Communist: "Praying! What good is that? You should be working, working for the benefit of your fellow man!"

Abe: "It's a sin to work today."

Communist: "It's a sin not to work. Isaac, come in and eat."

Abe: "I'm not allowed to eat!"

Communist: "Oh yeah! Who says so?"

And on it goes until Abe is finally convinced to go in. *(40 seconds.)*

At the start of each take, we can hear Abe inside the doorway, working himself up to anger: "The son of a bitch!" For two or three takes, Abe jumps down the last three steps of the stairway. Woody asks him to go down the stairs as fast as he has been, even faster, but taking each step; it is visually better that way. After each take, Jimmy Mazzola quickly repairs the fence so Abe can break it in once more.

The action is good. Woody asks the actors to accelerate the pace and exaggerate—"You must be really furious." He asks the Communist to react strongly at first, then suddenly to quiet down. After trying a few variations and finally getting what he wants, Woody asks the actors to improvise their lines at the end of the scene, just before they enter the house. "Come in," the Communist tells Abe, "I've got some literature."

(12 takes and 6 prints.) Completed at 12:00 noon.

12:30 P.M. Back on the roof to shoot the kids' POV of Miss Gordon's "striptease" (sequence 125). Sydney A. Blake (Miss Gordon) was the *Variety* reporter in *Purple Rose*. In real life, she lives in California and works at HBO as a story analyst. She had given up acting, but when Woody called her about this film, she couldn't resist; she couldn't resist Woody, that is, not the role.

Carlo enjoys working with Woody and finds they understand each other well. The experience, though, is entirely different from the ones he has had with Bertolucci and Antonioni. It's a much quieter set, and he likes it. I mention the beauty of the fog sequence he shot for Antonioni in *Identificazione di una Donna*. (1982). It's a wonderful scene, with a couple getting lost and separated in the fog. Woody liked it, too, and wants Carlo to do the same for him when Bea and her date Sidney Manulis get lost in the fog at Breezy Point, after the invasion of New Jersey by Martians (sequence 56).

12:35 P.M. Ready to shoot. The PAs have the portion of the street below blocked. Woody prepares to direct Miss Gordon's disrobing via walkie-talkie, but there is a last-minute problem. Miss Gordon wants to be alone in the room; she doesn't want men watching her. A PA explains that someone has to transmit the directions coming over the walkie-talkie. She holds her ground.

Kids, she doesn't mind, but no men. The Salad Sisters find the solution. Fern tells Miss Gordon that Richie Patrick and Jimmy Frederick are gay. The look on their faces! Miss Gordon submits.

Shot 125: Miss Gordon at the window, undressing. She disappears, returns wrapped in a towel, then drops the towel. *(20 seconds.)*

From the roof, we don't see a lot of the action, but the camera has a zoom lens to match the view through the kids' binoculars. Woody whispers directions into the walkie-talkie.

(4 takes and 2 prints.)

Shot 125A: Close shot. Miss Gordon reappears in the towel.

(2 takes and 2 prints.)

At 1:15 P.M., the striptease is over, and the five kids are brought back to the roof for some additional reaction shots. The young actors are feeling more and more at ease, bordering on the rambunctious, but Tom's booming voice quiets them down. Fern is there with Little Joe's teeth; Little Joe, in reality, has lost a front tooth.

1:45 P.M. The camera is ready. A carpet has been placed under the children so the camera, here on this old roof, will not pick up the vibrations of their footsteps. Woody acts out the reactions for each of the children's close-ups. They're supposed to see Miss Gordon's towel drop.

Shot 125B: Dave reacts: "Ah ma, Ah ma, Ah ma . . ."

Even Woody laughs.

(2 takes and 2 prints.)

Shot 125C: Burt (with a melancholy look): "I love you." And he blows a timid kiss.

The kids are having as much fun as we are. Woody asks Burt for a variation: "Ah bala bala bala . . ." Each time, Woody acts out the reaction before filming. He is nearly as funny as the kids.

(2 takes and 2 prints.)

Shot 125D: Andrew closes the series of reactions by sending Miss Gordon a big kiss and closing his eyes in rapture.

(2 takes and 2 prints.)

At 2:00 P.M. the kids are sent back to their tutor.

Last shot before lunch: A POV, through the kids' binoculars, of Rienzi the inventor adjusting his radio (sequence 128). Rienzi lives on the other side of Little Joe's house, in the middle of Beach 115th Street, next door to Mr. and Mrs. Silverman.

Shot 128A: Rienzi, seen through his window, manipulating his shortwave radio. *(2 takes and 2 prints.)*

We break for lunch at 2:30 P.M.

(L to R:) Andrew (Fletcher Previn); Burt (Sal Tuminello); Nick (Oliver Block); Little Joe (Seth Green); Dave (Maurice Toueg)

3:30 P.M. We are back inside the Communist's house for the scene in which Little Joe and his friends listen to a horror show on the radio (sequence 10).

The children are brought in so Woody can figure out the shot. He seats them in several different spots and moves them some more, using his hands to approximate the camera frame, panning from one of the boys to the next, trying different angles. Carlo follows him. The set is totally silent. After a few minutes, Carlo suggests a camera setup, the same movement Woody has been considering but from a different angle. Woody quickly agrees.

Carlo needs nearly two hours to light the room. The place is small, full of furniture, and in the film this will be a night scene.

4:40 P.M. Alberto Sordi is here. Nobody on the set, except Woody and Carlo, has heard of him. And yet he started his career at age thirteen, winning an MGM-sponsored contest by imitating Oliver Hardy. He also starred in two Fellini movies, *The White Sheik* (1952) and *I Vitelloni* (1953). Alberto Sordi is a great actor.

For Carlo it is a big reunion. Carlo was second unit director of photography on Mario Monicelli's Oscar-nominated *La Grande Guerra* (1959), in which Alberto Sordi starred. They kiss each other, they pat each other's cheeks, they hug—the Italian way. For Woody, it is more formal. He makes himself available and listens attentively; Sordi speaks English. The meeting is brief but cheerful. It's a nice scene—two great comics together in the middle of a set, with half the lights on.

5:15 P.M. Carlo is still lighting. Brian is massaging Liz's sore back. Woody sits in an armchair, hat over his eyes, between the children, who have become a little noisy. Woody seems thoughtful, yet happy. Burt announces that he has several girlfriends at school. Andrew seems dubious. Burt asks me if I have a girlfriend. Andrew waits for my answer.

5:40 P.M. Carlo is ready. Woody is called, having retreated to his trailer, and rehearsals begin.

Shot 10: The kids as they listen, horrified, to the radio program. The camera starts on the radio and moves to Burt and Andrew lying on the floor, to a profile of Nick, then on to the Communist's Son, and stops on Little Joe and Dave, sitting on the piano bench. Then, as the program breaks at a tense moment, Dave takes an ice cube from his glass and puts it down Little Joe's neck. Little Joe screams like crazy. *(42 seconds.)*

But the camera tripod has to be changed. Dickie is not happy with the shakiness of the pan.

6:00 P.M. The house is crowded and the kids are starting to get overly active. Carlo complains. Tom's voice booms, "Folks, we can't hear!" Woody waits. He takes off his hat and whistles, his head swaying to his own rhythm. Then suddenly he stops, and puts his hat back on, thoughtful.

6:15 P.M. Woody doesn't want to rehearse the kids anymore. The first take is shot. The kids listen to the playback of the horror show, then, at the end of the scene, the playback is cut so Little Joe's scream can be recorded cleanly. The main problem is with the scream. Originally, it was Little Joe who puts the ice cube down Nick's neck. But Nick doesn't scream well enough. Dave is tried but he's not good enough either. Finally, it is Little Joe who seems the best. Woody rehearses the scream with him, and we continue, though it is already the twelfth take.

7:20 P.M. Everyone is tired. It's a strange atmosphere—this overcrowded room, beautifully lit, with the echoing voice of the horror-show narrator. After each take, Woody turns to Dickie and asks, "OK?" to see if the camera was good. Kay has told me that even when he is acting, Woody does exactly the same thing. After finishing his lines, he turns quickly to the cameraman with an anxious "OK?"
(16 takes and 7 prints.)

At 7:25 P.M., "It's a wrap."

In the van back to Manhattan, Barbara is not happy. She doesn't like the van, but the station wagon she usually rides in has already gone. The van gives her motion sickness, she explains. Kay and Fern, exhausted by the day, don't show her sympathy. Within another few minutes, though, Barbara is laughing and having a good time, entertaining us. Little Joe, too, enjoys the ride; when the van hits bumps, he goes flying to the roof. That lasts until Fern decides she needs a cigarette. The windows are opened. Fern's cigarette becomes a major issue. Barbara's expression is that of someone experiencing the throes of death.
We all, however, make it back to Manhattan alive.

Friday, November 15, 1985

Fifteen thousand feared dead in Colombia as the eruption of a volcano creates torrents of mud. Four thousand bodies already found. (New York Times)
AND THE WHOLE WORLD BEGAN TO SCREAM (Daily News)
Ron says that his meeting with Gorby "can be an historic opportunity to set a steady, more constructive course in the 21st century." But Gorby still believes the United States is an implacable foe. (New York Times)

And girls in high schools throughout New York State will be allowed to play with boys in contact sports. (New York Times)

It's late call today because we have two night shots later. First a reshoot of Doris's kiss; in the dark, it wasn't clear that the black man was black. Then there's the scene of Mom and Pop watching searchlights. (sequence 117).

9:15 A.M. Rockaway. An amusement park on the shore, between Beach Ninety-seventh and Beach Ninety-eighth streets. There is a beautiful sun, so it's impossible to shoot. We move back to 115th Street, where some summer shots and interiors can be done while we wait for clouds.

10:00 A.M. On Rockaway Boulevard. The camera is set up in front of Woolworth's, shooting across the street. A table is set up in front of Cohen's Kosher Meat and the Neptune Bagel. Period cars are parked on the street. Jimmy Mazzola is ready at the end of the block to signal those cars that will be driving past in the shot. It's sunny, but cool now. Extras in summer clothes are poised for action.

Barbara is a PA today, helping with the traffic, a walkie-talkie at her side. "It's nice that they're considering me, at last, as a human being and not as Seth's mother!" she tells me.

Shot 15: Four men play cards at a table on the sidewalk, listening to a radio broadcast of the Yankee-Tiger game. A gunshot rings out. The men look toward a second-floor window. *(38 seconds.)*

Everybody is ready. Woody has given his directions to the four cardplayers and the few extras. But we have to wait while Cliff Schorr, the scenic artist, paints out the yellow line down the middle of the boulevard, so the street has the right period look. He'll have to paint it back as soon as the shot is finished.

10:30 A.M. Woody is standing, Jane at his side. An elderly, overweight little woman stops in front of him and starts telling him about the problems she's having with her husband, her children, her life. Woody listens, awkward but attentive. He doesn't know how to end this conversation; who would?

10:45 A.M. Ready to shoot: A PA, hidden in one of the shops and receiving directions from Woody via walkie-talkie, tells the men when to react to the gunshot. The sound effect will be added during postproduction. Between each take, while Jimmy Mazzola's cars go back to their starting positions, we let the regular traffic go through the setting.

(2 takes and 2 prints.) Completed at 11:00 A.M.

The camera is moved across the street, just in front of the tailor's shop. The tailor is not thrilled. He doesn't find movies "exciting" as Morton Nussbaum does; he is not "proud" as Leo Ingber is. "You're blocking my business!" he complains. "I'm going to sue!" He starts taking pictures on his lawyer's advice. "I've been here fifty years. I've always paid my taxes." Tim Bourne, the location manager, goes to negotiate while we continue to work. After about ten minutes, things have settled down and the tailor is cracking jokes with Tim.

11:20 A.M. Shot 15A: A closer shot of the players. Same action.

(3 takes and 2 prints.) Completed at 11:30 A.M.

12:30 P.M. Pop, Mom, and Bea have arrived. Woody relaxes in his trailer. And Ken Ornstein, the second assistant director, hurries past, followed by his newly recruited aide, Barbara!

1:00 P.M. The Waldbaums' residence. They are going to listen to Polly Phelps's story on the radio. The room is just too small. Richie guards the entrance, and we sit outside, on a small dirty staircase (Jane, Andrew, the two stand-ins, and the Salad Sisters, who go in and out) while listening to the action through Richie's walkie-talkie. Woody dashes by. Next week, Jane informs me, he is going to let me tell him about my plans for the book.

Shot 166A: Mrs. Waldbaum crosses the room and Mr. Waldbaum turns up the radio, totally attentive. *(10 seconds.)*

(6 takes and 2 prints.)

Shot 172B: The two are stunned by Polly's death.

(2 takes and 2 prints.) Completed at 1:15 P.M.

1:30 P.M. Summer in Little Joe's backyard. The grass is beautiful and green; some extra rolls of grass are piled on the side. There is a hammock and a bench, and flowers are everywhere. Santo's team finishes bringing summer to the yard so Bea can listen to beautiful songs on the radio (sequence A102).

Because of uncertain weather, the schedule is changing from hour to hour. Jimmy Mazzola begs for some advance notice so he can adjust his schedule. "Don't worry about the schedule, Jim. Just be ready!" Tom tells him.

Mario Mazzola, Jimmy's father (*Hannah* was his last film before he retired after thirty-seven years in the business), comes by the set to see how the boys are doing. They have the same stocky build, the same smile. Fern's parents are also visiting, and Carlo hugs Drew and kisses Bea's hand.

I am puzzled when I am asked to "pick up the cards." I learn that there is gambling going on behind the scene, handled by the sound department. Organized by Louis Sabat (the boom man), supervised by Jimmy Sabat (Louis's older brother), and "checked" by Frankie Graziadei (the sound recorder), the game works this way: A deck of cards is sold at $10 a card. Once done, someone not in the game chooses three cards from a new deck. The first person to have a card he bought chosen wins $300, the second $150, and the third $70. Today, Jimmy Mazzola wins first prize. Second and third prize go to a couple of teamsters.

1:45 P.M. The sun is beginning to disappear behind clouds. Woody is not satisfied with the set. We break for lunch.

4:00 P.M. It's getting dark, and cold, and boring. We're waiting for night for the last two shots, Doris's kiss and the searchlights (sequence 117). A flyer has been distributed in the neighborhood reading, AIR RAID SCENE TONIGHT. PLEASE TURN OFF ALL LIGHTS AT 6:00 P.M. OR CALL, AND WE'LL PLACE BLACK PLASTIC IN YOUR WINDOWS. Worse than Yom Kippur!

5:00 P.M. The boys have started lighting the street so we'll be able to see the black actor this time. The usual crowd hangs around. Jimmy Mazzola's friend has been with us all day. Another fellow has been hanging around for the past two days, and is constantly taking pictures of Woody. The other day, he was even on the roof next to us, and Tom had to ask him to clear the frame. But still he hangs on and has even begun making friends with some of the crew.

A ten-year-old, fair-haired boy skateboards up to me. "Is Woody Allen famous?" he asks. I tell him. The boy goes to Richie and asks him for a piece of paper. He goes to a policeman and borrows a pen. Then he goes to Woody, gets an autograph, and skateboards away. Brooklyn again!

5:30 P.M. We're ready to shoot the kiss. Doris is dressed differently and is with a different black man.

Shot R80: It's the same action as the first time, but they are going under a lamppost this time, so Mrs. Silverman can see it clearly and have her stroke.

(6 takes and 2 prints.)

Then we move to Little Joe's house for the searchlights.

6:30 P.M. It is definitely cold now. The street is dark, the searchlights are a block away, and Carlo doesn't want to shoot. The sky isn't dark enough, he says. But Woody wants to try.

7:30 P.M. It's freezing now. We've had to wait while a light three blocks away was extinguished; it was casting a shadow on one of the houses. The crowd is also waiting, wondering what's happening. Nothing is.

Finally, we're ready to try.

Shot 117A: Mom and Pop's POV of the searchlights. Tom directs, via walkie-talkie, a PA who is stationed by the searchlights over on Beach 117th Street. Occasionally, a real plane crosses the sky.

(1 long take.)

Shot 117B: The searchlights are seen over Mom and Pop's shoulders. The same action from the lights.

(1 long take again.)

Shot 117: Mom and Pop exit the house and discover the searchlights. It's beautiful. Mom wants to wake up Little Joe so he can see. *(27 seconds.)*

Two projectors shine across a white board, which throws a moving light on the couple, simulating the reflection of the beams.

(3 takes and 2 prints.)

At 7:40 P.M., we wrap.

Monday, November 18, 1985   *Third Week*

The death toll in Colombia is feared to be twenty-five thousand. (New York Times)

"Hell no! Cap won't go," Ron says after the letter Weinberger has sent him, urging that no accord be reached in Geneva, is disclosed in the press. (Daily News)

Lon Nol, seventy-two, former president of Cambodia, died yesterday in California.

And two Brooklyn brothers died this weekend.

Saturday, Louis Fleischer—one of the Fleischer brothers, Walt Disney's only real rival in the 1930s, and the uncle of director Richard Fleischer—died on the West Coast at age ninety-four. He and his brothers started as cartoonists on the Brooklyn Daily Eagle, and created Betty Boop, Popeye the Sailor, and the animated feature Gulliver's Travels. Before joining his brothers, Louis played piano for silent films.

Sunday, it was Jimmy Ritz, eighty-two, of the Ritz Brothers. Born in New Jersey and raised in Brooklyn, the brothers—Al, Jim, and Harry—gave their first performances at Coney Island. Their first movie together was Hotel Anchovy (1934), but Al had been an extra in The Avenging Trail (1918). Harry had the last film role, in Mel Brooks's Silent Movie (1976). Now, only Harry and sister Gertrude are left.

8:00 A.M. Rockaway. Once more, a beautiful sun! And the weather forecaster says it will be the same tomorrow. So tomorrow morning we'll stay in town and shoot interiors. Today, summer shots and a few interiors are scheduled.

Breakfast with Bobby Ward and Dickie in the production office. Dickie tells us about the nice little joint he went to Friday night with good food and good music. He asks me if I have made it to Pierre au Tunnel.

8:45 A.M. To be shot: an interior with the Dowdy Housewife listening to the Phyliss and Paul soap opera as she cleans her kitchen (sequence 11). It's a tiny room. Woody, Carlo, Tom, and the housewife are working out the shot. Woody, his hands approximating the frame, tries out some movement for the camera. He experiments with the blocking of the scene. He hangs the drapes, he puts the babies to bed, he picks a baby up, he goes through all the actions himself. Carlo watches and listens. You get the feeling that Woody is both precise in that he knows exactly the sort of effect he is looking for, and imprecise because he lets the atmosphere of the room lead him to that effect. And it doesn't take long for him to make up his mind. He has soon decided on a camera angle, and roughly the camera movement; now he lets Carlo work on the lighting and a more definite camera blocking. This is the first time I've witnessed the blocking process so completely. There's a feeling of quiet intensity on the set.

10:00 A.M. Carlo is ready. Once again, it's impossible for everyone to be in the room during shooting. Woody is crouched under the camera, and Tom is hiding himself amid the hanging laundry. The babies are brought by their mothers at the last moment. The soap opera is on the playback.

Shot 11: The housewife puts one of her babies in the playpen, puts dirty dishes in the sink, tests the babies' bottles, hangs wash. On the radio Paul asks Phyliss to come with him, to leave her husband and Little Tom, for their love . . . *(52 seconds.)*

The babies start screaming (perfect!). Woody asks the housewife to react to the radio lines. On "summer on the French Riviera," she'll be washing dirty dishes . . .

(7 takes and 4 prints.) Completed at 10:45 A.M.

11:15 A.M. The kids are back, along with Mom and Bea, for the shot we couldn't get Friday of Bea listening to songs on the radio. Carlo uses natural light, with one reflector trained on Bea, who sits on the porch. But he wants to wait for the sun to come out more, so it will give the house a better look.

Woody goes to chat with Bea. Barbara comes to me to complain about the slowness of the shoot. At Dubbins', property people are setting up boxes of fruits and vegetables for the afternoon scenes. The extras are relaxing down the block on the porch of the house that is being used as a holding area, taking in the sun in their period clothes.

12:05 P.M. The sun is taking a break, so we break for lunch. Woody goes off with Andrew, Bea, Mom, and Carlo. The photographer—the fellow who has been hanging around lately—stops Woody, introduces himself, and shakes hands. Woody makes a quick exit.

1:00 P.M. An older man asks me the name of the movie, then starts talking about the period cars and how it reminds him of the good old days when America led the world and World War II, when they "beat the shit out of" the Germans and the Japs, both.

His monologue goes on. Then suddenly he changes the topic to Woody, and tells me how much he liked *Annie Hall*.

Another guy approaches me—I'm the only one around who doesn't look busy—and asks if we're still hiring extras.

1:20 P.M. Shot A102: Bea is on the porch in an armchair, reading and listening to the radio. The kids race into the house, brushing past her, then return with cake and milk, go down the stairs and out of the frame. *(25 seconds.)*

A few variations are done. Carlo asks Bea, who is swaying to the music, to sway in and out of the light being reflected on her. Woody asks the kids to group themselves more tightly, and to start eating and drinking while they are running. For the last three takes, Mom rushes out the door and snatches back a bottle of Jack Daniel's that Burt has stolen, an idea Woody has come up with on the set. As usual, the kids enjoy doing the scene.

(10 takes and 7 prints.) Completed at 2:00 P.M.

2:30 P.M. We are ready to shoot Mr. Zipsky running down the street in his underwear, wielding a meat cleaver. This is the day of his nervous breakdown.

Shot F102: Mr. Zipsky, in his underwear and brandishing a meat cleaver, appears at his door and runs down the sidewalk, where he threatens a woman and her daughter. Then he enters Dubbins', reappears chasing a lady, and exits on the left side of the frame, only to return being chased by a policeman through the traffic. (Woody had also considered having him appear in his underwear in a synagogue.) *(45 seconds.)*

First Woody does the action himself, slowly, so Carlo can check the dolly and pans. Then, assistant cameraman Jay Levy plays the scene so Woody can view it through the camera. And finally, it's Mr. Zipsky's turn. (He looks perfect in his shoes, socks, underpants, and undershirt.)

Joel Eidelsberg (Mr. Zipsky) is not an actor by profession, but he is so naturally good (or the idea of the gag is so funny) that everyone bursts into laughter. "Very good—perfect," Woody tells him. But poor Mr. Zipsky is out of breath. Before the first take, Woody tells him not to stop by the lady and the little girl because it spoils the fluidity of the camera movement.

First take: Zipsky is still funny, but not as good. Woody tells him to just ignore the lady and little girl, and instructs the woman

being chased to come out of Dubbins' a beat later. Zipsky goes back to his house, exhausted. Dickie mentions to Woody that Zipsky shouldn't wave the meat cleaver too much; it creates bad reflections. Woody runs over to tell Zipsky.

3:30 P.M. Second take. "Good, Wood," Dickie screams. It looks excellent, as funny as ever. Woody wants to try again, but Carlo stops him. The light is gone. Earlier it was just right; now it is too late. Dickie thinks we have one good take at least. Woody is still not certain. Neither is Kay.

"He'll talk to you tomorrow," Jane tells me before leaving. We wrap.

Tuesday, November 19, 1985

*After the government suspended efforts to find survivors Sunday,
five more people, including an eighteen-month-old boy, have been
found alive by rescuers in Colombia.* (New York Times)

*To realtor Donald Trump, the 150-story tower he is going to
build—the highest in the world—on the West Side of Manhattan
will symbolize New York's power as well as his own.* (New York
Times)

In Geneva, Gorby has joined the joust. (Daily News)

*And another party is going on in Oman, where Sultan Qabus
bin Said is receiving representatives from some sixty countries,
including half a dozen heads of state, for National Day, which
doesn't mark any particular event, but coincides with the sultan's
birthday.*

*There will be camel races by the Bedouins, and a multimillion-
dollar, Hollywood-produced fireworks display. All the Bedouins
are in from the desert for the celebration.*

*In 1970 Sultan Qabus bin Said, helped by the British and a few
Bedouins, overthrew his father, Sultan Said bin Taimur—who
was the reclusive and curmudgeonly absolute ruler of Oman. The
old sultan forbade smoking, listening to the radio, playing drums
loud, and the wearing of eyeglasses or European shoes. He also
decided who could have a car, and allowed only a few of them.
Similarly, he decided who could get married, be educated, or le-
gally leave the country. For himself, he avoided the use of gas-
oline, preferring to have his automobile pushed along by slaves.*

*On the day of the coup, the old sultan, trying to pull a pistol,
shot himself in the foot, and became the only casualty. He left for
England, where he died in his suite at the Dorchester hotel two
years later.* (New York Times)

8:00 A.M. The whorehouse from *Purple Rose* is on West Sev-
enty-first Street, and belongs to Grace and St. Paul's Lutheran
Church, which uses it as a shelter for the homeless during the
winter. It's on the market for $1.2 million, and we're here today to
film people listening to the Great Tonino episode.

8:20 A.M. We're inside the house on the first floor. I get a nice
but distant good-morning smile from Woody. He decides on the

camera movement—a short dolly—then returns to his trailer.

An old couple are brought in and seated in armchairs near the radio. They must be nearly as old as this house (built at the end of the last century), and they appear to be enjoying the filming as much as the kids. They have brought their own camera and they ask one of the boys if he could take a picture of them as a souvenir.

Carlo goes to work. He'll need at least an hour, maybe an hour and a half. He is wearing a new mauve felt hat today, not his usual Tibetan-like one. His hair is already long, and he never cuts it during a shooting. We have three and a half months left.

The chaos begins. Lights are hung from the ceiling, the dolly track is laid, and wires are everywhere. Carlo, with Ray and Hammer at his side, walks and watches, as if he were on another planet. Because his English is not the best, he uses his hands—thin and beautiful—to get his meaning across, though Ray seems to understand before Carlo can even get three hesitant words out. And slowly, surely, the set begins to take shape.

9:20 A.M. Carlo is finishing up. Jeffrey is checking the costumes of the old couple. Jeffrey is, himself, always dressed elegantly and esoterically. Today he is wearing a Palestinian scarf.

9:30 A.M. Shot 2C: The old couple listen to the Tonino story through earphones. *(10 seconds.)*

There are no real problems, other than that the old man wants to act. He is making faces as he listens, and Woody wants him motionless.

(2 takes and 2 prints.)

Shot 8A: The old woman and the old man react to static on the radio. *(5 seconds.)*

(2 takes and 2 prints.)

We move to the other side of the room to shoot a young rich couple also listening to the Tonino saga. The camera setup—a short dolly again—is decided in two minutes. Carlo asks for forty-five minutes to light it. Woody dashes out.

10:50 A.M. Shot 2D: A young rich couple, looking elegant, finish tea as they listen to the radio. A maid comes for the tray. She exits. Zoom in to a close-up of the radio. *(5 seconds.)*

Jimmy Mazzola suggests a new liquid chemical for the tea cups; its smoke looks like steam. But it doesn't smell at all good, and no one is convinced by his demonstration. We go back to real hot tea.

(2 takes and 2 prints.)

For the second shot, where the young couple get radio static, Woody wants a pan of the young man going to the radio, hitting it, and turning it off. Carlo and Woody check the pan through the viewfinder, and finally decide on a simple wide-angle shot.

Shot 8B: Static. The rich man hits the radio, then turns it off. *(5 seconds.)*

(3 takes and 3 prints.)

We move downstairs to the kitchen, where a family is listening to the Tonino story on the radio.

Jane takes me aside. She asks me to tell her again exactly what I want. She wants to be sure she is conveying it correctly to Woody. In giving his OK for this book, Woody was vague, not telling me how long I could stay, not setting any guidelines.

So that's it! He doesn't want to talk to me. Or maybe there are things he is not going to accept. Is he already tired of me? Is he looking for a pretext to end the whole thing?

1:00 P.M. Shot 2E: A family—grandparents, parents, two children—are gathered around a table, eating in silence and listening to the radio. The little boy rises, goes to turn up the radio. *(5 seconds.)*

(3 takes and 3 prints.)

We break for lunch at 1:15 P.M.

It's the worst lunch of my life. People try to cheer me up, telling me not to worry, that it doesn't mean anything. "I'm seeing more of him than I do my own wife, and we never say a word!" says one. And Bobby Ward hasn't talked to him in the ten years they've worked together. Jeff Daniels, when he was playing Tom Baxter in *Purple Rose,* only heard from him to get directions. And then there is the Marshall McLuhan story. When McLuhan came to the set to reshoot his scene in *Annie Hall,* Woody didn't want to talk to him anymore. It was very embarrassing.

2:15 P.M. We are back on the set, in the street. Woody passes me, followed by Jane. There is a faint acknowledgment from him, but Jane is a little cold.

Sally (Mia Farrow) is here for the first time, with her six-month-old baby girl. She is beautiful, very fresh and natural, with her high cheekbones. Woody takes Baby Dylan in his arms and starts playing, making faces, putting his cap on her head. The baby enjoys it.

Carlo introduces me to his wife, Adriana, who is visiting. She is Italian and also speaks French.

Then we go back to the kitchen.

Shot 8C: The family's radio gets staticky. The little boy bangs it. The little girl joins him. (5 seconds.)

"More energy!" screams Woody.

(3 takes and 2 prints.)

We move to the second floor to shoot the Victrola experiment (sequence 40).

3:00 P.M. The scene will be done in two shots. The boys are setting up the camera on the stairway. The Victrola man, dressed and made up, waits in the next room, socializing with the crew. He is a nonactor, a producer of jazz and classical records at RCA, and this is his first movie.

Carlo comes and sits next to me. We talk about Adriana. She is a producer and distributor; her company distributed *Amadeus* and *Ran* in Italy. She is here on business, buying and selling movies, and to see Carlo, of course. She'll be coming back for Christmas. Over the holidays, Carlo is planning a screening of his film *Teresa the Thief*, with Monica Vitti. Liz told him I would like to see it.

Everybody is quite friendly toward me. Is this the swan song?

3:30 P.M. Shot 40: Long shot of the Victrola man at the controls of his radio. (15 seconds.)

No big problems, no major direction needed, except when the Victrola man performs his tasks with a little too much enthusiasm and Woody has to ask him to tone it down.

(5 takes and 2 prints.)

We move inside the room for the next shot. A short dolly track is being set.

4:00 P.M. Jane takes me to a corner of the room, hands me the script, and says, "This is for you. You must bring it back tomorrow morning." He's agreed to let me stay through until the end of the shooting. He'll take me to the dailies sometimes. I'll be able to spend a week in the editing room with him and see the rough cut and the final cut. And he will definitely be interested in seeing my manuscript before publication, which I had suggested.

4:30 P.M. Carlo is making his last adjustments. Woody jokes with Jeffrey. Seeing Romaine sitting on a bed, the bedroom door half open, a staircase in the foreground, Woody says, "It reminds me of a Hitchcock movie . . ." and he starts to describe the shot in *Psycho.* Then Liz tells him about a documentary, *Huey Long,* directed by Ken Burns, which had been in the New York Film Festival. Woody had asked for a print because Diane Keaton wanted to see it; she wants to do a documentary. Liz is a friend of Burns.

And they say he doesn't talk to anybody!

Woody passes near me. Holding up the script, I thank him. "Guard it with your life!" he tells me.

5:00 P.M. Shot 40A: The record producer puts a record on the Victrola, checks the level, then walks around the equipment, and adjusts the speaker. *(20 seconds.)*

Woody again has to ask the man to be more natural. The record producer wants to add flourishes, to look concerned. Woody is after simplicity.

(6 takes and 3 prints.)

"It's a wrap" at 5:25 P.M.

Wednesday, November 20, 1985

Israelis shoot down two MiG-23's in Syrian airspace. (New York Times)

Jesse Jackson, in an impromptu session, presses Gorby on Soviet Jews. (New York Times)

And PARTY TIME AT THE REDS (Daily News)

Picture of Ron and Gorby bursting into laughter on the front page of every newspaper.

One of the big questions that everyone is asking is just what did Gromyko mean when he said of Gorbachev, "He has a nice smile, but iron teeth"? Gorby answers: "As of now, I'm still using my own teeth." For the other big question, "Is the President wearing Kennedy-style long underwear?" Larry Speakes responds, "I think the President is wearing his customary underwear."

It is also learned that the President's son, Ronald junior, who was sent to cover the summit by Playboy, asked his father, "Are you ready, Dad?" To which the President replied: "Absolutely."

While their husbands party, Raisa and Nancy have tea. Nancy asks Raisa to come to America, and Raisa invites Nancy to Moscow. There is almond tea and freshly baked cookies. "I happen to love almond tea," Nancy says, but she tells Raisa if she doesn't like it, she can have coffee. Raisa enjoys the tea.

Finally, there are two letters sent by Soviet citizens to Gorby, urging peace at the summit. The first is from Soviet Jews who are asking Gorby to tell "the Zionist Reagan that Jews never had it so good. We dance, we sing, we eat kosher pickles." And the second is from inmates of labor camps who are protesting Reagan's Star Wars plan because it is "an assault on our liberties."

The two letters are, of course, spoofs. (New York Times)

8:00 A.M. We're back on the Rockaway shore, in front of Playland, to film the kids going to school.

The sky is beautifully cloudy. Woody arrives. He and Carlo go to set the shot. Jane comes directly to me and asks to have the script back. The first setup is decided quickly. The grips start laying dolly track.

8:30 A.M. The gambling is under way. Woody sends Jane to buy a card for him. Carlo buys two. I buy one. The deck goes fast. Teamsters, grips, the entire crew plays. Jimmy Sabat is also selling McDonald's chocolates for a fund-raiser at his son's Catholic school. "My wife asked me!"

Dickie is scandalized that I haven't been to Pierre au Tunnel. He tries to entice me by telling about the owner's daughter: "Her name's Jacqueline. Beautiful girl!" And Brian tells me his philosophy of life, his secret to good health. "Eat well, and fuck a lot. But no smoking, no alcohol, no drugs, and no men."

The onlookers have become numerous. There are the mothers of the youngsters in the scene, Jimmy Mazzola's friend, and the photographer who has been hanging around for a while now. A lot of pictures are being taken; there must be thousands of amateur pictures of Woody. Five adorable black children, ten years old, are accompanied by two white people, a fat, baby-faced man in his thirties, and a white-haired, warm-looking woman in her fifties. They're all watching Woody. "Do you want to be a star?" the woman asks. "Yes," the children answer together. "It takes a long time to do a movie," the woman goes on, "sometimes a year!"

9:00 A.M. The cars are in their starting positions. Jimmy Mazzola's friend, hat on, arm in the window, is ready to drive.
Shot 20: The kids go to school. The Masked Avenger, hawking his secret-compartment ring, will be heard on the voice over. *(20 seconds.)*
(2 takes and 2 prints.)
Shot 34: It focuses more on Little Joe. The camera tilts down from the roller coaster, then follows him until he disappears around the corner. *(8 seconds.)*
(3 takes and 3 prints.)
Shot 34A: Same action as above, but closer.
(3 takes and 2 prints.) Completed at 9:30 A.M.
And we move to the next location.

10:20 A.M. In front of the Needlemans' residence on Beach Ninety-sixth Street, by the radio-repair shop. We're shooting the truck full of gifts the burglars won on the *Guess That Tune* radio show (sequence 75).
Woody and Carlo work on the composition, first on the overall framing, then on where each of the prizes should be placed—the armchairs, the champagne cases, the kitchen set, the refrigerator. Woody wanders back and forth from the camera to the props. The action for the delivery men is blocked as well. We're in no hurry because the sun is back, and we need clouds. "It shouldn't be long," Ezra announces. "The forecast called for overcast."

11:00 A.M. The clouds are taking their time about showing up. I make friends with Frankie, Jimmy Mazzola's friend. He lives in Rockaway, but works in a Brooklyn hospital, where he has flexible hours. He was just passing by this morning, back from taking his son to school, when Jimmy asked him to drive a car in the scene. He had to hide his long hair for the shot. He asks me if I think the camera picked him up. He also tells me that this is not the only film to be shot in Rockaway recently. *Sophie's Choice* used a house on the beach, and parts of *The Flamingo Kid* were done in a restaurant here called the Sea Gull.
Jimmy Sabat points out a woman who has been with us since morning, in case I might be interested in her; I am French! "She's

beautiful, but I'm married," Jimmy tells me. The woman has gen-
erous curves, plenty of makeup, and resembles Gradisca in Fellini's
Amarcord.

I win third prize, seventy dollars, in the card game. Everybody
congratulates me.

11:30 A.M. It's getting sunnier and sunnier. Woody is sitting
in the director's chair. The amateur photographer goes to him and
shows him an album full of pictures of the previous day's shoot.
Woody looks at them. The man asks him to autograph one, and
Woody signs. Perseverance, it seems, has paid off.

11:45 A.M. The shot is abandoned, and we move to the cover
set: the Burglars inside the Needlemans' house, playing *Guess
That Tune* on the telephone. The interior is located on Beach 114th
Street. We move the equipment there, and break for lunch, giving
the Burglars time to get in from Manhattan.

2:00 P.M. Back on the set, waiting for the Burglars. Jimmy
Mazzola is fast asleep on the porch, face toward the ocean. Louis is
inside, sleeping next to the equipment. And Angela, one of the
PAs, is congratulating Santo for the work he did on *Singin' in the
Rain*, which is playing on Broadway. The real owner of the house
drops by, and is stunned by the disorder he finds.

All of Monday's work is going to be reshot. Mr. Zipsky's scene
was too sunny and the pace was off. And the Dowdy Housewife's
acting was not all it could have been.

3:00 P.M. Everybody is back on the set now. The camera is
ready, and we're waiting for the crooks to get in costume.

Ezra suggests to Woody that they shoot the zoo scenes tomorrow if the sun is out again. "It's not possible," Woody moans.
Tom sees me jotting down the remark. "This is unusual for an
American movie," he tells me, commenting on the filming's lan-
guid pace.

Tom is depressed. He's happy when things go well, when we
work efficiently, but this waiting for the clouds is getting to be a
little too much for him. At the same time, though, like all the
crew, he respects Woody's perfectionism. They all understand that
the delays aren't frivolous, that this attention to detail is what
makes his films of such quality. But still . . .

3:30 P.M. The Burglars (Mike Starr and Paul Herman) are in the house. The big one was in *Offbeat,* for which Carlo did the photography just before this movie.

Shot 72: The Burglars burgle. They're a little nervous, and then the phone rings (with the help of Jimmy Mazzola and a small battery). The crooks let it ring for a while, then the big one picks it up. "You, Mr. Marty Needleman. . . !" (Kay is the emcee here.) They listen to the tune, answer the questions correctly, and win! *(27 seconds.)*

There is to be no light at all, only the Burglars' flashlights. But first, "Just a sloppy rehearsal with the lights on," Woody asks. When they have finished, "I guess you congratulate each other at the end," Woody says.

Their performances are good. The few words of direction Woody has given have again proved sufficient. Now we have a run-through with the lights out. Carlo asks the Burglars to shine their flashlights on each other, the phone, and the radio. Woody catches a few details about the blocking, about where it would be best for the Burglars to deliver their lines, near the radio, near the phone.

(6 takes and 4 prints.)

Now we are to shoot the Needlemans returning from the movies to find their apartment robbed. Woody and Jimmy Mazzola get the place in appropriate disarray, and Carlo lights it.

4:30 P.M. The Needlemans are waiting outside on the porch. Martin Rosenblatt (Mr. Needleman) was Woody's uncle in *Annie Hall.* Helen Miller (Mrs. Needleman) was in *Purple Rose,* and was Woody's mother in *Hannah,* though she was not visible there; she locked herself in the bathroom after Woody's decision to convert to Catholicism. It's getting dark, and the Needlemans are getting a little tired of waiting. They haven't worked at all today.

"Look at her!" Fern says, nudging me. "Hanging around the candy again. She can't stay away!" Romaine is eyeing the sweets. (After lunch, Jimmy Mazzola has a box of candy brought for the crew.) Now it is Andrew who takes a handful and goes to give it to some delighted children in the crowd. He realizes that I have seen him and looks embarrassed.

Frankie and Gradisca have become friends, and are now chatting with just about everybody. "I saw you in several Woody Allen movies," Frankie says to me. Gradisca picked me out, too.

They ask me what my job is on the film, and I tell them. "Oh, a writer. I always wanted to be a writer, alone in a room . . ."

5:00 P.M. The scene is not shot. There are problems with the wiring in the old house, and it would take too long to correct them. A bad day for the Needlemans all around: First their home gets robbed and now they're robbed of the chance to perform.

We wrap.

Thursday, November 21, 1985

Good chemistry at the summit sessions. Nancy and Raisa are having almond tea again, and Ron and Gorby have spent almost five hours together. Pictures of them laughing together are in all the newspapers, even Pravda. *"The news is so good, we're going to hold it till tomorrow," Ron says.*

Asked whether interpreters had used microphones for recording purposes, a spokesman says of Ron, "If he's wired, he's listening to his Walkman." (New York Times)

European and American medical circles agree on the theory that AIDS began in Central Africa. The Africans vigorously disagree. (New York Times)

And: "I simply assume the responsibility," says Jesse (Jackson) in Geneva, when he is asked about a visit he paid to Jerry Falwell. And he adds that the question about where he gets his authority, his marching orders, is the same that was flung at biblical prophets. Asked if he was not afraid of being "used," he laughs and replies: "That's happened ever since I started dating in grammar school." (New York Times)

In the van with Mrs. Needleman, Mr. Zipsky, and Kay. Mrs. Needleman is complaining that Woody could have picked her a more handsome husband; Mr. Needleman has a weight problem. And Zipsky is a bit anxious; he hopes the first retake of his scene will be good because he hasn't run like that in twenty years!

8:15 A.M. Rockaway, Beach 115th Street. Breakfast at the production office. Carlo likes Drew. Every morning she gives him a big kiss. Mr. Needleman is having coffee and doughnuts. His wife is right; he should watch what he eats. Jeffrey is wearing a new tweed coat this morning. Woody's still wearing those same shoes.

8:45 A.M. Almost ready to reshoot Zipsky. Cliff is again getting rid of the yellow line down the middle of the street.

Shot RE102: The camera movement is simplified. Zipsky does basically the same action.

First take: Zipsky doesn't wear his glasses this time around. He makes his movements a little bigger, broader. He doesn't go into Dubbins', but stays in the middle of Rockaway Boulevard, swinging the meat cleaver.

Second take: Glasses back on. Same action. But this time with the policeman again at the end of the scene, appearing from camera left to grab Zipsky.

(3 takes and 2 prints.) Completed at 9:00 A.M.

The next shot will be the kids, in Cub Scout uniforms, collecting scrap iron for the war effort (sequence 110).

9:15 A.M. We are on the Boulevard. Jimmy Mazzola has put some scrap metal in a V for Victory container in front of Woolworth's. The camera is being set up. Cliff gets rid of a length of the yellow line, Jimmy Mazzola gets the cars ready, and the extras are put in their starting positions.

10:00 A.M. Shot 110: The kids go to the container. They drop off the scrap iron; there are period cars and pedestrians passing through the frame. *(25 seconds.)*

(2 takes and 2 prints.)

We move to Beach Ninety-sixth Street to shoot the scene of the truckload of gifts, which we couldn't get yesterday.

11:00 A.M. Tom and Carlo are having a drink at Murphy's bar. The loot on the truck is being arranged as it was yesterday. A Polaroid picture of the setting lets the crew match it exactly. Mr. and Mrs. Needleman are back, in nightclothes, on the balcony. Back, too, are Frankie and Gradisca, the amateur photographer snapping away, and the sun, shining and shining.

11:30 A.M. The sun hasn't let up yet, but we can see clouds on the way. Brian gets a picture of the camera department, with Carlo seated in one of the armchairs that the Needlemans have "won." Ray is chatting with Gradisca. She has definitely caught the interest of the boys. The black children are also here with their two chaperones. Woody is playing ball with Andrew. Woody plays quite seriously, with all the moves of a pitcher.

11:40 A.M. The clouds are here. Ready for rehearsal.

12:00 noon. The clouds are gone. Woody is back throwing the ball, but against a wall, alone.

12:05 P.M. The clouds return.
Shot 75: The Needlemans looking stunned at the deliverymen and the gifts. Two onlookers are in the foreground. *(15 seconds.)* *(5 takes and 2 prints.)*

We move back to 115th Street to shoot the kids collecting money for the Jewish National Fund, to build a homeland in Palestine.

12:45 P.M. We are at the intersection of Rockaway Boulevard and Beach 116th Street, in front of the drugstore. The store has been dressed as a luncheonette, and a newsstand has been built at its side. The camera is set a little up the street. These are not ideal conditions for shooting, because there's real traffic from four directions. Period cars are parked in front of the store, and others are readied to be driven into the shot. Dressed extras are poised to move in, too. The PAs have two barricades set up to keep the crowd out of frame, but it's difficult stopping all traffic at an intersection. At the moment, it's a jumble, this fake past and real present.

The PAs are continually asking people to step out of the shot or away from the equipment. In the confusion, Frankie and Gradisca are pushed back behind the barricades by Tom. A stray dog that has been adopted by the crew adds to the chaos. Ray notices Gradisca and rescues her, taking her to the gambling department. Frankie is left behind, dying of jealousy. Ray introduces Gradisca to Jimmy Sabat, trying to embarrass him. He succeeds; Jimmy mumbles a few words, then makes an awkward exit. Louis and Frankie Graziadei go to her. Woody notices her through a corner of his eye.

1:15 P.M. The shot is almost ready. Woody manages, in all the craziness, to abstract himself. Hands in his pockets, whistling, then thinking, he waits, Tom at his side. Frankie has made it back to us, and is with Jimmy Mazzola. Gradisca is just behind Woody, playing with the stray dog, staring at Woody's back.

Shot 36: Little Joe and Nick work the crowd with their donation cans, then Little Joe walks around the corner to Burt and Andrew, who have been getting donations from other pedestrians. (25 seconds.)

At the end of the second take, Little Joe doesn't hear, or doesn't want to hear, "Cut," and continues asking for money "for a new state in Palestine." An elderly woman, who is not in the film, opens her purse and gives him some change. Across the street, the crowd bursts into laughter. To be shooting a period film on such a crowded location, and have it work so well, seems almost miraculous. And the old woman, who would have been perfectly cast, has actually been cast.

(3 takes and 2 prints.) Completed at 2:15 P.M.

We move back to the quiet of Little Joe's house on Beach 115th

Street to reshoot the scene of Bea listening to the radio on the porch. Woody didn't like the lighting and the composition. Before we move, Gradisca approaches Woody. She blushes a deep red. They say a word or two to each other, but obviously, she is not Woody's type, and the encounter is soon over. . . .

2:45 P.M. In front of Little Joe's house. Bea is on the steps, chatting with Woody. Two houses down, on the porch of the holding-area house, Mr. Needleman is awakened by the screams of some young extras, and is not entirely happy. Gradisca appears and goes directly to the crew, ignoring me now that she knows more important people.

3:30 P.M. Shot RA102: Bea sits on the stairs, the radio next to her. The kids run into the house, then out, but no longer run to the street, going to the backyard instead, still eating cake and drinking milk. And Mom doesn't come out to grab back the Jack Daniel's bottle because Burt no longer takes it.
(5 takes and 5 prints.)
We break for lunch.

5:00 P.M. It's dark and cold. It has been a long day. A lot has been accomplished, though, and some of it hurriedly, all so we can finish the Rockaway scenes this week. No one will be too sad to leave this place. We are waiting for the dark so we can reshoot the searchlights.
Andrew has been hanging around with Drew a lot today.
Two teenagers ask me about Woody: "Is it true that he has two bodyguards? They say he comes by helicopter. Where is his limousine? Is it true that everybody has to stand up when he arrives?"

5:45 P.M. Ready to shoot. There are three searchlights this time. The lights and reflectors are moved closer.
Shot R117B: Over Mom and Pop's shoulders, looking at the searchlight.
(3 takes and 1 print.)
Shot R117A: Mom and Pop's POV.
(4 takes and 2 prints.)

At 6:00 P.M., "It's a wrap."

In the van back to Manhattan, with Mom, Pop, the Burglars, Kay, and Fern, we talk about Woody. They feel lucky to work with him, and they enjoy it. The big Burglar was very nervous during the shooting because Woody was not giving him a lot of direction, just asking him to improve and then not saying whether he liked the performance or not.

Friday, November 22, 1985

In Geneva, the party is over. "With their interpreters leaning over their shoulders, they laughed and exchanged pleasantries. After each had read a short statement, the other applauded. And just before they left the huge conference building, they retired to a private room, drank a farewell toast of champagne, and shook hands warmly." (In 1979, Leonid and Jimmy kissed.)

Though Ron didn't make it specific, it seems that the news that was "so good" he was holding it back, was that there will be more parties, in 1986 in New York, and in 1987 in Moscow. (New York Times)

In the black township of Mamelodi, South Africa, the police have shot dead at least 6 people. Hundreds of others have been injured. These new deaths bring the number killed by authorities so far this week to at least 23, and since September of last year, to more than 865, most of them black. (New York Times)

7:45 A.M. Breezy Point. The name says it all. Located at the end of the Rockaway peninsula, it is a summer resort from the early 1900s, abandoned in winter. We are having breakfast at the Surf Club, and nobody is looking forward to going out. It's very cold and raining; the sky is cloudy as only Woody could dream. The empty swimming pool and the beach huts that have fallen into disrepair are not the cheeriest atmosphere at 7:00 in the morning.

8:10 A.M. Woody and Carlo arrive, and out we go. Everybody is prepared for the weather except me. "Go see Jimmy Mazzola," I'm told. He gives me a beautiful yellow rain suit.

8:40 A.M. To shoot B102: A song on the radio reminds Little Joe of Little Evelyn (Rebecca Nickels), the girl he liked but who didn't like him, and Little Linda (Natane Adcock), the "pretty girl"

who liked him but whom he didn't like. It inspires him to rumi-
nate on the meaning of life.

The beach huts line a boardwalk across the sand. Two shots are
chosen.

9:40 A.M. It's still raining and colder. The equipment has been
brought across the sand in a four-wheel-drive pickup truck. The
boys had set a dolly track earlier, but it was neither long nor stable
enough. A wider base will have to be used.

Everyone wears the same-style yellow rain suit with hood. Andrew's is two sizes too large, and with his snow boots, he looks like
something from another planet. Woody has finally given in and
put on the rain pants, but still he wears his faithful leather shoes!
Carlo can't stand the pants either—it's so hard to move in them—
but he, too, has broken down.

(L to R:) Woody Allen; Carlo DiPalma

Huge umbrellas are set over the equipment. It's a strange scene, all these yellow creatures, waddling around like astronauts, in the rain, in an abandoned turn-of-the-century resort.

Little Joe, Little Evelyn, and Little Linda are staying warm in the truck, but the boys are still out in the elements working.

10:30 A.M. Woody's leather shoes must be soaking by now; mine feel like sponges. But he doesn't seem to mind; this weather is so ideal! The amateur photographer appears, but is hastily escorted out by Tom. The new dolly track is ready now. Little Joe is brought to his starting mark, a PA keeping him dry with an umbrella. The two girls are taken under the pier, and their pale, bare legs make us all shiver.

Shot B102: Little Joe runs along the boardwalk, then down the stairs and under the pier pilings to meet Little Evelyn and Little Linda. In front of Linda, who is pining for him, he tries to kiss Evelyn, who pushes him away roughly. *(20 seconds.)*

Little Joe runs fast, and Red and Bobby Ward have to push the camera like madmen. But the hard part is stopping when Little Joe runs down the stairs. Bobby Ward goes down, flat on his back, legs in the air!

(4 takes and 2 prints.)

The kids are taken back to the truck while the next scene is set up. The camera is put under the pier. Two arc lights are fired up.

11:00 A.M. Weatherwise, things are only worse. The rain seems colder now, and it gets under our rain suits and into our clothes no matter what we do. Under the pier, we're out of it but in a freezing draft. There's no winning this game. But the boys keep working through it all, and we're soon ready.

Shot B102A: Joe kisses Evelyn. She pushes him away. Linda steps back. Then Evelyn finally lets Joe kiss her. *(10 seconds.)*

There are little problems. Since we're closer, the acting and reacting have to be perfect—Evelyn's disgusted look when Joe kisses her the first time, the smile when she lets him, Linda's sad face as she sees that Joe is not interested in her, and of course, the way Little Joe kisses, a sweet, sensitive peck on the cheek: Joe's no Communist! Woody goes over it with the kids.

Little Evelyn is a petite, mischievous girl with red hair and strawberry freckles, like Little Joe, while Linda is the more romantic beauty. They are, once again, perfectly cast.

(12 takes and 2 prints.)
We leave Breezy Point with no regrets at 11:30 A.M.

12:00 noon. Back in Rockaway. It's supposedly our last day here. Since the weather is so beautiful—it's raining, but not quite so cold—we're back on the roof to reshoot an establishing shot of Rockaway. The gaffers (we're shooting with natural light) and the gambling department (no sound) have taken shelter, but the camera crew, Tom, Carlo, and Woody are out here in it. Even Andrew and Jane have disappeared.

Shot RA10: It starts on the foggy ocean, then pulls back for a long, high shot of the deserted street, with several parked cars, and a couple of extras running by in the rain. The view is rather depressing.

The PAs have stopped all traffic on Beach 115th Street and, when we are shooting a take, on Rockaway Boulevard. It is difficult, especially in the rain, to tell people that they can't return to their houses. The action of the extras has to be timed accurately, so they'll be in the designated spot when the camera pulls back.

(8 takes and 3 prints.)

2:50 P.M. The holding-area house is crowded with the Needlemans, their Burglars, Little Evelyn, and Little Linda, the girls' mothers, and a dozen extras.

Outside, we continue to work, to take advantage of the lovely weather. There's a rumor floating around that since the forecast calls for more rain, Woody wants to shoot Saturday. . . .

The camera has been moved to Beach 115th Street, near the ocean, looking in the direction of Rockaway Boulevard.

Shot RA10A: The opposite angle of RA10. The camera starts wide on the side of the street with Little Joe's house, then zooms to Dubbins' and Rockaway Boulevard.

Woody is in a great mood, whistling, joking with Jeffrey and Santo. He even talks with Drew: "Having a good time today!" he tells her. When Woody is up like this, he likes to walk among the crew, brushing past them, as though he were demarcating his environment, and showing them that they are part of it. He has just looked at me with a smile that said "Still there!"

(5 takes and 2 prints.)
We head for the beach.

3:30 P.M. The sky is beautiful in its own way: low, foggy, with a vague glow on the horizon. Woody is talking with Drew again when Barbara comes by to entertain him. At first, Woody listens to her monologue politely, then suddenly starts pulling back, closing up. He's saved by Jeffrey, who wants to ask him about Little Joe's costume.

It's a little warmer now, and the rain has let up somewhat. The atmosphere is improved, too. On the roof, with its cramped conditions, there was some tension.

Shot RA10B: Little Joe, in helmet and glasses, scanning the ocean.

A box is brought for him to stand on: He's not very tall.

(4 takes and 2 prints.)

We break for lunch at 3:35 P.M.

4:30 P.M. Beach 114th Street, back on the set. Inside the Needlemans' for their discovery that they've been robbed, the shot we didn't get Wednesday evening.

Carlo is joking in Italian, and even though nobody understands, it's still funny. Woody and Jimmy Mazzola are ransacking the set. "Hanging on! You're crazier than us," Ray comments to me. Everyone is tired and frustrated, but still at it. The prospect of leaving Rockaway helps.

The Needlemans' stand-ins complain about waiting under the porch in the cold, and are taken to the Needlemans' trailer.

Shot 74: It's dark. The light comes on and the Needlemans see the mess the room is in. *(10 seconds.)*

Jimmy Mazzola is outside in the rain, fanning with a board so the curtains will be blown by the open window. "Simpler and quicker than setting up a fan," he explained.

First take. The curtain wasn't blowing when the lights came on.

Second take. Again, no curtain action. "Jimmy Mazzola!"

Third take. Beautiful.

(4 takes and 2 prints.)

But Jimmy Mazzola keeps fanning. "Go on, Jimmy, stronger!" Ray yells. "Carlo wants to see it." And everyone, even Woody, laughs as Jimmy fans away frantically. A few minutes later, he comes inside, annoyed at having been the butt of the joke. "Everybody's having a good time!" he snarls. The boys quiet down quickly. Woody rereads the script with Kay.

6:00 P.M. Still setting up the next shot: the Needlemans listening to the Polly Phelps story on the radio. After this, we have to
go back to Beach Ninety-sixth Street to shoot the Needlemans
leaving home for the movies.

We're going to go on until 9:00 or 10:00 at least, and I have an
8:00 P.M. meeting in town. I take the subway back to Manhattan.
It's 6:30 P.M.

Monday, November 25, 1985   *Fourth Week*

In Malta, Egyptian special forces storm a hijacked Egyptian air-
liner: fifty dead. (New York Times)
And "Big Joe" Turner died Saturday at age seventy-four. His
career was launched in a concert he gave at Carnegie Hall in 1938,
"From Spirituals to Swing." His recordings of "Roll 'Em Pete,"
"Wooee Baby," and "Hollywood and Vine," established him as a
major-league jazz singer.

8:30 A.M. Madison Avenue and Twenty-fourth Street. We're
in front of the Fidelity Broadcasting building—actually the Metropolitan Life building—to shoot an establishing shot of the studio
where Biff Baxter (Jeff Daniels), the brave G-man who is 4F, takes
care of Japs and Nazis.

Shot 120: Same as for the RCA building on the first day, except reversed. Here, the camera starts on the entrance, then tilts
up the length of the building. *(7 seconds.)*

For this sort of establishing shot, the crew is almost more important than the director. Tom, Woody at his side, gives all the
cues. The PAs stop the real pedestrians and start the extras, and
Jimmy Mazzola conducts the car ballet.

Blocking the corners of two streets and the entrance of a huge
building at 8:30 in the morning in mid-Manhattan is not exactly
easy. So everything is done casually, at the last minute, as we did
on Rockaway Boulevard, and the real people who are still sleepy
and hurrying to work hardly notice.

(5 takes and 3 prints.) Completed at 9:30 A.M.

We move inside for the next shot.

10:00 A.M. We're inside the building, on the left side of the
ground floor, in a big Art Deco conference room, to shoot *The*

Court of Human Emotions and the World's Famous Counselor on Affairs of the Human Heart, Thomas Abercrombie (sequence 97).

Jane tells me that the filming ended at 9:10 P.M. last Friday. There was no trouble with the Needlemans listening to the Polly Phelps story, but it was a bit more complicated getting the arrival of the Burglars. The headlights of the Burglars' period car were not strong enough to cast the shadows Woody and Carlo wanted on the house. I mention my leaving last Friday. "I know," Jane says, "Woody noticed."(!)

The room is big, clean, and warm. It seems almost too easy working in such conditions. Woody takes off his green jacket, keeping on his cap, and walks among the boys setting up the camera and lights. Then, thirty seconds later, the jacket goes back on.

10:45 A.M. The camera is ready. Thomas Abercrombie (Martin Sherman) and the couple he is going to counsel are in position, Abercrombie behind the microphone. This is the first Woody Allen movie for Thomas; with his sweet and tolerant smile, he is, once more, beautifully cast. The couple has worked with Woody before. Maurice Shrog, the husband who wants his mom to live in their home, was one of Woody's fans in *Stardust* and the hypnotist in *Zelig*. Crystal Field, his cruel wife who can no longer stand her mother-in-law, was a member of the movie audience in *Purple Rose*.

First rehearsal. Woody is at the camera. The actors run through their lines. The camera starts on the announcer (Peter Lombard) introducing the show, then moves to Abercrombie and the couple, who then begin their dialogue. Woody is not happy with this much movement. The announcer is moved closer to Abercrombie's table. Woody goes over the script, checking the lines with the actors.

11:00 A.M. Woody rechecks the camera movement, while the actors run through their lines again. It's still no good. We go back to the original setup, and Woody goes back to the script. He asks the couple to improvise at the end of the lines.

11:20 A.M. Another rehearsal. Dickie operates the camera this time, but it's still not right. Woody is dissatisfied with the pace of the scene.

11:30 A.M. Back to the viewfinder. Woody and Carlo discuss the situation. A decision is made. The sequence will be done in two shots—first the announcer, then the show itself.

12:00 noon. Shot 97: The announcer introduces the show. *(15 seconds.)*
"OK?" Woody asks, turning to Dickie. "Yes, sir!" he answers. Woody: "Let's go to the next shot."
(2 takes and 2 prints.)
After an hour and a half of hesitating, waiting, changing, and changing again, the fifteen-second shot is finally in the can. And yet, during the delay, we never got the impression that Woody was lost or didn't know what he was doing, only that he didn't "feel" the scene, the movement, the pace.

12:15 P.M. Camera is ready. Woody checks the camera movement from Abercrombie to the couple. It meets his approval. He stands to the side while Carlo adjusts the lighting. Woody looks at the ground, seeming worried or thoughtful. He goes to the actors, stands in front of them as if he's about to tell them something important, but says nothing: He just looks at them. Then he starts whistling and walks away.
After three weeks, Woody seems more at ease, more relaxed, as if finally the filming is really under way. Carlo is moody today. Mornings are always difficult for him.

12:40 P.M. Shot 97A: Abercrombie, with his sweet smile, asks the couple to tell him everything. The couple starts arguing about the mother-in-law. The wife is fed up. "How can I throw my own mother out?" the husband says. "Grab her by the neck and push her into the street," the wife answers. *(25 seconds.)*
Take 1: Just before Tom screams "Action!" Woody reminds Abercrombie to keep his cheesy smile.
Take 2: Woody has asked the wife to be angrier. She complies, with a vengeance. After "Cut," everyone laughs. She's quite good.
Now that he has what he wants, Woody asks the actors not only to exaggerate even more but also to keep improvising. He suggests that the wife say she'll take a knife and put it in her mother-in-law's back if things continue the way they are. "Really furious, exasperated," Woody insists. The wife laughs. And to Abercrombie: "Just keep smiling."

Take 3: It works wonderfully. The wife has her anger controlled at the outset but becomes progressively violent. Woody is extremely happy; he nearly jumps with excitement.

Take 4: Woody has gone to the actors just before the take, but mostly to encourage them in the direction they've been going. By the end of the scene, the wife is almost in tears.

(Takes 2, 3, and 4 are printed.)

On that last take, she really seemed ready to do away with her mother-in-law.

1:00 P.M. Same setting and camera movement exactly, but now panning from Abercrombie to Mom and Pop arguing. Little Joe is imagining his parents in *The Court of Human Emotions.* But first, a "jacket crisis." Woody doesn't like the one Pop is wearing. A leather jacket is tried. It's no good. Finally he decides on a wool one.

Shot 98: The shot opens on Abercrombie nodding and smiling. Little Joe's narration will be put over this portion of the scene. Then the camera moves to Mom and Pop. Mom complains that Pop is a "business failure." Pop complains about her family living with them. Abercrombie concludes they deserve each other. So they turn on him: "We didn't come here to be insulted!" Pop says. "I love him, but what did I do to deserve him?" Mom asks. *(38 seconds.)*

Woody again yells at Abercrombie to "Open that mouth!"

After the second take, Woody asks only for more intensity.

For the fourth take, he accelerates the pace.

Mom and Pop are doing well, and seem to have things down pat. Woody goes to them with the script to check a few lines.

During the fifth take Woody almost cuts when Pop flubs a line, but he decides to let them finish.

In the sixth take, Mom misses her cue. "I am sorry," she says, as if a catastrophe has occurred. Woody laughs. Mom is very sweet when she's apologetic like this.

And on it goes. Mom is hilarious when she delivers her last line.

(17 takes and 6 prints.)

At 2:00 P.M., we break for lunch.

3:00 P.M. We're back in the conference room, but on the other side, for *The Whiz Kids* radio program (sequence 46). There is a long table, with nameplates for each of the children: JAY, 11; RO-MAINE, 10; FERN, 12 (a little nod to the Salad Sisters); GLENN, 10; SANFORD, 11.

3:15 P.M. The kids are brought in. There are four of them and only one girl. The final lineup is: Jay, Romaine, Glenn, and Sanford. Fern is out even before the first take!

These kids have nothing in common with Little Joe's scruffy gang. They're dressed in black caps and gowns, and they've been chosen for their looks; they resemble much more normal children.

3:45 P.M. Shot 46: The kids, as the Whiz Master introduces the show.
(4 takes and 3 prints.)
We move to kids being quizzed.

Carlo makes a few changes in the lighting. Tom is touching Liz's red hair; her hair is so startlingly red, you want to touch it just to prove to yourself that it's real. Doug is massaging Drew's back; earlier today, she was massaging Dickie and Louis. Woody is talking to Jeffrey, doing a hand trick with a dollar bill. It's been a relaxed day today.

4:15 P.M. Shot 46A: It opens on the Whiz Master questioning the kids, and then goes to them for their answers. "What are the moons of Saturn?" "Who said, 'Justice delayed. . .'?" And for Sanford: "Give me the square root of 1,963." *(26 seconds.)*

Sanford (Marc Colner) answers the question very somberly: "Well, it does not come out even, but . . ." "If he was my kid, I'd punch him in the nose," Carlo says. Woody asks Sanford to accentuate the superior tone even more.
(6 takes and 2 prints.)
Finally, Woody wants a shorter version, with only the last two questions.

Shot 46B: The camera passes the kids, and stops at Sanford.
(7 takes and 3 prints.)

At 5:00 P.M., "It's a wrap."
Woody puts his cap back on, his expression that of a cocky little tough kid. Jane smiles, finding it a bit vain.

Tuesday, November 26, 1985

Hijacking toll climbs to sixty. Tactics of Egyptian troops in assault are questioned. (New York Times)
    And radio performer/pioneer Ransom Sherman has died at the age of eighty seven. His shows included Club Matinee, Grapewine Rancho, Hap Hazard, Smile Parade, Mirth and Madness, *and* Fibber McGee and Molly, *on which he played Uncle Dennis. His film credits include* Swing Your Partner, The Bachelor and the Bobby-Soxer, *and* Always Leave Them Laughing.

    8:15 A.M. A day at the Prospect Park Zoo, Brooklyn, with Mom, Pop, Little Joe, Sanford the Whiz Kid and his parents, and a few extras. We're going to do the sequence where the two families meet and talk briefly.
    It's raining lightly and on the cold side. The carousel sequence of *Purple Rose* was shot in Prospect Park, in January. It turned too cold and rainy, though, and the carousel had to be rebuilt in a studio. Brian was born in this neighborhood; it has a reputation as a tough area. Woody was raised not far from here in Flatbush, which is just to the southeast.
    The breakfast table for the company has been set up in the zoo's Rhinoceros House, and the smell is almost overpowering. Woody is wearing a new, huge, gray fur-lined parka, wool gloves, and those same shoes. He has the hood on, and only his glasses show. He jumps from foot to foot, trying to keep warm.

    10:00 A.M. Shot 99: An establishing shot of Little Joe and his family at the zoo. The camera starts on the elephant, and moves to Mom, Pop, and Little Joe looking at it. Sanford and his parents step in front of them. Pop recognizes Sanford and approaches. They start to talk. *(28 seconds.)*
    First, however, we have to get the elephant out in the yard, and he likes the cold as much as he likes the rain. The keepers finally prod him out and close the door. Then the background action involving other parents and other children is not very active. "Remember, this is a zoo, you have to laugh!" yells Tom to the extras, who, like the elephant, are out in the rain only very reluctantly.

After a few takes, the elephant starts to improvise; he gets some straw in his trunk and puts it on top of his head. The effect is good, and Woody OK's it, but Dickie has to wait for the elephant to do it again before panning to the family. Fortunately, the elephant cooperates.

(10 takes and 2 prints.)

10:45 A.M. Shot 101: Front shot of Mom, Pop, and Little Joe talking to Sanford, seen over the shoulders of Sanford's family. Little Joe shakes hands with Sanford, who wipes his afterward. Pop is joking as usual. "Quick, what's one thousand eight hundred and sixty-six divided into . . ." he asks Sanford. The other family snubs them and moves on. Little Joe's family then moves on as well, Pop hitting Little Joe because he spends so much time in front of the radio instead of studying. *(42 seconds.)*

No problems for Mom, Pop, and Little Joe, but Sanford has a hard time getting through his lines.

(9 takes and 3 prints.)

Everyone stays in position.

Shot 101A: A pickup shot of the family leaving and Pop cuffing Little Joe.

For the second take, Woody asks Pop to really hit Little Joe. It gives a Grand Guignol effect to the scene, and Little Joe takes the blow like a trouper.

(2 takes and 2 prints.)

11:00 A.M. Shot 101B: The other family, seen over the shoulders of Mom, Pop, and Little Joe. Same dialogue.

The background is perfect; the rhinoceros is getting excited by the hippopotamus! But the problems are now starting. The Whiz Kid, the one with the 160 I.Q., can't get through his lines! "And now, if you'll excuse us, I'm sure you've come here to fulfill some purpose other than to obsess relentlessly over a celebrated personality."

The rain, though light, is still falling, along with the temperature. After three hours in this weather, everybody is just about frozen. But Woody hangs on. First he tries reciting the lines to Sanford just before the take. Then he shortens them. But the poor Whiz Kid can't get through to the end. Finally, Woody has to recite phrase by phrase.

(6 takes and 2 prints.)

Shot 101C: A pickup of Sanford and his family leaving.

At the end of the last take, Sanford gets through his lines perfectly. The rhinoceros laughs—really!—and everybody laughs
with him.

We break for lunch at 12:15 P.M.

An excellent caterer serves us at the Prospect Park picnic
house. There are forty extras, plus the mothers accompanying
children. Barbara is in charge of them. Ken is not happy because
some of the mothers have come with entire families, including
Grandpa, Grandma, uncles, and so on.

Woody wants to reshoot Breezy Point next Friday. Next Monday, we'll be shooting the opening sequence, the Astonishing
Tonino's scene. The script calls for pouring rain!

We have a quick trip in the van through Brooklyn to the next
location. We pass the arch at Grand Army Plaza, then turn onto
Bedford Avenue, moving through the different neighborhoods—
Bedford Stuyvesant, Williamsburg, and Greenpoint, where Henry
Miller grew up. We drive past the Brooklyn Church of Christ, the
Church of God in Christ Jesus Fair Deal Inc., the Church of God in
Christ on the Hill, the Church of the Open Door, the Church of
God and Christ International; the whole of Bedford Avenue has
been invaded. "The twenty-first century will be religious or will
not be," André Malraux said. In Brooklyn, as usual, they're far
ahead.

2:15 P.M. Kent Street, on the bank of the East River, to shoot
sequence A42: a broadcast antenna, for the sequence about the
history of radio. It's raining hard. Everybody is back in the yellow
suits. Jay carries the camera under his arm like a baby, Liz protect-
ing him with an umbrella.

Shot A42: The camera tilts up to the top of the tower, tilting
up at different paces with each take. The rain, of which there is
more than enough, will not show up on film.

(3 takes and 3 prints.)

And at 3:30 P.M. we wrap.

Wednesday, November 27, 1985

The space shuttle Atlantis *begins a seven-day mission.* (New York Times)

The Fashion Foundation of America in Brooklyn just announced its forty-fourth annual list of the world's best-dressed men, featuring Ron, Prince Charles, and inexplicably, Anthony R. Cucci, the mayor of Jersey City. The mayor was wearing flexible-waist polyester-blend slacks when he learned of his selection. Mr. Cucci said he was stunned and perplexed, and had no plans for a collection of Cucci wear. (New York Times)

Rajneeshpuram, Oregon. Guru Bhagwan Shree Rajneesh is back in India, and the eighty-five Rolls-Royces in which he enjoyed taking daily drives on the back roads of Oregon are for sale.

It all started when Ma Anand Sheela, the guru chief's aide, did "a lot of bad things such as plotting murder, tapping telephones, and grabbing power," the guru asserted. Then there was a federal indictment for immigration fraud. And finally the guru's followers (3,500 people) were told that their accounts had been frozen because the commune had current debts of about $1.5 million, and a long-term debt of $35 million.

Guru Bhagwan Shree Rajneesh left for India on November 14, saying he hoped never to return to America. The followers were told by the finance office of the community not to go to India. "This is very important. He wants to be left alone. Please respect his wishes," a spokesman said. Guru Bhagwan Shree Rajneesh is reported to be "in silence." (New York Times)

8:30 A.M. We are on the Lower East Side, in the basement of the synagogue Congregation Mogen Abraham, for Little Joe's Hebrew class (sequence 22) and his beating by Rabbi Baumel (sequence 38).

The basement is wonderful—a little dirty, but once again almost untouched since the turn of the century. There are scriptures on the walls and columns, huge beams, and a small altar in the middle of it all. Aged school benches have been lined up in rows, and the boys have started to bring the equipment in.

We're going to have to reshoot the Whiz Kids. Woody wasn't pleased with the look of the set. But the World's Famous Coun-

selor on Affairs of the Human Heart, Thomas Abercrombie, was
very good.

9:30 A.M. Carlo gets his morning kiss from Drew and feels
much better. I get one and feel better, too. Cliff is doing some
touch-up work on the ceiling, Barbara entertaining him all the
while. Jimmy Mazzola is taking out the too-modern windows in
the back and replacing them with wood-frame ones. The electrical
wiring is being improved. And the real rabbi is watching it all in
stunned silence.

Woody picks a Masked Avenger magnifying-glass ring for the
scene, while Jimmy Mazzola gives him a demonstration of his special-effects smoke. He'll cut a hole in Little Phil's shirt and insert a
plastic tube that will be attached to the smoke machine.

10:30 A.M. The children are brought in and seated at the
benches, with Little Joe just behind Little Phil (Josh Saviano).
Woody examines the children closely. He moves a few of them,
calling them "gentlemen," and then asks that they all put on their
yarmulkes. He has glasses distributed to most of them, and bit by
bit, the children, already terrifically cast, take on a more character-
istically Woody Allen look. When Woody works on such details,
his face is without expression; he never outwardly reacts to any of
it. He now stares at the children, and then turns to Carlo. "OK."

Rabbi Baumel (Kenneth Mars) arrives. He's immense, at least
six feet three, and wide as well; he looks a little intimidating here
among the small children. Since he's a bit hard of hearing, he has
to bend when talking to Woody. His head is quite near Woody's,
and Woody is all but trying to hide under the tweed cap. And
then, Rabbi Baumel puts his huge hands on Woody's arms.

11:05 A.M. Shot 22: Rabbi Baumel introduces his lecture. The
children will have to collect funds to create a Zionist state in Palestine. The Jews need a homeland. For, even here, they could be
persecuted.

Rabbi Baumel is superb. His theatrical inflections are perfect,
and Woody enjoys the scene. "Don't be stiff, kids," he says. Then
he congratulates the rabbi and encourages him along the route he
is taking. Baumel's resonant voice and the way he rubs his beard
are perfect for the character.
(4 takes and 2 prints.)

Shot 22A: Rabbi Baumel stands up to get into the subject. "Just as the German Jews said, 'I am a German, I am a citizen,' so the American Jews may one day have to say, 'But I am an American.' But it will not suffice . . ." *(1 minute and 5 seconds.)*

Rabbi Baumel does a great deal of stage work. For the closer shot, which includes the second portion of the lecture, he asks Woody if he might do the speech from the beginning. Woody OK's it.

Again, Rabbi Baumel is wonderful. At one point, he stops lecturing to blow his nose, then clean his glasses with his handkerchief. Woody starts laughing. He's seated on a bench behind the kids, and hides his laughter behind his cap. Woody looks entirely at ease, natural, spontaneous, almost childlike. Without understanding exactly why—is it the lines, the tone, the rabbi's face, Woody's laughter?—I start laughing myself.

(2 takes and 2 prints.) Completed at 11:45 A.M.

12:15 P.M. The lighting is being adjusted for a new angle. Rabbi Baumel relaxes, his stand-in taking his place. Woody goes to Mom, who has just arrived, to tell her that her scene with Thomas Abercrombie turned out well.

Shot 22B: The camera has been set in the aisle, behind the children, very low. Rabbi Baumel, now totally into it, explains to the kids what the Gentiles are going to do to them. "They will beat you up . . . they will drag you away . . . ostracized . . . degraded . . ." But suddenly, "What is that smoke?" Phil is on fire! Rabbi Baumel grabs Little Joe. *(1 minute and 2 seconds.)*

Rabbi Baumel is terrifying, and Woody again gets the giggles, hiding in the back of the class like a mischievous child. After the second take, Carlo asks the rabbi to move a bit from side to side, stepping in and out of a shadow. And things continue that way, the rabbi more and more terrifying, and Woody again and again dissolving into giggles.

(5 takes and 3 prints.)

1:00 P.M. Shot 22C: A medium long shot of the children listening to the rabbi, with Little Joe in the middle.

Woody takes Rabbi Baumel's place. He stares at the children, directing them verbally as the camera rolls: "A lot of staring," "A little open-mouthed," and so forth.

(1 take and 1 print.)

Shot 22D: A wide shot of the entire classroom listening to the rabbi, terrified.

It's the same process. Woody is off-camera, instructing the kids, "I'm not saying good things," "Look at my eyes!" "Move your eyes," "Everybody is watching me . . . I am the rabbi!"

(1 take and 1 print)

Shot 22E: A close shot of Little Joe and Little Phil, as Joe focuses the magnifying glass on Phil's shirt.

(1 take and 1 print.)

1:30 P.M. We move to the final shot for this sequence, in which Little Phil catches on fire. Jimmy Mazzola is at last allowed to make his smoke. He was so eager in one of the earlier shots, he brought on the smoke for no particular reason.

Shot 22F: Little Phil screams, "I'm on fire!" Rabbi Baumel runs over, sees what has happened, and, grabbing him by the collar, lifts Little Joe into the air. *(11 seconds.)*

Rabbi Baumel is quite strong, and Little Joe enjoys being lifted. *(5 takes and 2 prints.)*

We break for lunch at 2:00 P.M.

3:30 P.M. Back on the set. The next sequence has Little Joe and his parents in Rabbi Baumel's office, after he has used the money for a Jewish homeland to buy a Masked Avenger ring. It's going to be shot in the same basement, in another corner of the room. The school benches are being put aside, and Carlo is working on the lighting.

Mom's stand-in today is Nicole Stern. She was Barbara Hershey's stand-in on *Hannah* for almost two months, so she knows the whole crew. Her mother is French, from a small village in Brittany near the town of Quimper. She goes there summers to see her grandmother, who still lives alone on a farm.

Tom is explaining to Woody what a Louma is, asking if he will want one for the Tonino sequence next Monday. The Louma is a big flexible crane at the end of which the camera is fixed, allowing very spectacular movements. It was invented by two Frenchmen and was first used in America by Steven Spielberg for *1941*.

4:20 P.M. Shot 38: Rabbi Baumel's heart "is full of grief," it "swells with anguish." "Money for a Jewish homeland used to buy a Masked Avenger ring?" Mom doesn't know what to do with Little Joe, the way he listens to the radio every night. Radio is no good, states the rabbi, it induces "bad values, false dreams, lazy habits." "You speak the truth, my faithful Indian companion," Little Joe tells the rabbi. Rabbi Baumel, shocked, slaps him. Pop tells the rabbi not to hit Little Joe, he'll hit him, and he does. But Mom tells Pop not to hit Little Joe, Pop is too lenient; she'll hit him. And the rabbi gives another slap, then Pop, then Mom, until the rabbi suddenly becomes merciful: "Enough, enough! You'll hurt the boy." *(1 minute and 10 seconds.)*

During the rehearsals, the rabbi says "Masked Adventure" instead of "Masked Avenger," but he is otherwise perfect. The slapping goes fine, too. Everybody is enjoying it—the crew because the scene is very funny, the actors because it allows them to express themselves physically, and Little Joe because he seems to like getting knocked around, like in the van the other day. At the end of the slapping, Woody adds the rabbi's line: "Enough, enough . . ."

After three takes in which Rabbi Baumel speaks in a quiet, subdued tone, Woody asks him to try it angrily, more violent. After each of the takes, everyone laughs at the scene. Woody tells the parents: "You're too soft." "Too soft!" yelps Little Joe. "You guys are getting a kick out of it. I know you!" Little Joe seems a bit tired, but he is always the professional, and he continues to take the slapping.

Take 7 is fantastic. "You can hit him and you can twist him," Woody says, using his hands. We go on.

But just after take 9, it becomes too much for Little Joe. He is exhausted and breaks into tears. The adults had really been getting into the slapping scene, and Rabbi Baumel has such huge hands. At first, no one realizes what is happening. Everyone is too involved in the scene—the actors in their roles, the crew in their work, Woody in his direction, and the rest of us in being entertained. Pop is the first to be aware of it, and hugs Little Joe; Pop is a warm man. Woody talks to Little Joe: "Do you want to stop?" Little Joe asks only for a five-minute break. Rabbi Baumel is really worried that he has "hurt the boy."

Take 10. When the actors get to the slapping, they once again really do it, totally involved in their characters. Poor Little Joe is worn out, and once again he bursts into tears. Woody stops the scene. The atmosphere is awkward, uncertain. Rabbi Baumel is sincerely upset. He is a gentle man, but his hands are so huge and Little Joe is so small. It is very difficult for an actor involved in his part to maintain control. Pop takes Little Joe in his arms and goes to a corner. Little Joe recovers. Woody goes to him and jokes a little, but treats him as an adult. The slapping scene will not be done again, but the show must go on.

(10 takes and 5 prints.)

5:30 P.M. Shot 38A: A close-up of the rabbi, at the beginning of his speech.

Woody asks him for two versions, the soft one and the angry one.

(3 takes and 3 prints.)

Woody goes to shake hands with Rabbi Baumel and congratulate him.

"It's a wrap!" at 5:40 P.M.

Friday, November 29, 1985

"A dialogue of top leaders is always a moment of truth in relations between states," Gorby says in Moscow. He insists that the two sides should begin preparation for the 1986 party. (New York Times)

Archbishops in Rome call for more efforts to eradicate anti-Jewish sentiments in the Church. (New York Times)

Georgia Burke, 107, died yesterday in a Manhattan nursing home. She had auditioned for the Blackbirds, a black choir, when, on the basis of her audition song, "St. Louis Blues," she was hired away on the spot. She appeared on Broadway in such shows as Mamba's Daughters, They Shall Not Die, Porgy and Bess, Cabin in the Sky, *and she won the Donaldson award in 1944 for* Decision. *From 1934 to 1945, she appeared on radio as a nurse on* When a Girl Marries. *There are no known survivors.*

Dale Winter, ninety-two, died of heart failure yesterday. She and her husband, Henry Duffy, formed the Duffy Players in 1924 at the Alcazar Theater in San Francisco. In that company were such actors as Billie Burke, Otto Kruger, and Edward Everett Horton. She played the title role in the Broadway musical Irene *in 1920.*

In the van to Coney Island with Kay, Little Linda, and her mother. Because of the rain, Superman didn't make it to the Thanksgiving Day Parade yesterday. But everybody is happy because New York needed the water.

7:45 A.M. We are at a Coney Island fishing pier at Twenty-first Street and the boardwalk. The boys are sawing the aluminum handrails off the staircase. "Don't worry, we've got the authorization," Santo tells me. The producers are here today, along with Sandy Morse, Woody's editor since *Annie Hall*.

8:30 A.M. On the beach next to the pier, near the water, waiting for the equipment to make it down. Cliff, his bare feet in the freezing water, is getting rid of some grafitti on the pier pilings. Men working on the pier above start with their hammers and saws. Richie politely asks them to stop because we are about to film. They ignore him. Tim goes to talk to them, and they soon decide to go have coffee.

9:25 A.M. Shot 137: After the surprise of seeing Miss Gordon appear in their classroom, Little Joe and his gang go to the beach to talk about women. Andrew likes Rita Hayworth, Joe likes Betty Grable, and Nick likes Dana Andrews. He seems a little disappointed to learn that Dana Andrews is a man—"With a name like Dana?" Finally, Andrew, Nick, Dave, and Burt go back home and leave Little Joe alone to dream about Miss Gordon. *(38 seconds.)*

As the kids are seen walking along the edge of the water in a long shot, Woody puts earphones on to hear the dialogue, and runs back and forth to them when he wants to give directions.

A wild track (recording) of the kids' lines is done.

(4 takes and 4 prints.) Completed at 10:10 A.M.

Shot 137A: His pals are gone, and Little Joe, all by himself, dreams of Miss Gordon. He starts to talk to himself; of course, she is much older than he but . . . *(23 seconds.)*

Jimmy Mazzola rakes our footprints from the sand. Little Joe is seen much closer now as he continues to walk by the water. For two of the takes, Little Joe doesn't talk to himself.

(8 takes and 4 prints.)

Shot 137B: Close-up of Little Joe as, looking to the horizon and full of thoughts of Miss Gordon, a German U-boat rises from the sea in front of him! And he faints.

This is no problem for Little Joe. His eyes open wide, and he falls to the sand.

(3 takes and 2 prints.)

11:00 A.M. We are on the other side of the pier to shoot the background for the submarine. The U-boat will be a model that will be photographed later and superimposed on this image by Greenberg Associates, the lab that did all the special effects for *Zelig*. Sandy tells Carlo exactly what she needs. Woody lets them work.

12:00 noon. Shot 37: Little Joe's gang runs along the water and stops under the pier. They've just finished collecting funds for the homeland in Palestine, and are ready to count it to see if they have enough to buy the Masked Avenger rings. Maybe they should leave a little for Palestine, Little Joe thinks. Andrew wonders if they are sinning. The counting is quickly done. People gave only pennies for the Jewish homeland! Andrew sees Epstein, a kid from their Hebrew class, and fears he'll tell the rabbi. Little Joe is pretty sure Epstein didn't see them, though. *(22 seconds.)*

First Woody tries with all six kids, then keeps only the ones with lines: Andrew, Nick, and Little Joe. The shot is easy and the lines are not too difficult, but the blocking creates some problems. The kids have to stop at a precise spot, not hiding each other, keeping the composition the way Woody wants it. Woody first listens to the dialogue through earphones, but finds he prefers following them behind the camera.

(11 takes and 5 prints.) Completed at 12:50 P.M.

1:30 P.M. We are now on the boardwalk, just in front of a huge period facade with marble columns and a sign: ROCKAWAY BATH, to reshoot Little Joe kissing Little Evelyn with Little Linda watching (the shot under the icy rain of Breezy Point). The only set dressing required was adding the bath sign and repainting one of the marble columns.

Shot RB102: In a wide and very long shot, the three kids walk on the boardwalk, Little Joe clowning to get the attention of the girls. Suddenly, he tries to kiss Little Evelyn, who rebuffs him.
(2 takes and 2 prints.)

2:00 P.M. It's getting cold now. Boxes of hot dogs and French fries from Nathan's—in Coney Island since 1916—are brought in, while the camera is moved in for a closer shot of the kissing.

Shot RB102B: Little Joe kisses Little Evelyn on the cheek and she pushes him. So he tries again, and she accepts, giving a nice simpering smile.

On the second kiss, the camera zooms in on Little Evelyn's smile. It's hard getting the correct pace, and coordinating the camera movement with the action.
(12 takes and 2 prints.)

Next, Woody needs one more establishing shot of Rockaway.

Shot RA10: A wide shot of Little Joe, leather jacket and aviator glasses on, standing in front of the bathhouse, waving at the camera.
(1 take and 1 print.)

2:30 P.M. Again in front of the Rockaway bath, for a shot to be edited to the song "They're Either Too Young or Too Old."

Shot 151: Cousin Ruthie staring moon-eyed at a marine kissing his girlfriend. (11 seconds.)

The marine and his girlfriend have been waiting in the van for a while. They get into position. Woody briefly explains how they should kiss. The two seem to get along pretty well. They rehearse a little. Ruthie is in her spot, practicing her moon-eyed look. Woody OK's everything. Ready! "Rollin'!" screams Tom. Immediately, the couple start kissing. "I didn't say 'Action,'" Woody remarks.

(2 takes and 2 prints.)

We break for lunch at 3:00 P.M.

In the van to Rockaway to reshoot the Needlemans leaving their home to go to the movies, with the Salad Sisters, Mrs. Needleman, and Drew.

Mrs. Needleman brings to my attention the fact that she is Woody's mother in Hannah. (She hasn't seen the movie yet, so she doesn't know that she is only heard from behind the bathroom door.) Fern tells us about the time Woody put her in the party in Broadway Danny Rose. She had to wait almost an entire week, all dressed and made up. She even had to come back for the reshoot. And Woody cut her shot. Same thing for Purple Rose; she was in the theater crowd. Mrs. Needleman mentions that she, too, was in the audience, and was also cut. We talk more about Woody. Drew asks Fern if he's being paid for making his films. We answer that we think so. Then Drew, exhausted because her call is always one hour to two hours before ours, falls asleep. Her head falls on Mrs. Needleman's shoulder, and Mrs. Needleman puts her arm around Drew maternally. A little while later, Drew wakes up, and tries to sit up, but Mrs. Needleman won't let her, and she has to keep her head in the warmth of Mrs. Needleman's breast until we reach Rockaway.

5:30 P.M. Back in Rockaway at Beach Ninety-sixth Street, in front of the Needlemans'. And it won't be our last day in Rockaway. We learn that the searchlights will have to be reshot.

Shot R70: Front shot of the house. The door opens and Needleman appears, complaining because they're going to be late. Mrs. Needleman comes out, complaining because they're going to see another western; she likes love stories. They go down the stairs and leave the frame on the left. As soon as they're out, the headlights of the Burglars' car shine on the house. The car appears on the right of the frame, then the headlights are turned off.

Jimmy Mazzola is driving the car. Since they're not seen, the Burglars haven't come. A few takes are ruined when Jimmy can't get the old car moving. Woody is trying to get the Needlemans' lines and the timing perfect.

(10 takes and 5 prints.)

"It's a wrap!" at 6:15 P.M.

As for Monday, we don't know yet if the Astonishing Tonino is going to perform his stunt. It's all up to the weather. We'll have to call the office Sunday night.

Monday, December 2, 1985   *Fifth week*

Three high-ranked U.S. officers helped coordinate the Egyptian assault on the hijacked jet. (New York Times)

In Jewish-Gentile marriages, children often struggle to reach inner peace. (New York Times)

And yesterday was Woody's birthday: his fiftieth.

Big day today. The ADs and the PAs have to be on location at Rye Playland at 5:15 A.M., the Salad Sisters and Jeffrey at 5:30. The others—the mayor and his wife, City Councilman Arthur O'Donnell, the band (seven musicians), fifteen policemen, four newsreel cameramen, two lifeguards, the scientist, the radio crew, and a few onlookers—took a 5:30 bus from Manhattan. Mrs. Tonino (Camille Saviola), the press, and another contingent of the crowd took the 6:00 A.M. bus. Finally, the Astonishing Tonino (Verne G. Williams), Carleton Foxx, Mr. Rydell (Everett Quinton), the Italian man (Peter Lopicollo), the Priest, Dr. Max Kachaturian (the leading osteopath from Zagreb), and a few VIPs caught the 6:30 bus.

Jimmy Mazzola has a few props to bring, including twenty flash cameras, the musical instruments, three small boats, radio mikes and broadcast equipment, Movietone News cameras, the ambulance, the police car, the radio truck, the news truck, coffee and cups, hot soup, a corsage, a stethoscope, a straitjacket, chairs, the milk-can locks, and umbrellas.

Wardrobe must be ready for the mayor, his wife, and the city councilman to get some soup spilled on them, and they have to remember the green purse, the black scarf, and clasps.

Finally, because it is going to "rain," the crane to hoist the rain machines has to be there, too.

The big day has come. The Astonishing Tonino is going to do it.

8:00 A.M. Rye Playland. We're in the 1920s, on a huge, arcing beach with a building stretching out along the sand, a small restaurant in the middle, and dressing rooms on either side. Inland, there's the main building with its large ice-skating rink and two cabins flanking its entrance. On the beach side, the arc ends at a long pier, with a beautiful wooden pavilion at the head of it. And behind it all is a giant amusement park. It's a complete summer resort, but without the sinister look of Breezy Point.

9:00 A.M. We're working on the first scene, an establishing shot of the place where this extraordinary event is going to occur. One camera has been set at the end of the pier for a long shot, the other one near the main building, both focused on the curving beach. The crowd and the VIPs are brought to the beach and placed by Tom as Woody and Carlo work on the composition. Jimmy Mazzola brings the ambulance and the radio truck, but they get stuck in the sand, and the boys have to push.

10:00 A.M. Woody isn't pleased with the look and wants the scene moved to the end of the pier (where it was in the script). The beach is too flat, too big. Carlo agrees.

It is cold and windy, and could rain in a minute, so the weather is perfect right now. But the problem is that Woody wants the WPGT radio truck at the end of the pier, and the truck is too wide to make it between the pilings and too high to pass under the pavilion. First, we have to ask for authorization (Tim, as always) so Jimmy Mazzola can try to unscrew two or three pilings, which were screwed in a hundred years ago. If it doesn't work, they'll use chain saws, and the roof of the radio truck will have to be taken off, then put back on for the shot.

The faces of the producers are getting longer by the minute.

10:30 A.M. While Jimmy Mazzola works with the boys, Woody goes to record the wild track of the band on the beach. The band is perfect. The youngest members must be in their seventies. The musicians are wonderfully dressed: long overcoats and bowler hats. In the middle of the beach, instruments in hand and music on their stands, conducted by their leader, Harry, they start to play, "Limehouse Blues," "I Know that You Know," "The World Is Waiting for the Sunrise," "I'm Just Wild About Harry," "Stout-Hearted Men," "A Kiss in the Dark," and "Liebestraum." They are playing out of sync (is it on purpose?).

The clouds are closing in, but the band plays bravely on. "Is it overcast enough for you?" Bob Greenhut asks Woody. It's getting windy, too. Music sheets start flying. Sometimes one instrument stops while the musician runs after his sheet music. The scene becomes comic and pitiful. Even Woody, who is not in a great mood today, starts laughing. Now it is raining, but the band sticks with the piece till the last note. Then it starts pouring, and we hurry into the building.

"We made it," Harry says. Sandy thanks them; it was perfect. "We could have done better," says one. "I was handicapped," says another, showing his wide overcoat. But they are happy to have made it. We drink coffee. Up close they look like they must be in their eighties!

11:30 A.M. The rain has stopped. Four of the posts have been neatly taken out to allow the truck through. But the cab is still too high by maybe one inch, to get under the first beam. All the boys sit on the truck to make it ride lower. Bobby Greenhut watches. Still half an inch too high. The producer and I make the difference, each on one fender. The truck gets through. Bob Greenhut turns to me and says, "True madness, isn't it?" But you get the feeling that he's having fun, that he likes the challenge.

12:00 noon. The 120 extras are brought to the end of the pier near the radio truck. It's a very long, wide shot. Carlo works on the composition and Woody runs to get the exact placement for each of the extras. I look through the camera. It's a beautiful scene, with the pavilion in the foreground, the pier curving at the end, the activity around the radio truck in the background. But the weather is uncertain; the sky is dark, yet there is a light on the horizon. Woody wants only clouds.

It's cold and windy at the end of the pier. The producers are watching the clouds every minute. There's a good chance we won't be able to shoot.

12:30 P.M. A beautiful sun now. We're not shooting. The producers look dismal. The 120 extras are brought back inside (and the image was perfectly composed!), marching past us. One of the boys in the band comes over to me. "You look important. Do you know if we shoot on Saturday? Because I have a job at Joe's restaurant."

We break for lunch at 1:00 P.M.

Very good food is served to the crew and the 120 extras in a room on the second floor of the main building. I have lunch with Louis and Patti Eiben, the women's wardrobe supervisor. At the end of our table, the Priest is entertaining a few friends.

This afternoon Biff Baxter (Jeff Daniels) will be coming in. He was not scheduled today but when they saw the problems with the shot this morning, they asked him to hurry in.

2:15 P.M. We are in a locker room in the beach building to shoot Biff Baxter, G-man, passing an army physical so he can become a good soldier and "take care of" those Japs and Nazis (sequence 122).

The old rooms require little in the way of set decoration: Rows of lights hung from the ceiling, three tables, and a few chairs are added. Carlo is working on the framing, hanging the light fixtures at different levels, cheating on the perspective. Woody is discussing the schedule for tomorrow with Tom. Because the sun seems to be back for a while, we'll go to the cover set in Central Park with Kirby Kyle hunting, and to reshoot the Brummers Confectionary in Jersey.

3:00 P.M. Woody and Jeffrey inspect the seventeen extras, then Tom shows them their places on the set. The sergeant, who is a teamster and was Woody's driver during the production of a former film, sits behind his desk, and the doctor, who examined

Woody in *Zelig*, sits behind another one in the back. Then Biff Baxter appears in the same-style underwear that Zipsky wore. Woody checks the camera. "Good, good—but too many hats."

3:40 P.M. Shot 122: Biff Baxter is getting the army physical. The sergeant gives him a hard time. Biff panics: He has asthma, sinus, everything. Biff starts wheezing. The other men in line complain. Biff goes to the doctor, starts begging. But the doctor has already reached his conclusion. Biff Baxter is 4F, flat feet! *(45 seconds.)*

First rehearsal. Biff Baxter screams with joy when he learns he is 4F. Just after the hysterical yell he comes back to his very quiet self and looks at Woody. Woody is laughing; he likes the performance. But he has suggestions for the sergeant and the doctor.

For the first take, Biff Baxter kisses the doctor and puts his head on his shoulder. He's good but the background is too noisy and the sergeant and the doctor cannot be heard.

Woody and Carlo decide to move the dolly so the camera can follow when Biff Baxter runs to the doctor in the background.

For the fourth take, Woody signals to Tom that he is not happy because the background people, impressed by Biff Baxter's screams, stop acting and watch him act.

In the following takes, two versions are done, one where the background people are noisy, another where they whisper.

(7 takes and 6 prints.)

"It's a wrap!" at 4:30 P.M.

Tuesday, December 3, 1985

In the Philippines the court acquits the military and Marcos's cousin General Fabian Ver for the slaying of Benigno Aquino, and Marcos reinstates his cousin. (New York Times)

The three American officers, though in full battle dress, didn't participate in the storming of the hijacked plane. (New York Times)

And Rocky IV made $20 million over the weekend, $32 million for the five-day Thanksgiving holiday. A long way from when Sly was robbing old ladies on the subway in Take the Money and Run.

8:00 A.M. Central Park and 105th Street, on a freezing day but with a beautiful sun. Central Park is picturesque, and the location, with all the trees, looks like the middle of any forest in any part of the world, if you ignore the buildings in the distance. We are here to shoot Kirby Kyle's first accident, where, while hunting a rabbit, he loses one leg, but not his heart.

Woody and Carlo are walking near a ravine, followed by Tom, looking for the best setting and angle for the camera.

8:30 A.M. Woody and Carlo are still walking in the woods. They are now back by the ravine. They wander back and forth, and we decide to wait on the little hill while they make up their minds.

8:50 A.M. Kirby arrives. He's in a fancy hunting outift. Jimmy Mazzola gives him a gun. The woman who owns the two setters gives him one, then the other, so he can decide which one is best. He checks the dogs out, getting to know them, while Woody and Carlo continue to appear and disappear, then reappear five minutes later.

9:15 A.M. They are still wandering in the woods. Woody is like an animal ("like a dog," Dickie says) who instinctively feels something but doesn't know how to do anything about it. Jane goes to the trailer to take shelter from the cold. The boys are reading the paper in the cars and trucks. Kirby has stopped practicing with the dogs and waits, his gun ready. And Jimmy Mazzola discusses dogs with the owner. Jimmy had a training school for dogs and knows, naturally, everything on the subject.

9:25 A.M. It's a wrap. We won't shoot. Woody doesn't like the place. We move to the next location.

9:30 A.M. We're going to shoot. Jimmy Mazzola has to chase after the car with the dogs when it nearly leaves. Bob Greenhut has just arrived, and everybody has the feeling that he is responsible for the decision to film.

While the boys set the dolly track on the side of our little hill, Woody goes to his trailer. As he passes Carlo, he looks at him, resigned, shrugging his shoulders.

10:00 A.M. Shot 87: Kirby appears in frame, his gun ready, running behind his dog, who has smelled a rabbit. The camera tracks with him for a while, then lets him go out of frame. *(10 seconds.)*

Woody, more and more resigned, checks the camera and gives his OK. He's clearly depressed, and Bobby Greenhut goes to cheer him up.

(4 takes and 2 prints.)

At 10:15 A.M., we move to the next location.

In the van to Jersey City with Bill Christians (men's wardrobe supervisor,) Cliff, Kay, and Dvořák's "New World" symphony on the sound track. We drive through Central Park, which is dazzling today. When you're coming from the north, the buildings of Central Park South seem to grow from the ground like the stone monolith emerging in *2001*.

Cliff tells about the problems they had on *A Midsummer Night's Sex Comedy*. By the end of the shooting the trees were turning brown and yellow, so the leaves were painted green. But when the movie company left, the Rockefeller estate, which owns the property, complained because it didn't want its trees green in winter. So the company came back to paint the trees brown. The green paint was dye and difficult to get out. Then, when the rains came, the brown came off and the trees were green again, in the middle of January.

11:30 A.M. Back to Brummers Confectionary to reshoot the soda-shop sequence where Ruthie and her girlfriends are entranced by the Crooner singing "All or Nothing At All." Then we will shoot the black family listening to the Tonino story upstairs, in Grandma Brummer's apartment. (Grandma has gone away.)

Carlo needs an hour and a half to prepare. The disorder proceeds methodically. Bobby Ward and Ray, each balanced at the top of a ladder, scream for "Mickey, Dickie, Eddie, Jimmy," and more often "Moe," to get a small light, a reflector, a piece of wood. The closest crew member answers to whichever name: "Got it, Moe!"

Brummer junior and his eighty-year-old employee, who started with Grandpa, are watching the activity anxiously. Fortunately, they're doing some business with the boys, selling candies and chocolates.

1:00 P.M. Shot R13: Same action: The waitress turns up the radio, and goes to the back room. We see the faces of the five swooning girls. The camera angle is different.

The girls are brought in, and Woody inspects them. They're a different group from the first time. The background contains fewer adults, mostly young boys and a few girls. They are put in the back room. Finally, there is the waitress, who gives me a wink, and the counterman.

Jimmy Mazzola makes the ice cream floats (he loves it) with whipped cream, a little juice, and a cherry.

(3 takes and 3 prints.)

Before going to the next shot, we break for lunch.

3:00 P.M. We're back on the set. Jimmy Mazzola is getting the counter ready, setting out ice cream for the girls. The waitress is giving Dickie a wink now. Woody comes in and goes to give some directions to the young boys in the back room. The girls are giggling because the young boys don't understand what Woody wants.

3:25 P.M. Shot R13A: It starts on the boys, then moves to the legs and bottoms of the girls.

"You're really disgusted! You can't stand it!" Woody yells to the young boys watching the swooning girls.

(5 takes and 4 prints.) Completed at 4:15 P.M.

4:30 P.M. We're in Grandma Brummer's apartment to shoot the black couple in their kitchen listening to Tonino's story. Grandma Brummer lives in small rooms and it's getting crowded. I retire to the bathroom, and sit on the toilet seat to work on my notes, leaving the door open in case of anyone's emergency. Woody passes by. He gives me a small hello, the first today. I keep writing. Woody passes a second time. He seems to be looking for something. Suddenly I realize. I stand up and go to him. "I'm sorry, do you need the place?" He laughs. "No, no, I'm looking for Jane."

5:00 P.M. Woody's whistling again, playing with a package of Marlboros. The mood on the set is better than this morning.

Shot 2F: The black couple in their kitchen listening to Tonino's broadcast. The wife is serving her husband breakfast. *(10 seconds.)*

(4 takes and 3 prints.)

Shot 8D: The man leaves the room. The wife covers her ears because of the static. *(5 seconds.)*

(3 takes and 2 prints.)

And it's a wrap at 5:20 P.M.

Back in the van with Kay, the Salad Sisters, and the black couple. The Manhattan lights are beautiful, almost unreal. We talk about children, about Christmas shopping. The conversation moves to Sally (Mia Farrow) and her eight children, and the dog, cat, and parrot. She is looking for an old Checker cab so she can take everybody away for weekends. Sometimes Woody takes them in his limo. But does he take the dog, cat, and parrot?

Wednesday, December 4, 1985

"Outrage greets $1 fare scare. Ed boils in battle for freeze." (Daily News)

8:00 A.M. The McManus bar on Seventh Avenue and Nineteenth Street. The McManuses settled in Chelsea forty-five years ago but they started the business at the beginning of the century, on the East Side. When they first came from Ireland, they lived in Rockaway.

It's all wood, with beautiful old windows and lace curtains. The place is perfect, but it's small and not easy to light. To be shot: people listening to Polly Phelps's story.

9:00 A.M. The extras are brought in. Woody, Jeffrey at his side, selects the ones he wants, checks their costumes, and places them on the set. Jeffrey is all in fur today, with jeans, and the Palestinian scarf over his shoulder. Underneath, he's wearing a "Paris Sorbonne" sweatshirt.

Jane tells Kay that Mr. Needleman's first name has changed from Sol to Marty. And Jimmy Mazzola is working on artificial smoke, just in case.

9:30 A.M. Shot 168A: A wide shot of the patrons at the bar and back tables listening to the Polly Phelps story on the radio. *(5 seconds.)*
(2 takes and 2 prints.) Completed at 9:40 A.M.

10:00 A.M. Just outside, a breakfast table has been set up on Seventh Avenue. A street woman and a kid hang around. "Is it free?" the kid asks. The teamsters tell them to help themselves. The visitors take napkins, put two or three doughnuts on them, pour coffee, and disappear.

10:15 A.M. Shot 172C: The patrons are stunned to hear Polly is dead. They are gathered around the radio. *(5 seconds.)*

The shooting is disturbed by the McManuses' cook, who wants to go to his kitchen to start lunch. (We have the room only till noon.) The PAs try to explain to him that we are almost finished and that we need only two more minutes to complete this shot. But the cook isn't in the mood. "I have to work!" he yells, crossing the set, ignoring everybody.

(1 take and 1 print.)

We move to the next location.

In the van with the Effects Actress (Wendy Coates) and a few extras. The Effects Actress is really tiny, with a face like a doll, and very lively. She has a high voice, and she's telling a girlfriend about an audition she went to (she's also a singer and an actress), then about the problem she has with her cat. The girlfriend has stopped listening.

In the front seat, two aged extras are talking about the old times, about actors and agents. They talk about how nice it was being on the road and how, when the roadshow arrived in a new town, all the local people wanted to meet them, and invited them to parties. Now, touring doesn't pay anymore, except for somebody like Zsa Zsa Gabor, who's still popular because of TV exposure.

11:10 A.M. The back of the Good Shepherd-Faith Presbyterian Church, on West Sixty-sixth Street. In the basement is a spacious room with a sound booth, and there are a few old mikes and amplifiers that are used for conferences. All the accessories for radio sound effects are there—a house door, a car door, a telephone, bunches of straw, and gadgets for trains, horse hoofbeats, and so forth. Some of the props are numbered, having come from a museum. The real radio-effects man, with white hair and beard and in his seventies, explains the different effects to Santo.

12:00 noon. Carlo is lighting. The tiny Effects Actress is reading *People*. The Effects Actor (John Rothman) is also hanging around. In reality he was Meryl Streep's roommate at Yale. It's his fourth film with Woody. In *Stardust Memories* he was Jessica Harper's boyfriend, the screenwriting teacher at Columbia who thinks that comedy is hostility and that comedians like Laurel and Hardy, Bob Hope, or Woody are either furious or latent homosexuals. In *Zelig* he was Mia Farrow's cousin and the amateur film-maker who shot the famous white-room experiment; and in *Purple Rose* he was the producer's lawyer.

Kay gets ten blue pages from Jane, the rewrite Woody has done.

12:30 P.M. Carlo is ready. The real effects man gives a demonstration of the different sounds. Woody listens, interested. Then he pauses in front of the equipment, jotting notes on a yellow piece of paper. Tom asks for silence.

12:40 P.M. Now Woody is sitting in the back, looking over Kay's script. Jane brings him his hot water and toast. And he continues to work.

1:00 P.M. Woody needs more time, so we break for lunch.

2:15 P.M. Back on the set. On an old and small typewriter furnished by Jimmy Mazzola, Woody types what he has written on his yellow paper. He has kept his green jacket and his tweed cap on. He types with all his fingers, though not very quickly.

2:30 P.M. Woody has finished. Tom asks everyone to leave while the actors rehearse with Woody and Carlo. Photocopies of the new pages are given to the actors.

The new material is longer and quite different from what was in the script. Originally, a house was on fire, the guy and the girl were caught in a tornado, and Johnny, the bad man, was trying to shoot the hero. They were finally saved by the cavalry. "Oh, Tom, I love you," the girl said as the show ended.

Now, it is even more complicated. They are in their apartment getting ready to go to the country. They leave (front-door effect), take their car (car-door effect), and arrive at the station. The hero makes a phone call (a nickel in the phone). They take the train (a whistle). They arrive at the countryside (straw crushed), they ride horses (hoofbeats), and discover their house is on fire. It ends with the Sound-Effects Man doing the wrong effect.

In the corner, the real effects man looks on disapprovingly, while everyone else laughs at the new scene.

Woody decides to shoot the scene wide, and Carlo makes adjustments. Woody wanders around for a while whistling, then dashes out to his trailer.

3:30 P.M. Andrew is back with us after a few days' absence. (He still has to go to school!) He mingles, saying hello to everybody. Jimmy Mazzola is checking a stack of hundred-dollar bills. They are for Porfirio, the Playboy of the Western World, to use to light Irene's cigarette (sequence 65). The bills look real. Andrew and I ask where we can get some. But Jimmy Mazzola is evasive. "Some place in Brooklyn . . ."

3:45 P.M. Shot 45: Same action as in the rehearsal. The couple go to the country by train and find their house on fire. The Sound-Effects Man goes from one effect to the other, doing his job passionately. *(1 minute, 29 seconds.)*

Woody says he wants to shoot the rehearsal. After three takes and one good one, Carlo changes the pan from the actor to the effects man to a dolly shot. The track is set. Woody checks the camera, but doesn't like it, and we go back to the original setup.

Again, Woody tightens everything as he goes along. He cuts the car-door effect, he asks the actors to speed it up, he shortens the horse ride.

(10 takes and 4 prints.)

4:30 P.M. Woody goes to a corner of the room and starts writing another version. Two minutes later, he gives new lines to the actors. While the actors look over the lines, Woody goes over to Andrew. He likes talking to the boy, and the conversations seem to help Woody relax.

Shot 45A: It's much shorter. The hoofbeats of an army patrol. "Company, halt!" Tom screams. He's going overseas. The girl arrives: "Tom . . ." "Claire, you came," he says. Then the train leaves. "I love you, Tom." "I love you, too." Train whistle, and it's over.

(6 takes and 2 prints.)

"That's enough," Woody says.

It is a wrap at 5:00 P.M.

Thursday, December 5, 1985

8,239 people (7,298 men and 941 women) crowded into city shelters early yesterday. The temperature went as low as 25 degrees. (New York Times)

*Grigori Zolotukhin, seventy-three, minister of grain procure-
ment, will move to a less significant job, announces* Pravda. *He
will become minister of bakery products.* (New York Times)

*Anne Baxter collapsed yesterday morning on Madison Ave-
nue. She is listed in critical condition.* (New York Times)

*An Israeli computer programmer has built computer person-
alities of a Jewish mother and a Jewish uncle called "Mom" and
"Murray." Murray is a cartoon computer friend who sits on the
screen in his slippers, cracking jokes and conversing for hours with
whoever is at the keyboard. Mom sits in an overstuffed chair,
dispensing advice and making you feel guilty.* (New York Times)

*And Babi Burke, a forty-four-year-old nurse from Fort
Lauderdale, Florida, is taken away by Vatican security guards
after she elevates and consumes a communion host and then
raises and drinks from a silver chalice of wine. She is assisted by
her friend Marie-Therese, a former nun from Belgium. "Sexism,"
she declares, "is a sacrilege to the Gospel of Christ."* (New York
Times)

In the van with Kay and Angela. We are going back to Rye to
shoot Tonino's scene, with only seventy extras today, just enough
to make the pier look crowded. The sky is low and dark, with a
faint red sun.

Angela reads our horoscope in the *Daily News.* She knows
everybody's sign: Jane is, of course, Virgo; Sally and Andrew,
Aquarius; Woody, Sagittarius . . .

8:00 A.M. Beautiful sun, warm air, and the oily sea at Rye
Playland this morning. Despite the weather, the cameras are being
set up. The forecast said it should be cloudy by 10:00 A.M. Carlo
thinks maybe noon. Some good and unexpected news, though;
Woody liked the shot of Kirby in the woods (the one he didn't
want to shoot).

8:45 A.M. Woody is in his trailer. Bobby Greenhut and Ezra
are watching the sky. The clouds are creeping toward the sun. And
the boys—Mickey Green, the first assistant cameraman; Pete
Tavis, the teamster captain; Hammer; Woody's driver; and two
other teamsters—are playing hockey on the small rink.

The only thing Carlo misses about Italy is his little house in
Sardegna, he tells me. Carlo wants to stay here. He loves New
York. After this movie he might work on the next Antonioni

movie. In fact, doing one film a year with Antonioni and one with Woody would be a perfect combination for him. But Carlo won't do commercials. Whenever he agreed to do one, simply for the money, at the last minute he couldn't go through with it.

9:45 A.M. The forecast was right. Clouds are about to block the sun. The seventy extras are taken to the end of the pier, followed by the VIPs—the mayor and his distinguished wife, City Councilman Arthur O'Donnell, Carmella Tonino and Dr. Max Kachaturian, Mr. Rydell, Foxx, the Italian man, and the Priest, who looks a little "feminine," as Pop would say.

The blocking shouldn't take long, since it was worked out on Monday. This will be the opening sequence of the film: shot number 1.

10:30 A.M. Woody is dressed for frigid weather, and for the first time the leather shoes have been abandoned and replaced by snow boots. He has ski pants over his corduroy trousers, and he's wearing his huge gray parka. Under the hood, he has on a wool hat, and his black mittens are hanging from his belt. The string of the hood is tied under his nose and the only part you recognize are the glasses sticking out from the hood. Woody goes to check the two cameras.

11:10 A.M. There is a glow on the horizon between the sky and the sea, same as Monday. So we don't shoot: We break for lunch, hoping it will be gone in an hour. The seventy extras are taken back inside, passing in front of us.

The boys recall *Stardust Memories*. For nearly a week they went to the same location at 8:00 A.M. and left at 11:30 A.M. because Woody and Gordon Willis, the director of photography, found it too sunny. While waiting, the men played cards, or ball. Sometimes Woody played with them. Another time, a balloon was to go out on the right side of the frame, but the wind was blowing in the other direction. And there was also the time when Woody wanted twilight and overcast; it lasted almost another week.

"I thought those times were over," Ezra says, eyeing the horizon.

11:50 A.M. Back on the set. The extras are brought to the pier. Two local journalists are here, but they can't quite figure out what's happening.

12:10 P.M. It's decided. We won't shoot. The sky is dark enough but there is still that light on the horizon—a beautiful reddish light, but Woody doesn't want it. The seventy extras are taken back inside, passing in front of us in little groups for the fourth time today.

Bob Greenhut is taking it philosophically, but Ezra is totally depressed. "I'm going. I don't want to see this!" The boys are tossing stones into the water. Tom stays in his corner, depressed, too. Brian takes pictures of everybody. "Aren't we having a great time, guys!" jokes Bob Greenhut. The rumor is that the producers asked Woody to shoot another setup but Woody refused.

12:40 P.M. Ezra leaves. Bob Greenhut goes discreetly to Woody's trailer.

1:30 P.M. Still waiting. The seventy extras have been moved to a snack bar full of tables and electronic games, just in front of the rink. It's almost surrealistic. All these people in 1920s dress: Some are sleeping, others eat, the policemen are talking with the Priest. The Astonishing Tonino, in his bathing suit, is entertaining a young woman from the crowd. Old ladies are trying the video games and one of the boys in Harry's band is explaining to a policeman how they work. The lifeguards talk about bodybuilding. Some of the extras rent ice skates and try to enjoy themselves even though they can't skate. Upstairs, on the big ice rink, the New York Rangers team is practicing and the boys go to watch.

2:00 P.M. At the end of the pier. We are finally going to shoot the arrival of the Great Tonino (sequence 5). The camera faces in the opposite direction, the reddish horizon to our backs.

Both cameras are used. The extras, the officials, Foxx, Carmella Tonino, and some of the crowd are placed around the radio truck. The news cameramen are in front, ready to immortalize the day.

2:50 P.M. Shot 5: Everyone is waiting. Carleton Foxx is describing the scene for the listeners. Suddenly the Great Tonino is announced. The crowd becomes excited. And Tonino makes his appearance, running in his bathing suit between two lifeguards. The journalists converge on him, snapping pictures. Finally he reaches the radio truck, where Jeffrey puts a coat on his shoulders (it is really cold). *(10 seconds.)*

The sight is quite funny, if not astonishing.
(4 takes and 3 prints.)
Woody doesn't seem as resigned and depressed as Tuesday morning in Central Park, but you still get the feeling that the fact that we're shooting has more to do with Bob Greenhut than Woody. Woody and Bobby seem to have a nice, somewhat distant, but very respectful attitude toward each other.

We wrap at 3:15 P.M.

In the van back to Manhattan with the Astonishing Tonino and his wife, Carleton Foxx, Mr. Rydell, and two hairdressers who helped the Salad Sisters. The Toninos seem to get along pretty well. Tonino complains a little about the day: It was not very exciting running around in the cold in a bathing suit between two "pieces of meat" (the lifeguards).

In the back, the two hairdressers are talking about some of the actresses they have worked with—Rosanna Arquette ("She's nuts but she's OK") Madonna ("She's nice; she calls me her hero"), Rebecca De Mornay ("She's bad!").

Friday, December 6, 1985

Trump scores again: he gets the OK to build a $286 million sports dome. (Daily News)

And the twenty rabbis arrested in front of the Soviet Embassy protesting the treatment of Jews in the U.S.S.R. have been found guilty. Each defendant receives a fifteen-day suspended jail sentence, six months unsupervised probation, and a $50 fine. More than fifty rabbis have already been arrested in similar demonstrations. A second trial of twenty-five rabbis arrested on May 1 is scheduled for December 11. (New York Times)

In the van to Rye with Kay and Joanne Dillon (Eunice Cooper). It's Dillon's first film, her first acting job. She just got her SAG card. This morning, she got up very early to be sure not to miss the van. She looks a little like Diane Keaton, tall and slim, but maybe not quite as pretty.

We were supposed to give the Tonino scene another try today, but it's snowing over Manhattan.

8:15 A.M. A mantel of snow over Rye Playland. It's beautiful but the Tonino scene is definitely out. It's a pity because the sky is wonderfully dark. We are going to shoot on the two cover sets: the Cooper family amateur radio show with Eunice singing, and Kirby Kyle's third hunting accident, which blinds him.

Breakfast with Bobby Ward and Jimmy Sabat. These are two nice people, quiet, polite, and professional; maybe the two most likable boys on the team.

9:00 A.M. The Cooper family's home—"our garage, actually," as Mrs. Cooper would say—is located in one of the lodges at the entrance to the main building of Rye Playland, on the second floor. It was an abandoned room, which Santo has transformed, with a little furniture and some pieces of fabric, into an "amateur studio."

The piano tuner is working on the piano. Bald, a little hunchbacked, and in his seventies, he's a real character. He looks like Popeye, except that instead of a pipe hanging from his mouth, he always has a drop of moisture hanging from his nose. Ken and I are worried that it will drip into the piano. His tools set in front of him, he tests the piano, absorbed in his job, ignoring Carlo and the boys at work on the lights.

9:45 A.M. Two extras stand in for the Coopers. Jimmy Sabat whispers to me that the woman looks exactly like Jack Lemmon in *Some Like It Hot* ("Well, nobody's perfect!"). Woody comes in to check the camera movement and framing, then dashes out to let Carlo finish his work. The room is small and difficult to work in. Ken is working on the call sheet for next Monday. We are not coming back, for the moment, for another try on the Tonino scene.

Jeffrey's outfit today consists of rain rubbers over his shoes, gray corduroy trousers, a sleeveless leather jacket over a fur-lined parka, white shirt, a dotted tie, a red wool sweater with black-and-white checks, and a fur hat on his head.

11:00 A.M. Carlo is ready. Woody returns, and the Cooper family arrives. Mr. Cooper, a shy man, goes to sit behind his radio transmitter. Mrs. Cooper (Alice Beardsley) starts practicing "Roses of Picardy" on the piano, and Eunice waits behind her mike. Jeffrey and the Salad Sisters have done a good job on Eunice, but not to her advantage. She now looks like a cross between Diane Keaton and Shelley Duvall.

11:15 A.M. Shot 41: the Coopers' amateur show, featuring Eunice's rendition of "Roses of Picardy." Mrs. Cooper opens the show, then starts to play. But Eunice is shy, like her father. "Go ahead, dammit!" Mrs. Cooper says. Eunice does it. *(1 minute, 36 seconds.)*

Mr. Cooper has to change his shirt because the white is too bright for the lights; it reverberates on film. Woody goes to Eunice, who listens to him carefully, then he goes to the corner and starts whistling "Roses of Picardy" with tremolo.

First rehearsal: Woody wants to start shooting immediately, but Dickie needs one rehearsal for the camera. Eunice is perfect, as is Mrs. Cooper. But there is a problem with the old mike. The room is too small and the piano too strong: It drowns out Eunice's voice. Jimmy Sabat has to hide a modern, more sensitive mike.

11:45 A.M. Ready to go. Carlo signals Mickey when to zoom by tapping his shoulder. "Beautiful," Dickie screams after the first take. He is talking about the camera movement, not Eunice. The second take is not so well timed. The third take moves a bit faster. "One more and we're finished," Woody says.
(5 takes and 3 prints.)
We break for lunch at 12:00 noon.

Lunch in the main building from the same caterer. Tim is not pleased. Tonino's extras ate like crazy and there isn't enough food left for the crew.

After lunch, the boys go back to the hockey rink for a little break. Tom and Ken are playing but not as well as Mickey, Pete, or Jimmy Sabat's fourteen-year-old son, who has come to see if the boys have any potential. Tim, always tough, is at the goal with no protection.

Downstairs in the lobby, the owner of Kirby Kyle's dog is breast-feeding her baby.

1:30 P.M. Back in the woods for Kirby's third accident, in which he will lose his sight. Actually, we are at the end of Rye Playland's parking lot, at the edge of a lake, where there is a small forest. It has stopped snowing, but a light rain is falling. Woody has put on a green cape with a hood and looks like Little Red Riding Hood. Rumor is that the opening sequence, the Great Tonino, might be dropped for now and filmed in April during the reshoot.

Brian alerts me that Mike Tyson, the boxer, is fighting tonight. He shows me the article in the *Daily News:* "He is going to be the best." Brian and Tyson are from the same Brooklyn neighborhood.

2:00 P.M. Kirby arrives with one leg and one arm, helped by Ken and Jimmy Frederick. They set him, with the dog and the gun, behind a bush at the edge of the lake. In the script, Kirby was hunting deer, but now it will be duck.

Shot 91: Kirby is at the edge of the lake, half hidden behind a bush, waiting for ducks to approach, his gun ready. *(5 seconds.)*

Jimmy Mazzola throws bread in the lake, so the ducks can be in the frame. It works so well he is soon being followed not only by a herd of ducks, but also sea gulls. "Forget the sea gulls, Jimmy, just the ducks!" screams Tom. But the birds are not fully cooperative, and Jimmy Mazzola is running out of bread. The ducks come and go, so Dickie stays ready to film. "The ducks are coming. The ducks are coming . . ." screams Woody, having as much fun as the rest of us.

(5 takes and 5 prints.)
And "It's a wrap" at 2:30 P.M.

Monday, December 9, 1985   *Sixth Week*

Trafficking in children is discovered in Yugoslavia, and AIDS is discovered in Russia. (Radio report)

"Moscow yearns for Stallone," and Rambo *videocassettes sell well on the black market. (New York Times)*

Ed closes second gay bath in AIDS battle. (Daily News)

Poet Robert Graves, author of I, Claudius, *died Saturday in Majorca.*

And Jack Skirball, former rabbi who became an Oscar-winning film producer, died Sunday. He headed a reform congregation in Evansville, Indiana, during the twenties. In the thirties, he left the rabbinate to distribute educational films. In 1942 he produced Alfred Hitchcock's Saboteur *and* Shadow of a Doubt. *He made a second fortune in real estate. In 1976 he co-produced* A Matter of Time, *the last film by Vincente Minnelli.*

8:00 A.M. John Jay College of Criminal Justice on West Fifty-sixth Street. Founded in 1964, it was originally the Twentieth Century-Fox headquarters. The conference-room scene of *Zelig* was shot upstairs in Spyros Skouras's old office. We're working in Darryl Zanuck's secretary's office, to shoot the Reba Man (sequence 48). Darryl Zanuck's office next door, with its huge "medieval" chimney, stained-glass windows, and sculpted wood paneling, has become a conference room.

8:45 A.M. Woody is in a fine, almost mellow mood this morning. He plays with a couple of dollar bills as he jokes with Bob Greenhut. They discuss the shooting schedule. It's definite now; we'll shoot the Tonino scenes in April. The one we have shot—Tonino's arrival between the "two pieces of meat"—has turned out well, but weather conditions make the rest too risky, too dangerous to film now. Woody does a few tap-dance steps.

9:45 A.M. Molly Regan (Jessica Dragonette) arrives, arm in arm with Jeffrey, and heads for the makeup department. An actress and voice coach, she went to school with Jeffrey; he was the one who told Woody about her. While the boys are making last adjustments, Woody starts rehearsing with the Reba Man.
When Woody talks with Carlo, it is always in fragments of sentences, more expressions of feeling than anything intellectual: "We could . . ." "You know . . ." The conversations—incomprehensible to the outsider—always end the same way.
Woody: "You know what I mean?"
Carlo: "Yes, of course!"

10:15 A.M. Shot 48: The announcer: "And now, everybody's favorite maid—Reba!" The camera moves to a man (Jerry Sroka) doing all the voices: (As the playboy) "Reba! Is my breakfast ready?" (As Reba, the black maid) "Comin' Missah Bill . . . I do declare . . . you was out late last night." (As playboy) "That's none of your business, Reba. I have a hangover." (As Reba) "Yassuh . . . yassuh!" Then the man starts to talk, normally, to the camera: "We were voices . . . They didn't know our faces . . ." *(33 seconds.)*

The room is small. Woody is right next to me during the first take, so near our elbows are touching. But he didn't say hello this morning. During a break between the first and the second take, an extra gets into the room and starts to watch. Woody looks at him. "Who is this?" "I'm waiting to be made up," the extra answers, terrified. "Out!" Woody replies, and turns back to his work, a little proud of his tyrant number. It's funny for us, but the poor extra. . . .

No problem with the Reba Man. He is good both as the playboy and as Reba, his maid.

(4 takes and 2 prints.) Completed at 10:30 A.M.

11:15 A.M. The main lobby of John Jay, a colorful, almost baroque hall. To be shot is a scene of Jessica Dragonette singing the "Italian Street Song" (sequence 43). Even with the problems of last week, we are still on schedule. When Woody is satisfied, things move quickly and he manages to make up lost time. Sandy is here, as is Bea, dressed comfortably in a man's extra-large tweed jacket, a tartan skirt, wool stockings, and Hush Puppies. She gives Woody a little hug, and goes for makeup.

12:00 noon. Jessica Dragonette is on the set. Her musicians are going to their instruments. Jessica's dress is beautiful, with flowers on the breast. Jeffrey designed it and had it made in the "costume shop," a department put together especially for the movie. All the dresses for Sally and Bea, for instance, were made in the shop, as were the dinner clothes for the male principals for the sequence in the King Cole Room. The shop people started working long before the shooting, but they have to keep working because changes are always being made. Even when costumes are rented for the big scenes with hundreds of extras, there are always alterations.

12:20 P.M. Shot 43. The camera starts close on Jessica as she sings the "Italian Street Song," and finishes on a wide shot with the orchestra. *(1 minute, 25 seconds.)*

It is Jessica's voice on the playback. Usually Woody prefers direct sound, but the acoustics here would not allow it. Jessica is good, and everyone applauds the performance.

(3 takes and 2 prints.)

Shot 43A: A close-up of Jessica singing.

No problems with her.

(2 takes and 2 prints.) Completed at 1:00 P.M.

Two musicians ask to be photographed with Woody. Brian uses their camera to take the picture. Woody, wearing his green jacket and tweed cap, has his usual glum look. The two musicians, in black tie, smile and smile.

Brian tells me Mike Tyson is supposed to come to the set this afternoon.

We break for lunch.

2:30 P.M. We're at the Horn and Hardart Automat ("This is world famous!") at the corner of Forty-second Street and Third Avenue. Built in 1938, this is one of the last of the original Automats. At the time, since these places were unique to New York, it was one of the biggest tourist attractions in town. We have the whole restaurant for the afternoon, and outside on the sidewalk a crowd is gathering and looking at us through the windows. We are in the 1940s, just after Mom has had her baby, and Bea, accompanied by her new boyfriend Sy (the married one), has taken Little Joe for a tour of Manhattan (sequence 157). The scene will take place next to the food dispensers. A simple pickup shot of Bea, Sy, and little Joe walking among the other patrons, looking at the choices. Carlo goes to work.

3:15 P.M. "Good seeing you," the Hebrew tutor tells me. He is a tall, handsome young man who looks like Mandy Patinkin in *Yentl.* He teaches Hebrew and Jewish literature in three synagogues. Today he is lightly unshaven, wearing a tweed cap like Woody, and reading *High Spirits* by Robertson Davies. Barbara comes to say hello, too, but the last few days have not been good to her. She and her son were on hold all of last week. Little Joe was tutored at the hotel, and she had to hang around. This weekend they went back to Philly, but two days aren't a lot of time. Her daughter, who is staying at home down there, has started complaining. Fortunately, she has a meeting with some people from the Whitney who are interested in her work (Barbara is a painter, too), and that helps her spirits a little.

Andrew is back and still hanging around with the women, especially Drew. Jimmy Sabat is reading his racetrack news. Brian is flirting with Jane. And Carlo and the boys are working.

4:00 P.M. Carlo will be ready in ten minutes. Woody is back and so are the three actors. Bea, as usual, ignores Sy (Richard

Portnow). Little Joe entertains him. Andrew is talking to a teamster now. He likes to go from one to the other, and he does it in a gentlemanly way, always reserved, but spontaneous.

4:10 P.M. First rehearsal. Woody is on the dolly. The shot is a little difficult but beautiful. It plays with the mirrors that cover the huge pillars in front of the food dispensers. It starts on a shot of Sy and Little Joe walking toward the camera, on the left side of the frame, looking at the food, while on the right of the frame we see a reflection of Bea coming toward them. When all of them are close enough, the camera moves back, following the actors, retaining on the other side that same sort of image—half reality, half reflection in the mirror. But it seems it is too complicated, and the shot is too busy with all the other patrons.

4:30 P.M. Woody and Carlo have tried another camera setting but have finally come back to the original, simplified.

Shot 157: The camera moves along the food dispensers with patrons passing by and reveals Bea, Sy, and Little Joe in mirror reflections as they look at the food dispensers. (20 seconds.)

(6 takes and 4 prints.)

We wrap at 5:00 P.M.

Mike Tyson is here with a pal. He is not big, but you wouldn't like to meet him in a dark alley. Brian introduces him to Woody. They shake hands, exchange a few words, then Woody dashes out.

Tuesday, December 10, 1985

Apparently distraught over finances, an Iowa farmer kills his banker. (New York Times)

A Japanese puzzle—the vending-machine murders. Haruo Otsu went fishing one recent morning and stopped along the way for drinks at a vending machine. Halfway through the second bottle, Mr. Otsu started to feel sick. A few hours later he was taken to the hospital. The next night he stopped breathing. The poison was paraquat, a deadly herbicide, and it had been put into or near the vending machines deliberately. Vending machines have killed ten people and left thirty-five seriously ill in the last few months.

"They cynically enjoy superiority by imagining the victims groaning, and do not feel any remorse," stated Professor Susumu Oda, *a mental-health specialist. Bottlers are inclined to blame the victims for having been careless: "If only consumers were more cautious, they would have seen that some tampering had been done,"* said Takeo Mizuuchi, a spokesman for the Japan Soft Drink Bottlers Association. (New York Times)

8:00 A.M. The Savoy Manor on 149th Street, in the Bronx. BALLROOM, MARRIAGES, PARTIES, 4 CHURCH FUNCTIONS, the sign says. In the back, about 150 extras have parked themselves on chairs in the middle of the vast room. On one side, a dozen hairdressers are "conducted" by Romaine. On the other side, another dozen makeup artists are "directed" by Fern. This is the kingdom of the Salad Sisters.

It's an incredible atmosphere. There are all types of military uniforms, and pretty girls everywhere. Some have been to makeup and the hairdresser, but not wardrobe—and vice versa. Richie passes by screaming for numbers to get in line, then checking names; the extras are being kept track of numerically. A sailor tries to get something started with a pretty girl while she's fixing her stockings. The period skirts the ladies are wearing are sexy, and everybody is having fun.

The set is the grand ballroom of the Savoy Manor, just to the right, off the lobby. At the far end there is a stage with a piano and drums, and a huge USO banner on the back wall. On the side, a few posters read LOOSE LIPS SINK SHIPS and WHEN YOU TALK TOO MUCH, YOU GET INTO TROUBLE. In the middle of the ballroom are tables and chairs. We are in the forties to shoot Sally singing "I Don't Want to Walk Without You" for the USO (sequence 143). Popeye the piano tuner is back and doing his job.

8:20 A.M. Sally arrives with Baby Dylan in her arms. Woody says good morning to the baby, taking her in his arms. Then Sally rushes away to get ready.

8:35 A.M. The lighting of the room is under way, and should take a long time. The boys hurry in with the rest of the equipment. Unshakable, Popeye keeps working on the piano.

In the back room, the atmosphere has quieted down. Most of the extras are ready. Some of the girls read, others chat, still others flirt with the soldiers. The makeup and hair people relax, too. They were here at 6:00 A.M. and haven't stopped working since. Jeffrey and Bill pass by, distributing hats and checking costumes.

9:30 A.M. Popeye has finished and tries the piano. (Chopin's Waltz in C Sharp). I approach and tell him I like this piece. "You know this guy was not happy in his life. He had this woman on his mind. What's her name. . . ?"

Sally comes in, beautiful in her red skirt. Woody looks at her, taking her by the hand. They have a sort of removed attitude with each other, but with a lot of attention given on both sides. You have a feeling that Woody is proud of her, and impressed by her, too. Sally wants to rehearse the song, and goes to the stage, where the two musicians wait. Everything will be recorded live. Woody checks the camera movement. It's nice, this image of Sally singing "I Don't Want to Walk Without You" in her high voice before a ballroom empty except for the boys, who continue to work, and Woody, who is looking for another camera angle.

Sally finishes. Woody goes to her, takes her hand, and guides her to a corner. She's cold, and Woody gives her his jacket.

10:15 A.M. Carlo will be ready in ten minutes. Jimmy Mazzola and his men are filling glasses and putting Lucky Strikes and Camels without filters on each table. Brian assures me that Tyson (nineteen years old) will be world heavyweight champion next year. Dick Hyman is here with Sandy.

The extras are brought in. Most of them are couples, soldiers with girlfriends. While Woody is at the camera, Tom seats them. Sally is back on the stage. Tom explains the scene to the extras. They just have to be lively and listen to Sally. They should drink, smoke, and have fun.

11:00 A.M. First rehearsal. Woody rides the camera. Sally sings her song. At the end, everyone applauds, enthusiastic. Tommy has to stop them.

Woody works with Carlo on the composition for the final part of the scene. A few extras are moved. Now is the last chance for hair, wardrobe, and makeup, because the next one is "pictures."

Shot 143: The camera, looking from behind the audience, starts on a wide angle of the whole room, and moves to a closer shot of

Sally as she sings "I Don't Want to Walk Without You." *(1 minute, 35 seconds.)*
    (3 takes and 2 prints.)

12:05 P.M. In the back room, the excitement is gone. These people have been here six hours now and they're beginning to get tired. Stockings are falling down and the girls have to keep tugging at them. Sally has gone back to her trailer. Kay introduces me to the interviewer (Ken Chapin) for the scene this afternoon. He's her husband in the real world.

12:50 P.M. Shot 143A: Sally sings the song, seen from another angle. Only half of the audience is brought back. The musicians listen to a little of the playback to get the rhythm. Sally goes on again. She is really charming, and she does have beautiful cheek-bones.

(3 takes and 2 prints.)

There is not much directing in this scene—just of the camera movement. It's strange how Woody cuts very quickly after the song is finished, as though certain he will not need more of the scene for the editing. He has been doing it this way all along; as soon as the action is over or the lines are said, he cuts.

The camera is moved again for an even closer shot of Sally. The audience is taken away. Sally stays on the set and Baby Dylan is brought in. Woody plays with the baby. He makes faces, and six-month-old Baby Dylan, who has a good sense of humor, bursts into laughter. Then he takes her in his arms and makes her walk on the table. Sally looks very proud of her.

1:45 P.M. Shot 143B. The camera moves along the stage. It starts on the musicians, passes Sally singing, and finishes on the right edge of the stage, on a sailor standing against the wall by a war poster.

(3 takes and 1 print.)

We break for lunch at 2:00 P.M.

In the van to Manhattan with Kay, her husband the inter-viewer, Mr. and Mrs. Globus, Mr. Brooks, and the Bigot. Danny is offering us the overture of Mozart's *Cosi Fan Tutte.*

Kay's husband was Woody's father in *Stardust Memories* and then an interviewer in *Zelig.* Mark Hammond (Mr. Brooks) was a customer at the cafeteria where Sally worked in *Purple Rose.* Mar-tin Chatinover (Mr. Globus) was the endocrinologist in *Zelig* and George Hamlin (the Bigot) was the chemotherapist. It's the first Woody Allen movie for Armellia McQueen (Mrs. Globus). She is a Broadway actress and lived in Paris for nine months when she was on tour with *Harlem Swing* at Le Theatre de la Porte St. Martin.

The talk is about religion. Nobody except Mrs. Globus knows who Father Divine was. Mrs. Globus has a line about him in the next scene. Father Divine was an evangelist who had a lot of fol-lowers during the forties, she tells us. Next, we're talking about Guru Bhagwan Shree Rajneesh and his eighty-five Rolls-Royces.

3:30 P.M. Columbus Circle and Central Park West, next to the park entrance. A camera truck is already there, but it is for a TV show, *Mike Hammer*, with Stacy Keach. Their second unit is shooting the fourth take of scene 155: Stacy Keach arrives by taxi, gets out to buy a hot dog, exchanges a few words with the vendor, and leaves in the taxi. The director is tall, tanned, and bearded. There are a lot of photographers and the public is much more interested in Stacy Keach than in Woody, who has just arrived and is discussing the setting with Carlo a few yards away. Lauren Hutton is also around (is she on the TV show?). She leaves in a limousine.

Manhattan has become Hollywood.

4:30 P.M. It's getting dark. The TV crew has gone now, and the public starts gathering around our PAs' barricades. Stacy Keach has stayed and is chatting with Brian. Andrew comes by, directly from school. Barbara arrives from the hotel to help.

A kiosk is dressed with period papers and magazines and the subway entrance is blocked. A guy wants to buy a paper and Richie has a little trouble explaining that they are not real. "We're shooting a movie."

5:00 P.M. We'll be ready to shoot in ten minutes. It's quitting time in Manhattan and the crowd of onlookers has swollen dramatically. All the producers are here: Jack Rollins, Bob Greenhut and Ezra. They have come from the Fifty-seventh Street office. The atmosphere is spectacular, with the lights (one is on the top of a truck), the period costumes, and the public. Mr. and Mrs. Globus, Mr. Brooks, the Bigot, and a few extras are put in position to form a group, with the interviewer in front of them.

5:15 P.M. Shot 111: A street interview for the radio, just after the declaration of war. Mr. Globus thinks they're gonna "knock the hell out of those Japs and Germans." Mr. Brooks wonders if America is doing "the right thing," and why can't "Europe fight its own war." The Bigot agrees, and says Roosevelt is the one who led them into the war, along with the monied interests, "and those people know who I'm talking about!" Finally, Mrs. Globus confesses she never liked those Germans. "They got Hitler," she says, "but we've got Joe Louis. And the Japs have got the emperor, but we got Father Divine." (*35 seconds.*)

Woody puts on his earphones. We can't hear anything because of the traffic. It must be hard for the actors to concentrate.

(*10 takes and 3 prints.*)

We move to the newsman in his kiosk listening to the Polly
Phelps story (shot 168B).
(1 take and 1 print.)
Jane goes to Woody and asks him something. He gives her an
OK. She returns with two adorable, fair-haired little twins
(Hannah's twins in *Hannah*). "Hi, fellows!" Woody says.

We wrap at 6:05 P.M.

Wednesday, December 11, 1985

*"Tycoon [Mr. Delacorte, aged ninety-two] and wife mugged in
Park: cash robbed, mink stolen."* (Daily News)
*Soviets mark human rights day: A contingent of
plainclothesmen and uniformed police wait. Whenever a potential
demonstrator draws near, he or she is whisked off to a waiting
bus. After eleven people have been taken away, a middle-aged
man announces that he wants to recite some poetry, a practice
that is not unusual at the Pushkin statue in the square. But before
he can do anything more, two plainclothesmen throw him to the
ground, a third punches him, and all three drag him away.*
*Pravda reports: "The repression of 'dissidents' is being inten-
sified in the U.S.A. and other Western countries, police attacks on
peaceful demonstrations by antiwar activists are becoming more
frequent, an assault is being waged against the rights of trade
unions, and acts of terror are being organized against progressive
social activists."*
*The Soviet rights record is lauded at a news conference by a
panel that includes Metropolitan Filaret of the Russian Orthodox
Church, Samuel Zivs of the Anti-Zionist Committee, an auto-
plant worker, and a woman from a collective farm.* (New York
Times)

8:15 A.M. Manhattan Center on West Thirty-fourth Street.
The camera is being set up in the lobby of the theater. First we are
going to shoot an establishing shot, where Sally begins to tell us
how she became a radio personality (sequence 139).
Angela is wearing a white Basque beret this morning. Jimmy
Mazzola is being massaged by one of the caterers, who's an expert.
Jimmy has scoliosis and two broken vertebrae from a motorcycle

accident. I split a card with Frankie. Dickie complains that he hasn't even come close to a winning card in the last ten years. Andrew is already here—perhaps he has no classes—and Jane was robbed yesterday. The thieves came in through the window and took her TV and VCR.

9:10 A.M. The extras are brought in. They are the patrons waiting to get into the theater. Sally arrives. Woody takes her by the hand to the center of the set and explains the action. Woody is very considerate with Sally, completely different than with Bea. With Bea, it is more of a game, a pal relationship. He just looks at Sally, stares at her, touches her as if she were not real. There is respect and admiration in his behavior—at least that is how it seems at first glance.

9:20 A.M. Shot 139: Working as an usher, Sally takes tickets and lets people into the theater. After the last of them, she closes the door, walks toward the camera, and starts to talk: "When I came to New York, I wanted to get into radio so badly . . ." But she couldn't break in, she continues. She also had to support herself, working as a cigarette girl and a paid laugher, while taking acting classes. She even went to broadcasting class to improve her elocution. *(33 seconds.)*

First rehearsal: It doesn't work. The pace is too slow. There is total silence while Woody thinks. But he still notices two people from wardrobe walking by in the background.

Second rehearsal: Woody asks Sally to start talking as soon as she closes the door. It's no good. The extras are taken away. Sally sits in a chair. She doesn't like the high heels she has to wear. While Carlo works on a different camera setting, Woody talks to Sally.

9:50 A.M. Instead of having Sally walking toward the camera, the camera will dolly in. The track is being set. Sally sits in the director's chair, singing low. Brian brings a videocassette of Tyson's fight last Friday for Woody; it's a gift from Tyson. Sally gives a little hello to Andrew but he stays with us.

10:00 A.M. "Let's stand by for pictures!" No more ticket line. Sally just lets the last two patrons in, then closes the door. Woody has her talk as soon as she closes the door. It starts wide on Sally as she closes the door and dollies in on her as she says her lines.

Take 1: Stopped by a noisy bus outside.

Takes 2 and 3: Good. Woody changes a few of the lines. "Keep the second one for a voice test, but the third one is the only good one," he tells Kay.

Take 4: Faster and with more energy.

Take 5: Sally doesn't make it through. Woody goes to her. They rehearse. He puts his hand on her shoulder, the way he does with Andrew.

Take 6: Her voice is higher, more fragile, more naïve.

Takes 7 and 8: More and more emotion. Almost desperate, nonplussed.

Because this is the first dialogue scene we are shooting with Sally, Woody is looking for the voice he wants her to use for the rest of the film. When he has a good actor at his disposal, he feels totally free to ask the person to change the least nuance. But he still wants control of the performance. He mimes the scene, he says the lines, he acts it out himself, showing the tone he wants. Often, the result can be (as with Renoir or Truffaut) that the actors, while they keep their personalities, develop a similar tone: the Woody touch.

Take 14: Same mannerisms, but more energy.

Take 16: Sally is going back to her real voice, much lower. Before each take, Woody starts reading the *Daily News*. Tom screams, "Rollin'!" Woody is still reading. "Action!" And at the last second, Woody raises his head from the paper to watch, as if the more he was involved in the details of a scene, the more he tries to detach himself from it until the last moment so he can judge with a certain distance. "Don't worry about the mistakes," he tells Sally, who is getting a little tired of her lines. And we go on, reviewing all the possible deliveries: from very low to very high, from naïve to femme fatale.

Take 22: Back to a desperate, broken voice.

"This is the last one, I promise," Woody tells Tom.

Take 23: "This is it, definitely!" Woody says loudly. Then as Tommy screams, "Action!" Woody mumbles to himself, "This is it, this is it!"

We'll go on for three more.

(26 takes and 19 prints.)

We move to the next location at 11:00 A.M.

12:00 noon. The Casa Galicia on East Eleventh Street is another of those old places untouched since the twenties. Pictures of dancers hang in the lobby, Astaire and Rogers among them. We are shooting in a small ballroom with a stage. Santo has built, three feet from the real one, a wall with a huge window full of green and red neon, to give the effect of a street. The sign reads: PARADISE DANCE PALACE. We are here to shoot another segment of the day when Bea and Sy take Little Joe all around town (sequence 158).

While the set is being readied, Woody and Carlo discuss the camera angle. Woody then goes off with Ezra to talk about the schedule for the following day.

We break for lunch at 1:00 P.M.

2:30 P.M. Back to the Tango Palace. Dick Hyman is in with Sandy. This will be a live recording of a three-woman band. "Not so unusual at the time," Dick says. The tango teacher is here, too, wearing a navy-blue velvet suit with a handkerchief in the breast pocket, a gray turtleneck, and black Italian moccasins. With all this and his white hair, he looks like Italian director Vittorio De Sica. Little Joe is massaging the neck of our caterer/masseuse. Then it's his turn, and he sits on her knees so she can work on his neck. From a distance it looks a little like Faye Dunaway giving Dustin Hoffman a bath in *Little Big Man*.

3:00 P.M. Though he isn't working today, Pop is visiting, and Woody chats with him while the extras (more girls and soldiers) are brought in for the first rehearsal. Bea sulks and, of course, ignores her date, Sy, who is entertaining Little Joe with an imitation of Bogart. The three female musicians (Barbara Gallo, Jane Jarvis, Liz Vochecowizc) go onstage. They look perfect. Woody is in another good mood today. He talks to the dancers. He shakes Little Joe's hand, then wipes his own on his sweater, looking disgusted.

3:40 P.M. Shot 158. The camera starts on the band, then moves to reveal the dancers. *(1 minute, 20 seconds.)*

Woody asks the woman drummer to smoke. Then he shows a dancing couple precisely where to dance. Tom pushes another couple into the frame at just the right moment. The tango teacher

wants to practice the dance a little with Bea, but it's too late. *(4 takes and 4 prints.)*
We move to the next shot.

4:20 P.M. The tango teacher congratulates the band: "I love the way you are playing." Woody plays ball with Little Joe, and Carlo dances with Bea to show Dickie how it looks. In a corner, Andrew is sitting beside Jimmy Sabat and, earphones on, listens to the sound track of the previous shot.

Shot 158A. The camera starts on a sailor at a table, passes Little Joe sitting alone, and moves to Sy and Bea dancing. Then it comes back, following Sy and Bea in a close shot, between the dancers, leaves them, and ends on Little Joe. *(1 minute.)*

The only problems are with coordinating the focus and camera movement. After the first take, as he often does, Dickie asks everybody to hold their positions so Woody can check the framing. *(4 takes and 2 prints.)*

We wrap at 5:15 P.M.

Thursday, December 12, 1985

Nuclear accident in Jersey, but damage is called "minuscule." (New York Times)

New York City will not be able to pay for AIDS expenses— health insurance companies are going to go bankrupt—and studies show that AIDS can infect the brain. (New York Times)

A Jersey panel recommends a ban on boxing. (Daily News)

At the Second Stage, Jeff Daniels (Biff Baxter) and Jill Eikenberry (Pop's real-life wife) are receiving great reviews in Lanford Wilson's Lemon Sky. (New York Times)

Diplomatic incident between U.S. and China: The State Department expresses regret to China today over the arrest of a Chinese student by campus police in Berkeley, California. China, in an unusually harsh protest issued in Peking, accused the police of beating the student, and demanded an official apology. The student, Li Hizhi, was arrested by a campus policeman because he was suspected of peeping through a woman's dormitory window, but it was later determined he was innocent. (New York Times)

10:00 A.M. The Paradise Garage on King Street, the oldest and best-known gay disco in Manhattan. We're there to shoot the *Breakfast with Irene* [Julie Kurnitz] *and Roger* [David Warrilow] show (sequence 58). The disco's bar has become Roger and Irene's apartment, from which they broadcast the show. Using only the glass brick walls, the bar, a new carpet, and adding the first steps of a staircase and some beautiful Art Deco furniture, Santo has transformed the very rough disco into an elegant set. He was influenced, he tells me, by the Paris apartment of French architect Pierre Chareau.

The way Santo uses an existing environment (a bar) and, by mixing it with a few accessories, transforms it into something entirely different (a sophisticated apartment) is much more fascinating than a fully built set. Carol Joffe, who is the former wife of Woody's manager, and who started with Woody in *Stardust Memories*, also had a hand in the set. She is the set decorator and works directly with Santo.

The view of New York from the window, which is in reality the front door of the bar, is made of a huge transparency (a black-and-white picture of the period enlarged and then painted). To light it, hundreds of bulbs are put behind the photo, and can be rearranged to achieve different lighting effects. It is less expensive than building a complete set, but it still costs approximately twenty thousand dollars.

12:00 noon. Carlo is working on the general lighting, highlighting the glass walls by putting projectors behind them. It will be a slow process.

There is a rumor that we will be reshooting the USO scene. Woody didn't like the way Sally looked. She was wearing too much makeup. As Fern says, "He likes her with no makeup, like she is when she gets out of the shower." In fact, Woody likes Sally in reality, when she is Mia, with her extra-large dresses, no makeup, and her hair uncombed. Makeup tests were done on Sally, but Woody has a concept of Mia and a concept of Sally; it is always difficult to make the two concepts work as one. Fern and Jeffrey don't know what to do anymore!

Ezra and Tim are discussing the schedule for the coming days. They have to worry about the weather and the reshoot. And the constant changing of schedules is hard on all the departments, sometimes causing nightmares for each of them, what with canceling extras, booking more makeup and hair people, being ready with every kind of costume, and so on.

2:00 P.M. Shot 58: The camera will record a 360-degree pan. It starts on a painting of Roger and Irene. Irene (off-camera): "I'll have a little coffee, darling." Roger (off-camera): "Sure, sweetheart . . ." The camera passes the adman (Alan Altshuld) and the stage manager (Steve Kronovet). Woody has the adman walk to the stage manager to help the look of the pan. We still hear Roger and Irene's voices. Roger met Walter Winchell last night, and he said he'll try to be at the Stork Club tonight. Irene loves the Stork Club. The camera passes the technician, then the black maid; Woody has the maid walk by the bar for the same reason. Tomorrow morning, Roger says, they'll tell us everything about the new Moss Hart play, which he heard was "just divine." The camera is on them. Irene: "This is Irene Draper . . ." Roger: ". . . and Roger Daily . . ." End of the show. We move to the announcer (Ken Roberts): "Swanson's Tooth Powder, the tooth powder with the larger-than-life smile, has brought you Broadway's most fascinating couple . . ." *(34 seconds.)*
Woody lies behind the sofa at the feet of Roger and Irene, so he can see but not be seen. I am with Ezra under the piano (with the 360-degree camera movement, there is no choice but to hide). The rehearsal goes fine but Woody doesn't like the red shirt the adman is wearing.

2:20 P.M. Second rehearsal: There is a problem with the sound now. Jimmy Sabat hears the generator from the street. It's just as well because Woody doesn't like the adman's new blue shirt anyway.
We break for lunch at 2:30 P.M.

4:00 P.M. We're ready to shoot now. The actors are back in position. The sponsor's man has a gray shirt on, and Woody is back behind the couch.
There are no big problems other than the camera movement and getting the actors' blocking right. After the second take, Woody gets behind the camera, moving with it, to check the blocking. Woody asks for a few takes at a faster pace.
(8 takes and 4 prints.)

4:45 P.M. The announcer is Tony Roberts's father. Woody

chats with him. Brian takes a picture. Angela and Patti are reading *World Tribune,* the Buddhist newspaper. Though both were raised Catholics, they have become Buddhists. But they are very tolerant of infidels and invite me to one of their seminars.

5:00 P.M. Ready for rehearsal.

Shot 58A: They are not "on the air" anymore. The adman goes to congratulate the couple, but the tone has changed. "You louse! Don't ever call me darling, you two-bit bum!" Irene says to Roger. "Don't call me a bum, you third-rate phony!" Roger tells her. They go at it physically. The stage manager and adman are stunned. Roger and Irene throw the rest of the breakfast at each other. The adman and stage manager break it up. Irene finally disappears upstairs and Roger quiets down. "They came in like that this morning," the stage manager remarks. "Something must have happened last night at that nightclub. . . ."

Woody explains when and how he wants the fight—two beats after the announcer stops talking so the jingle can be added later. Then Irene "could" exit upstairs at the end. He tells them what the camera is doing—but remains very vague. "We'll play around with it," he adds. To Carlo he says, "We should rehearse several times so everybody gets comfortable with it."

First rehearsal: Everybody is ready. Just before "Rollin'," Woody announces: "It will probably be wrong, or a little clumsy, but we'll correct it." At the end, Woody turns to Carlo: "It was good." The first try is frequently good, and this may be why Woody so often wants to shoot the rehearsal. But in this case, he didn't know how the fight would go and he prefers being able to control things at the beginning and avoid having the scene go wild. Woody suggests that Roger and Irene throw plates and other objects at each other. He also decides to have the black maid join the fight at the end. While the last adjustments are made for the first take, Woody yawns, gives me a nice smile of complicity, and begins to walk back and forth amid the activity, whistling.

5:45 P.M. Ready to shoot. Everybody sits on the new carpet. Together in a corner are Andrew, Jane, Liz, Patti, Jeffrey, and me. The actors are good; the scene is funny and spectacular. Woody is pleased. It's a nice, family atmosphere.

Take 1: Good. But Dickie points out that the maid blocks a little too much of the fighting by being in the front.

Take 3: Jimmy Mazzola mentions that he doesn't have a lot more plates. And Roger has hurt his foot. "Did I do it?" asks Irene.

Take 5: It's very violent: "That was weird," concludes Irene. Now she hurt her foot when Roger grabbed her.

Take 6: Woody suggests to Roger that he take the shovel from the fireplace and threaten Irene with it. "Last one," Woody says before "Action!"

Take 7: Again, it's very violent. When the adman grabs Roger to break up the fight, Roger hurts himself on a chair. He complains to the actor, asking him to take it easy. The tension is growing—a little like the slapping scene in Rabbi Baumel's office. Woody doesn't pay a lot of attention to it but does ask the adman not to hold Roger too tightly.

Take 8: "That was good," Roger says to the adman.
(11 takes and 8 prints)

We wrap at 6:30 P.M.

A cake is brought for Nick's birthday. Everybody sings "Happy Birthday" except Woody. But when everyone applauds, he whistles two or three times, then dashes out.

Friday, December 13, 1985

"258 G.I.'s died amid scattered guns and toys." (Daily News) They were coming back for Christmas from the Sinai, where they were on duty with the international peace-keeping force. Their plane crashed on takeoff at Gander, Canada. They had been stationed at Fort Campbell, Kentucky. (New York Times)

Anne Baxter, sixty-two, died yesterday following her stroke last Wednesday.

Max, Mon Amour is being shot in Paris. It is the passionate love story, both sexual and emotional, between Margaret (Charlotte Rampling), the wife of an English diplomat, and Max, a monkey. There are some love scenes between Max and Margaret, which include some very intimate caresses. The scenes are quite touching and moving, asserts a journalist who saw the dailies.

"The main subject of the movie is the difficulties individuals have communicating with each other, accepting each other, and developing links with people apparently very different," says di-

rector Nagisa (In the Realm of the Senses; Merry Christmas, Mr. Lawrence) *Oshima.*
    "If millions of people are capable of falling in love with E.T., why couldn't they fall in love with Max, who lives on earth?" asks the producer, Serge (Ran) *Silberman.* (Le Monde)

In the bus to Rye Playland with the seventy-five extras for the roller-skating scene (sequence 51). Another bus, with the forty-five extras for the clam-bar scene (same sequence), left half an hour ago. One extra is reading a play, another reads music sheets, listening to a tape recorder, and Angela has her Walkman on. A truck passes us. On its side, in big letters: WALDBAUM'S FRESH PRODUCE.

11:00 A.M. Breakfast in Rye with Kay, Tom, Ken, and Ezra at the Coopers', where Eunice sang "Roses of Picardy." We're shooting the clam bar downstairs. Kay asks if the dailies were good yesterday. "I didn't go," Ezra answers. "I can't stand it anymore. The tension, waiting to see if it is going to be good, with no influence on the situation. I wait for Bob to call me, and as soon as he says hello, I know the answer."

11:20 A.M. The clam bar. Once again Santo and his team have done a good job transforming an unexceptional space into a beautiful set with only a few accessories, including the paintings on the tiles behind the bar, the chandeliers, the tulip-shaped glasses, and flowers. "Giovanni's Clam Bar" seems the perfect place for a romantic date for Bea and Sidney Manulis.
    Woody passes by to look at the set, then leaves. "Don't move anything at Casa Galicia!" Santo says to his assistant. "He wants to look at the dailies once more."
    On the beach, it's a beautifully cloudy and foggy day; it would have been perfect for Tonino.

12:00 noon. We're being delayed because the electrical truck has broken down on the road, and the equipment is being transferred to another truck. "The truck is good news," Ezra says. "Insurance will pay." But the other news is that Woody finds the skating rink too small, so we aren't shooting it, and it will be rebuilt in the studio. The roller-skating rink was constructed in the middle of the amusement park, and once again it is a beautiful job—the paintings, the colors (gray and white), the lights. But it is true that it looks rather small.

In Giovanni's Clam Bar, Jimmy Mazzola is testing the fog. The terrace is filled with smoke. Jimmy asks Carlo if it's enough! It smells like peppermint. "I have peppermint, vanilla, strawberry," he explains to me. "I had it shipped in from California."

1:00 P.M. We're still waiting. In the main building, the New York Rangers are practicing on the ice rink and the extras from the clam bar are either watching the Rangers or playing computer games. The roller-skating extras were sent home. In the building just next door, where Jeffrey and the Salad Sisters have their head-quarters, everybody is also waiting. It is impressive to see the line of shoes, dresses, and all the accessories—all this for a scene that might be on the screen ten seconds and for extras who will be seen only in the back of the frame. And yet, it is the quality of each of these details—haircuts, makeup—that, taken together, give the images their richness and texture, and that finally contribute to the overall quality of the movie.

1:30 P.M. It's raining now. The electrical truck is not going to be here for a while. The producers wanted to break for lunch but the catering was only scheduled for tonight and is not ready. "It's Friday the thirteenth," Tom says. We could also say, "It's Rye Playland!"

At 2:00 P.M., we break for lunch.

3:15 P.M. The truck has just arrived. Carlo needs half an hour, he says. Jimmy Mazzola and his boys are preparing the shrimp and oyster plates. There is also a big plate for the crew.

3:40 P.M. Everything smells like strawberries, even though Carlo has asked Jimmy to keep the fog outside for the moment. Bea and Manulis (Andrew Clark) arrive, along with Woody. Bea is very friendly with Manulis, and one must admit that Manulis is something. He is six feet four, a little heavy (but it is all muscle), has a great, curving moustache, an infectious laugh, and is always at ease in any situation.

Tom is setting the background extras at the table. Woody doesn't like the curls of Manulis's moustache and asks that they be cut. Manulis is disappointed; he had grown them for the film, he tells me later, and certainly for Bea. Bea asks to look through the camera. Jimmy Mazzola is overdoing it out there; the fog starts seeping into the room.

3:50 P.M. Shot 51: The camera starts on a waiter, following him for a wide shot of the restaurant, and then moves closer to Bea and Manulis eating, chatting, and drinking. *(15 seconds.)*

First rehearsal: They are both excellent but Woody isn't pleased with Bea's haircut or hat. Jeffrey and Romaine go to work on it. This scene is crucial because it is the beginning of a long sequence (shots 51 to 57) of Manulis and Bea going on an "exciting" date.

4:15 P.M. Second rehearsal: Bea has more modern hair and a flower on her hat. She is perfect in the part of the scene when she tries to hide the fact she needs glasses. Carlo is a little nervous. "Madonna! Doesn't understand my English." The waiter is not hitting his mark and misses the light. Carlo turns to us. "My English is no good?" The poor waiter, not knowing Carlo's humor, is a tad overwhelmed. And the strawberry smog continues to surround us. "No more fog, Jimmy!" Ray shouts.

4:30 P.M. Ready to shoot. "Drink that beer," Woody yells to Manulis. Then he makes him finish all the glasses on the table, including Bea's. But Woody also lets them improvise, encouraging them to enjoy themselves. And it works.

(10 takes and 4 prints.)

It's a wrap at 4:50 P.M.

Tim introduces Woody to the general manager of Rye Playland, who also wants a picture with Woody. Woody puts on his Zelig face.

Monday, December 16, 1985   *Seventh Week*

Two writers read their stories for PEN. Yesterday evening, John Updike and Woody Allen, invited by Norman Mailer to raise money for the weeklong forty-eighth International PEN Congress next January, read their stories on Broadway. Norman Mailer, as master of ceremonies, first reads his poem "Ian Fleming Revisited." Woody reads two unpublished stories.

The first concerns fifty-three-year-old Sid Kaplan, a lawyer who has suffered "rejections so numerous they had to be delivered by the Santini brothers." Mr. Kaplan's fantasies have been ignited by catching a glimpse of a beautiful young woman in the elevator of his Park Avenue co-op.

In the second work, Phil Feldman's hostility manages to escape while he is sleeping. In the form of a hairy black blob with red eyes, it goes racing down Lexington Avenue to inflict revenge on Mr. Feldman's psychiatrist, his parents, a fast-food restaurant, a litterbug, and a teenage boy who is force-fed the radio with which he had been disturbing the peace.

Mr. Updike reads a portion of the trials of his fictional Henry Beck, the writer from Ninety-ninth Street and Riverside Drive, who marries and moves to Ossining, New York, and who "had the true New Yorker's secret belief that people living anywhere else had to be kidding." (New York Times)

Bruce Weintraub died of pneumonia last Saturday in Los Angeles. A native of New York, Weintraub was set decorator on films such as Blowout, Hardcore, Cat People, Scarface, The Natural, for which he was nominated for an Academy Award, and Prizzi's Honor. He was production designer on Summer Lovers and Cruising. He was to have been associate producer of John Schlesinger's soon-to-roll picture, The Believers. Bruce Weintraub was thirty-three years old.

9:00 A.M. We return to the Good Shepherd church's back room for reshoots of the sound-effects studio and The Whiz Kids show. The Sound-Effects Man's face did not show well. And for the other show, Woody did not like the background (a World War I commemorative plaque) and the way the kids moved.

We're beginning the seventh week of a fifteen-week schedule—nearly halfway. We had a late call today, a slow start, like all Monday mornings. The boys are bringing the equipment in, and Bob Greenhut, Ezra, and Tom talk over the schedule for the week. The white-haired effects man, the real one, is back with us.

10:00 A.M. Woody wanders among the period sound-effects devices, jotting notes, ignoring all the activity around him. Is he writing a new scene? People are amazed by the sight, and the producers are in agony.

10:05 A.M. He's finished. He gives the yellow sheets to Kay for typing and goes to talk to Brian. He must have been checking a few things on the spot. But for a moment, everybody thought . . .

10:35 A.M. First rehearsal: The actors read their lines with little intonation. Dickie wants the clock on the wall behind the Sound-Effects-Man moved up and to the center. And Woody asks for an "On the Air" sign. But Jimmy Mazzola doesn't have one. He decides to modify an exit sign from above the door. Cliff writes ON THE AIR on a piece of black posterboard and starts cutting it out.

11:15 A.M. The Effects Actor tells me that he is auditioning this week for the new Andy Bergman play that Mike Nichols is going to direct on Broadway. Barbara is back with us; Little Joe is in a scene not in the script that we are going to shoot this afternoon at Rienzi's place. Jimmy Mazzola is atop the ladder adjusting the red "On the Air" sign, and Woody, a little impatient, goes to ask him when he'll be ready.

11:35 A.M. Shot R45: We are back to the shorter version. No big changes. Tom, whose name is now Paul, arrives with his troops. "Company halt!" (Horse hoofbeats.) Then Claire arrives: "Paul . . . Paul." "Claire . . ." (The train.) They have to part. "I love you." "I love you, too . . ." It ends with the Sound-Effects Man blowing his version of a train whistle.

After two relatively flat takes, Woody asks them to do it louder and with more energy.

Take 3: Woody stands before the actors, silent for about half a minute, and then asks Paul not to cup his hand to his ear.

Take 4: It's much better. Woody lets them improvise some. He only asks for more energy.

It's always the same. Woody, most of the time, starts out low-key and vague. All his comments are in the most general terms. Then, progressively, he tightens everything, corrects little details with little strokes. You have a feeling that up to now he has been studying the potential of the actors, the way he stares at them. At the end, he achieves a precision, a total control of the scene. But he needs time to build up to it.

(8 takes and 6 prints.)

11:55 A.M. Shot R54: It's the same camera setting, but with a few variations in the action. After Claire and Paul meet, after the hoofbeats and before the train, they go to a field to talk (straw crushed), the Sound-Effects Man's expressions matching the emotions in the lines.

Take 2: Seeing the Sound-Effects Man's face, Woody is laughing under his tweed cap as he asks Dickie if he is following the blocking well. The actor does have an amusing face and he seems to be having great fun with the sound effects.

Take 3: Woody cuts. The Sound-Effects Man leaves too soon.

Take 4: Woody asks him to crush the straw differently.

(5 takes and 2 prints.)

12:15 P.M. *The Whiz Kids* show is going to be shot on the other side of the room. A large curtain is hung from the ceiling for the background, and the big table and chairs have been brought from the other location. The camera, sound, and lighting equipment have to be moved. Woody and Carlo choose the camera placement, and Woody disappears.

Jimmy Davis has worked for Rollins and Joffe since *Zelig* as a production assistant. On this film, he works with the location staff, flitting between sets, getting ready for our arrival. Tomorrow, there are two difficult locations to deal with. One is a ship, the *Intrepid*, where he has to deal with the unions, and the second is a private house whose owners are anxious because this is the first time they've dealt with a movie company.

Santo is also nervous today. When I asked him if the reshoots and changes of schedule were making things more difficult, he just answered, "Yes," and went on with his work. And Jimmy Mazzola has a sizable problem that he submits to Mickey and me: What should he give his wife for Christmas? "I already gave her a sports car, a fur coat, a diamond ring . . ."

1:00 P.M. While Carlo finishes his work, Woody stands across the table from the kids. The kids are talking to each other, becoming more at ease. They start calling him "Woody." Woody asks one of them to repeat after him "William Gladstone" until the child has it down pat. All the while, Romaine works on the young-ster's hair. Sanford is back and seems to know his lines. No prob-lems with the little girl (Tannis Vallely) either; she's a pro. She has just finished a film with Gerard Depardieu *(Une Femme ou Deux)* directed by Daniel *(The Return of Martin Guerre)* Vigne.

Shot R46: The lines are the same but the camera movement is entirely different. The scene starts on a side angle of the kids with the Whiz Master in the background. Then as he starts asking the questions, the camera loses the Whiz Master, facing the four kids.

First rehearsal: Woody has the kids fight, knocking hats to the ground, punching and pinching each other, while answering the questions. At the end of the rehearsal, the kids burst into laughter. He shows them what kinds of things they should do to each other. They find it very funny and become a little giddy. Woody whis-tles, fingers in his mouth, to get their attention.

Take 1: "A little bit at first, then very angry at the end. But real!"

Take 3: "Don't get mad at first, build up to it."

Take 4: "Don't fake it," Woody says to Sanford, referring to the punching. "Make it real."

For the five final takes, Woody makes a couple of small changes: The Whiz Master asks only two questions, so there will be a shorter version, and Sanford doesn't participate in the fight-ing. He sits straight and impassive. "Hold that look," Woody tells him.

(10 takes and 6 prints.)

We break for lunch at 2:00 P.M.

3:15 P.M. Little Joe and his gang (Dave, Nick, Burt, and An-drew) are back with us to shoot their breaking into Rienzi's apart-ment, just after spotting him from the roof, working at his radio equipment. Since he must be a spy, they have to take the risk. Biff Baxter or the Masked Avenger would have done it (sequence 133).

Rienzi's apartment is also in the Good Shepherd church, in a room just next door. Carlo and Woody choose two shots—the kids entering the building by a small, dingy staircase, and the other inside Rienzi's apartment. The boys go to work. It's going to take awhile because the room is small, and the lights will be difficult to hang.

4:00 P.M. The staircase is cramped, grimy, and in bad shape. So Carlo has to work hard to make it a pretty kind of dirty. Woody, with Jeffrey at his side, checks the actors' costumes. The kids are OK, but Rienzi has to change.

In the back, a little chapel is used as the holding area. The Salad Sisters have set up shop under the cross. Dave's mother is here with his aunt, who speaks French, and Burt's grandfather. Rienzi (Alfred De La Fuente) keeps to himself; he must be in his eighties, and already seems exhausted.

4:30 P.M. Shot 133: The gang sneaks around the corner, then exits to the left. The camera watches them from a low angle. *(9 seconds.)*

It would be easier if the place wasn't so cramped. "Look around before you come out," Woody tells the kids.

(5 takes and 3 prints.)

4:45 P.M. Inside Rienzi's apartment, for a rehearsal with the actors. The room is tiny. Inside are Tom, Kay, Woody, the kids, and Rienzi. The dialogue is wonderful. The kids discover the radio equipment and a lot of other suspicious stuff. "Look, he *is* a Nazi spy," Andrew says. "We have to call the FBI," Burt says. "He's going to turn us over to the Nazis," says Little Joe. Rienzi appears. "Thieves!" he screams at the kids. They accuse him of being a spy. But everybody finally quiets down, and Rienzi explains that he is an inventor. He shows them a few of his creations. "This is an electric shaver for a horse. I've worked on it for a long time." And then, "I also have a cigarette lighter which works underwater. Not yet!"

Woody is concentrating. He wants the kids intrigued, but not too excited, and it's difficult. The dialogue is changed. Burt now says, "Oh God, if he catches us, he'll turn us over to the Gestapo." The words are hilarious from his mouth, but Burt has trouble getting the delivery right. And Rienzi doesn't have all the energy he needs.

5:00 P.M. Carlo works on the lighting. He and Woody have finally agreed on doing the scene in two shots. Carlo wanted only one, but Woody thought that it would be too difficult for the children.

Woody sits and chats with Jeffrey and Brian at the Whiz Kids' table. Behind the curtain, we can hear Richie coaching the kids with their lines.

6:15 P.M. Shot 133A: The camera is in the door frame. It tracks the kids as they enter, following them and revealing Rienzi's apartment. The kids look around, inspecting the equipment, making comments. *(35 seconds.)*

Woody, Tom, and Louis are the only ones in the room. The hallway is getting crowded, and Carlo, who needs space, begins to get nervous. It's also difficult for Dickie and Red because the doorway is narrow and the dolly track goes through it.

6:35 P.M. The first take is not good. Burt misses his cue.

While the camera is rolling, Woody directs them verbally until just before their lines: "Look around slowly. . . . The guy is not there. . . . Start to come in. . . . Look scared. . . . Don't look at the floor, look at the room. . . . Go ahead, kids. Look at the room. You don't want to get caught!" He is concentrating hard, looking at each of them.

6:50 P.M. Take 8: Burt is not getting his lines right. Woody gives them to Little Joe. It was funnier from Burt's mouth, but there will be fewer problems with Little Joe.

Take 9: The first good one. Woody throws up his arms. The kids get excited. Now they scream together as Tom says, "Rollin'!" Carlo gets more and more nervous; he thinks we should kill the kids.

A lot of takes are not completed, because of both the acting and the camera.

(19 takes and 6 prints.)

We move on to the arrival of Rienzi, but Carlo needs half an hour to adjust the lights.

7:20 P.M. Woody reads *The New York Times*. He has a nice smile for me, but he seems exhausted. Behind the curtains, Richie is coaching Rienzi and the gang again.

7:45 P.M. Shot 133B: Rienzi catches the kids in the act. "Thieves!" he screams. "You're a spy!" the kids yell back. Finally, everybody quiets down. "I am an inventor," Rienzi explains. He starts showing them some of his inventions, and the kids become interested. *(45 seconds.)*

Woody sits on a little box just under the camera and has to

keep his head bent most of the time. Tom and Louis are crouched in a corner.

The first completed take is the sixth. And on it goes. Woody tightens the scene; the electric horse shaver and the cigarette lighter that works underwater (but not yet), are out. Everybody— the kids, Rienzi, Woody—is exhausted. But, as usual, Woody hangs on.

(16 takes and 4 prints.)

We wrap at 8:15 P.M.

Tuesday, December 17, 1985

Rub out: Mobs hit Big Paul. (Daily News)

As Big Paul and his associate, Thomas Bilotti, stepped out of a limousine in front of a restaurant on East Forty-sixth Street near Third Avenue shortly before 5:30 P.M., three men approached, drew semiautomatic weapons from under their trench coats, and opened up a barrage of gunfire at close range. Big Paul and Tommy were each shot about six times in the head and upper body and fell dead beside the open doors of their black Lincoln. Big Paul, seventy years old, was the godfather of the Gambino family and had been on trial in Federal District Court in Manhattan since September. (New York Times)

Black-market trade in children in El Salvador: The demand for adoption has become greater and greater in the United States, Europe, and Canada, and people are willing to pay the highest fees. "Baby facilitators" try to persuade destitute mothers to give up their babies, or they just kidnap them. The kidnappings have reportedly increased in recent months. In poor neighborhoods, women have to keep their children indoors.

Lawyers often charge a $5,000 to $10,000 fee, and on top of that, they claim large additional expenses like "baby care, and paying off judges." (New York Times)

9:00 A.M. Inside the *Intrepid* on the Hudson River, at Forty-sixth Street. The camera has been stored under the wing of a McDonnell Douglas A4 (used in Vietnam) while the location is being prepared. On the set there is a huge poster reading WINGS OVER AMERICA: AIR CORPS. US ARMY. In the background are a few

American flags and two period cannons. We are shooting Bea, Sy, and Little Joe continuing their tour of New York (sequence 156).

I again ask Jane about the dailies; I was supposed to see the Tonino sequence. She looks embarrassed and says, "He thinks that it would be better another time. But I'll mention it to him again."

Sy is back, too, but Bea still ignores him. He just doesn't have the charm of Manulis. Little Joe is entertaining Woody, who seems to enjoy it. As they have for several mornings now, Bobby Ward, Jimmy Sabat, and Richie Baratta, Tim's assistant, ask if they can have a quick look at the business section of my *New York Times*. The boys need to know how their stocks are doing.

10:15 A.M. Shot 156. Amused, Bea watches Sy showing Little Joe how the cannon works. *(20 seconds.)*

There is no sound, so Jimmy Sabat can read his racing form. Just before the take, Woody goes to Bea, whispers something in her ear that makes her laugh, and then goes back to the camera, looking at her critically. Poor neglected Sy is a little awkward and embarrassed, but Woody is having a good time.

(3 takes and 2 prints.)

We move upstairs.

10:45 A.M. On the deck of the *Intrepid*, to do a shot to be edited to "I'll Be Seeing You," after the declaration of war. A sailor is kissing his girl good-bye.

There is a beautiful sun, and a beautiful view of Manhattan, the Hudson River, and New Jersey. But it's freezing. Everybody hops from one foot to the other to keep warm. Woody walks back and forth and does some of his tap dancing. The camera is hurriedly set. The sailors are brought in. In the end, the girl is not in the shot.

Shot 107: The camera starts on the top of the ship's tower, and tilts down to some sailors waving good-bye. *(15 seconds.)*

On some takes, they don't wave and just stand looking toward the camera.

(8 takes and 3 prints.)

We rush downstairs to the next location. To speed things up, everybody grabs a piece of equipment.

In the bus to the next location with the cultured family and the rich family. They are already in costume. The rich couple are in

long dress and black tie, while the cultured ones are dressed casually. The cultured son is entertaining the rich young woman.

12:00 noon. The O'Keefe residence on West Eighty-sixth
Street, a vast, elegant house with high ceilings and parquet floors.
There are quite a few tenants living here these days, but the place
still looks handsome.

We are shooting in the big sitting room on the second floor,
street side. The room itself, with the sun streaming through the
window, looks beautiful. But the equipment is being brought in,
and the place quickly becomes a mess, with cables everywhere and
lights hanging from the ceiling. "Good," Carlo remarks, "no see
the ceiling." Two huge lights are set outside on the street to take
the place of the sun, and in a few hours, the place will look even
better than the real thing.

1:00 P.M. The rich family makes its entrance; two rich couples,
parents and children. They look distinguished. It's amazing how a
"rich"-looking costume instills a natural sense of being rich in
anyone's behavior. The young rich girl and the rich woman are
not truly beautiful; they are less beautiful than the sailor's girl, or
Doris, the Communist's daughter. The butler's name is Billy.

Shot 166C: While playing cards, the rich family stiffly listens
to the Polly Phelps drama. The butler serves them more iced tea.
(45 seconds.)

Woody seats them, shows Billy the butler how to enter and
leave the room. He does it himself, taking the appropriate attitude.
Then he tells the two couples to just listen to the radio, drink, and
play, but to stop from time to time to listen again.
(5 takes and 2 prints.)

1:30 P.M. Shot 172D: The family hears that Polly Phelps has
died. A closer shot of the five people, stunned. "Take a deep
breath," Woody tells the butler. "Put your hand on the lady's
shoulder—don't be so stiff."
(1 take and 1 print.)
We break for lunch at 1:40 P.M.

3:10 P.M. We use the same sitting room for the cultured family, but the drapes, the furniture, and the picture on the wall have
been changed to create a cultured atmosphere.

Dickie is recuperating—sleeping—in the dining room with all the equipment. Woody passes by to discuss the camera setting, but Carlo is still working with Santo on placing the furniture. Woody goes upstairs on business. Jimmy Davis complains to me about the way his day is going. This morning, he had trouble with the ship owner and the local union representative because there were supposed to be thirty of us and we were fifty instead. And we shot on the upper deck without telling the ship owner beforehand. Now, the owner of this house is upset about all the disorder we are creating, and concerned about damage we might do.

4:00 P.M. Woody comes in and puts the cultured family where he wants them, so Carlo can light them. He then quickly chooses the camera setting, and goes back upstairs for a conference with his accountant, who has just come in.

It's getting dark outside, but the sun is shining—our sun—two arc lights in the street. We shot the night scene of the rich family during the day and now we are shooting the day scene of the cultured family at night.

4:45 P.M. First rehearsal: The cultured son is smoking a pipe. His father looks like a university professor, his sister is not really pretty but is beautifully cast, and his mother is very proper and staid. Woody listens to the Mozart quartet, Number 19 in C, which the family will hear. He tries having the family mime playing instruments as they listen to the music. Carlo likes it. Then Woody pauses. He stands silently in front of them, looking at the ground. Now he asks the family to just sway their heads to the music. Finally, he gives the father a book and the son a cigarette. Woody's accountant passes by, watches for a moment, then moves on.

5:00 P.M. Shot 16: The cultured family listens to the Mozart quartet with silent intensity. *(10 seconds.)*

Take 2: Woody asks the daughter to eat a grape, in rhythm to the quartet.

Take 3: Woody asks the daughter to take more grapes. She may not be pretty but she is funny.

Take 5: No cigarette for the son and no grapes for the daughter.

After the sixth take, Woody starts laughing to himself. "I've got an idea." He goes to the mother and tells her. She starts laughing, too. Then he goes to the father and tells him. The father laughs. We are waiting. But when Woody tells it to Carlo, Carlo says he'll need half an hour to adjust the lights. So Woody drops the idea (we are already on overtime), figuring he already has what he needs.

(6 takes and 5 prints.)

"It's a wrap" at 5:25 P.M.

Woody had wanted the father to fall asleep. Then the mother would stand up and slap him in the face. (Falling asleep, listening to Mozart!)

Wednesday, December 18, 1985

Cops have a line on Big Paul: Mob families OK'd hit. (Daily News)
It is a dispute over control and direction of the Gambino family between Big Paul and a rival faction led by John Gotti. A new tourist attraction has emerged in Manhattan: the spot where the killing took place. (New York Times)
Gretchen Sinon, ninety-two years old, has been taking "Writing Non-Fiction" at the New School for the past eight years. Born in New Jersey in 1893, she was influenced early on by teacher Rebecca Reyher, author of Zulu Women. *She accompanied her on a four-month trip to Africa to study women tribal leaders.*
"She was a dyed-in-the-wool Republican before she started at the New School," says her daughter Mary Louise. "Now she is a dedicated Democrat." Her teachers recall her offering excuses only twice. In the first instance, Gretchen apologized for submitting a handwritten paper, explaining that her typist had died. In the second, she notified the professor that she would be attending a wedding in Colorado and would fly back in time for class, hoping he would understand if she was a little bit late. She still travels some, but Gretchen refuses to leave the New York area while the class is in session. She even attends twice a week during the summer term. "I hate to miss a class," she comments. "It's just so interesting."
Gretchen has been working on her autobiography. It begins

this way: "When I was nine years old, my father bought his first automobile. It was a 1902 one-cylinder Knox." Even if it's far from finished, Gretchen plans to continue the book as she goes on perfecting her writing in the New School. (The New School Observer)

8:00 A.M. We're on West Twelfth Street at the New School, the first university for adults, founded in 1919. The first degree programs, initiated in 1934, originated as the University-in-Exile, a haven for European scholars who had fled Nazi persecution.

We are in the small New School theater auditorium, which has a stage and an oval ceiling. It's a nice design, and the acoustics are said to be very good. Today, we are shooting Bea playing *The Silver Dollar Jackpot* and, thanks to Abe, winning (sequence 160). It is part of the New York tour with Sy and Little Joe. There are 150 extras today. The Salad Sisters and wardrobe started work at 5:00 A.M.

9:00 A.M. Two cameras: One is upstairs on the balcony, the other is in the crowd. Carlo is lighting. Sandy, Frankie, and Kay check the playback of the opening fanfare with the band's conductor. The jingle will be dubbed in later. Woody pops in to check Kay's script, then zooms out. Then the prop man (where is Jimmy?) shows Kay the stuffed fish. He apologizes for being able to find only five types of fish, instead of the six wanted.

10:00 A.M. The orchestra, then the crowd, are brought in and placed. *The Silver Dollar Jackpot* emcee, Max (Tony Roberts), arrives and chats with Brian. Since they made *Annie Hall* together, Woody and Tony Roberts have been calling each other "Max." Max is tall and personable-looking. He kisses Kay and gives Bobby Ward a strong handshake.

10:30 A.M. The audience is in position, placed so they fill the frame. The theater holds about 250. Bea comes in, followed by Sy. Little Joe takes Max by the arm to talk to him; Max is impressed! And Woody goes to talk to Bea, who seems to be in a bad mood today.

11:00 A.M. Shot 160: Bea comes onstage as the fanfare introduces her. The audience applauds. *(9 seconds.)*
(2 takes and 2 prints.) Completed in two minutes.

11:15 A.M. Carlo adjusts the lighting for the next shot. Woody and Max have gone back to their chess game upstairs. Bea has gone to her room, too, and Sy eats a cracker as he watches the boys working.

Jane tells me the dream she had last night. At the end of the day, after having wrapped and left quickly, she realized she had forgotten something and went back to the set. She discovered me, taking pictures of the set with a huge camera. She put her hand over the lens . . . (No comment.)

11:45 A.M. Shot 160A: To start, Max asks Bea a few personal questions: "You're from Rockaway? And what do you do, Bea?" "I am a bookkeeper," Bea answers shyly. "Oh, for a minute I thought you said 'beekeeper.' I'd hate to get stung!" The crowd laughs. *(30 seconds.)*

Woody: "Max, you look silly."

Max: "Yes, I know, Max."

It is the first time, after seven weeks, that I see Woody unrestrained. Sitting in the first row, he is laughing alone, cracking jokes with Max, teasing him.

Woody to Bea: "We're keeping you up?"

Max: "Not really, Max."

And Max doesn't give Woody a chance. When Woody comes on the stage to direct them, Max takes on Woody's attitude (the Zelig cowering look, hands folded in front of him, shifting from one foot to the other, head bent to the side.) Max improvises, overacts, complains. He is good, though. Woody cuts him off in the middle of a sentence. Their private show is quite funny.

(4 takes and 3 prints.)

12:10 P.M. Shot 160C: Bea chooses fish because of Abe. The game starts. Max, disgusted, holds up the fish, one after the other, to Bea, who identifies them all. *(43 seconds.)*

No problem. Max is good and funny. Bea is perfect as she squints through her glasses at the fish.

(4 takes and 3 prints.) Completed at 12:20 P.M.

12:45 P.M. Carlo sets the lights for the next shot, another long shot of the audience. Bea stays with us this time. She sits in the auditorium, chatting with the Salad Sisters. Here and there in the room the crew, some "fellow musicians," and a few of the extras are becoming friends. Sy has finally decided to try another girl. It's a nice scene, this mixture of period and contemporary people getting to know each other.

1:05 P.M. 160D: Bea identifies the final fish. She wins. Closing fanfare. Applause. *(15 seconds.)*

No problems. Max shows off a little for fun. The crowd likes him. After the applause and Woody's "Cut," he continues to improvise.
(2 takes and 2 prints.)
Woody to Max and Bea: "Thanks a lot, kids."
We break for lunch at 1:15 P.M.

3:00 P.M. Back on the set. Bea and Max are gone. The only shots left are reaction shots of the audience (sequences 160B and 160E), with Sy and Little Joe in the middle of the crowd. The crew is on the stage, and the show is the audience. The audience is again arranged to make the theater look full. Woody is on the stage conducting their laughter and applause, signaling them when to increase the level. Sometimes, it is Tom who directs the extras, with Woody whispering in his ear. They have to listen, then applaud lightly, then laugh, then laugh louder. . . . Tom: "Those born in January, laugh! . . . Now the February ones! . . ." One long shot. It will be intercut with Bea's scenes.

The audience is good at laughing and Woody laughs with them.

We wrap at 3:50 P.M.

Thursday, December 19, 1985

Millions of mice are committing suicide by throwing themselves from a cliff in Israel. (New York Times)

A ferry carrying 177 people from Manila to a southern Philippine island sinks: 124 dead and 53 saved. (New York Times)

Ed restores Dr. Elliot Gross to job, citing fairness. (Daily News)

Dr. Gross, New York's chief medical examiner, has been subject of city and state inquiries for almost a year. "He's been through the fires of hell," Ed says. "How long do you keep the guy roasting?" (New York Times)

Four Afghan children just arrived at Kennedy International Airport to receive artificial limbs.

Zarmina, four, was playing outside when a bomb fell; she lost a leg. Utmakhail, ten, lost her right arm to cannon fire. Shafiullah, seven, lost a hand in the bombing of her village. And Mozafar, ten, lost his arm.

These four children are the lucky ones. In the village, they make tourniquets. Then they burn cloth and use the ashes to stop the bleeding. To make the pain go away, they pray. Thousands of children have died on their way to Pakistan.

"Even though I lost my arm," Mozafar says, "I can fight with my other arm." "The people who did this are nonbelievers," says Shafiullah. "The children here are a part of the struggle," says Dr.

Mojaddidi, who counts ninety-four family members killed in the fighting. "Whatever we have, we sacrifice for Allah. When a man loses a son, he sends the second son. When he loses that one, he sends the third one. When he loses that one, he sends the next son. And the next, and the next, and the next. And only the mother and the father are left." (New York Times)

10:00 A.M. We are at the Tisch School of the Arts of New York University, on Second Avenue and Seventh Street, for four days. Today we're shooting the string quartet that the cultured family was listening to on the radio (sequence 17), and Sally going to adult class to improve her elocution (sequence 140). But for the final three days, we will be shooting *The Herbie Hanson Show* (sequences 103 to 106).

Barbara Heller, one of the location people, introduces me to Santo's driver, because he's a writer. He writes for the cultural section of *Vogue* magazine. He also free-lances.

In the wardrobe room, which also serves as the holding area, the quartet musicians are tuning their instruments. Four extras are also hanging around. They have been with the movie four days now, at Rye Playland and at the Good Shepherd church, and have yet to work. True, they get paid, but they don't want to make a career of not working. They hope today will be their day. Walkmans on and books in hand, they wander.

Two more reshoots have been announced—the sailors on the deck and the Rienzi scenes.

11:00 A.M. The quartet's scene will be filmed in a dance hall; we're shooting in a corner. Carlo lights and Frankie complains about the acoustics. Woody stays with us during the preparation, not returning to his trailer as he usually does. He huddles in a dark corner, sitting on a box, rereading Kay's script. He has kept on his jacket and cap. He looks like Charlie Chaplin sitting on the stairs, freezing in the dark.

Bobby Ward tells me about the time he worked with Boris Kaufman on the early Sidney Lumet films: *Twelve Angry Men* (1957), *That Kind of a Woman* (1959), and so on. Boris Kaufman is Dziga Vertov's brother and was the director of photography on French director Jean Vigo's films. He won an Academy Award for *On the Waterfront* in 1954.

11:30 A.M. Shot 17: A wide shot of the musicians playing Mozart's quartet Number 19 in C. *(20 seconds.)*

The quartet is formed of two couples, one young and one old, mirroring the cultured family. The older woman complains that the way the chairs are lined up in a row is not accurate. Before playing, the musicians listen to the playback the cultured family heard, so they can get the same tempo.

Take 1: Woody beats time with a clothespin, and eventually hangs it on Jeffrey's sweater.

Take 2: Woody asks for a faster version with more energy.

Take 3: Woody asks the musicians to exaggerate their movements even more, to become caricatures of themselves. It makes the old woman laugh.

(The 3 takes are printed.)

12:00 noon. The adult-education class will be shot one floor up in a similar room with a hardwood floor. It looks like a small gymnasium. Two walls have been built to form a smaller space for the classroom. After choosing the first camera setup with Carlo, Woody paces for a while, sees the piano, hesitates—I am just behind it—then dashes out of the room.

12:30 P.M. Books have been placed on each desk for the class, *The Voice: Its Production and Reproduction,* by Douglas Stanley and J. P. Manfield. At least that's how the cover reads. The title page says "How to Make It When You Are Cash Poor."

Two huge neon letters—OT (from hotel)—are being set up outside the window, hanging from the crane of a truck parked on Second Avenue. A couple of grips are working on them. Carlo seems to have finished, but we are waiting. Someone says it is because of the sign, others say it is for the lights in the room (Carlo wants to use the chandeliers, but they don't have the right bulbs), still others say that it is for Sally.

Kay works on her notes, Louis is dreaming, Frankie reads *Stereophile* magazine, and Dickie is with his *New York Times.*

1:40 P.M. Sally arrives with Andrew, Baby Dylan, and a beautiful *au pair* girl, a model type.

We break for lunch.

3:30 P.M. Lunches are longer when Baby Dylan is around. The delay, it turns out, was caused by the chandelier bulbs. The electricians did not have the right size. The adult students make their entrance. First the background, then the terrible man (Bill Hugh Collins), the housewife (Yvette Edelhart), the teacher (Edward S. Kotkin), and students #1, #2, and #3. The two extras who were complaining about not working are in at last. Woody, Carlo on his right and Jeffrey on his left, seems satisfied. The actors are seated. Sally is not in the shot. Woody doesn't want to rehearse: "Picture," directly.

Shot 140: The camera is behind the students, looking over their shoulders to the teacher saying, "Hark! I hear the cannons roar. Is it the King approaching?" (4 seconds.)

(5 takes and 2 prints.)

4:00 P.M. Carlo is working on the lights for the next shot. Jaqui Safra (student #3), the one with the French accent, was the husband of Woody's sister in Stardust Memories, the one who never stopped having heart attacks but was still exercising in his bedroom. He appears to be a good friend of Woody and Sally's, and while they are talking together, Brian makes his move on the au pair, but cautiously. She is very beautiful. She is tall and slim, wears no makeup, and stands like a dancer. But she follows Woody and Sally next door, and Brian shifts to Drew.

4:30 P.M. Carlo is ready. Two huge lights on the roof are lighting the facade of the buildings across Second Avenue, illuminating the whole street. But it's not dark enough yet and the next two shots will include the outside. So we wait for night to fall.

In the room next door, Woody is playing with Baby Dylan. Louis, Andrew, Mickey, Hammer, and I are playing hangman. No producer today. Maybe it's better this way.

5:10 P.M. It's dark enough. The adult students are brought back in.

Shot 140A: It starts on a wide shot of the class, then zooms in to the terrible man reciting the quotation. (11 seconds.)

Sally is a little tired. She puts her head on her arm, gracefully. Water is poured on the wooden floor so it is not noisy when the dolly rolls.

Woody asks the terrible man sometimes to say the quote right, sometimes to mangle it. "Arg, the King approaching. Is the cannon moving?" the terrible man says. Dickie has the giggles behind

the camera. And with each take, the man varies his delivery.
(3 takes and 3 prints.)
Shot 140B: A close-up of student #1, the good one. He delivers the line perfectly. *(4 seconds.)*
Not funny.
(2 takes and 1 print.)
Shot 140C: Now an old lady. *(4 seconds.)*
She is an extra, and was not supposed to have a speaking part. But she gets through the quotation with no problems.
(2 takes and 2 prints.)
Shot 140D: The student with the French accent, also seen in close-up. *(4 seconds.)*
Now it's Woody and Sally's turn to get the giggles. In fact, everybody is laughing to some degree or another. The repetition of the quotation is already funny, here on the set, without the benefit of editing.
(5 takes and 4 prints.)
Shot 140E: The housewife's turn. *(4 seconds.)*
"I hear the cannon roar. I think somebody is coming!"
Now everybody is in stitches.
(4 takes and 3 prints.)
For the last shot of the series, because Sally is in the back of the class and Carlo wants her to photograph well, the camera has to be moved and the lighting adjusted.

6:15 P.M. Shot 140F: A close-up of Sally repeating the quotation after the teacher says it offscreen. *(10 seconds.)*
"Arg, I hear the carriage arriving . . ."
No problem with Sally.
(3 takes and 3 prints.)

"It's a wrap!" at 6:30 P.M.

Friday, December 20, 1985

TED NIXES '88 RUN FOR PREZ (Daily News)
There were 200 on the Philippines ferry but 85 were rescued. Only 125 dead. (New York Times)
A Disneyland is going to be built on the outskirts of Paris, France!

9:00 A.M. We're back at the Tisch School of the Arts, on the sixth floor, for *The Herbie Hanson Show* (sequences 103 to 106). A set has been built for the show consisting of high, pink wood panels and drapes, a small stage with "Herbie Hanson" stands for each musician, rows of seats, and the technician's booth in the back. The floor is covered with shiny black plastic. Carlo and the boys have started lighting.

In the holding area. The 120 extras are in. Woody described them as a "casting nightmare" in the script, and they certainly are; Todd Thaler, who is in charge of casting them, has really outdone himself. The Salad Sisters don't have a lot to do to make the extras into the nightmare Woody has requested. You wonder if some of them are going to make it through the day: old, young, frightening-looking, crazy-looking, half-witted, crippled (an eighteen-year-old girl). They've been here since 6:00 and the PAs and makeup and wardrobe people are already exhausted. There are not a lot of pretty girls here; Brian is not hanging around.

Rebecca, the beautiful *au pair* girl, lives in Brooklyn. Actually, she's a painter and only takes care of Baby Dylan on the set when Sally is working. She is also interested in movies. She made a few shorts when she was taking a class at the New School, and this is why she took the job.

11:00 A.M. Liz has just told me that Rebecca is Arthur Miller's daughter!

Carlo is ready, and Woody is having all the extras pass slowly in front of him so he can put them in one of two groups, A or B, to be placed in different parts of the room. Woody's face is impassive. It is both funny and pathetic to see the way they look at Woody. Most of them have already worked with him, on the train in *Stardust Memories*, for instance, and, since Fellini doesn't work in New York, Woody must be the only one who will give them a job, outside of horror-movie producers.

11:30 A.M. Shot 104: The entrance of the audience. The camera is in the studio. The doors open. The casting nightmare stampedes to the seats. *(20 seconds.)*

They have been asked to rush to the seats, and they do it beautifully in rehearsal. Tom asks them not to overdo it and to be careful of the dolly track. Some of the old ones walk with canes.

Take 1: An old lady falls, tripping on the dolly track. Nothing

serious, but it creates a jam and we have to stop. It is really impressive to see this horde of crazy people invading the room. "They are like the Huns," Pop would say.

Take 2: No good. Sam, who is pushing the paralytic in a beautiful wooden wheelchair, didn't start at the right time. And some of them are smiling. "You shouldn't smile," Tommy cautions them.

Take 3: Problems with the camera movement.

Take 4: Good.

(Takes 2 and 4 are printed.)

As always, Woody cuts quickly at the end of the shot. For the last take, Woody stays alone in a corner, looking lonesome. It appears the shot is depressing him a little.

11:50 A.M. Jane sits in the director's chair in a corner of the lobby, tickling little Moses, who seems to enjoy it. Moses is Sally's seventh child in the real world. He is eight years old, Korean, with big glasses, and a crippled leg.

Jane takes him to the set to Woody, who is sitting thoughtfully in his chair. Woody welcomes the boy warmly, takes him by the hand and hugs him. The child's face lightens, as does Woody's. It's a wonderful image—little Moses' smile and Woody's warm, open, natural, and unexpected behavior. Woody jokes with the boy, makes faces, and the child laughs. Now Andrew, Moses' older brother in real life, joins the group, and stays at their side, serious, responsible, watching, and not at all jealous.

12:15 P.M. Shot 104A: Same action (the crowd entering) but the camera is in the back of the room, looking from a different angle.

A woman slips and lands on her forehead. She seems to have hurt herself, but she goes on.

(1 take and 1 print.)

We move to the next shot.

1:50 P.M. We are ready to do the reaction shots of the *Herbie Hanson* audience and the paid laughers. Woody always shoots the reaction shots to a show separately, and shoots the show without the audience. In *Annie Hall*, during his stand-up routine, he was doing his jokes to an empty room. And when the audience was finally filmed, they didn't know what they were laughing at.

The paid laughers come in, two women (Amelia David and Robin Smith) and one man (Steve Leibman). Then Sally, who has also taken a job as a laugher, enters all in red. Woody has her put on a coat, and they all go to take seats in the middle of the casting nightmare. Brian asks me to guess which is the man dressed as a woman—the wardrobe department noticed him this morning. I can't find her, or him. He points her out to me. He, or she, looks beautiful! On *Manhattan*, they chose a beautiful woman to be Mariel Hemingway's stand-in and it turned out she was a man.

Shot 106A: The audience applauds.

(1 take and 1 print.)

Shot 106B: Same action but the camera pans over the audience to a closer shot of Sally and the paid laughers.

One woman is falling asleep. Tom's booming voice takes care of that.

(2 takes and 2 prints.)

Shot 106D: A concert of laughter.

Woody is in front of them, conducting.

Take 1: The four paid laughers, Sally included, laugh alone. The audience doesn't react.

Take 2: They still laugh alone; the others turn to them.

Take 3: The paid laughers laugh. The audience begins laughing with them. Then everybody is laughing.

(The 3 takes are printed.)

Shot 106E: Sally starts to laugh. The paid laughers join her. Then the crowd.

(2 takes and 2 prints.)

Shot 106F: The first paid laugher starts laughing, then stands up, still laughing—and the audience applauds him. The second does the same, then the third. And then Sally gives the last laugh and is applauded, too. *(20 seconds.)*

(4 takes and 3 prints.)

We are all laughing now.

"Excellent," Woody says.

We break for lunch at 2:00 P.M.

3:30 P.M. I'm walking up the stairs with the paid laughers. "We are very good at parties," one of the women tells me. But the man is exhausted; laughing is hard work.

On the set, Woody is playing chess with Ezra, the board set on top of the piano. And the extra who plays the paralytic is stuffing tissues into his shoes(?).

4:00 P.M. Shot 106H: The audience leaves the room after the announcement that war has been declared. *(10 seconds.)*

Between takes, Woody goes back to the chess game.

Take 1: Woody to the crowd: "I have some bad news for you." They listen, learn of the war, then leave.

Take 2: Woody asks them to leave the room at a quicker pace.

(The 2 takes are printed.)

Woody hurries back to the chessboard.

4:30 P.M. A Christmas special today on the game—one card, twenty dollars. The first prize is six hundred dollars. I don't play.

Moses and Jane continue playing together. The band leader for *The Herbie Hanson Show* is the one from the *Silver Dollar Jackpot* show. He is in reality the music arranger for the film and works with Dick Hyman. He is a little tired of pretending to conduct and a little disappointed because he is not sure he will appear on-screen very much.

While Carlo sets the lights for the next shot, Woody and Ezra continue the chess game. Woody seems a little moody today, and appears almost uninterested in the shooting. When Tom asks him a question, he answers briefly, as if it's painful, then goes back to the game.

And Jane is exhausted. She often works till 10:00 P.M. as well as weekends, and she has only two weeks off each year—when she

takes them! She has been working with Woody since *Broadway Danny Rose;* she arrived in the middle of the shooting. Before, she worked at NBC on *Saturday Night Live*. But she's happy working with Woody and has become more of a friend to him. I tell her she should be the one to write the book. But she says she can't. She would be sued. She knows too much.

In the holding area, it is a "catastrophe!" as Carlo would say. The 120 extras are being released. They have to turn in their costumes, fill out forms with their names and addresses. Some of them have trouble doing it because of physical or mental handicaps. The PAs are at their wits' end. They have been handling them for nearly twelve hours now.

5:30 P.M. We're ready to shoot Herbie Hanson's (Steve Mittleman) arrival onstage. The camera faces the other direction now, with the backs of the crowd in the foreground. Ten people make up the audience, arranged to fill the frame. The transvestite is still with us and sits next to a tiny man who does not seem bothered. Does he know?

Shot 106C: The announcer (Ed Herlihy) introduces the show, "The Associated Life Insurance Company presents . . ." The audience applauds. The band plays the jingle. Then he reads the life insurance commercial, "When you die, pass away, leave this earth forever . . ." And the speech ends, ". . . remember, life is short, but death is forever! And now, here's Herbie Hanson!" Over the applause and the band playing (faking it), Herbie makes his entrance. He opens with a few jokes.

(3 takes and 2 prints.)

And it's a wrap at 6:00 P.M.

On the staircase, I bump into Woody and little Moses. I thank him again and I tell him I'll be away for a week. Woody wishes me a nice trip and a merry Christmas.

Monday, December 30, 1985   *Eighth and Ninth Weeks*

Last Friday, terrorists hurled grenades and fired submachine guns at crowds of holiday travelers at airports in Rome and Vienna in attacks on check-in counters of El Al Airlines: 16 dead and 113 wounded. Ron blames Libya.

Two hundred and thirty-five Polish tourists on a shopping ex-cursion on Christmas Eve failed to return to three ships docked at a West German port. (New York Times)

Ron and Gorby agreed to exchange three to five minutes of videotaped New Year's Day greetings that are intended for broad-cast in the United States and the Soviet Union. (New York Times)

"The thing is, we are killed by both parties. As both parties are killing us, we don't like both parties." Caught in the middle of the fighting between the Front for the Liberation of Mozambique (government) and the Mozambique National Resistance (rebel army), civilians are fleeing from Mozambique to South Africa. The soldiers and insurgents usually come at night to kill, rape, and burn, so the civilians spend their nights hiding in bushes where they are eaten by lions and other wild animals. More than 100,000 people have fled in the last year. (New York Times)

8:30 A.M. The Julia Richman high school on East Sixty-seventh Street.

Back on the set after a week's absence. Everybody is warm, friendly. We shake hands with Woody; it seems he had his hair cut over Christmas. Barbara, as always, is everywhere at once. Jimmy Sabat's son is visiting again.

Not a lot was accomplished during Christmas week. On Monday, the company finished *The Herbie Hanson Show.* Tuesday, Woody was sick and nothing was shot, for the first time in Woody's career. Thursday morning, it was the reshoot of the USO with different makeup for Sally, and she sang "I Don't Want to Walk Without You" at a much slower pace, totally changing the atmosphere of the scene. In the afternoon, it was *The Gay White Way* show (sequence 144), where Sally, a radio star now, did her "Hedda Hopper"-like show. Friday morning was *Guess that Tune,* where the Burglars win the jackpot while robbing the Needlemans (sequence 73). And in the afternoon, the *Amateur Talent Hunt* (sequence 47), with the singing housewife, the dentist who plays the harmonica, the telephone operator who talks like a monkey, and the others.

We're here to shoot all the classroom scenes (sequences 21, 35, and 134). We are on one of the upper floors of Julia Richman, where a few of the classrooms have been decorated with period posters. There are thirty-seven children today, with thirty-six mothers, and Burt's grandfather listening to a Walkman. Two reshoots are planned: *Herbie Hanson* (Woody wasn't pleased with the set) and *Rienzi.*

9:50 A.M. Shot 21: The teacher (Mindy Morgenstern) is writing on the blackboard. Masked Avenger whistle rings are heard whistling throughout the room. The teacher turns abruptly, trying to catch one of the kids. *(11 seconds.)*
It goes smoothly.
(3 takes and 2 prints.)
Carlo works on the next shot, the camera focused in the other direction.

10:40 A.M. All the kids are back, including Little Joe, Burt, Dave, Nick, Andrew, Little Evelyn, and Little Linda, Little Arnold (David Mosberg), Little Ross (Ross Morgenstern), and others. They are in the classroom, each with Masked Avenger rings ready and their eyes on Woody, who directs them from beside the camera. He makes a few seating changes, then he's ready to shoot.
Shot 21A: POV of the teacher: A wide shot of the classroom, with Little Joe and his gang spread out. They whistle with the Masked Avenger rings, then, quickly hiding them, they put on innocent faces.
(2 takes and 2 prints.)

11:10 A.M. The kids remain in the room while Carlo makes some adjustments of the lighting.
Shot 21B: Same wide angle, but the teacher appears in the frame, walking down the aisle looking for the guilty parties. When she reaches the end of the room, the kids behind her blow their whistles again. She spins around, furious. The camera zooms in on her face. *(20 seconds.)*
It is Woody who cues the kids. The shot is a little troublesome because some of the kids are looking either at the camera or at Woody.
(7 takes and 3 prints.)
Woody gets a wild track of the whistling. And the kids are taken out so that Carlo and Woody may set the next shot, Show and Tell (sequence 35B).

11:30 A.M. Carlo and Woody are alone in the classroom, discussing where to put the camera. Woody walks through where each kid will be. First he's Little Evelyn going to the blackboard, then he goes to Little Arnold's seat in the front row, then to Little Ross's, who sits in the corner talking about the Masked Avenger ring, and finally he shows Little Joe's reactions. Carlo watches. There is a minimum of words. Everything is done with gestures— the camera angle, the camera movements—and always in as few shots as possible. It's decided that the scene will be done in two shots. A master shot for the three students and their Show and Tell: Little Evelyn and the ship-in-a-bottle her brother made, Little Arnold with the contraceptive he found in his parents' bedroom, Little Ross with the famous Masked Avenger ring he got for fifteen cents, then finally a second shot of Little Joe reacting to Ross's Masked Avenger ring. Carlo goes to work.

12:00 noon. Because the real sun is shining through the window more and more and interfering with our sun (the huge lights set on the crane in the street), Carlo wants to wait for dusk. We move to the next scene, Miss Gordon's arrival in the classroom (sequence 134), to be shot in another room down the hall, the windows of which look onto another street.

12:30 P.M. Miss Gordon, in high heels, is talking to tiny Principal Peters (Henry Cowen) outside the classroom, while Woody chats with Brian. But Principal Peters is not very talkative, and Miss Gordon and I, who both live in California, start to socialize. She tells me she did a voice over in *Zelig* and that after her striptease in Rockaway, she went back to Los Angeles. She doesn't regret having quit acting, and likes her job at HBO as a story analyst. Miss Gordon's mom is Italian (she was born in Rome herself). But her Pop, like Polly Phelps, is from Pennsylvania, and she prefers mellow California.

Meanwhile, the boys are moving the sun to the other street.

1:00 P.M. The kids return to the classroom and take their seats. Woody joins them, acting like a schoolkid (going to his seat, with a childlike walk). It's very funny, but few notice it. Woody doesn't mind; he's enjoying himself.

Shot 134: A wide angle of the kids, chaotic. Little Joe yells, "Here comes the principal," and they quiet down. *(15 seconds.)*

The kids start talking, growing noisy. Woody tries to get the camera rolling without their knowing, but it can't be done. Prin-

cipal Peters sometimes peeps through the door and smiles, finding the whole thing a little insane. Woody is having trouble getting exactly what he wants—a real uproar and an abrupt end to it.
(14 takes and 7 prints.)
We break for lunch at 2:00 P.M.

3:30 P.M. Shot 134B: A wide angle of the class reacting to the entrance of Principal Peters and the substitute teacher, Miss Gordon. The camera zooms in on Little Joe, Burt, and Andrew, who are stunned.

Woody explains the scene to the kids. Then he walks down a row, playfully pushes Burt, and takes his seat, to show them how to do the scene. He plays it broadly. He bites his book, makes faces (like the Tex Avery cartoon wolf seeing a pinup). The kids burst into laughter. It's funny and Woody enjoys doing it. The kids applaud. Then Woody goes back to his director role, very serious. When he puts on these sorts of displays, it's always unexpected. He does them both spontaneously (he needs to do it and enjoys it) and to play to an audience (the kids and us).
(5 takes and 3 prints.)
And now a series of close-up reactions of Little Joe and his gang.
134C: A close-up of Little Joe and Andrew. *(5 seconds.)*
Once again, Woody tells them precisely what to do—to bulge their eyes and drop their mouths—directing them verbally during the take since no sound is being recorded. Because Little Joe is more of a professional, Woody lets him improvise.
(3 takes and 3 prints.)
134D: Close-up of Burt.
He already has such an incredible face, with his buck teeth, that anything Woody asks of him guarantees excellent results.
(1 take and 1 print.)
134E: Close-up of Nick.
(1 take and 1 print.)
134F: Close-up of Dave.
(1 take and 1 print.)
All these reactions are in the same spirit as when they saw Miss Gordon through the window; it's just not as cold here.
For each take, Carlo has to adjust the light a little.
The sequence is completed at 4:45 P.M.

5:00 P.M. Shot 134G: A close-up of two little girls reacting to Principal Peters's entrance.

(3 takes and 3 prints.)

Now the camera is moved for a reverse angle, toward the blackboard, and Carlo gets it ready.

Principal Peters is neither a principal nor an actor; he is a regular person and this is his first movie role. He was having dinner with his wife, who is an actress, in a restaurant in Greenwich Village and Woody was with a party of eight at the next table. When he and his wife left the restaurant, Jane followed them into the street and asked him if he would like to be in a Woody Allen movie. What is even stranger is that a year ago, he was stopped in the street by another woman called Helen or Eileen—he doesn't remember exactly—who told him he would be perfect for a role in a Woody Allen movie! She took his number but never called. Principal Peters is having fun, but he is still a little anxious because his wife coached him on his lines yesterday, and this morning he was given new ones.

5:30 P.M. Jimmy Sabat's wife and daughter are visiting. Woody is very gallant with Miss Gordon ("He is the sweetest director I know," she told me earlier), and Kay is having a nervous breakdown. "Wasn't Miss Gordon saying this line?" she asks Woody. "She is going to say something else," he replies. "It will work," and, indicating his head, "it's all up there." Woody is improvising everything and seems to be enjoying it. He is also editing the movie while shooting, getting exactly what he needs, and no more. It's sometimes difficult for Kay, even after ten movies, to figure out what exactly is happening "up there" in Woody's head.

5:45 P.M. Shot 134A: A wide shot of the classroom over the kids' shoulders. Principal Peters enters and tells them that they are going to have a substitute teacher. *(18 seconds.)*
It is much shorter than originally planned; in the script, two kids were fighting and Principal Peters had to shut them up before announcing Miss Gordon.
(3 takes and 3 prints.)

6:00 P.M. Woody is in a great mood. He whacks the table with a ruler to get attention, and calls the kids "monsters." Kay has given up following what's going on.
Shot 134H: The camera starts on a master shot of Principal Peters, who asks Miss Gordon to come in. "They're all yours," he says. The camera pans to the door and zooms in as Miss Gordon appears. She goes to the desk as the principal exits. The camera stays on Miss Gordon, who, after having given a beautiful smile to the little monsters, turns to write her name on the chalkboard. *(35 seconds.)*
In the script, she asked the monsters their names, and when she got to Andrew, he couldn't get it out. As she goes to the board, Miss Gordon sways her hips as Woody has suggested. The kids appreciate it. No difficulties here, other than tightening the pace of the entrance and exit.
(6 takes and 6 prints.)

6:15 P.M. A poster above the blackboard reads BE A LOYAL AMERICAN. Carlo works on a closer shot of Miss Gordon. The kids are gone, and Woody is sitting on a bench reading a math textbook he found on a table. He seems fascinated. The title of the chapter is "Inflexible Logic."

6:30 P.M. Shot 134J: A closer shot of Miss Gordon turning to write her name on the board and, while turning back, reacting to the kids' appreciation of her backside.

Woody checks out the swing of her bottom and asks for a faster version. Between each take, he returns to "Inflexible Logic."

(5 takes and 4 prints.)

We wrap at 6:45 P.M.

Tuesday, December 31, 1985

9:30 A.M. We're back at the Julia Richman school. The background kids are brought in while the Salad Sisters check the principals, Little Joe and Miss Gordon. Lark, the eldest of Sally's real daughters, is visiting because her cousin Stephanie, daughter of Sally's real brother, is in the class. The kids are happy to be back at school together and are no longer overly impressed by the camera, the crew, or even Woody.

Shot 134K: Miss Gordon picks Little Joe, and asks him to come to the board. She will not tolerate any foolishness, just because she is not the regular teacher, she tells him. But Little Joe starts to imitate her dancing under the shower. Miss Gordon looks at him, shocked. (33 seconds.)

At the beginning, the scene doesn't work at all, but progressively, detail by detail, Woody adjusts it. He has Little Joe resist a bit when Miss Gordon calls him up ("Me. . . ?") then he has Miss Gordon start talking before she sits. And finally, Little Joe adds to his imitation of the striptease: "With the towel . . . baba poo . . . under the shower . . . baba poo . . . on the floor!" Miss Gordon seems to have fun acting horrified when she realizes that Little Joe must have seen her. Once again, it is a matter of tightening the scene and accelerating the pace, adding some actions and shortening others. "Keep it alive," Woody tells Little Joe when he dances in front of Miss Gordon.

(16 takes and 8 prints.)

10:15 A.M. Shot 134L: A close-up of Nick reacting to Little Joe's dancing around and saying, "Oh God! That kid is going straight to hell!" *(3 seconds.)*

Just out of the frame, Woody repeats the line before Nick says it.

(3 takes and 2 prints.)

10:30 A.M. While Carlo does his work, Woody sits in Little Joe's place, in the middle of the kids (who now consider him one of them), and starts chatting with Stephanie, who sits in front of him.

Shot 134M: Close-up of Little Joe reacting to Miss Gordon's sashaying.

Little Joe makes his faces. Miss Gordon, helping out a fellow actor, starts to move her bottom.

(1 take and 1 print.)

We get a wild track of the classroom sounds. Nobody moves, and the sequence is over.

11:00 A.M. Woody and Carlo discuss the camera setting for the next shot. It is a scene to be used as a substitute for the one of the waitress showing her new WAC uniform to the girls at the ice cream parlor, which we did on the second day of shooting (sequence 108). Woody will now use a scene of the students pledging allegiance to the flag. They decide on a pan starting on the BE A LOYAL AMERICAN poster and moving across the classroom as the kids and the teacher recite the pledge. Carlo goes to work and Woody looks for the math textbook so he can finish reading about "Inflexible Logic." After searching a few of the desks, he finally finds it, sits, and starts reading.

11:15 A.M. Barbara introduces me to her rabbi, who has come by with his wife and daughter. Rabbi Cohen is of the Reform branch, and does a lot of social work. He is a fan of Woody's and quotes him in his lectures, Barbara tells me. Barbara asks me to tell him how Woody works.

12:00 noon. The camera movement isn't working. It's too complicated, and too difficult to light because of the windows. Anyway, Carlo doesn't feel it. These are the most interesting moments, when there are difficulties, when they begin the arduous search for solutions. Woody has to put "Inflexible Logic" aside. But this is not an important shot, and the solution is soon found by abandoning the BE A LOYAL AMERICAN poster and simplifying it.

12:10 P.M. Shot R108: The camera starts on the American flag, then moves back to reveal the teacher and the kids standing, hands to their hearts, pledging allegiance to the flag. *(15 seconds)*. *(3 takes and 2 prints.)*

12:30 P.M. We're about to move to the Masked Avenger ring scene, in the room at the other end of the hall, when Woody and Carlo realize that we are going to have the same problem with the sun as yesterday. So they decide to stay here. Jimmy Mazzola has to redress the room, because the next sequence takes place before the declaration of war.
We break for lunch.

2:30 P.M. Back on the set. Woody had lunch with Gene Siskel of the *Chicago Tribune* at the Fortune Garden, a Chinese restaurant on Third Avenue. He had a double order of shrimp dumplings, won ton soup, and spring rolls, chased down by a Heineken beer, Siskel said, but he seems OK.

3:00 P.M. Shot 35: The teacher asks the kids to come to the board with their Show and Tell items. Little Evelyn is first, with the ship-in-a-bottle her brother built. Then Little Arnold is a big hit with the contraceptive he found in his parents' night table. And finally, Little Ross shows the Masked Avenger ring. *(53 seconds.)*
The shot is almost a minute long. No problem with Little Evelyn: She says her lines very naturally. Little Arnold doesn't have a lot to do. But Little Ross can't seem to get through his lines. Poor Little Ross—he either forgets the words or he mispronounces them. He almost panics. But Woody likes the effect. He shortens Little Evelyn's lines, asks Little Arnold to take the contraceptive from his pocket sooner, and uses the timidity and hesitation of Little Ross to comic effect. Between takes, as usual, Woody reads *The New York Times* entertainment section, which has a big ad for Sylvester *(Take the Money and Run)* Stallone's film *Rocky IV*. (Sometime next year, on the set of his next film, Woody will be reading a *New York Times* with an ad for *Rocky V*.)
(12 takes and 3 prints.)

4:10 P.M. Shot 35A: The camera zooms in for a close-up of Little Joe, totally enraptured with the Masked Avenger ring. *(4 seconds.)*

No problems.

(3 takes and 3 prints.)

Now a wild track of Little Ross: Woody sits in front of him and explains, very quietly and seriously, the importance of the Masked Avenger ring and its secret compartment for small messages. He repeats the lines before the take, and tries to put Little Ross at ease. It's difficult, but the boy makes it.

We wrap at 4:30 P.M.

There is champagne and cake. Everybody wishes everyone a happy New Year. Adriana comes by to pick up her husband, Carlo. Woody offers a very discreet general happy New Year and escapes. I end the year 1985 with a big kiss from Barbara.

Thursday, January 2, 1986

Ron and Gorby's pledge for '86: year of peace. (Daily News)

Ron taped his remarks Saturday in Los Angeles against a dark background with family pictures and a vase of flowers, while Gorby spoke against a green-and-gold tapestry. The two men wore dark suits and white shirts. (New York Times)

Swearing to do better, Ed begins third term. (Daily News)

Ed presents a dual message: "A firm sense of pride" in his record and concessions that difficulties remain. (New York Times)

If New York is Hollywood on the Hudson, Jersey City is little Hollywood on the Hudson. Woody Allen wrote and directed a film in Jersey City. Among the films shot on location were Perfect *with Jersey native John Travolta, and such epics as* California Girls, Doubletake, *and* Kane and Abel, *which starred Peter Strauss and Veronica Hamel. Then there was a film shot for European television in which a replica of part of the Berlin wall was built on Jersey City's Exchange Place. (Daily News)*

And two entertainment personalities died on New Year's Eve: Ricky Nelson, forty-five, in a plane crash; and Oscar-winning producer Sam Spiegel, eighty-two, whose films included John Huston's The African Queen, *Elia Kazan's* On the Waterfront, *and*

The Last Tycoon, *and David Lean's* The Bridge on the River Kwai *and* Lawrence of Arabia.

8:30 A.M. We're back at the New School, in the basement, in a circular room painted two colors so it can be used for two radio-show studios. On one side, chairs and orchestra stands have been set up. To be shot are scenes of a radio songstress singing "I'll Be Seeing You" and "They're Either Too Young or Too Old" (shots A107 and 149), and Bill Kern telling the Kirby Kyle story (sequence 84). Woody, in a beige Shetland sweater and tweed cap, is having his breakfast, hot water and toast, while talking to Andrew. Jeffrey is next to them, dressed very casually today in light-brown boots, faded jeans, a beige vest and jacket, a black shirt, and a metallic cowboy tie.

From time to time one of the teamsters or the *Vogue* magazine writer (Santo's driver) comes to inspect the set. And Andrew is hanging around with Drew again.

9:30 A.M. The radio singer (Catherine Hayes) is here. She's in her thirties, a little overweight, with an amusing face. When she was interviewed, she said she was a singer but when they tried to record her, she was terrible. Woody has kept her because of her looks but he'll have to use another voice. Jeffrey has put a flower-pot on her hat, emphasizing her offbeat looks. Frankie has her listen to the playback, with the orchestra conductor at their side.

10:30 A.M. The musicians are brought in.

Shot A107: The radio singer singing "I'll Be Seeing You" in playback. *(20 seconds.)*

The singer's lip sync is not without flaws. Woody, as usual, cuts as soon as he has the twenty seconds he needs.

(5 takes and 2 prints.)

The singer goes to change for the next song, while Carlo sets up for another camera angle.

After nine weeks, we have shot 120,000 feet of film, which means that we are averaging less than 2,000 feet per day. The reason is that Woody doesn't cover himself, doesn't do a lot of takes, and, knowing exactly what he wants, shoots only what he needs.

11:15 A.M. Everybody is back. The singer makes eyes at Carlo, but he doesn't seem interested.

Shot 149: The radio singer sings "They're Either Too Young or Too Old." *(20 seconds.)*
(3 takes and 3 prints.)

12:00 noon. We are facing the other side of the room now, and Bill Kern is going to tell us the story of Kirby Kyle, the pitcher who had heart. Guy Le Bow (Bill Kern) is in his early sixties, a former sportscaster, with a limp and a warm face. Now he owns and runs a radio station. Jimmy Mazzola seats him on the set behind the table and Carlo starts working. Woody gives Bill Kern the script. Bill reads it and starts laughing. He will read from the pages on-camera.

12:15 P.M. I am sitting in one of the musicians' chairs from the previous shot, taking notes. Woody goes to the conductor's stand, and in front of the empty seats, with me in the corner, he takes the baton and, very seriously, starts to conduct. The boys keep working and don't pay any attention to him, and Woody continues conducting, not paying any attention to me. Suddenly he stops, and starts pacing, whistling.

12:30 P.M. Pictures directly—no rehearsals.
Shot 84: Wide shot of Bill Kern telling Kirby's story. *(1 minute, 13 seconds.)*
Bill Kern's voice is warm and personable, while the lines are absurd, grave and funny. Again, as in Rabbi Baumel's scene and the Polly Phelps episode, Woody plays with ambiguities. There is emotion in Bill Kern's voice, and there is emotion on the set while we are shooting.
Shot 84A: A closer shot of the same scene.
(2 takes and 2 prints.)
We break for lunch at 1:00 P.M.

In the van back to the Good Shepherd-Faith church, with Little Joe, Nick, Dave, Burt, the Communist's Son, a few mothers, and Rienzi. Danny lets us hear Jean Pierre Rampal playing two Bach sonatas. Rienzi congratulates Danny on his taste. The Communist's Son is a bit withdrawn. Nick is very hotheaded, and never stops teasing Burt, who is getting tired of it. Little Joe plays the boss, and Dave is subdued. The radio announces that *Play It Again, Sam* is showing at a local theater. "Let's go now!" Rienzi

suggests. The vitality of the kids makes him younger. But poor
Rienzi still has difficulties getting out of the van with his costume
on and extra clothes in his arms.

2:30 P.M. In the holding area of the church, in one of the back
rooms, in complete silence, Nick, the Communist's Son, and Burt
are doing their homework. The math-and-science tutor is keeping
an eye on them. Little Joe was tutored this morning at his hotel
and is now rehearsing his lines in the chapel next door, while
Rienzi, seated under the cross, is eating a banana.

3:00 P.M. I AM FOLLOWING JESUS
           ONE STEP AT A TIME
           I LIVE FOR THE MOMENT
           IN HIS LOVE DIVINE
           WHY THINK OF TOMORROW?
           JUST LIVE FOR TODAY
           I'M FOLLOWING JESUS
           EACH STEP OF THE WAY.

It's written on a blackboard in the room where we shot the
sound-effects studio and the Whiz Kids. Woody reads it all the
way through but it doesn't seem to convert him, and he walks
away, whistling and flipping a nickel.

Carlo is lighting Rienzi's apartment. It is difficult because everything—the lights, the props—has to match what we shot the
other day. We are reshooting only the last shot, where Rienzi
shows up after the kids have come into his room.

5:00 P.M. Shot R133B: Rienzi sees the kids. "Thieves!" he
screams. Then he enters the room. An argument begins and the
kids surround Rienzi. Nick: "You're a Nazi spy." Rienzi: "I hate
the Nazis, I am an inventor." Then he shows them the mike that
makes voices come out of the radio. Little Joe: "Can I borrow it?"
Rienzi: "I guess so."

The hall is getting crowded, the kids are getting active, and
Carlo is getting nervous ("Madonna!"). To calm himself, he rubs
Liz's red hair.

The camera is again in the door frame for the same movement
as before. The problem with the first version was the acting and
the lines, which have been simplified. Once more it's difficult for

Woody, with Rienzi's age and the kids getting more and more restless. Woody plays with the tone of the scene. The fight at the beginning is exaggerated, then it suddenly becomes calm and the parties are willing to talk. The abrupt change of tone is quite funny, as if each of them has forgotten the argument of moments before. At one point, Woody asks Rienzi to improvise.

(17 takes and 5 prints.)

We wrap at 5:30 P.M.

Friday, January 3, 1986

West Virginian inmates who took over their penitentiary agreed to release all hostages and to relinquish control of the prison to the authorities. In return, Governor Archibald A. Moore agreed to the prisoners' demand that he meet them on Friday to discuss improving their treatment. They demand "decent meals" and at least one hot meal a day. The agreement was signed on live television yesterday. (New York Times)

Chilean air force personnel recovered the bodies of the eight American tourists who died on New Year's Eve when their Cessna Titan 404 crashed on an Antarctic glacier. The victims had planned to spend New Year's Eve among the penguins in Antarctica. (New York Times)

8:30 A.M. The King Cole Room in the St. Regis–Sheraton hotel on East Fifty-fifth Street is a big, pink, Art Deco restaurant with a stage, a dance floor, and mirrors on the walls. Above the mirrors, there are murals of Old King Cole. The tables have been dressed with small lamps. Two rows of huge chandeliers running the length of the room and floor lamps around the dance floor have been added.

All the interior scenes of the nightclub will be shot here, including Irene and Roger having their little affairs with Porfirio and Sally (sequences 60 to 65), and the end of the movie, where the radio personalities gather to celebrate New Year's Eve (sequences 175 to 179). All the King Cole roof scenes will be done in the studio in late January. We are settling into the King Cole Room until Wednesday.

Carlo has started to light. Popeye, always unshakable, his nose ready to drip on a moment's notice, does his job. Jimmy Mazzola and Jimmy Frederick are pouring the wine (grape juice), and at one of the tables, Bob Greenhut, Woody, and Tom are discussing the shooting schedule.

A Chihuahua is brought to Woody for approval. The *Vogue* writer comes to check the set, followed by one or two teamsters.

9:30 A.M. The bar downstairs, a chic room all in wood with tables and dim lighting, is being used for the holding area. In the middle, there is a huge square bar, where uniformed hotel waiters are serving coffee, tea, and hot bagels and cream cheese on the beautiful hotel china. The more than one hundred extras, all in black tie and long dresses, appreciate the way Woody is treating them. Everybody is chatting, having a good time. The Latin band members have joined the party. It's an incredible atmosphere, but nothing like the USO back room, where the girls were fixing their stockings and the boys were making their moves. It's the formal clothes that account for the change; the extras act in accordance with what they are wearing. This sixty-year-old man, white-haired and distinguished, could be the chairman of the board of a corporation, and this wistful young lady, a rich heiress. The party is disturbed, from time to time, by a few teamsters who have decided that coffee and hot bagels served with class taste better.

10:00 A.M. The *au pair*, Rebecca, passes by with Lark to have a look at the set. (I get a distant little smile.) She is still beautiful, but more groomed today, her blue earrings matching her blue shirt.

The *Vogue* writer, who is having his breakfast of coffee and doughnuts at one of the tables on the set, is being jostled a bit by Ken.

10:30 AM. Carlo will be ready in ten minutes. Jimmy Mazzola is setting the first course (a cold plate of salmon, artichokes, and macédoine of vegetables) on the tables.

Brian shows me an article in *The Sporting News*, IS THERE A HEAVYWEIGHT CHAMPION BEING BORN?, and the cover of *Sports Illustrated* with a big picture of Mike Tyson ready to fight under the title KID DYNAMITE.

10:45 A.M. The extras are brought to the set in little groups and directed to the tables, a few of them being sent to the dance floor. Then come the waiters, followed by the Latin band. The

conductor is Tito Puente himself. The Latin singer, who was in
Hector Babenco's *Kiss of the Spider Woman*, sits on a chair on the
stage, her little Chihuahua on her lap.

Roger and Irene arrive from their rented hotel rooms upstairs.
Roger's black-tie jacket is double-breasted and Irene wears a flashy
dress with a lot of jewelry. They are chatting with the maître d'.

Shot 60: A long and wide establishing shot of the King Cole
Room. Roger and Irene, Broadway's most fascinating couple, appear at the door. The maître d' leads them to a table. *(13 seconds.)*

The band mimes the music, which will be recorded and added
later. So Roger and Irene arrive to complete silence. The band is
not even in the shot, but one can see the reflection of their colorful
costumes in the mirrors. The extras are not having enough fun
(smoking, laughing, sipping wine), not showing enough energy.
And they're supposed to be doing all that without making any
noise, as Tom reminds them, so the dialogue can be recorded clean.
Again, Woody cuts very quickly once Roger and Irene have started
to follow the maître d'. The fifth take is the first good one.

(6 takes and 2 prints.)

The extras are brought back downstairs so the boys can work
on the next setup, the camera getting a reverse angle.

12:00 noon. While Carlo continues to work, Roger and Irene
stay with us and relax at one of the tables (Roger has taken off his
jacket.) Irene would prefer not to do the tango scene with Porfirio
today because she needs to practice more with the tango teacher.
Roger makes fun of her jewelry. *"C'est de la camelote"* ("That's
junk"), he says.

Roger speaks fluent French with practically no accent. Born
British, he lived in Paris several years as the assistant to *Réalité*
magazine's editor-in-chief. He met Santo in a production of *As
You Like It* in Minneapolis, and it was Santo who introduced him
to Woody. Roger is a stage actor, and has worked in both Europe
and America. Samuel Beckett wrote *Solo* for him, and just after
the shooting, he is scheduled to go to Paris to play Marat in
Marat/Sade at Le Theatre de Bobigny. He is a little concerned that
Woody will keep him too long, because the *Marat/Sade* rehearsals
started January 2. But since he'll be sitting in a bathtub for the
whole play, he doesn't think the blocking will be too much trouble.

1:00 P.M. The shot is difficult to set because of all the mirrors,
though Carlo loves them. The background is brought in. Sally is in

the scene and arrives in her short, pink cigarette girl's skirt. She looks adorable. And Bea is visiting today. She wanted to see the beautiful people.

1:45 P.M. Ready to shoot. "Romaine, Fern! Make her prettier," Woody commands, pointing to Sally, and he starts pacing. Sally doesn't look impressed by his performance.

Shot 60A: Roger and Irene follow the maître d'. Then Roger spots Richard (Terry Lee Swarts). "The show at the Morosco was . . . smashing! You were right," he tells him. Irene thinks she saw Ernest Hemingway at the bar. The camera follows them. Irene meets Margaret (Margaret Thomson) and stops to chat with her. "Cigars, cigarettes." Sally appears around the corner. Roger goes to her, asking for cigarettes: "Where have you been? You never return my calls!" But Sally is firm: "I told you it was over." "Don't say that!" Roger begs. "I meet you in hotel rooms, in the back of cars, in stalled elevators!" Sally says, "You're gonna lose your respect for me!" But the love duet is interrupted by Irene; their table is ready. (30 seconds.)

The problems come primarily from the blocking. Roger is turning too wide and goes out of frame, and when the camera pans to follow them, it must use their bodies to hide its reflection in the mirrors. It is taking time to adjust, but it's worth it. As for the actors, everything's fine; Sally is the perfect ingenue. When Woody rehearses with Roger and Sally, he stands very close and acts their parts, saying their lines, making faces, always caricaturing a little. He looks nothing like he looks when he is acting in a movie, but still, there is that intonation, that voice. It's quite amusing to see him doing it.

Tom has to wake up the background actors, who are getting tired of waiting. "Ken, tell the dancers to smile. They look like they're going to the chair!" The Spider Woman and the Chihuahua are getting along well. The first good take is the seventh one. The first very good one is the twelfth.

(17 takes and 5 prints.)

We break for lunch at 2:35 P.M.

4:00 P.M. Sally, back in her extra-large street clothes, introduces me to Baby Dylan, who gives me a wonderful smile. Adriana, Carlo's wife, is here, too. She is very excited because her company invested in Max, Mon Amour. She is set to go to Paris next week to see the dailies.

Carlo is working on the next scene, which is Roger and Irene at their table with their party. Margaret (the friend Irene met in the previous shot) is now her stand-in, and Nicole, Mom's stand-in in Rabbi Baumel's scene, is in the scene, at a table next to Roger and Irene's.

Downstairs in the bar, after ten hours, the atmosphere is still respectable. Little "affairs" are blooming, though, and the young heiress is listening to rock 'n' roll on a cassette player.

5:00 P.M. Woody rehearses with the actors while Carlo finishes setting up. He explains the sequence and how we are shooting it. At Roger and Irene's table, we'll do three sequences that will be intercut with the two of Roger and Sally arguing about their love affair, and with some shots of the band. Woody has the whole scene edited in his head. As with Rabbi Baumel, he is happy with the way Irene and especially Roger play their parts. Once again, it's the perfect marriage between great lines and characters, and Woody has to work out only a few details. It's fascinating how much he enjoys working when the conditions are as good as these. "Like a child with his construction game, the director detaches himself from the immediate world and builds another one as he sees it," as François Truffaut once said. Woody gives me a smile, rolling his eyes heavenward.

Shot 60C: The couple sits. "The ball at the Waldorf was dull, Margaret said," Irene tells Roger. But Roger is distracted. A friend, Gail, joins them. "It's been so long . . ." Suddenly Roger realizes he paid the girl and forgot the cigarettes! He exits. *(28 seconds.)*

Victoria Kennedy (Gail) is tall and beautiful. She is a young model just out of high school, and this is her first film. Roger seems interested. But Tom is, too (he was talking to her a moment ago). In fact, everybody is interested in her, but Gail has eyes only for Woody.

There's a little problem with Gail's lipstick now. When she gives Irene a kiss, it leaves a perfect red spot on Irene's cheek. *(6 takes and 3 prints.)*

6:00 P.M. In the bar downstairs, after twelve hours, the atmosphere is still respectable, but a few of the men have slipped off their jackets and a few women have pulled up their long dresses. Most of them have not worked since this afternoon at 2:30, because the camera has been moved closer, and there's no need for all the extras.

On the set, Sally and Baby Dylan come to say good-bye.

Shot 63: At Roger and Irene's table, Tom (Ed Silk) and Jessica (Janet Frank) have joined the party. Roger comes back from his first argument with Sally. "Leonard Lyons sends his love," he says to Irene, who wonders what took him so long. Tom and Jessica have just come from the Lunts' party. "It was divine," Jessica says. "Jed Harris was there and said he was interested in my new farce *The Christmas in the Congo*," Tom says. But Roger thinks he just saw Dick Rodgers: "Perhaps he'll come on our show." And he goes back to Sally, while Tom continues to talk about his farce. *(34 seconds.)*

Woody sits next to Nicole, at the edge of the frame. Again, no problems.

(5 takes; the last 2 are printed.)

6:30 P.M. The next shot is Porfirio's arrival at Roger and Irene's table. The camera setting is different, taking in the whole room. Carlo and the boys are working.

Gail and Woody are in the middle of a heavy conversation. Roger interrupts them to ask for an autograph. Then they start again. Jane, Jessica, and Tom (Ed Silk) keep discreet distance. Woody has on his concerned face as he listens to Gail.

6:45 P.M. The background is brought in. Woody and Gail are still talking. Another woman approaches and joins the conversation, but Gail is still the one. Tom (Ed Silk) has moved closer, too, and I suspect he is eavesdropping.

6:50 P.M. Tom Reilly is still placing the extras. The second woman, who is as tall as Gail, is persevering. Gail doesn't appreciate it. Woody seems to enjoy the situation. But Gail has to join Roger and Irene's table so Carlo can make some final adjustments on the lighting. And the other woman stays alone with Woody. . . .

7:15 P.M. Woody checks the camera movement. He OK's it, then goes to talk with the actors.

In a corner, Jimmy Mazzola is aging the hundred-dollar bills. He soaks them in cold tea, then he dries them over a lamp. Andrew helps him.

7:30 P.M. Shot 65: The camera starts on a wide long shot of the whole room, looking toward the entrance. When Porfirio and

Brenda appear, the camera moves to a close shot, and follows them
to Roger and Irene's table. "This is Brenda Tracy and Porfirio,"
Jessica says, introducing the new couple to Irene. "Porfirio is the
Playboy of the Western World," Jessica adds. They sit. Irene takes
a cigarette and starts to light it, but Porfirio takes the lighter from
her hand, gets a hundred-dollar bill from his pocket, sets it on fire,
and lights Irene's cigarette with it. The party is impressed. *(45
seconds.)*

Dimitri Vassilopoulos (Porfirio) has a history of hanging
around nightclubs; he did it in *Stardust Memories*. Even if he has
a great sense of humor, lighting cigarettes with hundred-dollar
bills, Porfirio is very serious because of his Spanish blood, and he
rarely smiles. Porfirio is also quite masculine; it is 7:30 P.M. and
Romaine has to shave him.

Woody is lying next to Louis at the foot of the table, which
amuses the party. The difficulty is once again the fluidity of the
camera movement, and getting the blocking of Porfirio and Brenda
right. For the fourth take, Woody adds a waiter passing by. After
each take, Woody emerges from under the table with his questioning face: "OK?"

(9 takes and 5 prints.)

"It's a wrap" at 8:00 P.M.

Monday, January 6, 1986   *Tenth Week*

Mother Teresa to Ed Koch: "Give me all the AIDS convicts."
(New York Post)

*Troublesome gulch. Gary announces he will not run for the
Senate this year. "Does that mean I'm making some announcement about '88? Nope. Does it mean I still have an interest in
being President? Yep."* (New York Times)

*Soviet poet Yevgeny Yevtushenko denounces Sly for his two
films* Rambo: First Blood Part II *and* Rocky IV, *reproaching him
for killing " 'Reds' and Russians not for money, but with a kind of
perverse relish."* (New York Times)

*The Universe could be composed of gigantic "bubbles," with
the stars and galaxies, probably including our Milky Way, gathered on the surface. "If we are right, these bubbles fill the Universe like suds filling the kitchen sink," says John P. Huchra of the*

Harvard-Smithsonian Center for Astrophysics. (New York Times)
   The Bears beat the Giants (21–0), and the Patriots beat the Raiders (27–20).
   And Una Merkel dies at eighty-two. She began her film career as a stand-in for Lillian Gish in D. W. Griffith's Way Down East *(1920), and made her stage debut as a cigarette girl in* Montmartre *(1922) at the Belmont theater in New York City.*

8:30 A.M. We're back in the King Cole Room. The singer wasn't convincing, and her lip syncing was too far off the mark. Since all the radio performers will be gathering here tomorrow for New Year's Eve, Woody is casting a new singer tonight. The reshoot of Rienzi's scene, however, has turned out well.
   Moses is with us today, and Woody is wearing a green Shetland sweater, light-green corduroy trousers, but still those same shoes. And the gambling department is pushing a new game, a Super Bowl pool. They're charging twenty dollars per box.

9:45 A.M. The extras are brought in. We're doing the scenes in which Porfirio makes his move on Irene, using his irresistible charm and humor, while Roger and Sally are doing it on the roof. The tango teacher is back with us to supervise Irene and Porfirio's dancing, and the Spider Woman singer is back onstage with the Chihuahua.
   Shot 67: Porfirio is having a lot of success at Irene's table; Gail, Brenda, Tom, Jessica, and especially Irene are absolutely enthralled by his charm, as he mixes his favorite cocktail, a champagne martini. Then lust takes over, and Porfirio takes Irene (who doesn't know if all this is such a good idea) to the dance floor. They start dancing the tango. *(1 minute.)*
   Woody asks Porfirio to dance with Irene more energetically. The tango teacher practices with Irene, to show Porfirio how. But neither of the actors is very good. Woody doesn't seem to mind, as long as Porfirio shows energy. The second take is better. "One more and we're finished."
   Between each take, Woody goes back to Moses. He talks and jokes with the child (again shaking hands with him and wiping his hand on his sweater with a disgusted look) up to the last moment, until the camera rolls.
   (6 takes and 5 prints.)
   Nobody moves. The next shot must be matched perfectly: an-

other angle of Irene and Porfirio dancing the tango. The camera is taken to the middle of the dance floor. While the boys set up the camera, the background and the band stay motionless and silent. The tango teacher, who is not exactly proud of his pupils, tries to show Porfirio how to make his dancing look better.

It's suddenly getting chilly. An extra, gallantly, puts his jacket over his date's shoulder. The gambling department, always ready to help damsels in distress, picks out the prettier ones.

Shot 67A: The camera follows Irene and Porfirio as they dance the tango, looking into each other's eyes.

(6 takes and 4 prints.)

11:30 A.M. The extras are back in the bar downstairs. It is their second day, and the ice between them has been broken. Jimmy

Davis is getting a haircut, Richie chats with Brenda (Porfirio's date), Nicole reads Shirley MacLaine's *Dancing in the Light*, a young woman is practicing sign language from a book, and Tom (Ed Silk) chats with Gail (he must be talking about his new farce, *The Christmas in the Congo*).

12:00 noon. Woody is talking to Little Moses the way he likes to with Sally or Andrew, face to face, a hand on his shoulder. Moses hugs him. They stay that way for a moment, then Woody grabs a sheet of yellow paper from the table next to him, does a quick drawing, and gives it to the boy.

12:30 P.M. Woody is face to face with Sally now, talking to her while the Salad Sisters make her prettier. Sally has a bad cold today, and she's tired.
Shot 61: Sally approaches; "Cigars, cigarettes," and leans against one of the mirrored columns. Roger comes up behind her. He is in love with her, he explains. So Sally asks him to marry her. But he can't, he says, the ratings of the show are too high. An old lady buys some Lucky Strikes and tells Roger that Billy Rose is here. But Roger stays with Sally. He reminds her about the good time they had that weekend in Havana. But Sally reminds Roger that he promised to get her into radio. She doesn't want to sell cigarettes all her life; she is a natural talent. She starts to walk away. *(54 seconds.)*
"I think she should be selling cigarettes before the dialogue," Woody says. "So, let's try it." In the background, the extras and the band fake a good time in silence. Roger and Sally are excellent, consistently believable.
(5 takes and 3 prints.)
The background extras are released for a while. The musicians, tired of having pantomimed all morning, start playing. They're improvising, but quite well, and Woody enjoys it. Carlo works on the next setup, but it will be shot this afternoon.
We break for lunch at 1:35 P.M.

3:00 P.M. Woody is looking at a proof of a *Hannah and Her Sisters* advertising poster. Little Joe is visiting, and Patti is giving Sally a set of fake fingernails. Roger has taken his shoes off and is relaxing. And Carlo and the boys are still working on the shot.

3:30 P.M. Ready to shoot. No rehearsal. Everybody is in position. While Carlo makes some last adjustments, Woody holds Sally's cigarette tray and has her go over her lines. In the back, some extras are falling asleep. Tom goes into action.

Shot 64: Roger is back behind Sally. He's "exploding with desire." Roger has spoken to the head of the agency about her, and he wants to meet her. Sally becomes more considerate of his needs. But she is on her shift. "There must be a place," Roger says. Sally has an idea. (1 minute, 30 seconds.)

Once again, Roger and Sally are very good. After the fourth take, Woody asks Sally to play up the naïveté. On the seventh take, Sally, who is exhausted, misses her cue. But Woody already has several good ones.

(7 takes and 5 prints.)

4:30 P.M. Easy day today. The mood is good because Woody has gained a day. We were scheduled to come back on Wednesday, but we should be done by tomorrow night.

Sally, Baby Dylan in her arms and Rebecca following, comes to say good-bye. All the principals (Roger, Irene, Porfirio, Brenda, Tom, and Jessica) have left. The only shots left today are of the band.

5:00 P.M. Woody is whistling "Titina," the nonsense ditty Chaplin sang as the waiter in *Modern Times*. We are going to shoot the Spider Woman singing "Tico Tico."

Shot 62: The Spider Woman sings along with the playback. *(1 minute.)*

The Spider Woman gives her Chihuahua to Tito and starts

singing for the first rehearsal. She is great, but Tito isn't too delighted to be conducting with the Chihuahua in his arms. Moses has gotten a little lonesome; Woody notices and goes to him. For the first takes, the Spider Woman sings with her veil on, taking it off halfway. The last ones are done with no veil.

(5 takes and 3 prints.)

5:30 P.M. The pianist for the Monica Charles (Diane Keaton) scene tomorrow is from California. He phoned to say he couldn't take the early flight, and would arrive tomorrow at 6:00 A.M. Monica Charles insisted on having him! Woody and Tom decide to have a backup ready (Dick Hyman, for instance; he is a great pianist) just in case. You never know what to expect from California!

6:00 P.M. Moses likes the Chihuahua. He is playing with it on the dance floor. Woody, on the other hand, doesn't like it, so when he goes looking for the boy and sees him with the dog, he keeps his distance.

Shot 62A: A closer shot of the Spider Woman singing "Tico Tico."

The Chihuahua is now sleeping in Tito's arms.

Woody asks the Spider Woman to exaggerate.

(4 takes and 2 prints.)

6:20 P.M. Woody has given in. He goes to Moses and the Chihuahua. The dog wants to lick Woody, but Woody won't let it.

Shot 60B: The band is playing. The camera zooms in to Tito and the piano player. *(10 seconds.)*

They are allowed to play anything. They start with "They're Either Too Young or Too Old," since the music sheets are on their stands. But it is too slow, so they switch to a fox trot.

(4 takes and 2 prints.)

"It's a wrap!" at 6:25 P.M.

Tuesday, January 7, 1986

Four killed, fifteen wounded in attacks in Punjab, India, including a sixty-year-old woman who was stabbed to death. Nearly sixty people have died since October in attacks attributed to extremists fighting for an independent Sikh nation in Punjab. (New York Times)

After a faulty valve thwarts the launching, the shuttle is delayed again. (New York Times)

Ed calls federal government's expected cuts in aid "Rambonomics." (New York Times)

If a major nonnuclear conflict breaks out between the United States and the Soviet Union, the navy might seek to attack Soviet nuclear submarines. The contemplated action would be intended to tip the nuclear balance in favor of the United States, and induce the Soviet Union to end the conflict on terms favorable to American forces. (New York Times)

9:00 A.M. We're back in the King Cole Room. It's New Year's Eve, 1943, and everybody—Jessica Dragonette, Herbie Hanson, the Masked Avenger, Max—is here. Champagne and balloons are everywhere.

In the bar downstairs. "Ten-minute warning! Everybody wake up!" The forty new extras and a hundred from the previous day have been here since 6:00 A.M. Richie walks back and forth before the group screaming, "I need a woman!" "I need a man." The St. Regis waiters mix with the 1943 waiters, and the atmosphere is turmoil.

9:45 A.M. Max is here, elegant, in black tie. Monica Charles (Diane Keaton) is onstage, all in white like a bride, and the pianist from California has finally arrived. Sally has come to watch, too, but in civilian clothes; she wears an oversize dress, no makeup, and her hair is wild and uncombed. While the extras are put at tables, Woody watches carefully and regularly checks the framing through the two cameras. Jimmy Mazzola distributes party hats and cigarettes.

10:15 A.M. The room is half full, with only enough extras to fill the frame. Pictures directly.

Shot 175: Monica Charles sings "You'd Be So Nice To Come Home To." *(1 minute.)*

Monica sings in a high, almost fragile voice, but perfectly in tune. Everybody (the extras, the crew, Sally, Bob Greenhut, Max, and Sandy) listens in a reverent silence. This is the first time Monica has been back with Woody since *Manhattan*. At the end of her song, she gives us her little *Annie Hall* laugh ("Oh God!") and there is some applause. Woody goes to her and asks her to sing a more animated version.

For the second take, Monica is more at ease, and the effect is stronger. More applause at the end this time. It is strange and fascinating to see Monica Charles and Sally at the same time. They're so different, especially today, with Monica's white dress and Sally's baggy clothes. Sally still has her cold, and Max looks at me wondering what and why I am writing!

(3 takes; the last 2 are printed.) Completed at 10:35 A.M.

Monica Charles goes back to her room. Her part is over, and the pianist can go back to California.

10:45 A.M. Woody writes a few words on a sheet of paper, and gives it to the band leader.

Shot A175: The band leader introduces the evening and "our songbird," Monica Charles. *(30 seconds.)*

The band leader's new lines are much shorter. Max has gone out and bought *The New York Times;* yawning and bored, he starts reading it. "You've been great so far, Max," Woody says to him as he passes by.

(4 takes and 2 prints.) Completed at 11:00 A.M.

Now, a change of camera setting. The extras are sent back downstairs.

11:30 A.M. Woody's accountant, dressed in black tie, seems to have a part in the movie.

Shot 177: Irene is on the stage, telling everyone her wish that

1944 will bring peace and bring our boys home, once and for all.
(12 seconds.)

(4 takes and 3 prints.)

Now we get ready for the New Year's countdown. All the extras are brought in. Jimmy Mazzola distributes more hats and confetti.

Woody doesn't like the snap-on ties; Max and the accountant are given real ones. Tom continues to place the couples in the room. Woody goes to talk with his accountant, and Max is getting bored. A new cigarette girl is here, but she's not as pretty as Sally, who's now a radio star.

12:00 noon. Max complains that he has nothing to do, and Woody, after checking the frame, goes to talk to him.

Shot 181: While the band plays "Auld Lang Syne," the crowd, kissing and hugging, celebrates New Year's Eve. *(1 minute.)*

The crowd is asked to kiss, scream, and cheer, and they really get into it. Woody whistles, with no great results, to end the first take.

For the second take, Dickie gets creative. He asks Nicole, who is in the foreground, to give her date "a big long kiss" when he pans to her. The date likes it.

(2 takes and 2 prints.)

1:00 P.M. In the bar downstairs, it's "break for lunch" for the extras. The room is quiet and nearly empty. The accountant, glasses on, works on a file. Richie reads the *Daily News*, which announces that Orion's stock is going up. Either, they say, Orion has a film that's going to make a lot of money this year (*Hannah and Her Sisters*, for instance), or Cannon Film Group is going to take over.

We break for lunch at 1:10 P.M.

2:30 P.M. We're back on the set. Woody's accountant watches Carlo rehearsing the camera movement with Sally's stand-in. It seems he finds it all a little ridiculous, and has begun to tire of his experience as an actor.

3:00 P.M. The radio stars come in, the men in black tie and the women in beautiful, long dresses: Jessica Dragonette, all in green; the new singer (Maureen Sadusk), a little overweight but with a less comical face; Herbie Hanson and the Reba Man; the Tiny

Man, Nick Norris (Ronald Leir), and the Pretty Girl (Shelly Delaney) from his show; Roger and Irene; Bill Kern; and Max, in the scene at long last!

Woody seats them around the table. Jessica chats with her neighbor, the Reba Man, but Bill Kern isn't socializing with his neighbor, the Pretty Girl, so much. The accountant joins the group. Nick Norris, the Tiny Man (who looks bigger sitting), is at one end of the table, and Max is at the other end, between Jessica and the accountant.

To be shot is Sally's arrival at the table with her date, the Masked Avenger. Wallace Shawn (the Masked Avenger) was the "oversexed, brilliant kind of animal" whom women found devastating, in *Manhattan*.

3:30 P.M. The French-accented student from the adult-education class is visiting today with Jean Doumanian, a good friend of Woody's. Woody is having his picture taken with them by Brian, as always with that Zelig look.

Shot 176: Sally comes in with the Masked Avenger to the King Cole Room, where she used to work as a cigarette girl, and joins the table of the radio stars, now welcomed. *(20 seconds.)*

In fact, the accountant is the only one of them who really acts in the scene. He stands, gives his seat to the Avenger, and sits in the next chair. After two or three takes, he introduces himself to Sally, who hadn't recognized him.

Most of the problems come from the camera movement. Woody has all the actors deliver their lines sooner, before Sally and the Avenger sit.

(10 takes and 5 prints.)

While the next shot is being set up, the party is asked to wait on the side. Carlo is exhausted; he still has his cold and has been working hard and fast for the past three days, but he's happy because the dailies look good.

4:30 P.M. The radio stars are back around the table. Woody goes to crack a joke with Max, but Carlo is trying to check the framing; Tom asks Woody to move. Woody leaves, with a guilty smile. The radio performers are amused.

Nick Norris has put on a hat that makes him look even bigger. His diminutive size is still obvious, though, because he's sitting between tall Herbie Hanson and the overweight singer.

Shot 178: The radio personalities are drinking and laughing,

and enjoying each other's company. The Masked Avenger announces that he's already drunk. *(26 seconds.)*

Dickie calls Nick Norris "little fellow," but Nick doesn't seem
to mind. No problem with this shot. Max is, of course, entertaining everybody. Hidden behind some flowers, the Salad Sisters are
enjoying the scene.

(6 takes and 3 prints.)

5:30 P.M. Carlo is setting up the last shot of the sequence,
where the whole party decides, on Sally's suggestion, to go to see
the roof.

In the bar downstairs, the atmosphere is a little like the one of
Buñuel's *Exterminating Angel*, cups, glasses half empty, and plates
with scraps of food everywhere. The men have taken their jackets
off and the women have lifted their dresses over their knees. In a
corner, the Reba Man is cracking some jokes with Herbie Hanson,
who loves it. Barbara and Little Joe have joined the party.

6:00 P.M. Shot 179A: The radio stars are still enjoying themselves. Sally suggests going to the roof, where there is a beautiful
view of the city. The Masked Avenger wonders how she knows
about the roof. Everybody decides to go have a look. *(40 seconds.)*

The "little fellow" is out: One of the cameras is set at his
place. While the first camera follows the radio stars, the second
one films the background.

(4 takes and 3 prints.)

The party is over. Woody kisses Sally good-bye, thanks his
accountant, and shakes hands with Max, then cleans his hand on
his sweater.

We get a few wild tracks of the background, babbling and applauding.

And "It's a wrap!" at 7:00 P.M.

Wednesday, January 8, 1986

*Ron belts Libya, and orders Yanks to pull out. "I think he's not
only a barbarian, but he's flaky." Ron says of Qaddafi. (New York
Times)*

A fifth force, a function of the mass and the atomic composi-

tion of a given object, challenges both the findings of Galileo and a fundamental element of Einstein's general theory of relativity. (New York Times)

And when Pegeen Fitzgerald began to broadcast her radio show from her home with husband, Ed, in 1937, Eleanor Roosevelt went to their apartment to watch.

Pegeen's topics are eclectic. An electrician walks in during the program; she says he looks like a delightful man, "very charming," and interviews him. She discusses a fat man working on the veranda who got stuck crawling back in the window; the exciting social life of her neighbor, bachelor George Porgie; her cleaning woman, Mrs. Woo; her apartment decor; or her cats. Pegeen has 390 homeless cats and 118 dogs on her Last Post Estate in Falls Village, Connecticut. These are the things she discusses on the air.

One day, their live-in housekeeper, Frances, died right before air time, and the corpse lay in the next room during the show. "I made no mention of it," Pegeen says. "I didn't want to upset them." Another day, Ed became so angry during a breakfast show that he went back to bed, leaving her to solo.

Ed died in 1982. But Pegeen goes on daily. Among other issues discussed today are the Ice Palace construction, Albert Einstein's cat, T. S. Eliot plays, and Mrs. Woo's whereabouts. (New York Times)

8:30 A.M. The Manhattan Center on Thirty-fourth Street, on the eighth floor. We're back in the theater where Sally used to work as a page, in a small upstairs studio, to shoot Uncle Walt (sequence 94) and the *Future Stars* show (sequence 69). Popeye is already at work on the piano.

The holding area is just next door, on the balcony of the huge theater/ballroom of the Manhattan Center. The Ventriloquist (one of Broadway Danny Rose's clients, the stutterer) is combing his puppet's hair. The puppet is appearing on the *Future Stars* show.

Good day for the gambling department. The spaces on the Super Bowl pool are filling up, and Louis has sold almost all the cards in fifteen minutes.

9:30 A.M. The *Future Star* girl (Danielle Ferland), in a pink dress, comes in so Woody and Carlo can decide the framing. Behind her, there is a big billboard for WHOLE WHEAT CEREAL WITH DELICIOUS NEW FLAVOR, "IT'S BITE SIZE." Carlo suggests a camera angle. Woody changes it, wanting it wider. But Carlo prefers his. Woody accedes, and lets him work. And Carlo starts complaining: "No chandeliers, no mirrors! No funny. Get another cameraman."

10:00 A.M. Shot 94: The *Future Star* girl sings "Let's All Sing Like the Birdies Sing." *(34 seconds.)*
The pianist plays off-camera. The little girl is a professional, and looks at ease when she finishes. Before he says, "Cut," she turns to Woody for his reaction.
Woody: "Is that all?"
The girl (a little panicked): "Am I supposed to sing it twice?"
Everyone laughs and applauds. She's good. Woody asks her "to give a bigger performance" for the second take.
(3 takes and 2 prints.)
Woody goes to thank her and shakes her hand, a sign he has liked her. "Nice to have met you," she tells him before she leaves.

10:30 A.M. The *Vogue* writer reads *The New York Times*, sitting next to Uncle Walt (Richard Shull), who is having coffee. The Ventriloquist is still here, but Woody has decided not to use his puppet for the *Future Star* show. Popeye sits next to him, in silence, until he is asked to tune another piano.
Popeye puts all his instruments on the piano and begins. The boys watch. It's fun seeing him work. He really only comes alive when he tunes a piano.
There's a certain carelessness in Jeffrey's outfit today. His jeans have a hole in the back pocket, his jacket looks like he cut the sleeves off with a kitchen knife, the metallic cowboy tie is OK, but the light-brown shirt doesn't match the rust-colored sweater, and he hasn't shaved.

11:00 A.M. Carlo is ready, but Popeye is not. The room is small and the piano loud. Carlo is not happy and greets each chord with a "Madonna!"
Woody checks the camera, and makes some adjustments, which Carlo OK's.

11:30 A.M. The piano is still being tuned. Everybody is a little overwhelmed by the noise. But Popeye is unshakable. Ken asks him how much longer it will take. Ten minutes, the tuner announces.

The past three days have been exhausting for his department, Jeffrey tells me. They had the black ties and long dresses to alter for the two hundred extras. And Monday, when Woody recast the radio singer, five people worked overnight to make alterations on the costume.

12:00 noon. We're ready to shoot. Dick Hyman has composed the music, and is checking it with the pianist. Uncle Walt, seated at the on-camera piano, can sing, but does not know how to play. Woody wants to shoot directly, but Uncle Walt asks for a rehearsal.

Shot 69: It's the end of the show, and time for the kids to go to bed. But before going, Uncle Walt sings the "Uncle Walt Squirrel Rangers' Club Song." At the end, Uncle Walt reminds the kids "to pay attention to Mom and Dad, and to eat all your cereal. . . . Good night, little Squirrel Rangers!" He waits a moment, then, turning to the technicians in the booth, says: "That ought to hold the little bastards!" But he's still on the air! *(1 minute, 36 seconds.)*

Originally, Woody had wanted to break the shot into two parts, first a wide shot, then a close-up. But after the second take, he decides it would be safer with two cameras, so the cuts will match perfectly.

After the fourth take, Woody is satisfied. But Uncle Walt begs for another try: He feels he didn't say "little bastards" right.

(7 takes and 3 prints.)

Woody goes to thank Uncle Walt and the technicians. Then Louis asks him to pick up the cards. He does so, then races out. Jane wins!

We break for lunch at 12:45 P.M.

3:00 P.M. The River Diner on Eleventh Avenue and Thirty-seventh Street is a small snack bar built in a trailer in the middle of a no-man's-land. To be shot is a customer listening to Polly Phelps's story.

Carlo is happy because last summer he shot *Offbeat* here (Martin Scorsese's *After Hours* was also shot here) and the owner recognizes him, immediately bringing him a cold Heineken. I ask him how he got into movies. The youngest of eight children, he was raised in the film world. His father repaired cameras, and his brother managed a movie studio. In the early 1940s, all the men were off to war and he got a job, at age fourteen, as focus operator on Visconti's *Ossessione* (1942). One day, Visconti offered him one hundred lira if he could keep the camera in focus during a long traveling shot of Clara Calamai singing. He did it, got the money, and decided to stay in the business.

3:30 P.M. The place is tiny and crowded. Carlo is almost ready. The *Vogue* writer is not pleased because he has had to run back and forth from one location to the other with Santo, and he didn't get much lunch. Dickie is sleeping among the equipment.

Shot 168C: A woman customer listening, rapt, to the Polly Phelps broadcast. *(5 seconds.)*
(2 takes and 2 prints.)

"It's a wrap!" at 4:00 P.M.

Thursday, January 9, 1986

Mother Teresa persuades Greenwich Village to allow the St. Veronica's church to open its rectory to fourteen prisoners who are dying of AIDS. The first three have arrived from the state penitentiary at Ossining, just released by Governor Mario Cuomo. (New York Times)
    Ron freezes Libyan assets. (New York Times)
    And Jean Tugend dies at eighty-two. She was producer Harry Tugend's wife, and a general manager for Jed Harris and Billy Rose.

8:45 A.M. At the New Yorker hotel on Eighth Avenue and Thirty-fourth Street, we're back to *The Herbie Hanson Show*. The new set is entirely different. While the previous one was built in a studio, this is a real theater/ballroom, with Roman columns and a promenade. It is much larger. The *Guess that Tune* and *Amateur Talent Hunt* shows were shot in this hotel during Christmas week.

9:10 A.M. Upstairs, the "casting nightmare" is less pathetic than last time. The holding area is bigger (three huge reception rooms with Chinese murals) and the more crippled of the extras are not being used this time around. The problem is that half of them are OK, and the other half are mentally slow. With the latter

group, you have to take time with each word, repeating everything. It's sometimes difficult to discern one from the other, and
you find yourself talking to one of them slowly, as if to a little
child, until he cuts you off, saying, "It's OK, dear. I understand."

Ten-minute warning. "If you want to go to the
bathroom . . ." screams Richie. The one hundred extras hurl
down the stairs all at once.

10:00 A.M. Woody has simplified the shot. The audience will
already be in the theater. The three paid laughers are brought in
first, then the musicians, and finally the audience. The difference is
that now the crowd members are no longer crippled, but only a
little misshapen. There are a lot of old people, too.

Herbie is rehearsing his jokes on a corner of the stage. The
conductor of the band is still the film's music arranger, Dick
Hyman's assistant. The *Vogue* magazine writer is having a late
breakfast. Dickie asks me (it's been awhile since he's done this) if
I've been to Pierre au Tunnel. When I tell him I haven't had the
chance yet, his opinion of me seems to drop another notch.

10:30 A.M. We are shooting with two cameras.

Shot R106: It's the same as the first time. The announcer introduces the show, "The Associated Life Insurance Company presents . . ." The audience applauds, the band plays the jingle, then
he reads the commercial, and Herbie makes his entrance.

The audience is in a good mood; they even applaud Tom's
jokes. After the first take, Woody asks the announcer to be even
more dramatic when he reads the commercial. Woody doesn't
seem very happy with Herbie's entrance, but he applauds him with
the crowd.

Woody cuts the fourth and goes to talk with Herbie.

For the fifth take, Woody lets the cameras run, but he is nervous.

Another take is done. But Woody is still unsatisfied. He asks
for Santo, but Santo is gone. We move on.

(*5 takes and 3 prints.*) Completed at 10:45 P.M.

The audience goes back upstairs.

11:10 A.M. Shot R106A/R106B: Herbie cracks a few "good"
jokes like, "The traffic is so heavy in midtown Manhattan that
Broadway looks like one big parking lot," and "I saw one woman

stick her hand out the window, I thought she was signaling for a
turn . . . but she was drying her nail polish." At first, of course,
nobody laughs. Then the paid laughers go into action. And before
long, they're stealing the show from Herbie.

Herbie is onstage. Woody sits next to Kay and her script in the
fifth row. The audience is gone. Herbie is telling his jokes to an
all-but-empty room. Then Woody goes over the jokes with Herbie, helping him with his delivery by repeating the lines, the camera already rolling. Herbie says to the crowd, who are now
reacting to the paid laughers, "May I remind you there is a show
up here!" Woody: "Bigger. . . . Angrier. . . . With this kind of a
look." The lines are repeated several times, the camera still rolling.
And Woody seems to get what he wants. Herbie to the paid laughers: "At least they like me in section four!" The camera is still
rolling. "Keep going," Woody says, and he shows the facial expressions he's looking for. "Say something like, 'Jesus!'" It seems
to work at the end, and Woody laughs.

"Let's stop for a moment." Woody goes back to his script to
double-check. But it's OK; he has what he needs, and it's over at
11:20 A.M.

Herbie Hanson, in real life, is a stand-up comic, not an actor.
That's why Woody directs him so painstakingly to get exactly
what he wants. In half an hour, Woody's mood has totally
changed; he now does a little tap-dance number for Jane and
Jeffrey.

11:45 A.M. The audience comes back in.

Shot R106C: After having gotten over the paid laughers, the
audience is back with Herbie, ready to give him a chance. Herbie is
starting all over again, but a man runs from backstage, pushes
him, and begins to read the special bulletin: ". . . in response to
the Japanese bombing of Pearl Harbor, President Roosevelt has declared war on the Axis . . ." The audience begins to run in all
directions. Herbie is stunned, but he still tries to get in a few good
ones.

After the second take, Carlo mentions that the audience is not
leaving quickly enough, making the scene a little static. Some
chairs are removed so the audience can really run out.

(3 takes and 3 prints.)

The audience goes back upstairs. The cameras are going to
focus in the other direction now, and the lighting has to be

changed. The band and the conductor are released. As before, the band has been faking the tune ("Fine and Dandy").

12:45 P.M. Woody arrives to check the camera framing, Baby Dylan in his arms and Sally at his side. Sally, not yet in costume, wears one of her usual oversize outfits. Baby Dylan is having as much fun as ever. While Woody works, the two ladies go to sit with Jimmy Frederick. Sally gives me a nice hello smile, and Baby Dylan starts flirting with Jimmy.

We break for lunch.
The next shot will be done first thing this afternoon.

2:30 P.M. Woody and Carlo are working on the composition of the frame, placing and replacing the extras. The room is not full and they have to cheat with the frame, making it look crowded and visually right.

I am sitting in one of the musicians' chairs on the stage. Woody turns suddenly in my direction, saying to Carlo, "Just an idea . . ." I start to move. "No, no. You can stay here," Woody tells me. This happens periodically, such as when I was on the toilet seat in Grandma Brummer's bathroom, and since we don't often talk directly, it's sometimes a little disconcerting.

2:45 P.M. We're waiting for Sally. The Salad Sisters are working to "make her prettier." Dickie wants to check the framing. "Kenny, take Sally's seat, and try to look like a blonde," Tom says. One of the paid laughers cracks a joke to the two other paid laughers, who, silently, laugh. Woody is just in front of me (I'm almost on his back) reading the Daily News.

3:00 P.M. Shot R106D: The camera looks at the audience over Herbie's shoulder. He cracks two jokes; they don't react.
Woody sits on a stool, and Tom is in the director's chair. The camera rolls, but just before action, Woody stops. He wants more glasses on the extras' faces. Wardrobe acts. We start to roll again, but Woody cuts one more time; he doesn't like the way Jeffrey has distributed the glasses. Here comes the "glasses crisis." Woody gives out the glasses himself, followed by Jeffrey with a basket full of them. Jeffrey is very tense; he takes this kind of little thing to

heart. But Woody doesn't think anything of it; he just wants the glasses distributed differently!
(4 takes and 2 prints.) Completed at 3:10 P.M.

3:20 P.M. Now we're back for the laughers' symphony.
Shot R106E: One camera takes in the whole room. The other one focuses on Sally and the three paid laughers. It's the same action as before. One paid laugher, then two, then three go into action. The crowd reacts to them, applauds.
"I'll pretend to tell a joke," Woody tells the crowd, standing on the stage, holding his script. He conducts with his hands and his face, telling them exactly the length and the degree he needs. Sally does a great laugh at the end, arms outstretched, just as Woody mimes to her.
(3 takes and 3 prints.) Completed at 3:35 P.M.

3:45 P.M. While Carlo finishes his work, Woody goes behind me to play the xylophone. It's an awkward situation again. Should I compliment him? But he doesn't play very well!
Shot R106F: The exit of the crowd after the declaration of war, seen from another angle.
(1 take and 1 print.)
Woody: "That's fine with me."
Tom: "You don't want to do another for security?"
Woody: "No. With the two cameras and the other point of view, it should be OK."
Tom: "You promise me we won't reshoot?"
Woody: "This—no."
And he dashes out.

"It's a wrap!" at 4:00 P.M.

Friday, January 10, 1986

The U.S. backs away from asking Western Europe for curbs on Libya. Shultz says the Allies balk. (New York Times)

8:45 A.M. In the empty, sixty-foot-high Grand Foyer of Radio City Music Hall, Andrew is getting a guided tour from Woody. We'll be here for two days. To be shot today are the dreamed cocktail party where the Jackhammers (Irving Selbst and Hope

Sacharoff) run into Max Harris (sequence 19), and also a scene where a few women in a beauty parlor listen to the Tonino broadcast.

It's the usual routine. Dickie is resting in a comfortable armchair in the Grand Lounge, and Louis is selling cards and also working on the Super Bowl pool; a number of boxes are not yet sold. Woody bought one for himself and one for Andrew. But Louis is confident that next week, when we're in the studio with all the boys there, the boxes will go fast.

It is really exciting to have all of Radio City Music Hall to ourselves. It was built in the late 1920s and the quality of the construction is amazing; it was beautifully restored in 1979. The two twenty-nine-foot chandeliers, the twenty-four-carat-gold-leaf ceiling, the marble panels from Africa, and the bronze on the doors of the auditorium are elegant. But perhaps most extraordinary and unexpected are the restrooms and the lounges, decorated with beautiful murals and furniture. The only regret we have is that the Rockettes are not onstage rehearsing. The stage is currently being prepared for the Reverend Dr. Martin Luther King, Jr., birthday tribute, set for the twentieth of this month, featuring, among others, Tito Puente.

9:45 A.M. Because we couldn't get in the building before 8:00 A.M., the holding area is located a few doors down, at the Women's National Republican Club, on West Fifty-first Street. In the lobby there is, naturally, a huge, colorful portrait of a very grave Ron, along with an announcement of yesterday's schedule:

At noon: The women's propeller club in the ballroom.

At 2:00 P.M.: The opera club in the solarium.

At 4:00 P.M.: The Irish institute in the Lincoln room.

We are using two big rooms upstairs. For both the beauty-parlor scene and the party, Jeffrey went for style. The costumes are beautiful, and even more beautiful are the hats; Jeffrey likes hats. There are some nice women, too, but nothing compared to the USO girls. Mrs. Jackhammer is really impressed. But she is also a little worried because she can't find her shoes. They were too tight and somebody was supposed to stretch them, but now she can't find the person!

10:15 A.M. The party is going to be shot in the Ladies' Lounge, just off the Grand Lounge. Given the murals, the eight lamps, the mirrors, and a few sofas, Santo has only to add flowers and a table in the middle to give the lounge a perfect cocktail-party atmosphere.

Jimmy Mazzola has brought the drinks and food: Boxes of petits fours (with one for the crew), Champagne Cordon Rouge, Scotch, martinis . . . The table is being dressed and everything prepared so the Jackhammers' dream to meet Max Harris can come true.

10:40 A.M. The extras are seated in chairs grouped in a corner of the Grand Lounge. Max Harris (Marc Goodson) and the Jackhammers are staying aloof over by the "dancing girl" statue. Max Harris sits in the director's chair, smoking a cigar, and checking out the room with a blasé look. He has come with a very chic friend (blue blazer, striped shirt with club tie, blue-and-white shoes) and doesn't socialize with the Jackhammers. Mr. Jackhammer is, in the real world, in the men's-clothing business, but because of his strong character face, does bit parts here and there. He was in James Goldstone's *The Gang that Couldn't Shoot Straight,* and was an agent in *Broadway Danny Rose* until the scene was cut.

Woody comes to check the Jackhammers' outfits, then those of the extras. They are lined up, men on one side, women on the other, and like a general, with Jeffrey at his side, Woody reviews. Then Woody goes to the set to discuss the camera movement with Carlo. Tom calls for silence; the set is cleared. And Woody and Carlo start their discussion, consisting mostly of gestures, onomatopoeic mumbling, and some whispering. They both seem to need and enjoy these quiet, serious times where they try to "feel" the room.

11:15 A.M. The Jackhammers try to start a conversation with Max Harris, but Max is standoffish. Ethel Jackhammer is a subdued person, always following her husband and not entering the conversations. I compliment her on her hat. We share an admiration for Jeffrey. "And he's such a sweet man, too," she says.

I ask Jane a third time if I might see some of the dailies. She tells me she hasn't gotten an answer yet.

The extras are brought to the set. It's funny how when the boys recognize an extra from another film, it's always a pretty girl. Jimmy Mazzola serves the champagne. Once again, Carlo has used only the existing lighting: two chandeliers, the eight lamps on the side. But he adds a small spotlight hung from the ceiling for the Jackhammers and Max Harris when they start their dialogue.

Ethel's hat is being changed. It was too beautiful. They should look like "they don't belong in this world," Jeffrey insists. Suddenly I am being drafted by the gambling department to hold a cable. "It's about time!" Ken comments.

12:30 P.M. Shot 19: Listening to *Breakfast with Irene and Roger*, the Jackhammers begin to dream, and then here they are among the beautiful people, but not very at ease. Their breakfast sausages are replaced by champagne and caviar. And here is Max Harris coming over to talk to them. "I'm going to do Eugene O'Neill's new play. It's a searing piece of work about lost souls in a waterfront dive and their self-deception." Jackhammer tries to rise to the situation. "How intensely profound—right, Ethel?" *(36 seconds.)*

The problems are with the camera movement and the blocking of the action. The actors have to enter the frame at the right moment to give a fluidity to the image's changing composition. The camera wanders through the party, Fellini-style, before finding the Jackhammers. Max Harris delivers his line perfectly, and the Jackhammers easily manage to look as if they don't belong to this world.

(9 takes and 4 prints.) Completed at 1:00 P.M.

1:15 P.M. The beauty parlor is in the third-mezzanine powder room. Once again, given the beautiful murals (Kuniyoshi's) and the mirrors (Deskey's), Santo has only to add a few pieces of black lacquer furniture to create a beautiful new location. Woody seems satisfied.

Tom: "What are we doing now?"

Woody: "Lunch."

Tom: "You want to have lunch?"

Woody (leaving): "Movies! It's not just suffering, it's torture!"

We break for lunch.

3:00 P.M. Ray has started lighting the Grand Foyer for Monday. We have only one shot this afternoon, with no sound; the gambling department has left for the weekend. Adriana comes to say good-bye; she is going to Paris to see the dailies of *Max, Mon*

Amour. And Woody's nephew, his sister's son, is visiting us with his girlfriend.

4:00 P.M. Carlo is ready. The extras are brought into the parlor. There are five patrons—not very beautiful but very chic—and four beauticians. The camera is in a small corridor, and, since Carlo is using the reflections in the mirrors, no one but the actors can be in the room. It becomes crowded. Carlo tosses out "Madonna!" and "Take it easy!" a few times, then threatens to kill a few people. Woody's visitors are impressed.

Woody is very social with his guests, explaining that it's not a very interesting day to watch because of the short scenes and the lack of directing. The eighteen-year-old nephew is shy and respectful with Uncle Woody.

4:30 P.M. Shot 2G: The camera pans around the beauty parlor, the clients listening to the Tonino story. *(20 seconds.)*

Woody asks one attendant to tune the radio, but nothing else. Jimmy Mazzola serves the rest of the champagne in the back during the take. It helps Carlo take it easier (us, too).

(3 takes and 3 prints.)

"It's a wrap!" at 4:50 P.M.

Monday, January 13, 1986   *Eleventh Week*

Early Friday morning, Donald Manes, the Queens borough president known as "The King of Queens," was found bleeding in his car near Shea Stadium with a slashed wrist and an injured leg. City police had stopped the weaving car, behind the wheel of which was a semiconscious Manes. It is not clear yet if he was victim of a crime or if he inflicted the wounds himself.

Saturday Manes' condition delayed the inquiry. Ed hastened to Manes' hospital bed. He kissed him on the forehead. "Don't worry about anything, Donny," he said, "we all love you."

Sunday, Manes was moved to the cardiac unit.

Now, on Monday morning, his knife cuts appear self-inflicted. His wristwatch had been removed and his socks rolled down. The cuts had been made inside the car by a sharp kitchen knife found there. Manes says it happened between midnight and 1:00 A.M.

Don has been weak since an operation to remove a polyp last November, Ed notes. (New York Times *and* Daily News)

City offers help in bribe probe. (Daily News)

The shuttle should be in space after seven delays. The astronauts will launch an RCA satellite. (New York Times)

Two hundred forty-five Bolivia drug police are held in a three-day siege by cocaine growers. (New York Times)

After Big Paul's death last December on East Forty-sixth Street, John Gotti, an ex-convict, is said to have taken control of the Gambino crime organization. (New York Times)

The "Mighty Mike" has struck again. Saturday night, Mike Tyson tied Marciano's KO record. (Daily News)

And Czech poet Jaroslav Seifert, 1984 Nobel Prize winner, died Friday.

8:45 A.M. We're back at Radio City Music Hall. Two sequences will be shot. The first one is part of the series in which songs remind Joe of people and events from his youth (sequence 102). Today Bea and her new date, Chester, take Little Joe to a movie at Radio City Music Hall. The second sequence is another person listening to the Tonino broadcast, a rich woman in her bathtub.

Woody, in dark-blue corduroy trousers, green Shetland sweater, and those shoes, whistles and walks alone in the Grand Foyer, using his hand for the frame, looking for different camera movements and angles, while Carlo, with Ray, Hammer, and Bobby Ward helping, finishes the lighting. The Grand Foyer is taking on a new and nice look. The *Fountain of Youth* (a sixty-by-thirty-foot mural by Ezra Winter) over the huge staircase begins to come alive.

9:45 A.M. There is big news today. It was kept secret from us all until the last minute, but the deal was closed last Thursday. Woody has chosen one of his longest collaborators for the role of Chester—Jimmy Sabat! Dressed by Jeffrey in a double-breasted pale-blue suit, yellow British shoes, and striped shirt, and with heavy makeup on his face and grease in his hair, Jimmy feels perfectly uncomfortable.

10:15 A.M. Having been dressed and made up at the Women's National Republican Club, the 125 extras are parked in chairs in the Grand Lounge downstairs. There are men and women of all ages and kids with their mothers. They have started waiting. Jeffrey is distributing the accessories—watches, bags, jewels, gloves, glasses.

10:30 A.M. The Music Hall pages are first brought to the set and stationed on the huge staircase. Woody tries them in different spots—along the left wall of the Grand Foyer, only on the staircase, one every two steps, and so on. Bea, all in pink, and Little Joe, in knickers, check the camera. Now the audience is brought in in little groups and placed here and there.

Baby Dylan arrives with her mother and goes directly to Woody's arms. Woody continues working as he holds her. He carries her low, and from a distance it looks a little strange. But Baby Dylan doesn't seem to mind. Putting her head on Woody's chest, she sucks her thumb, listening to Woody's heartbeat.

Finally, there are no pages on the stairs, and a lot fewer people in the middle of the Grand Foyer. Woody looks through the camera and again adjusts the position of each group.

Sally is really overdoing it today. As soon as she returns to real life, she goes to the other extreme. As usual, she has no makeup and her hair is uncombed, but she now has glasses at the end of her nose and braces on her teeth. And still, she looks charming!

10:45 A.M. One of the two huge chandeliers is being lowered, and Ray is changing some of its bulbs. A friend of Woody and Sally's is visiting and holds Baby Dylan. Woody looks a little jealous. He starts making faces to attract attention, but Baby Dylan, for once, is unimpressed. So Woody noisily kisses her belly, and, at last, gets a smile.

11:05 A.M. It's the last chance for makeup and wardrobe before "pictures." Jimmy Sabat complains because Romaine is putting too much grease on his hair. Now she puts some black on his bald spot. He doesn't realize what she's doing, but everybody else enjoys it. Jimmy is very low-key, never raises his voice, always does his job quietly and professionally, and never calls attention to himself. That makes the situation all the funnier.

11:30 A.M. Shot F102: Bea, Chester, and Little Joe enter the lobby. We discover the Grand Foyer along with them. They walk to the staircase. *(20 seconds.)*

No problems with the acting.
(2 takes and 2 prints.) Completed at 11:40 A.M.

12:00 noon. After discussing the possibility of a shot showing
the trio's point of view of the room, Woody decides to put the
camera halfway up the stairs. Carlo likes the idea because there are
some mirrors he'll be able to play with.

Jeffrey's outfit today consists of black boots, black leather trousers, black silk shirt, black tie (with two small spots of yellow), and
a waistcoat of an undetermined dark color.

12:30 P.M. Ezra's sister is in the crowd. The boys are putting
black tape on the handrail to kill the reflections, and Brian is taking

pictures of Woody talking to Kay and Ezra. And though no one is going to tell him so, none of us is convinced that Jimmy is a great actor. The last time he appeared in a movie was *Serpico*, he tells me.

Shot F102A: We see the trio as they approach the staircase, coming from the middle of the Grand Foyer. They climb the stairs. *(18 seconds.)*

(5 takes and 4 prints.)

And we break for lunch at 12:50 P.M.

Walking down Sixth Avenue to buy a newspaper after lunch, I come across Woody and Bea returning to the Music Hall. Woody gives me a smile and a "You here! How come?" face. Running behind are Tom, Jane, and Ezra. "Hurry up! You're going to be late," Ezra yells to me.

2:45 P.M. We are on the staircase leading from the Grand Lounge to the Grand Foyer to shoot the scene after the trio's arrival, when they arrive at the top of the stairs.

Shot F102B: They climb the stairs to the second floor, then walk onto the balcony and exit the frame on the right. *(24 seconds.)*

There are no problems other than getting a good blocking with the actors and the extras passing by. For the third take, after the trio exits the frame, Woody has Little Joe come back for another look at the immense lobby.

(5 takes and 4 prints.)

3:30 P.M. We are in a hall on the third mezzanine. Woody proposes an ambitious shot of Bea, Chester, and Little Joe arriving from the end of the corridor with other people passing by. As they approach, the camera dollies back in advance of them. At the end of the hall, the camera stops and pans as they walk by, with one of the grand chandeliers seen through the railing. The camera continues to pan, first losing them, then picking them up from behind on a mirror as they walk away. Carlo needs two hours, and that makes Tom nervous because the rich woman in the bathtub will have to go on overtime. So Woody cuts the end of the shot, the reflection of the trio in the mirror, and stops the shot on the chandelier. But before doing that, we go back downstairs for a point of view of the trio in the Grand Foyer.

4:15 P.M. The extras are brought in and placed in the Grand Foyer. Woody checks the camera, but he doesn't like the shot. He seems suddenly out of sorts, as though he has decided to not care about the shooting. While Carlo works on another setting, Woody chats with Bea, Brian, and Andrew.

4:30 P.M. Everything is at a standstill. The one hundred extras are in position and Carlo has finished setting the shot, but Woody still doesn't feel it. Nobody knows exactly what is happening. Woody appears to have lost interest in the whole thing. Everybody waits.

The same thing happened on *Annie Hall*, I'm told. It was a scene in an amusement park on Coney Island, with two hundred extras; everyone stood around all morning, and finally nothing was shot.

5:00 P.M. Woody comes back to life. Most of the background extras are sent back to the holding area. We keep only nineteen of them and the ushers. Woody, with a smile of relief, goes to Little Joe. "This is completely different," he tells the boy.

The idea now is this: The song reminds Joe of the day he went to Radio City Music Hall, but as with all memories, it comes back to him distorted, idealized. He remembers a Radio City Music Hall they'd had all to themselves, with the ushers lined up waiting for them, with the Grand Foyer looking unrealistically beautiful.

5:15 P.M. Shot F102D: The lobby is empty, except for the ushers lined up on the side. Bea, Chester, and Little Joe walk through. *(15 seconds.)*

(4 takes and 2 prints.)

Now we move back to reshoot the first establishing shot, as they enter the lobby, with the Grand Foyer empty this time.

5:40 P.M. The atmosphere is more relaxed now. Bea tells us that Chester/Jimmy is very good because during each take, he finds something different to talk about. For the last take, he was inviting her to go to the races. The nineteen ushers are lined up along the left wall and on the steps. Woody, checking the camera regularly, goes to place them exactly where he wants them. The Grand Foyer, with the line of ushers standing to attention on the side, wonderfully lit and empty, indeed has a surreal beauty.

It's almost 6:00 P.M. and Chester, who is a masculine South American like Porfirio, needs a shave. Fern covers his dark beard with powder. Woody sits alone in a corner, as if exhausted by too many emotions. "Are you ready, Woody?" Tom screams. "Yeah!" Woody screams back, staying seated, and giving me a tired smile.

We are going to reshoot all the scenes done in the morning, this time with only the trio. But Woody has everything printed (the scenes with all the extras), in case the last-minute idea doesn't work.

"It's a wrap!" at 7:00 P.M.

Something new happened today in Woody's career: He started reshooting on the same day!

Tuesday, January 14, 1986

Manes: "I was kidnapped." He says two men abducted and beat him. (New York Times)

"I am the boss of my family—my wife and kids at home," *John Gotti said as he arrived at Brooklyn federal court to face a variety of racketeering charges yesterday.* (Daily News)

9:45 A.M. We're on West Forty-fourth Street, between Broadway and Eighth Avenue, in front of Sardi's, next to the Helen Hayes theater. The theater has been transformed to "The Little Theater." The play is now *Arsenic and Old Lace*, a new comedy by Joseph Kesselring, produced by Howard Lindsay and Russel Crouse, with Boris Karloff, Allyn Joslyn, Josephine Hull, Jean Adair, and John Alexander. On the same side of the street, all the signposts that would have been in the shot have been taken out, and a huge poster for "Panama Hattie" hides the modern background. Jimmy Mazzola has lined up his cars. We are in 1942 to shoot a pickup shot of Sally walking in the street while she tells us her story (sequence 143). For the moment, the modern traffic passes through.

10:30 A.M. The holding area is inside Sardi's. The receptionist looks like Madonna, and her sweater opens enough to suggest she might be a "Communist." Breakfast is being served at the bar on the left. In the second-floor dining room, the fifty extras for to-day's scenes are ready and waiting. On the third floor, in the Renaissance reception hall, with old Broadway stills everywhere on the walls, the wardrobe and makeup departments are tidying up.

Carlo tells me Antonioni has called him about his new film. He should be ready to shoot in April or May, and he's coming to New York in February. It will be an American production, and the prospective actors are Jessica Lange and Richard Gere.

11:00 A.M. It's freezing. The dolly track is set up on the sidewalk and Sally's stand-in, an attractive red-haired young woman, waits in front of Sardi's so Woody can check the camera. Woody is back in his huge gray parka, and Pop is visiting.

11:30 A.M. The extras are in position. The traffic between Eighth Avenue and Broadway is stopped.

Shot A143: Sally walks past The Little Theater and Sardi's. *(13 seconds.)*

(6 takes and 4 prints.)

Before he dashes out, Woody is handed a copy of next Sunday's *New York Times Magazine* with a picture of him on the cover and the headline AUTEUR, AUTEUR: THE CREATIVE MIND OF WOODY ALLEN. We are stationed just in front of a *New York Times* truck garage.

We move to Grand Central Station for the next shot.

12:30 P.M. Grand Central Station, tracks 34 and 35. The entrance has been dressed with an arch of little lights. In the hall leading to the train, a few lamps have been hung, along with a few posters: YOU'LL BE HAPPIER IN NASH; DON'T LET THAT SHADOW INK THEM. BUY WAR BONDS (with three children holding war toys); and the one that was on the RCA building the first day, WAR BONDS: TO HAVE AND TO HOLD.

We have the track to ourselves, and a rope barricade has been set up. People have begun to stop and look. Tom tells them that nothing will happen for at least another hour. But there are plenty of people around because it is lunch time, and the rumor that a Woody Allen movie is being shot has already spread.

We are here to reshoot the pickup shot of the sailors we did on the deck of the *Intrepid*, to be edited to "I'll Be Seeing You" (sequence 107). Originally it was a girl kissing a sailor, but the girl was not used on the *Intrepid*. She is back to kiss several soldiers, but now she is Sally. Woody has written a new scene consisting of several shots, still to be edited to the song.

1:30 P.M. There are a lot of spectators now, blocking the way for the real passengers. Some have brought lunch (pizza, sandwiches) and are watching; it's noisy.

Sally is going "to make our boys happy." She's going to start with a soldier, continue with a sailor, and conclude with a marine. For the moment, she is still in the hands of the Salad Sisters. The boys are ready, and waiting . . .

2:00 P.M. Shot R107: It's after the declaration of war. All our boys are leaving for the battlefield. Under the arch of lights, Sally and Charlie the soldier stand arm in arm, looking in each other's eyes. "Are you going to wait for me?" asks Charlie. "Do you love me?" "Oh, Charlie!" Sally answers. "Nobody ever made love to me like this!" The camera zooms in as they kiss. *(30 seconds.)*

For openers, there is not enough smoke from the trains. "Jimmy Mazzola!" Then Tom has to ask for silence between each take, explaining to the crowd that we are recording dialogue. The public is cooperative enough, but they can't hear the lines, and they're a little disappointed by the lack of action and the brevity of the shot.

Sally's stand-in, the pretty redhead, plays a passerby in the scene. Charlie (Danny Aiello, Jr.) is the son of the actor who played Sally's husband in *Purple Rose of Cairo*. Charlie, though tall and strong like his dad, has a kind of baby face, and seems a little embarrassed to be kissing Sally. It's funny to see them arm in arm, waiting for action. Sally acts a little motherly with Charlie, but Woody doesn't seem to mind.

After the fifth take, we have to stop because a train is arriving on our track. And the real travelers exit the train through the set, not realizing at first what all the lighting, the crew, the period costumes, and the crowd behind the barricade mean. More and more people get off the train, and Woody, seeing that and feeling that he already has a few good takes, decides to move on.

(5 takes and 3 prints.) Completed at 2:30 P.M.

3:00 P.M. Sally has changed clothes and is ready for the next man.

Shot A109: Sally is now with Tom the sailor. Same blocking, same sort of dialogue ("Oh, Tom! Nobody . . ."), and same action, with the zoom in on the kiss. *(16 seconds.)*

Tom (Garrett Brown) is at ease, chewing gum and talking non-stop to Sally between takes. She looks impressed. Tom is the relaxed type. On "Action," Tom gives Sally "a big long kiss" and such a strong one that Sally has difficulty keeping her mouth shut; she is out of breath at the end. But that's what Woody wants!

(3 takes and 3 prints.) Completed at 3:05 P.M.

Sally gives Tom the sailor a solid handshake. Woody thanks him, and the man leaves happy.

3:15 P.M. Sally has already changed her blouse. Now it's the marine's (Matt Mulhern) turn.

Shot A110: Same blocking, same lines. They kiss, the camera zooming in. Then Sally turns to the camera. "You cannot say that I didn't do my job to keep our boys happy!" *(20 seconds.)*

Woody decides that while they are kissing, two or three of the soldiers passing by should say, "Hi, Sally!" After the second take, he asks Sally to drop the "that," and change "job" to "part."

(6 takes and 4 prints.)

It's a wrap. We move to the final location. To be shot are Bea, Sy, and Little Joe exiting Macy's, after Bea has bought Little Joe a chemistry set with the money she won on the *Silver Dollar Jackpot* (sequence 161). But since it is a night shot, and we cannot shoot before Macy's is closed, the call is for 6:30 P.M.

Woody and Sally dash away, and are followed by some of the crowd. It's incredible; people are literally running after them.

6:30 P.M. West Thirty-fourth Street, between Sixth and Seventh avenues, in front of Macy's. Santo has dressed the window on the right of the entrance: MACY'S URGES YOU TO BUY EXTRA WAR BONDS. There is an illustration of an airplane flying through a huge one-hundred-dollar bill.

The crew's food is served on the sidewalk. It's cold and Barbara is having hot soup. Naturally, a street person approaches. Tim reacts automatically: "It's for the crew." Then he realizes the person's situation and adds, "You know what, babe? Dig in."

The boys have started setting up the camera and the lights. Three lights are being set on the trucks' roofs, on the other side of West Thirty-fourth Street. The boys are in an unexpected and amazingly good mood, as if they've used the past three hours toasting each other's health.

7:30 P.M. Waiting inside Macy's.

Rachel is the name of Sally's cute red-haired stand-in. She is an actress but she doesn't want to do theater, only film, television, and commercials. She is the bride in the opening sequence of Mike Nichols's *Heartburn*. Kay, Tim, and Richie Baratta talk about the two movies in a row they did together just prior to this one, Brian DePalma's *Wise Guy* and *Heartburn*. Jimmy Sabat complains because his coat has been stolen from the trunk of his car in a parking lot near Grand Central Station. And the *Vogue* writer confesses to me that he is making more money as Santo's driver than as a writer for *Vogue*.

8:30 P.M. Shot 161: Bea, Sy, and Little Joe, proudly carrying his chemistry set, exit Macy's. Little Joe walks on ahead. Sy assures Bea that next week, he will be free, unmarried. *(44 seconds.)*

There's a lot of noise in the background, so Woody listens to the dialogue through earphones. The sidewalk has been blocked, but the modern cars continue down Thirty-fourth Street.

(7 takes and 4 prints.)

We wrap at 9:00 P.M.

Wednesday, January 15, 1986

After Manes recalls being slashed in his car near Shea Stadium, Ed says he won't cast stones, ". . . even if the Queens Borough President was with a hooker." "People who have any brains," he continues, "know that we're all—what's that Catholic term?— weak vessels. We all have infirmities. We're all human. We're all sinners." And he concludes: "I am not going to pass judgment." (Daily News *and* New York Times)

" 'Hannah and Her Sisters' is one of Woody Allen's great films, the answer to the prayers of Allen fans who have found his work since 'Annie Hall' and 'Manhattan' a bit slight. This should score more decisively at the box office over the long haul than his last several pictures. For the first time in a decade, Allen has not had Gordon Willis behind the camera, but Italian lenser Carlo Di

Palma has done an exemplary job in his stead. Like all of the director's films, it looks and, with a sound track loaded with old show tunes, sounds great. (Variety)
And Donna Reed died yesterday at sixty-four.

9:00 A.M. We're on the third floor of the RCA Recording Studio on West Forty-fourth Street. I'm sitting next to Dickie, who is getting some sleep as Mozart's Concerto Number 15 in B Flat for Piano and Orchestra is being played in the next studio. Above us are the National Academy of Recording Arts and Science's "Hall of Fame" awards won by Victor records. Among them are Paul Whiteman's recording of George Gershwin's *Rhapsody in Blue* (1927), Duke Ellington's "Take the 'A' Train" (1941), Toscanini and the NBC Symphony's Beethoven's Symphony Number 9 (1927), Caruso's rendition of "Vesti la Giubba" from *I Pagliacci* (1907), and "God Bless America" (1939) by Kate Smith.

To be shot today are the Biff Baxter radio show (sequence 121), and Sally singing the commercial for the laxative, "Get Regular with Re-Lax" (sequence 142). Tomorrow, we go back to Radio City Music Hall. Woody liked what we shot last Monday with Chester. But it seems that in the end, the first version with all the extras looked better than the reshoot with the empty lobby! In any case, Woody needs more scenes to cover the song. And we have to shoot the rich woman listening to the Tonino broadcast in her bathtub.

10:15 A.M. The studio has been dressed with a new carpet, new wallpaper, seven period lamps, and a few accessories. The camera is in the technicians' booth, looking through the window to the recording studio. Woody wants to see the technicians' reflections in the window over the action in the studio. Carlo does it by lighting the technicians in the booth, but leaving the camera in the dark. It's not easy because there is a short dolly. Then Woody says he wants the reflection of an "On the Air" sign flashing in the window.

11:30 A.M. Woody is rehearsing lines with Biff Baxter. Carlo makes final adjustments, and Jeffrey compliments Liz on her trousers. The Victrola man comes to visit; he works in the building.

Shot 121: Biff Baxter, G-man, is facing a group of Axis rats. The Germans, led by Herr Himmel, are numerous, and the Japs are armed with Samurai swords. Herr Himmel tells Biff Baxter he hasn't a chance, but Biff is not scared. *(12 seconds.)*

Seen from behind and through the window, the German (Kuno Spunolz), the Japanese man (Henry Yuk), and Biff Baxter deliver their lines while the announcer (J. R. Horn) and the effects man remain poised for action. After the first take, Woody tightens the pace: The Japanese man was fine but the German was a little slow. *(5 takes and 3 prints.)*

Now the camera is in the studio, looking the other way, facing the actors. The lighting has to be redone.

12:00 noon. In the lobby, the Japanese man chats with the technician, the German smokes a cigarette alone in a corner, and Biff Baxter discusses the Super Bowl with the gambling department. They are all agreed that the Bears are going to kill the Patriots, but Jimmy Sabat thinks that if the Bears get hit first, they could collapse. Biff, disgusted by such nonsense, goes back to his room downstairs.

Sandy is here today, along with Dick Hyman, for the recording of "Get Regular with Re-Lax." She is all in curls, with a white Pierrot shirt and a red blazer.

12:30 P.M. One floor down in the holding area, Biff Baxter is alone, reading in his dressing room, and the *Vogue* writer is lying on the floor, sleeping. The union woman, who comes to the set from time to time, complains to Jimmy Davis that there are not enough rooms for the actors.

Today, I split a card with Nick Bernstein. Nick started at age fourteen as a production assistant on *Manhattan*, and worked summers on Woody's movies. His father wrote *The Front*, and is scheduled to have his next script produced by Robert Benton and directed by Peter Yates this summer. Nick complains to me that it is not always easy for him on the set because the crew has known him since he was a kid (the Salad Sisters are like mothers to him), and nobody takes him seriously.

Sally shows up, Baby Dylan in her arms, followed by pretty Rebecca. She invites Biff Baxter to come to her room to say hello to the baby. Informed by the walkie-talkie network of their arrival, Woody runs up to give Baby Dylan a few good-morning kisses.

1:00 P.M. We're almost ready to shoot. Sally comes to watch. She's still in street clothes, and Woody touches her, hugs her, kisses her, and whispers things in her ear that make her burst into laughter. But Sally has to leave to get into costume.

Shot 121A: Biff Baxter teaches the German and the Jap a thing or two. The three actors do the yelling, and the effects man works on his effects—breaking glass, clanking swords, and so on. Biff wins, and the announcer closes the show. The producer comes from the booth to congratulate Biff, but the G-man starts feeling weak; he's anxious about the army physical tomorrow. Everybody, including the Jap and the German, cheer him up and remind him he has every malady. Yes, but what if it doesn't work? What if he gets inducted? *(1 minute.)*

Stephen Defluitter (the producer) was one of the doctors in *Hannah.* Woody cuts the first take because the effects man is doing the wrong effect. The second take is OK, but Woody asks the Japanese man, the German, and the announcer to sympathize more with Biff at the end. Otherwise, their yelling during the fight was great. For the third take, Woody doesn't cut as quickly as usual, and lets Biff improvise. The fourth take is no good; the producer didn't wait long enough before coming in (we need time so the jingle can be dubbed in later). The fifth take is good. "One more and we're finished."

(6 takes; takes 3, 5, and 6 are printed.) Completed at 1:20 P.M.

Shot 123: Biff Baxter's show is in progress (after the physical, after he's been declared 4F because of flat feet). He is "beating " the German, and the Jap is already dead. *(11 seconds.)*

(2 takes and 2 prints.)

A quick wild track of the Jap yelling. And we move the equipment upstairs for the laxative commercial.

2:15 P.M. In a huge recording studio, all in wood, divided by tall curtains, and with a big booth, a drummer and xylophone player are rehearsing, playing "Angel Eyes," while the boys move the equipment in. Woody and Carlo decide the setting for the first shot; the camera will be in the booth.

We break for lunch at 2:30 P.M.

4:00 P.M. Back on the set. Nick comes over to me and gives me $150: We have won first prize. Immediately, the gambling department encourages me to continue, and I buy a box with Kay for the Super Bowl. As Nick says of winning, "It makes it a nice afternoon."

Downstairs, in the holding area, Rebecca is trying to get the baby to go to sleep, but Baby Dylan is not interested. Jeffrey is working on the costume of Doris, the sponsor's wife (Hannah Rabinowitz), the one who doesn't like Sally. The whistler (Philip Shultz) is also perfectly cast; at the moment, he is wandering around, rehearsing his part.

5:00 P.M. Sally says she wants to practice the laxative jingle with the musicians. Dick Hyman watches, satisfied. He composed "Get Regular with Re-Lax," music and lyrics, and all the musicians are his friends. There is Derek Smith at the piano, Phil Bodner on clarinet, Howard Alden on guitar, Dick Romoff on bass, Dave Carey on xylophone, and Ted Sommer on drums. The band performs here and there in Manhattan. "They're one of the best," Dick Hyman says. Now the whistler joins the rehearsal.

5:30 P.M. Sally is sitting on the piano bench as the musicians continue to play other tunes, improvising and enjoying themselves. It makes for a nice atmosphere. Carlo is in the booth, having trouble lighting the sponsor (Ira Wheeler) and Doris, who have been seated now for nearly an hour, motionless.

6:00 P.M. Shot 142: Sally, seen through the window of the booth, sings her song. At the end, the creative people start arguing. The director asks Sally for more feeling, adman Bill wants the product pronounced more clearly, adman Tom wants to edit the jingle, the songwriter refuses, the director asks Sally to go again. (50 seconds.)
Adman Bill has been cast as a woman (Mercedes Ruehl). The actors are good, but Woody asks them to be more violent in their arguing. "You should be in love with the song," he says to the songwriter (Greg Gerard) And to adman Tom (Bruce Jarchow) and the director (David Cale): "Really angry!"
(3 takes and 3 prints.) Completed at 6:15 P.M.
Jane approaches and says Woody has suggested that I come next week to see dailies for the King Cole roof scenes. I can jump in Jeffrey's car at the end of the day to go to Woody's screening room.

7:00 P.M. Shot 142A: We are in the studio, with Sally and the whistler in the foreground and the creative people in the booth in the back. Sally sings the song, the whistler whistles, but the director stops her in the middle. "No! No! . . ." *(30 seconds.)*

The whistler is not that great at whistling but the way he looks at Sally is quite funny.

(3 takes and 3 prints.) Completed at 7:15 P.M.

Sally, the musicians, and the whistler are finished. We move back inside the booth for the last shot, the one where Doris gives her opinion of the show.

7:30 P.M. Adman Bill has a show tonight, but since she doesn't appear until the second act, she hopes to make it. She is socializing with the sponsor. But wife Doris doesn't seem to mind; she has her own problems. First, her stockings are sagging. Second, she didn't think this was going to run so late, so she didn't bring enough money to take a cab back to Brooklyn, and she doesn't want to take the subway. She also wants to call home. "My father must be frantic by now," she says.

8:00 P.M. Shot 142B: Adman Tom thinks the problem is the girl. The director defends her; she is the best they auditioned. Adman Bill turns to the sponsor to get his feelings. The sponsor thinks Sally is perfect. The others agree. Then he turns to his wife: "What do you think, Doris?" "I don't like her," Doris says. "Get rid of her," the sponsor concludes. (20 seconds.)
Doris is great.
(4 takes and 2 prints.)

"It's a wrap!" at 8:15 P.M.

Thursday, January 16, 1986

Parking Bureau boss is booted. Deputy Chief of Parking Bureau Geoffrey Lindenauer is charged with extorting five thousand dollars in the bathroom of a Manhattan restaurant. Department of Transportation Commissioner Anthony Ameruso fires Shafran. Manes moves to NYU Medical Center. There is the first hint that the mystery of Manes' slashed wrists and the growing parking-kickback scandal might be related. "I believe this is an honest government," Ed says. "When you are dealing with millions of dollars, corruption will surely exist." And Ed concludes: "Fortunately, few people are corrupt." (New York Times and Daily News)
At the PEN Congress, Michael Scammell, chairman of International PEN's Committee on writers in prison, cites "a general deterioration in the situation of writers and journalists around the world." Four hundred fifty writers are known to be in prisons, labor camps, special mental hospitals, internal exile, or are thought to have been kidnapped. The proportion of imprisoned writers is highest in Eastern Europe and the Middle East, and in such nations as the Soviet Union, the Philippines, Iran, Romania, Turkey, Poland, and Cuba. (New York Times)
And a car goes out of control this morning at 8:20 A.M., killing one pedestrian on Fifth Avenue.

8:00 A.M. We're back at Radio City Music Hall, to shoot some more scenes of Bea, Chester, and Little Joe, and the rich woman in her bathtub. The Salad Sisters take Jimmy/Chester to be dressed and made up. He looks like he's going to the electric chair.

9:30 A.M. Woody arrives late. His driver was sick and never showed up this morning. Then his substitute driver got caught in the traffic jam caused by the accident on Fifth Avenue. Everyone goes directly to the third mezzanine, to the hall where Woody wanted his difficult shot last time. The movement is simplified, but Carlo still has to relight the Grand Foyer, and will need at least two hours.

Bea has settled into the beauty parlor, which is now back to a powder room. Bea doesn't feel well today; she has a cold and a stomach ache. So she goes to get some sleep, covered by her coat, on a sofa next door in the dark gentlemen's room.

10:30 A.M. The rich woman's bathtub is on the second mezzanine, in the oval Ladies' Lounge. Using the mirrors for effect, Santo has simply added a huge black bathtub in the middle, a little furniture, and a new carpet. It looks beautiful.

Ray, Hammer, and all the boys are still working on the lighting of the Grand Foyer. Three huge lights are directed toward the balcony of the third mezzanine, and three small ones, hanging from the fourth mezzanine, focus on the balcony below. We (the gambling and camera departments, and a few PAs) are launching paper planes in the Grand Foyer, but none of us are doing it too well. Tom declares himself the champion, though his demonstration is not exactly convincing.

11:30 A.M. Carlo is about ready, and Woody comes to check the camera. The extras are brought in. Director James Toback, in a three-piece dark-blue suit, comes to visit. He goes directly to Brian, gives a little hello sign to Tom, but doesn't greet Woody. Brian introduces me, and we shake hands. Then they disappear to the back to talk.

Shot F102G: Little Joe, Bea, and Chester approach in the hall. As they pass by on the balcony, we hold on the huge chandelier, and they go out of frame. Little Joe comes back to gawk. Then Bea comes back to get him, and they leave the frame. (30 seconds.)

The first take is not good: Little Joe is not on his mark. For the second take, he doesn't stay out of the frame long enough before he comes back. The two following takes are good.

(4 takes and 2 prints.)

Shot F102H: Same action exactly, but this time with no extras, just a couple of ushers in the back. *(30 seconds.)*

(1 take and 1 print.)

Now we move inside the theater, to see the three entering and being seated. The boys start moving the equipment.

We break for lunch at 1:15 P.M.

3:00 P.M. We're back on the set.

Shot F102J: Inside the theater. The show is on, one of the doors opens, and Bea, Chester, and Little Joe appear. Behind them, we see the chandelier. They take their seats as another couple enters. *(15 seconds.)*

The first take is not perfect. The other patrons come in too quickly, and we can't see the chandelier well enough. For the second take, the couple is "a pinch late," Dickie says.

(4 takes and 2 prints.) Completed at 3:15 P.M.

"Get a rest, guys," Woody says to the trio. Then to Tom: "We should go to the tub."

4:00 P.M. George Manos is visiting. He played the press agent in *Purple Rose,* and is Rollins and Joffe's associate in the real world. Woody wants more yellow flowers by the bathtub; otherwise, he thinks, with all this black, it will look like a funeral home. He also wants another radio; Jimmy Mazzola produces several of them.

The rich woman and her black maid are waiting in the Gentlemen's Lounge next door. The rich woman is not very beautiful (perhaps it is because she is rich?). A parrot is put in a cage on the set, and Jimmy Mazzola fills the tub.

Jeffrey's outfit today consists of yellow-brown boots, jeans, beige cashmere sweater with nothing under it, and a green military jacket with gold stripes.

4:30 P.M. Carlo has used only one light, reflecting off the ceiling, and the existing lamps.

Shot 2H: The camera starts on the parrot, and pulls back to reveal the rich woman in a bubble bath, with the maid passing through. They are listening to the Tonino broadcast. *(10 seconds.)*

The rich woman, wearing flesh-colored tights, gets in the tub. Jimmy Mazzola stirs the water for bubbles. Woody is talking to the black maid. The rich woman is very relaxed (perhaps because she is rich?). Between each take, Jimmy Mazzola works on the bubbles and the steam. He also has to tease the parrot, who, ignoring us, keeps showing his back.

(3 takes and 3 prints.)

The rich woman goes to have her hairstyle changed. In the next shot, she will be listening to the Polly Phelps story, still in her bath, but twenty years later. The radio is updated, and the towels are changed.

Shot 168D: Same camera movement and action. *(10 seconds.)*

The rich woman gets creative. "Just listen to the radio. . . . Don't smile, . . . Wash yourself slowly," Woody tells her. All this is done without sound, and she doesn't know what she's listening to. But she seems to enjoy taking her bath in front of everybody (perhaps because she is rich!).

(1 take and 1 print.)

"It's a wrap!" at 5:00 P.M.

A slow, easy, boring day, with no real directing. Tomorrow, we move to the studio, and will be there for the final four weeks.

Friday, January 17, 1986

Goetz gets off. "An individual is justified in using deadly force when he reasonably believes he is being robbed," Justice Stephen Crane says. (Daily News)

The cops believe Manes did it to himself. (New York Times)

And at the PEN Congress, the women are demanding a greater role. Betty Friedan, author of The Feminine Mystique *and* Second Stage, *assumes the leadership and makes it clear to Norman Mailer and the others that "if they will not give our representatives room on the platform, we bodily will take the platform. . . . The men are friends of ours," she continues, "and they even believe in social justice. Yet, there really is a failure of their own creative imagination."* (New York Times)

8:30 A.M. We're at the Kaufman Astoria Studios in Queens. The Astoria Studios were opened September 20, 1920, as part of the Famous Players–Lasky Corporation's huge empire. Famous Players was Adolph Zukor's company and was founded with the profits he made as American distributor of the French film *Queen Elizabeth* (1912) starring Sarah Bernhardt. In 1916, Zukor merged with Jess Lasky. In 1919, Famous Players–Lasky acquired their distributor, Paramount Pictures Corporation. But they changed their name to Paramount Famous Lasky only in 1927, and to Paramount Publix Corporation in 1930. As early as 1927, they began moving their activities to the West Coast, where their main studios were. And while between 1920 and 1927 over one hundred silent films were produced in Astoria, with stars like Rudolph Valentino and Claudette Colbert, the studio was primarily used to test Broadway performers. In 1929, the Marx Brothers, while playing in *Animal Crackers* on Broadway, made their film debut in Astoria with *The Cocoanuts*.

In the early thirties, the studio was rented to independent producers; *One Third of a Nation* (1939) with Sylvia Sidney and Sidney Lumet was produced here. Then the Astoria Studios were more or less abandoned. In 1942, Paramount gave the facility to the U.S. government, and it became the Army Pictorial Center. During the World War II era, Kitty Carlisle Hart came to the lot to sing to the troops on celluloid, and the army used the facility until 1969, when it was abandoned once again. Thanks to a group of people—among them Queens Borough President Donald Manes, Larry Barr (a business representative for the Motion Picture Studio Mechanics Local 52), and director Sidney Lumet—the studio was reborn in 1977 with the shooting of Lumet's *The Wiz*. Then several movies followed, using studio facilities to some degree or another, films such as Miloš Forman's *Hair*, Bob Fosse's *All that Jazz*, Lumet's *The Verdict*, Francis Ford Coppola's *The Cotton Club*, and more recently, Richard Benjamin's *The Money Pit*.

In the past Woody has shot some scenes at Astoria, for *Zelig* and *Broadway Danny Rose*, but this is the first time he has used it so extensively. We have three of the four main stages, the fourth being used by *Ishtar*, the Elaine May/Dustin Hoffman/Warren Beatty/Isabelle Adjani comedy, which, it is said, has cost $12.5 million even before anything has been shot. Beatty and Hoffman are getting $5 million each, and the director half of that! On stage E (26,040 square feet), we have two sets: The King Cole roof over Times Square, and Little Joe's house in Rockaway. Stage G (12,000 square feet) will be used first as the roller-skating rink we didn't shoot at Rye Playland (sequence 51), then as Breezy Point, where

Bea and Manulis get lost in the fog (sequence 52), and finally as the Pennsylvania field where little Polly Phelps has fallen into the well (sequence 163). At the moment we are upstairs on stage F, a much smaller area (5,000 square feet). To be shot, the *Nick Norris—Private Detective* show, the new singer singing "I'll Be Seeing You" and "They're Either Too Young or Too Old," and the Crooner singing "All or Nothing At All."

9:30 A.M. Ezra is less anxious now—no worries about the clouds or the sun anymore. He chats with Woody. Carlo finishes lighting the set, which is two wood panels put at an angle, one of them with glass, to form a technicians' booth. Carlo doesn't like shooting in studios; they have no soul, and he doesn't feel comfortable ("No real!"). Nick Norris (the Tiny Man) is talking with the Big Man with the Oriental voice (his assistant). The Big Man has huge hands but small feet, and Nick has a loud voice. The Pretty Girl is not ready yet; the Salad Sisters are making her prettier.

10:15 A.M. Woody checks the camera, then goes to the actors and tells them what the camera is seeing, how and when it will move. It is time for the first rehearsal. Just before it starts, the Big Man goes to Woody. He has brought his sister, and asks if she can come and watch. "Sure," Woody answers.

Shot 42: The announcer introduces the show. "The maker of Sloan's liver pills presents *Nick Norris—Private Detective.*" The Pretty Girl begs for Nick's help; her brother has been murdered. She'll pay anything. "OK, sugar," Nick answers in his deep, loud voice, "c'mon in and sit down." And the Big Man with his high Oriental voice says: "Shall I warm up the car, boss?" *(20 seconds.)*

After the first rehearsal, Woody shortens the lines of Nick and the Pretty Girl.

Take 1: No good for Dickie. But it's a chance for Jimmy Mazzola and Kay, who had forgotten to set the clock to 1:00 P.M.

Take 2: No good for Dickie again; the camera movement could be better. But the acting is fine for Woody.

Take 3: Nick Norris hesitates a little on his first line. "Once more," Woody says.

Take 4: The first good one.

Take 5: The announcer's necktie, a real one, is getting loose. Jeffrey acts. But the take is still good.

Take 6: Nick waits too long to start his lines, but Woody still prints it. "One more and we're finished. Really hit it this time," Woody announces.

Take 7: Good.

(The last 4 takes are printed.)

Shot 42A: Same action but seen closer. *(20 seconds.)*

(2 takes and 2 prints.)

11:30 A.M. The technicians of the *Nick Norris* show are getting friendly with the Big Man's sister. Woody is eating a fattening-looking cake while giving me a smile of complicity, the first in two or three days.

Jeffrey's outfit today: reddish-brown boots, jeans, a western-style denim shirt, the metallic cowboy tie, and a colorful sleeveless sweater over it all.

11:45 A.M. We're still in the *Nick Norris* studio, but with new technicians and shooting from a different angle. The new singer is ready. The song is on the playback, but this time it's her own voice on the tape. Woody wants the technicians to smoke more.

Shot RA107: The new singer sings, "I'll Be Seeing You."

Unlike the first one, the new singer has a good voice. The whole crew stops to watch her. The song is a little wistful, and it affects everybody. Is it the nostalgia of the song? The quality of her singing? But she has everybody's attention, and it's nice seeing the faces of the boys turning almost solemn, contemplative.

(2 takes and 2 prints.)

The singer goes to change for the next song; the studio will be the same. We wait. "It ain't over till the fat lady sings!" Jimmy Frederick says.

12:15 P.M. Shot R149: Different camera setting. The singer sings "They're Either Too Young or Too Old."

Take 1: She sings it Mae West–style, more vulgar, winking, rolling her hips. It's funny. Carlo loves it.

Take 2: Woody asks her to hold her music sheet closer in front of her, and to look at it more.

(The 2 takes are printed.)

"Perfect." Woody gives the singer a little sign of thanks, and we move to the next set at the other end of the stage.

12:45 P.M. We're moving fast today. This is already the last shot scheduled. The Crooner studio is a simple, back-lit wall with an Art Deco clock and a shiny black floor. A flashing red "On the Air" sign will be reflected on the wall.

The Crooner (Todd Field) is quite young. He will sing in playback, but it will not be his voice. He made a recording of the song, but his voice was not right.

1:30 P.M. Woody checks the camera. He asks for a bigger "On the Air" sign. Jimmy Mazzola doesn't have one. By moving the existing one closer to the wall, the reflection becomes a little bigger. But Woody wants it bigger still. "How long would it take to make a bigger one?" asks Woody. Jimmy says fifteen minutes, but Cliff asks for an hour because he has to cut the letters. Woody hesitates. He asks to see how the sign would look higher, and decides to go with that.

Shot 12: The Crooner sings "All or Nothing at All." (20 seconds.)

Woody needs only the beginning of the song—the rest of it will be over the images of Ruthie and her girlfriends listening in the soda shop. The Crooner is very shy, tense, and intimidated by Woody; he seems paralyzed. Woody asks him to be more expansive, to keep looking upward, but he is not very good at putting people at ease, and the crooner has a hard time being "real mellow." And there are more problems with the "On the Air" sign. Sometimes it stops blinking.

(9 takes and 6 prints.) Completed at 2:00 P.M.

Before breaking for lunch, Carlo and Woody go downstairs to stage E to have a look at the King Cole roof. We're shooting there the first thing Monday morning.

And "It's a wrap!" at 2:15 P.M.

Lunch at the commissary with Drew, Ken, Angela, Doug, Richie, and the Crooner. The Crooner has been a Woody Allen fan since childhood. He worked with a stage company, doing Shakespeare, but he wants to go into movies now because it's more fun. He has a test with Disney in Hollywood next week, and wants to move out West permanently.

On the different stages, Santo and his team are finishing setting up everything.

Stage G: The entire roller-skating-rink structure has been moved from Rye Playland; new panels have been made, and it is three to four times bigger. Since the rink is supposedly outdoors, long black drapes surround it for the dark sky.

Stage E: On one side, there is Little Joe's house. It's a perfect replica of, if a little bigger than, the one in Rockaway. When the owner of the one in Rockaway came to see the set with his daughter, the three-year-old girl didn't understand what was happening and was upset to see her house brought to the studio; he had a hard time explaining to her that it was only a movie. It is a work of incredible precision, where the smallest details (an ashtray, items in a cupboard, a toothbrush in the bathroom) have been duplicated. There's an amazing feel to it, a feeling of, well, reality, the reality of the thirties and forties. The rooms are bigger than the original, so it will be easier to work in. There's no ceiling, so Carlo can hang his lights, and if he needs more space, he can move any of the walls. Santo is having a good time. While making *Desperately Seeking Susan,* his department didn't have any money. Here, they have plenty!

On the other end of stage E is the King Cole roof. On the right, there is a huge Camel billboard with the face of a soldier, his mouth open, blowing smoke; on the left, several other billboards; and in the back, a huge transparency made of an old still of Times Square. At the Vaudeville, they're playing *Destry Rides Again* with Marlene Dietrich, and Benny Fields is appearing onstage.

Monday, January 20, 1986   *Twelfth Week*

In Lebanon, Moslems fight President Gemayel, resulting in thirty-two dead. (New York Times)

Ed urges Manes to tell all about it. (Daily News)

A fifty-nine-year-old construction worker on Staten Island wins the New York State Lotto jackpot: $30 Million. (New York Times)

"It's very difficult to have more than one wife if you have only one household," Colonel Qaddafi says. In Libya, the People's Congress tries to limit polygamy by requiring a man to obtain the permission of his first wife before taking a second. (New York Times)

There to fight against the "sinners," "the forces of Darkness," and "the allies of Satan," American Protestant sects "who were called by God" are becoming more and more active in El Salvador. (New York Times)

Prince Rainier has landed "Kid Dynamite" for a bout in Monaco on March 29. "Monaco may be tiny, but you can bet a solid left hook that there won't be anything small about the purse." (Daily News)

And Norman Mailer concludes the PEN Congress: "One of the ways in which everything is deteriorating is that manners in the world are getting a lot worse." (New York Times)

9:15 A.M. On the King Cole roof at Astoria Studios. It is going to take all morning to light it. Ray, Hammer, and all the boys are working hard, while Carlo, his mauve felt hat on, sits in the director's chair in the middle of the roof, checking the work.

It's Martin Luther King Day, and there is no school. Sally has come with four of her eight children—Baby Dylan, Lark, Daisy, and of course, Andrew. Andrew complains to me about yesterday afternoon when his mother took him to a boring concert where Daisy was playing piano.

11:00 A.M. The look of the King Cole roof is improving. We're going to shoot the New Year's Eve party, where all the radio stars decide, at Sally's urging, to go see the view from the roof (sequences 180 and 183). Woody decides on a rough blocking, showing Carlo approximately where the actors are going to say their lines, so he can start to make some adjustments. Santo asks for some details on the set decorations. Jimmy Mazzola asks Woody if he wants the ground wet. Woody quietly answers everyone's questions, then goes back to his room. This shot is the last image of the film, and therefore important.

12:00 noon. *Ishtar* next door has already started shooting. Like us, they moved into Astoria this morning. They've just returned from location in Morocco, and will stay in the studio three weeks, before filming in New York City for a few more weeks. They're using two soundstages. One is next to our roller rink, and some of our dressing rooms are next to theirs. The director of photography is also Italian, a friend of Carlo's, the Oscar-winning *Apocalypse Now* Vittorio Storaro. But he has brought his Italian camera crew, and American unions have required hiring an American camera crew, even though there is nothing for them to do. It's depressing for this second team to hang around, so they come to say hello to our boys, most of whom they know.

Nicole is back with us, and helps the other stand-in, Myla Pitt,

rehearse her lines for George Furth's *The Supporting Cast*. The
two of them met on *Hannah*, where they worked as stand-ins for
almost two months and became friends. Nicole wants to do only
film, but Myla prefers theater and is working in films for the
money. Stand-ins are paid about a hundred dollars a day.

Biff Baxter, very elegant in his black tie and tortoiseshell
glasses, comes to the roof to have a look. He checks the three pages
of the script with his lines, and tries to get a better grasp of what
the scene, and in fact the film, is about. Woody never gives the full
script to actors: they get only their scenes. Louis gives us Xerox
copies of the Super Bowl pool. All the spaces have been bought up.
Now it's Max's father (Roger and Irene's announcer) who comes to
see the roof. He's impressed. He, too, is elegant in black tie. Romaine finds it exciting with all these handsome and well-attired
men everywhere.

1:10 P.M. Carlo is almost ready, and the radio stars are waiting
downstairs. Roger and Irene are there, of course, along with Herbie Hanson, the Polly Phelps Newsman (Ivan Kronenfeld, who
played Barbara Hershey's husband in *Hannah*), Sanford the Whiz
Kid, Abercrombie, and the rest—except Woody's accountant, who
decided that enough was enough!

They're all socializing. The Masked Avenger is having a serious discussion with Bill Kern; the overweight singer talks with
the tiny Effects Actress; and Max is having coffee with his dad.

Woody is already on the roof. Tom wonders if we shouldn't
break for lunch before starting anything (we're already on overtime), but Woody wants to set the blocking. The company is
brought in. Their arrival is fantastic. Most of them are seeing the
roof for the first time and are overwhelmed.

1:20 P.M. Woody, script in hand, stands in front of the group.
He tells them in general terms what he wants them to do, where
they should stand, and for the ones who have lines, where to deliver them. Woody decides to rehearse, with Carlo behind the
camera.

The first rehearsal doesn't work. Woody, still with script in
hand, gives a few indications of blocking to the ones with lines—
Sally, the Avenger, the singer. It takes three more rehearsals. Each
time, Woody becomes more precise about the blocking. But there
are odd moments when he stands before the group, in silence, re-

reading the script, staring at them for a couple of minutes. You're tempted to think that he doesn't know what he is doing. It's difficult to pin down just when it is that he becomes more precise, because it is done by little touches, a bit at a time.

There is a fourth rehearsal, and it is good. Woody turns to Jimmy Sabat to check on the sound: "Is it going to be OK for the lines with the background noise?" Then he asks how it looks for the camera. Carlo thinks the camera should follow Sally and the Avenger to the Camel billboard, instead of staying on a wide shot of everybody. Woody rereads the script, checks the camera, and decides to cut the scene into two shots. He goes back to the actors. "That blocking is not going to work," he says.

The first shot will be of everyone arriving. Then the camera

will follow Sally and the Avenger. The dialogue of the others will
be filmed afterward, in different spots. "I've got it," Woody says,
turning to Tom. "Maybe we should go to lunch first," Tom suggests. Woody laughs; Tom is embarrassed, but there is the overtime. A deal is struck; we do one more rehearsal with Woody at
the camera. The scene is rehearsed twice more, and at 2:00 P.M.,
we break for lunch.

Lunch in the commissary with Nicole and Myla. Warren
Beatty (tennis shoes, a light jacket, hair uncombed) is having a
salad with a friend at the next table. Nicole is very excited, but
Myla doesn't find him so attractive.

3:15 P.M. Bill Kern has stayed on the roof for lunch time because of his bum leg. He is talking sports with Hammer and Louis.

I show Roger the roller-skating rink, and he lets me touch his hair; the Salad Sisters have put some gel on it so it stays put. It is as tough as wood! Roger can't stand it. We talk about London, Paris, and New York. Roger never reads papers or watches TV and, like Jimmy Sabat, feels much better for it. He is leaving on Thursday for Paris; the premiere of *Marat/Sade* is February 18.

4:00 P.M. Everybody is back on the roof. Tall Jessica Dragonette is talking with tiny Nick Norris, Abercrombie chats with Roger and Irene, and the Reba Man cracks a few jokes for the Pretty Girl.

Two more rehearsals for Dickie and the camera. Then we're ready to shoot. Makeup and wardrobe check the actors. Jimmy Mazzola waters the floor, while Jimmy Frederick pours the champagne (apple cider again) and hands out cigarettes. There's a little problem, though—nobody here smokes. The courageous little Effects Actress volunteers. Now Jimmy Mazzola goes to stir up the pigeons, those "rats with wings."

Shot 180: The party arrives on the roof through the small door. Everybody is a little drunk, laughing and enjoying life. Sally and the Avenger go to the edge to see the view. The Avenger still can't figure out how Sally knows about this place. "It's a long story!" she tells him. *(28 seconds.)*

The pigeons are causing most of the problems. Woody wants two or three of them flying near Sally and the Avenger at the end of the scene, but they're not listening. And, as with the ducks at Rye, Woody is enjoying the trouble.

(8 takes and 6 prints.)

Woody goes back to his script. Everybody stays on the roof. Abercrombie is now entertaining Jessica, and Sally seems to have gotten a little tired of the Avenger. Max asks Woody when it'll be over.

Woody: "Don't worry, Max, we're just gonna keep you a few hours more and then you'll be free."

Max: "You're worse than Josef Mengele. You're gonna pay for it, Max. Everybody has to pay someday."

Woody, laughing, goes back to his script, and Max, disgusted by such impertinence, goes to talk to Bob Greenhut and Ezra.

Woody complains to Tom that there are too many people on the set. But everybody is part of the crew, Tom explains. Woody doesn't push the issue, but it bothers him.

The next shot is set. A first rehearsal with everybody, but it's decided that only a few of them will be in the frame. So Bill Kern, Sally, Biff Baxter, and Max are free. Woody goes back to his room to let Carlo set up.

"Are we doing another shot afterward?" Woody asks Tom before leaving. "It depends. Let me consult the money people." Tom goes to Bob Greenhut.

6:00 P.M. Shot 180A: The atmosphere is mellow. Herbie Hanson, the *Guess That Tune* announcer (Don Pardo), Irene, and the Polly Phelps Newsman exchange some melancholy comments on how time goes so fast, how the years pass "so quickly . . . and then we're old . . . and we never knew what any of it was about. . . ." (*25 seconds.*)

"I've got a double dip, and she's giving me a floating job,"

Dickie screams to Woody after the first take. There is a moment of stunned silence as everybody looks at everybody else, to see if anyone has understood. Then, a big laugh. After a few clarifications from Dickie, Woody figures out what happened. The double dip refers to Irene and Herbie, who hide each other when they cross the frame, and it is the overweight singer who is giving Dickie a floating job (moving too much) as she crosses the frame.

But the problems are only starting. Most of the players are real radio announcers or stand-up comedians, and don't have much acting experience. They lack presence. Woody tries hard—"Use your own words"; "Do you feel comfortable?"; but it doesn't work. Then, there are a couple of other problems. Jimmy Mazzola's wind fans are noisy, and the actors aren't speaking loudly enough. And before each take, we have to wait until the huge mechanical top hat going up and down in the background is in the right position. So between the double dips, the floating jobs, the fans, the top hat, and the actors, Woody is exhausted. He keeps at it, though, going to the performers one at a time, having them rehearse, saying the lines for them, acting out their parts. A lot of takes are not completed.

Finally, at 7:00 P.M., Woody stops. We have done fifteen takes, and none is good. Only the last one will be printed for a test. Woody disappears quickly. This has been the most difficult shot of the movie so far.

"It's a wrap!" at 7:10 P.M.

Back in the van with Sanford the Whiz Kid and his mom. Sanford is from Maryland and is a professional actor, though this is his first film. He proudly shows me his picture on the cover of a 1940s *Life* magazine, printed up for the film. He had a nice day today; it was fun to be in black tie on the roof with the beautiful people. And this morning, he was entertained by two charming ladies, Lark and Daisy, who gave him a tour of the studio.

Tuesday, January 21, 1986

City contracts: Big probe set. Ed cancels a $22.7 million contract with Citisource Inc. when he discovers it has neglected to say that one of its directors and the largest single stockholder was his pal Bronx Democratic leader Stanley Friedman. (Daily News)

Cannon Films plans to produce King Lear *from a script by Norman Mailer, starring Dustin Hoffman, and directed by Jean-Luc Godard.* (New York Times)

9:30 A.M. Shot 180B (to replace 180A of yesterday evening): same camera movement, blocking, and action, but different actors. Max's father takes the place of the *Guess That Tune* announcer. Irene takes the place of Herbie Hanson, Roger the place of Irene, and Biff Baxter the place of the Polly Phelps Newsman. *(25 seconds.)*

No more problems. Each of the actors has a real presence now, and gives the scene the important mood of nostalgia it was lacking yesterday. The overweight singer has been replaced by tiny Nick Norris, who doesn't give Dickie any floating job, and the Reba Man is still flirting in the back with the Pretty Girl. Woody tries different variations of tone for Biff Baxter at the end of the scene.

(6 takes and 5 prints.)

10:45 A.M. The rumor is that Woody didn't like the dailies of the singer. It was not that she was bad, but he didn't feel the atmosphere was right.

Everyone is back on the roof now. Biff Baxter reads *You Know Me Al* by Ring Lardner, and Abercrombie, smiling as usual, chats with Nick Norris. Mom and Pop have come by to see their house next door, and also to watch the beautiful people on the roof.

11:45 A.M. Shot 180C: Sally, the Avenger, and Max look at the beautiful view from the edge of the roof. The atmosphere is nostalgic. After Biff Baxter's comments about the years passing, Bill Kern says they're all becoming history. The singer tries to cheer everybody up. Max starts his speech: ". . . we have it pretty good . . . we're the voices all America listen to . . ." Sally thinks Max is a little drunk. The Avenger wonders if future generations will ever know of them. Sally falls into the mood. The singer cheers them up again: "Listen. We're here to celebrate New Year's Eve!" *(1 minute, 35 seconds.)*

The camera is on the outside edge of the roof, on a man lift, and Woody, less than four feet from Sally, the Avenger, and Max, stares at them as they go over their lines. His face is expressionless, only his eyes darting from one actor to the other.

The first four takes are done with few comments from Woody; the actors are good. After the fifth take, Woody suggests that Sally and the Avenger relate more to one another. Then he asks Max to do a livelier version. Woody also changes a few words here and there as the takes go on. Max adds some flourishes to his performance, and Woody seems to approve.

(12 takes and 8 prints.)

The actors go back downstairs while Carlo and Woody decide on the camera setting for the last shot of the film (sequence 183).

They find a spot near the back wall. While Carlo watches through the viewfinder, Woody goes through the action. He "acts" the entire scene, all the different parts (miming the actions, laughing, drinking), but approximately and quickly. Though Woody stays quite serious, it looks funny. Maybe it's the way he walks, bent slightly forward, arms hanging forward, with short steps, making a few constrained faces.

After three minutes, the camera movement is agreed upon, and while the boys go to work, we rush to see yesterday's dailies. I follow, a little thrilled, since it's my first time.

12:00 noon. Inside the Zukor theater. The fifty-seat studio screening room is already crowded: Sally, Jane, Tom, Mickey, Dickie, and the entire gambling department. Woody is tense; he is very anxious to see how the roof looks. The screening starts. But the door opens and closes as more people come in, and that's too much for Woody. He asks that the screening be stopped. And immediately, Tom acts. Everybody has to leave, even Sally and Jane! Only Woody, Carlo, and Tom remain. A trip for nothing. . . .

We break for lunch.

Woody is spending lunch time with Baby Dylan in Sally's room. The rumor is that he doesn't like the look of the roof.

At the commissary, Carlo is having lunch with Vittorio Storaro. Max is at a nearby table with his dad.

2:15 P.M. Back on the set. Jean Doumanian is visiting again. Dickie is having his after-lunch nap near the camera. And Al, the special-effects man ("He's the best," Jimmy Mazzola tells me), is giving Woody a snow demonstration. Three large tubes equipped with three fans each drop plastic snow from a structure built over the set. Woody describes the snowfall rate he wants.

2:50 P.M. All the party is back with us, gathered before Woody, listening with great attention as he explains the scene.

Woody speaks slowly, softly, as if embarrassed by all the beautiful people. He coughs, hesitating ("You know . . .") They have to be lively, congratulating each other. It's New Year's Eve. Then the snow starts to fall. They go back down the staircase, laughing, drinking, joking. And Sally stays alone with the Avenger, who launches into his signature phrase: "Beware, Evildoers, wherever you are!" At the end, Woody remains silent for about a minute in front of the waiting party, as if he's thinking of anything he could add. Max, as always, takes advantage and rouses Woody: "Ready to shoot?"

Woody goes to the camera and starts composing the shot. The Reba Man and the Pretty Girl are positioned near the water tank, Sanford and the *Guess That Tune* announcer near the staircase, the singer with the ever-smiling Abercrombie, Sally between Biff Baxter and the Avenger in the foreground. Max is with his dad not too far behind. The short Effects Actress is with tall Herbie Hanson, Nick Norris with Jessica Dragonette, and Roger and Irene are finally back together.

3:00 P.M. There is a problem. At the end of the shot, after the Masked Avenger has yelled his warning across New York, the roof stays empty with the snow falling. But the huge transparency of Times Square in the background doesn't look real enough for Woody. The party is asked to step down from the roof for a moment so we can work on two things. First, make the top hat move more slowly so it will hide the phony background more, and second, improve the lighting of the transparencies.

3:45 P.M. "It's beautiful like that, but it's not what he wants. He wants the real Times Square of 1944!" Tom says. Carlo and Ray think it looks OK, but Woody is adamant. He tries to find another angle. There's something nice and winning about his stubbornness, because he stays very quiet, very low-key, and looks somehow desperate as he searches for another solution.

Finally, Woody gives up. The hat will do what it can. The party is brought back for a first rehearsal, Woody at the camera, without the snow and the fans so Jimmy Sabat can record a clean sound track. But Max starts again. Now he wants to have a picture taken with Woody next to his dad and himself. Woody stands between the two (they're very tall), looking frightened. And now the rehearsal can start!

Abercrombie is not fast enough going down the stairs, and the whole party has no energy: "There's champagne downstairs," Woody tells them. A second rehearsal, again recorded by Jimmy.

4:20 P.M. Shot 183: People are drinking, laughing, and enjoying each other now. It's 1944! "If this damn war doesn't end this year, I'm going to enlist!" Biff Baxter decides courageously. But the snow starts to fall. Max gives the signal. And everybody goes down the little staircase, disappearing one by one. The Masked Avenger is the last out. Before closing the door, he yells to Manhattan, "Beware, Evildoers, wherever you are!" and laughs his memorable laugh before disappearing. The camera pulls back for a wide shot of the roof, the snow falling more heavily, and the top hat going up and down. . . . (2 minutes, 13 seconds.)
    Max is at it again:
    "How am I going to know when it's snowing?"
    "I'll cue you," Woody tells him.
    "I like that!"
Jimmy Mazzola distributes the party hats and pours the champagne. Somebody has said that the plastic snow can be harmful, and we all put on little protective white masks and party hats since the snow is falling on us, too. The show becomes equally funny on both sides of the camera. "Don't swallow the snow, Max!" Woody yells. "Are you trying to gas us?" Max complains, seeing us in masks.
    After each take, the snow has to be removed. Jimmy Mazzola and his boys start their vacuum cleaners. Woody keeps teasing Max, but Max finds him silly now. In one take, the snow doesn't fall enough. And in another, Max is too late announcing the snow. After each take, Woody lets the camera run. And for one minute, we stand, in silence, on the King Cole roof under the snow. It's beautiful.
    (5 takes and 4 prints.)

5:30 P.M. Several wild tracks. First, the two tough guys:
    The Masked Avenger: "Beware, Evildoers, wherever you are!"
    Biff Baxter: "If this damn war doesn't end this year, I'm going to enlist!"
    Then Max: "It's going to snow. Let's go downstairs!"
    "Great Max," Woody says, encouraging him.
    And everybody is released except Max. Woody needs a wild

track for the *Silver Dollar Jackpot* scene: "OK, little lady. You chose fish." But first Jimmy has to get the same antique mike used in the scene.

We wrap at 5:45 P.M.

Back in the van with the singer, the Polly Phelps Newsman, Abercrombie, and Sanford. Abercrombie asks me how he was. He also tells me that he was in *The Cotton Club* in a scene at Richard Gere's table, but the scene was cut.

Wednesday, January 22, 1986

Manes did it. "The truth of what happened to me on the night of January 9 is as the police said. The wounds I received that night were self-inflicted. There were no assailants, and no one but me is to blame." (New York Times)

And twenty-two people were killed by a car bomb in East Beirut. (New York Times)

9:00 A.M. We're back on the King Cole roof. To be shot: Sally taking Roger (who is "exploding with desire") to the roof so he can relax (sequence 66). The soldier smoking on the Camel billboard is now a civilian; we have moved back earlier in the film, before the war. It is the first time in the movie that we see the roof.

Woody is thinking about doing the scene in one very complicated shot. Sally and Roger appear at the staircase door, walk left and around the structure, looking the roof over. They disappear behind the staircase structure, then reappear on the other side. Roger starts to hug Sally, and finally they go at it. Visually, it's a little too much, too much camera movement, so the sequence is broken into two shots. First, they discover the roof; second, they start at it.

9:45 A.M. "Catastrophe!" Sally took some medicine yesterday, and it turns out she's allergic to it; her eyes are swollen. The doctor is on his way. She isn't feeling well. We're trying to get the Crooner so we can reshoot "All or Nothing At All" (Woody didn't like the recording-studio background). Carlo leaves with the boys for stage G to start lighting the roller rink, and Woody is going to record some wild tracks of Roger and Irene for their *Breakfast* show. Roger is getting nervous. It's looking as though he could miss his plane tomorrow, and not be in Marat's bathtub on Friday as he promised!

11:45 A.M. Sally is feeling better; the doctor gave her some more medicine. The Salad Sisters are working on her. Dickie is sound asleep on the camera dolly (it doesn't look very comfortable). Sally's stand-in reads the complete works of Tennessee Williams. Roger's stand-in is working a crossword puzzle. And on a half-lit set (the lights are being saved), the top hat continues up and down.

12:00 noon. Woody and Roger are back on the set. We're waiting for Sally. She comes in, looking beautiful.
Shot 66: Roger and Sally come through the door and discover the roof. Roger is already feeling much more relieved: "Under the stars, the orchestra's playing." Sally reminds him she only gets a ten-minute break. *(25 seconds.)*
Take 1: The actors are good. But there are problems with the hat. It should come up just when they come onto the roof, so the transparency of Times Square doesn't look too obvious.
Take 2: Woody cuts because of the hat again. When it's not ducks or pigeons . . .
Take 3: Now it's Jimmy Mazzola who is overdoing it with his fans. Jimmy Sabat can't get a clean sound track.
Take 4: Sally walked too far away. She looks tired. Woody: "Are you OK?" Thanks to Jimmy Mazzola, who waters the floor between takes for the reflection and who is blasting her with wind so her hair will look good, poor Sally is suffering.
Take 5: The first good one. "One more and we're finished."
Take 6: Good again.
(Takes 5 and 6 are printed.) Completed at 12:30 P.M.

1:00 P.M. We are waiting while the boys bring the smoke machine from the billboard to the roof, so the smoke rings will be intact when they enter the frame. A piece of the roof edge is removed.
Sally rests under the water tank, chatting with Roger; she's feeling much better. She socializes a little with me, too. She is

quite like Andrew when she talks or listens to you; both look at you very seriously, with their eyes blinking, head a little to the side, and also in the way their legs bend backward.

I get confirmation that it's OK for me to go to the dailies tonight. I'll have to jump into the second car with Fern and race to Woody's cutting room on Park Avenue to get there on time. Woody starts looking at the dailies the minute he gets in.

1:30 P.M. The smoke-ring machine is set. The rings are reaching the frame, but they are not perfectly formed anymore. And the noise . . . Jimmy Sabat asks if it's a joke! We abandon the smoke.

Shot 66A: Roger makes his move, but Sally's cigarette tray doesn't make things easy. And Sally would like to hear more about the head of the agency. But nothing can stop Roger when he is in a mood like this, and Sally is always ready to make the boys happy. They go to the edge of the roof. *(30 seconds.)*

A first rehearsal for the actors. Woody shows Roger how to hold Sally with his hands firmly on her bottom. Roger, a little embarrassed, asks how far he should go. "Don't worry. It will be cut," Woody tells him. Carlo simplifies the shot; no dollying forward, just a pan and a zoom. Woody suggests they go to the edge of the roof next time so they'll be more comfortable making out. Between each take, Woody gallantly goes to hold Sally's cigarette tray so the strap doesn't hurt her neck. And Roger discreetly departs.

After the second take, Roger starts really getting forward. Woody likes it. Sally doesn't mind being hugged and kissed, and "doing everything to make our boys happy," but when things are as they were with the sailor the other day and now Roger (so demanding!), she gets a little worn out.

The third take looks very good. Roger really grabs her. "Did you get hurt?" Woody asks Sally. And to Roger: "Good. But even more energy. Really do it." And on his delivery: "Give her assurance."

Take 4: Good. "One more and we're finished."

Take 5: Woody cuts. Roger is too soft.

Take 6: "That's good. That should be the level—real committed."

Take 7: "Perfect."

(Takes 3, 4, and 7 are printed.)

We break for lunch at 1:50 P.M.

3:05 P.M. We're back on the set. Woody comes in and asks Tom for his pages of the script. After reading the scene, Woody talks briefly with Carlo. To be shot: After having done the deed, Roger and Sally find themselves stuck on the roof because the door doesn't open from the outside (sequence 68). It will be done in a simple pan. Carlo goes to work, and Woody hurries back to Sally's room to play with Baby Dylan.

3:30 P.M. Santo's team is finishing Little Joe's house on the other end of the stage. It's a strange feeling to see it inside the studio. From the exterior, the replica is perfect, with the porch and the staircase where Bea was listening to the radio.

The actual house itself is well built, and it's sad to know that it will be destroyed after the movie ends, unless someone buys it. After *A Midsummer Night's Sex Comedy*, a man bought the house for five thousand dollars and moved it to another location to live in. He just had to reinforce it and install water and electricity.

4:15 P.M. The camera is set just at the edge of the roof. Woody courageously goes to check it. He OK's the setup, then checks the pace of the smoke rings. Jimmy Mazzola shows him the pieces of debris with which Roger will try to open the door. Woody goes back to Sally and Baby Dylan. Carlo needs fifteen more minutes to get everything ready.

Jimmy Mazzola waters the rooftop. Roger's stand-in reads *Overruled* by Bernard Shaw (he has an audition next week). And the hat continues tipping.

4:45 P.M. There are problems. To create the night-sky background, huge black drapes have been hung. And since there are so many lights on the set and the drapes are not far enough back, they show up on-camera. Santo is brought in. But little can be done. The only way would be to hang the black drapes much farther away. But Little Joe's house is just behind. Woody asks if Santo could use a big billboard in the back to hide the drapes, but that would take at least two hours to rig. Tom and Bobby Greenhut are getting nervous. We have already spent two hours on this shot. The framing could be changed, but it looks beautiful the way it is. Carlo tries a tighter framing, but Woody agrees it's not as good. Carlo is pleased; today, he's the one who doesn't want to give up. Woody is more open to suggestions, and willing to discuss the situation. Bob Greenhut goes to check the tighter framing, and thinks it looks good. "If you need me, I'll be in the Jackhammers' kitchen," Santo says.

5:15 P.M. The actors are back in. Carlo has tried to fight the reflection on the drapes with a more indirect lighting. The sequence has been cut in two shots, with different camera angles.

Shot 68: Roger and Sally put their clothes back on after their brief interlude. Sally comments how fast it was. She thinks it might have helped that she had the hiccups. Roger, now satisfied, is anxious to go back downstairs. He goes to the door, and finds it locked from the inside. *(11 seconds.)*

Jimmy Mazzola sprays his water. "Looks good," Dickie says, checking it through the camera. Woody undresses his actors—one stocking for Sally, unzipped trousers for Roger. "You don't have to say 'I have to go back to the table,'" Woody says after the second take. Then, after a few seconds' pause, "Do as you feel." "Tell me what you want," says Roger. Woody, looking embarrassed, doesn't answer.

Take 3: The first really good one.

Take 4: Dickie cuts, not happy with the camera movement.

Take 5: Dickie is still not satisfied.

Take 6: "Could do better," Dickie says. Maybe lunch was too good?

Take 7: "Right on!" Dickie almost screams. "We move on," Woody decides.

(Takes 2, 3, and 7 are printed.) Completed at 6:00 P.M.

6:30 P.M. Woody is working on the blocking of the next shot, where Roger and Sally try to break the door down. Script in hand, Woody has the actors say their lines, showing them approximate spots and actions. He follows them around the set. Once a rough blocking is decided, Woody goes to the camera to watch through it. Roger and Sally rehearse their lines several times. But Woody is not satisfied with the movement: "It's not going to work."

These moments are the most interesting ones. Woody looks truly disturbed, and he doesn't bluff or try to hide it. Roger and Carlo make suggestions about new blocking or camera movement. But Woody seems not to understand, or listen. He acts like he is in another world. It is as if he is refusing to talk or think too much about it, but is again trying to feel the space, to get the atmosphere. He's trying to find a solution not through words but through emotion. Everybody waits in silence, while he rereads the script, there in the middle of the set, with everything ready, lights, actors, crew.

6:45 P.M. The shot is divided into two. Woody has decided on the first one, but he doesn't want to think about the second one now. Carlo needs thirty to forty-five minutes.

7:30 P.M. Everybody is ready. Jimmy Mazzola sprays the floor, the Salad Sisters polish Sally, and Ezra (we're on overtime) is ready to ring the bell that sounds before each take to let everyone know we're "Rollin'!"

Shot 68A: The door is closed from the inside and the couple is stuck on the roof. "The trick is not to panic!" Roger, who is totally out of control, says. He suggests they climb down the side of the building. Sally refuses categorically. Didn't she know the door closed from the inside? But this was Sally's first time, too. (27 seconds.)

Take 1: Good. But Roger is too fast, and doesn't hit his marks exactly.

Take 2: Woody cuts quickly. Sally doesn't hit the door strongly enough, and Roger doesn't emphasize enough. "The trick is not to panic!"

Take 3: Little problems with Roger, always with the blocking. Woody cuts. Roger comes from the theater; he gets entirely involved, and forgets to check the marks put on the floor to show him where to stand so the framing will be right.

Take 4: "No good, fellows," Woody says. There are more problems with the blocking.

Take 5: Good! First one. Woody reminds Roger to be forceful on his line "The trick is not to panic!"

Take 6: Very good. Roger could do better on "The trick . . ." But Woody seems satisfied.

Take 7: Dickie wants one more. Woody goes to encourage the actors.

Take 8: No good for the camera. Roger forgot about "The trick . . ." and was not hitting his marks well. Woody saw that immediately and made a frustrated little movement. He acts out the exact pace for Roger, and shows him the spot at the edge of the roof where he wants him to be.

Take 9: "Right on!" Dickie says. Woody: "One more and

we're finished." Across the set, Jimmy Sabat is arguing with
Jimmy Mazzola about the noisy fans.

Take 10: No good for the camera. And Roger was great! "God-
damn," Woody mumbles to himself. First time he has lost any
control.

Take 11: Roger's blocking is again not perfect.

Take 12: Again.

Take 13: Perfect.

(Takes 5, 6, 9, 11, and 13 are printed.)

We wrap at 8:10 P.M.

Woody dashes out. Fern, Larry (Jeffrey's driver), and I race
after him. But when we get to the door, he is already gone. Larry
drives full speed. We have to arrive on time, because we cannot get
in once the dailies have started. Jane lets us into Woody's cutting
room "Just in time!" and the screening begins.

It's a small room, dark-green velvet on the walls, dark-green
carpet. On each side, four or five comfortable swivel armchairs. At
the end, a sofa. The cutting room where Woody has edited all his
films since *Manhattan* is to the left. There is a small kitchen area
on the right. The space is neither very big, nor very luxurious, but
comfortable and functional.

Woody and Carlo sit on the sofa. And in the armchairs are
Sandy, her assistant Marty Levenstein, Ezra, Jane, and the other
three of us. The projection system is very high quality. We look at
the first shot of Tuesday morning, where Woody had changed all
the actors (shot 180B), then the following one, when Sally, the
Avenger, and Max grow melancholy looking at Times Square (shot
180C), and finally, the last shot of the movie, with everybody
going down the staircase, and the snow falling (shot 183). Most of
the takes of the first two shots look great. Woody is whispering to
Carlo. He stops the screening after two takes of the last shot.

Woody doesn't like the last shot, though Carlo thinks it's OK.
Ezra, of course, loves it (to reshoot with the whole cast will cost a
lot). But Woody still thinks the transparency doesn't look real. We
leave discreetly.

Dailies are always a little disappointing, because in seeing the
rough material, take after take, you can pick out every imperfec-
tion. But Sally looks beautiful, as does the last shot with the snow,
though Woody is right; it looks a little unreal.

Thursday, January 23, 1986

Government soldiers kill four children in Uganda. (New York Times)

Seven black South Africans are shot by police after two white policemen are killed. (New York Times)

Kate Mostel died yesterday at sixty-seven. A former Rockette, she was the wife of Zero Mostel, an actress herself, and Abe's real mother.

And three quarters of last year's 4,369 aspiring cabbies in New York were immigrants. They came from eighty-two countries, from Albania to Yemen. The median age was thirty-three, and more than half had completed two or more years of college. Languages included West African dialects of Ga, Efik and Kru; and the Indian languages of Gujarati, Telegu, and Malayalam. (New York Times)

9:00 A.M. Two Moroccans, dressed in their *jellabas,* are visiting Little Joe's house. They were brought from Morocco by *Ishtar,* as extras. Now they want to stay in America. In one month here, they have made more money than they'd make in five years in their country.

It's still up in the air whether or not we'll reshoot the last scene with the snow. The problem is that with all the beautiful people, it would cost another eighty thousand dollars. For the moment, there is no reshoot, says Ezra. Carlo is going to make a few tests this afternoon, and Woody will look at them.

Jeffrey is back with us this morning (he was absent the last two days) in a white shirt, black tie, red sweater, a black safari jacket, checked trousers, gray socks, and black moccasins.

10:15 A.M. Carlo is almost ready. Woody, Sally, Roger, Porfirio, and Irene are on the King Cole roof. Woody takes Sally by the hands, and brings her aside to rehearse her lines. He stands facing her, holding her hands, playing with them as he listens. He asks her for several readings of "We're going to be electrocuted," trying different tones.

Porfirio and Irene are rehearsing in another corner. They like rehearsing together. Now the Playboy of the Western World puts her through tango steps, though it is not in the scene.

Shot 68B: Roger and Sally are still stuck on the roof. Sally's ten-minute break is up, and she says she's going to lose her job. Then lightning strikes. "Lightning is attracted to the highest point." Sally has read it; "It's a fact." They're going to be electrocuted. While Roger again tries to break the door down, Sally goes to the edge of the roof and starts screaming for help. It makes Roger furious. They argue, Sally in tears because she's going to lose her job, and Roger afraid that if Irene finds out, she'll divorce him and the show will be over. Suddenly they hear voices from the staircase. "If you've never made love under the stars before, you're in for an experience," a male voice says. "Can't we just get a hotel room tomorrow?" answers a woman. The door opens, and it's Irene and Porfirio! *(1 minute, 2 seconds.)*

Take 1: Cut. Sally went out of frame.

Take 2: Dickie has a problem: Irene is so much bigger than the Playboy of the Western World that in the close shot her hands hide Porfirio's face. Otherwise, Sally and Roger are good.

Take 3: Problems with the lightning—it's not big enough. Roger didn't react. And the door is opened too soon, before the camera has time to finish its movement. Woody is also unsatisfied with Irene and Porfirio's arrival. He rehearses, trying it with Porfirio appearing first, then Irene first. Irene makes suggestions. Woody stays silent, staring at the actors. Then he goes to Carlo: "I try to make it as real as possible."

Take 4: Very good.

Take 5: Brian saw the shadow of Louis's boom. Nobody else saw it?

Take 6: Good. "Let's do it again," Woody says. He doesn't seem satisfied yet by Porfirio and Irene. Sally is being freshened up by the Salad Sisters. Woody again stands facing her, his hand on her waist, watching her in silence.

Take 7: Very good. "One more and . . ."

Take 8: Good.

(Takes 4, 5, 6, 7, and 8 are printed.) Completed at 11:15 A.M.

We're finished with the King Cole roof until the reshoot. Roger is leaving for Paris this afternoon. He shakes hands with everybody. People have enjoyed having him on the set.

11:40 A.M. A visit to the *Ishtar* set. They are setting a shot in a Moroccan restaurant. Dustin Hoffman's and Isabelle Adjani's stand-ins are there. Vittorio Storaro works with two video cameras, a walkie-talkie in his hand. There are plenty of people everywhere. Woody would have a nervous breakdown! Dustin Hoffman is wandering around in the hall, dressed in a black shirt and a red headband. Since we are shooting the roller rink now, we are on the stage just next to them.

12:00 noon. Seventy-five extras, in period dress for the roller skating, are waiting in the Zukor theater. There are the usual problems. One of the extras is cold (he's just arrived from California) and wants his jacket back. And Angela wants to kill another one who said he could roller-skate beautifully, when he can't even stand up on the things. "Let him go. He'll kill himself all alone!" says Stephanie from wardrobe.

12:15 P.M. The roller-skating rink looks beautiful with all its lights. On each side there are two counters full of sweets, popcorn, and cotton candy. (Two cotton-candy and popcorn machines are in the back.) On the other end of the stage is the Jackhammers' apartment set, a huge wall totally covered by an advertisement for pinking shears. In the middle of the advertisement, there is a small window that opens onto the Jackhammers' kitchen, the interior built behind it.

Manulis is practicing alone in the rink. He is not a champion, but with his six-foot-five, 230-pound frame, his moustache, and his laugh, you can understand why Bea is so impressed. Bea is eating cotton candy in the director's chair, entertained by Jeffrey, who, of course, has his arm around her.

Woody decides on a long traveling shot, and the boys go to work. Bea puts on her roller skates and enters the rink, led by Jeffrey, who also has on roller skates. Jeffrey tries to impress Bea with a few fancy moves. He's good. Poor Manulis; I go to compliment him. "That's only practicing. You're gonna see the performance!" he tells me.

Susan Joffe is here today. She is the daughter of Woody's producer and manager, Charles, and Carol (the set designer who works with Santo). From time to time, Susan helps with the wardrobe. Today, for instance, she worked on aging the roller skates. She has known Woody since she was a little girl, and tells me that one day Woody hit her sister with a lollipop and broke it on her head. That was back when Woody didn't like children. She admits, though, that she and her sister were giving him a hard time.

1:00 P.M. We're in the Jackhammers' kitchen. Carlo thinks that a long shot of the rink from their window could be nice. The boys bring in all their equipment. Santo is not very happy; he has just finished dressing the set with dirty dishes and dirty laundry. Once again he has done a great job and created perfection to the last dirty detail. The camera is being set up among the hanging laundry. Downstairs, Jimmy Mazzola tries the fog, rose-scented today.

We break for lunch at 1:35 P.M.

3:00 P.M. The seventy-five dress extras are practicing. Because the roller-skate wheels are wood, it's very noisy. First, we'll record some wild tracks of the organ.

The extras are asked to stand on the side, silent and motionless. Woody goes with Jimmy Sabat to the organ. The organ player (Lee Erwin) begins with "Shadow Waltz," and then plays "The Very Thought of You," "You Must Have Been a Beautiful Baby," "You're Getting to Be a Habit with Me." The rink, all lighted, with everybody standing still, looks magical.

Shot A51: Wide establishing shot of the skaters skating. *(30 seconds.)*

The camera is looking from the Jackhammers' kitchen. The fog has been abandoned. No big directing is required. The skaters skate, Manulis in the middle. Woody considers having some of them fall, but he drops the idea.

(2 takes and 2 prints.)

Shot A51A: The camera follows Manulis for half a spin around the rink. The camera is in the middle of the rink now. Again, there is not a lot of directing. Woody makes a few suggestions to Manulis.

(5 takes and 2 prints.)

Shot A51B: The camera tracks Manulis and Bea, skating arm in arm.

(2 takes and 2 prints.) Completed at 4:00 P.M.

Tom is relieved. We can release the extras now. And we should be finished with the film's big crowd scenes. Bea takes some popcorn and cotton candy home, and Manulis gives me a cheerful "See you next week!"

Carlo starts the lighting for the last shot for today: an establishing shot of Jackhammer having his breakfast, seen through the window (sequence 18).

5:00 P.M. On stage E, the King Cole roof is dark now, possibly awaiting a reshoot before being dismantled. Without lights, it has lost its magic, a little like a glamorous star with no makeup.

On stage F upstairs, the designers are working on tomorrow's shots. For the third reshoot of the singer, they are repainting the studio. And the Crooner will have a new background for his reshoot: a big Pepsi-Cola billboard. Just next to these two sets, the hospital room is being dressed to welcome Little Joe's family, who will be visiting Mom after she has given birth to Little Joe's sister (sequence 154).

Andrew thinks Dave is too fat, Burt is a little young, and Little Joe too noisy. And he thinks Manes isn't clean. Andrew doesn't want to be a musician like his father (André Previn), or an actor like his mom (Mia Farrow). For him, the thing is directing. But Andrew has principles. He wants total control on his films—writing, directing, final cut, and publicity. He doesn't want to write his own scripts, though, and suggests I write them for him. Of course I accept, and suggest he should hire Woody and his mom to act in the movie. He agrees, but "not Bea," he says. I tell him she is a good actress. "Yes," he replies, "but she flirts with Woody."

6:30 P.M. Ezra is beating Woody at chess. Carlo is almost ready. Dustin Hoffman, in jeans and black leather jacket, has finished his day and is going home. And Andrew, Jimmy Sabat, and I are having a club soda next to the organ.

Shot 18: Jackhammer having breakfast seen through the window.

The image is quite funny because the window is in the middle of the pinking-shears advertisement. Woody wants smoke from the two chimneys in the background. At the moment, there is smoke everywhere, except from the chimney. "We want smoke, not fog!" Tom yells to Jimmy Mazzola. It seems there is a leak in Jimmy's smoking system, and the Jackhammers' building looks like it's on fire. "Easy on the smoke," Woody says. Finally, we make it.

(3 takes and 2 prints.)

We wrap at 7:00 P.M.

In the station wagon, racing to the dailies (Woody is, of course, ahead) with Bob Greenhut, Fern, Jeffrey, and his assistant, Judy.

Larry is driving. Bobby is satisfied with the first reviews of *Hannah*, but gets nervous when writers start commenting on its "Chekhov" spirit and making comparisons to the three sisters in *Interiors*. Bobby is not convinced that making *Hannah* look like a sequel to *Interiors* would help at the box office.

Then we talk about the day. Fern overheard this exchange between Bea and Woody this morning:

Bea: "I hope you don't expect any grace from me today!"

Woody: "I stopped expecting any grace from you after the first two weeks of *Hannah*."

We arrive in time to see Roger and Sally making it on the roof (sequences 66 and 68). No problem—both are very good. We also look at yesterday's dailies again, the last sequence in the snow. It looks much better the second time. "We won't get anything better with the transparency. We'll have to build something," Woody says to Bob Greenhut, who doesn't react.

Friday, January 24, 1986

A Queens collection-agency executive accuses Manes of extortion. He states that Manes has demanded payments (about thirty-six thousand dollars) be made to Geoffrey Lindenauer, the deputy chief of the Parking Violations Bureau arrested last week, and a good pal of Manes'. Ed, who last week saw nothing wrong with a political figure having business dealings with the city, is backing off. He now suggests that Manes could step down. (Daily News *and* New York Times)

Five more killed in Lebanon clashes. (New York Times)

And the mystery of Dian Fossey, the American zoologist killed at her research camp in Central Africa, begins to clear up. The woman struggled eighteen years to protect "her gorillas" against poachers who made souvenirs of the animals, or sold them to zoos. And she had kidnapped the young child of a suspected poacher who had seized a baby gorilla. Her intention had been to make an exchange. (New York Times)

8:30 A.M. Woody is playing chess with Abe. Mom is in the hands of the Salad Sisters; the Crooner is next. Liz is happy because she just got her copy of Vincent Patrick's *Family Business,* signed by the author (who is Richie's dad). Since it's supposed to snow this weekend, Tim has gone to look for a location in the neighborhood for the snowman with the penis (sequence D102), and Carlo is lighting the Jackhammers' kitchen.

9:45 A.M. The Jackhammers' kitchen is a little crowded, and Carlo is ready to kill anybody. Kay asks Jimmy Mazzola if the sausages are cooked. They are being kept warm in doggy bags downstairs at the roller-skating rink. The Jackhammers come in, she in her nightgown, he in his underwear, followed by Woody and Bea, who has come to "flirt"! The Jackhammers are much more relaxed today than at the party with Max Harris and the beautiful people.

Shot 18A: The Jackhammers are having their morning meal while listening to *Breakfast with Irene and Roger* on the radio. *(41 seconds.)*

Woody doesn't have to do too much to make it funny. The way Jackhammer eats, the way Mrs. Jackhammer passes the food to him, and the voices of the most sophisticated couple in town in playback on the radio are enough to make everybody laugh after each take. Once again, the combination of a great but simple idea, and a beautiful cast, are all but enough. Jackhammer's line, "Gimme another sausage, willya!" over the distinguished voices of Irene and Roger, is irresistible. Woody then works on the details. One take is done with them not talking. Another, where they argue.

(5 takes and 4 prints.) Completed at 10:15 A.M.

10:45 A.M. We are upstairs on stage F to reshoot the Crooner. He will sing this time in front of the huge Pepsi-Cola billboard: BIGGER AND BETTER. The camera is being set in the technicians' booth, to shoot him through the window.

Louis asks me to pick up the cards. With all the boys in the studio playing now, he sells his deck within twenty minutes, and I arrived too late to buy one. Jimmy Sabat is a little worried; too many horses look like winners today. Jane has an eyepatch on this morning because of a cornea problem. And Barbara is back with us, busy taking orders for lunch from the PAs and the actors who have to stay on the set.

Sandy is here today, because of the music, and for the sake of

the Crooner, who was very tense the other day. She tells me that
Woody, too, liked the shot with the snow better the second time.

11:30 A.M. Shot R12: The camera starts on the control console,
then moves up to the Crooner singing "All or Nothing At All."
Woody lets him sing a little longer this time. He asks him to
loosen up.
(5 takes and 4 prints.) Completed at 11:50 A.M.
Woody thanks the Crooner. And we move next door to the
hospital room. The camera setting is quickly decided. We'll do it
before lunch, then move downstairs to Little Joe's house.

12:45 P.M. The pink hospital room looks almost too pretty.
"We're about ready to place the bodies," Tom says. The "bodies"
are the whole family. It's the first time they have been together.
They don't know each other very well yet, and exchange first
names. The new ones for us are Grandma (Leah Carrey) and
Grandpa (William Magerman). All together, they make for a wonderful group.
First Myla, the stand-in, who has been cast as Mom's roommate, gets into one of the beds. Then the nurse stands next to her.
Mom gets into bed, and the family gathers around her. A lot of
people are on the set today, and Woody is getting nervous. He
notices a new face, signals to Tom. The woman in question works
for Jeffrey. Woody lets it go, but Jeffrey asks her to move a little
more toward the back.
Shot 154: Mom has given birth to Little Joe's sister. The family visits, gathered around the bed. Abe has brought flowers, and
Bea chocolates. *(15 seconds.)*
No dialogue. There will be a voice over. Woody asks them to
be lively, to cheer Mom, letting them improvise. There are a few
problems with the blocking (Grandma hides Ceil) and with the action (Abe gives the flowers too soon). During the shooting, Woody
plays with a piece of the red ribbon from Bea's chocolate box, making it into a knot, pulling it, undoing the knot. Then he looks
around surreptitiously to see if anybody was watching.
(5 takes and 4 prints.)
We break for lunch at 1:30 P.M.

3:00 P.M. We're in Little Joe's living room. With Woody,
Carlo, Tom, Jimmy Mazzola, and Bea to discuss the establishing
shot of the family (sequence 24). Woody, script in hand and fol-

lowed by Carlo, looks for spots where the actors could say their lines, and for the right angle for the camera. All this is done in perfect silence. As usual, everything is set in approximate terms. Woody doesn't talk much, showing the camera movement with his hands. Carlo "listens." They decide on a dolly shot. And Woody disappears to his room.

(TOP, L to R:) Pop (Michael Tucker); Mom (Julie Kavner); Bea (Dianne Wiest); Ruthie (Joy Newman); Ceil (Renee Lippin); Abe (Josh Mostel) (BOTTOM, L to R:) Grandpa (William Magerman); Little Joe (Seth Green); Grandma (Leah Carrey)

Carlo not only has to light all the rooms on the first floor (since the camera will see everything) but he also has to worry about the exterior lighting, the sun shining through the window. It will take at least two hours.

4:00 P.M. Jeffrey is giving his arm to Mom to go to wardrobe now. The Salad Sisters are working on Grandma and Ruthie. And

LITTLE JOE'S HOUSE

BACK YARD

1ST FLOOR

Grand-parent's

Toilet

SINK

RADIO

FRIDGE

Kitchen

Dining room

RADIO

ALLEY

Sitting room

Hallway

SOFA

PORCH ON STREET

2ND FLOOR

Bea's

BED

Abe & Ceil's

BED

Bathroom

Mom & Pop's

BED

Little Joe
& Ruthie's

BED

BED

Little Joe invites Woody's nephew and his friend, who are visiting again, to his room.

The snowman has arrived. He is on a table in the carpenter shop: He is made of three synthetic balls of different sizes to be covered by real snow, and his huge penis is erect! Everybody goes to pay him a visit.

The exterior lighting is completed, and Carlo is working inside now. All the boys are hard at it: Ray, Red, Bobby Ward, Mickey, Eddie, Jimmy, and even Hammer!

5:00 P.M. It's all happening at the Salad Sisters' place. If you want to learn something, you just hang around their rooms. You'll meet Grandma in her nightgown, Grandpa in his underwear, Woody's nephew, and all the stars. You'll hear stories about Sly (Fern worked on him in *Nighthawks;* she says he was "OK"), Dustin, Dudley, Liza, and others. Pop is talking about *The Manhattan Project*, which he saw yesterday; his real wife, Jill Eikenberry, is in it. It was directed by *Annie Hall* and *Manhattan* co-writer Marshall Brickman, and is to be released in June.

6:00 P.M. We're in the house. Grandma is in her bedroom, Grandpa on the staircase, and Ruthie on the phone, ready to listen to the Waldbaums' party line. Ceil is in the kitchen, and Mom and Pop are in the dining room. Woody, Kay's thick script in his hands, asks the actors to run through their lines. Without acting, they go through the scene several times. Woody observes.

Grandma is now upstairs, and Grandpa is in the living room reading his paper. "It's going to be fine," Woody says. He goes behind the camera, asks them to run through their lines again, slowly, so he can check the framing and decide the exact blocking. Jay puts marks on the floor, and Mickey checks the focus. The movement is complicated (dollying and pans back and forth) but it creates a linking of action (one actor brings the camera to another one, then another one passes in the frame and the camera follows him . . .), which could be beautiful and a perfect way to introduce each character and create an atmosphere at the same time. (It's the same kind of establishing shot as the one in the castle in Renoir's *The Rules of the Game*, where each actor serves to introduce the other, the action choreographed like a ballet.)

The one who's really getting depressed is Jimmy Sabat, with people moving and talking all over the place, Louis can't follow each of them with the boom microphone. Even having Frankie with another boom will not be enough. Jimmy has to hide mikes in every corner. He'll have to mix all five tracks while shooting.

Carlo checks the camera and gives Woody a few suggestions. The actors go through their lines again. Woody watches them, quietly repeating their lines to himself, and making faces. A last rehearsal for Dickie, and we are ready to go. I am just behind the dolly track, with Woody's nephew and his girlfriend. Woody, though very concentrated, takes a moment to chat with them from time to time. The uncle and the nephew have a distant, but respectful attitude toward each other.

7:00 P.M. Shot 24: Pop is dictating a business letter to Mom in the dining room. "We take great pride in announcing Coronet cultured pearls . . . make that genuine pearls." Mom stops typing. Pop can't say "genuine" pearls if they're cultured; he'll go to jail. Pop insists. Mom argues. She thinks the whole letter is no good; they're going to be stuck with those pearls like they were with everything else. Mom goes to the kitchen. Pop is furious: "This time I've got the right item at the right price!" He goes to the living room to light a cigarette, passing Grandpa, who is reading his paper. "Nathan . . . Nathan!" Grandma yells from upstairs. Grandpa, mumbling, stands up, and goes to the staircase (Little Joe crosses in the background, running), passing by Ruthie on the phone as she announces that Mrs. Waldbaum is going to have her ovaries out. Ceil appears from the kitchen to hear more about Mrs. Waldbaum's health. *(1 minute, 10 seconds.)*

Before the first take, Dickie, who has a problem following Grandpa with the camera when he stands up, gets creative: "You don't jackrabbit after forty-five years," he tells Grandpa. "I don't with my wife."

Take 1: Woody cuts. Everything is wrong. The pace, the blocking. They have to go faster.

Take 2: Pop doesn't go far enough to get his cigarette, and his hands are seen in the frame while Grandpa is standing up.

Take 3: Grandpa is too late reacting, and "It looks like you're waiting for her cue," Woody tells him.

Take 4: Woody cuts. "You've got to really read your paper," he says to Grandpa, who is getting a little tense.

It's now 7:30 P.M. Ezra is here. He's in a corner discussing overtime and penalties with Tom and Hammer (the union representative). Woody goes on. Takes 5, 6, 7, 8, and 9 are not completed because of problems of pace, actors flubbing their lines, blocking, or Grandpa, who is a little lethargic.

Take 10: The first good one.

Take 11: Problems with the dolly. Red is getting tired. And Mom goes to the kitchen so quickly, it's hard keeping up with her.

Take 12: Pop makes a mistake on his lines. Everybody is tired now.

Take 13: Little Joe falls while crossing in the background. And Cousin Ruthie muffs her lines on Mrs. Waldbaum's ovaries.

Woody's nephew has stopped watching, but his girlfriend hangs on. Woody walks back and forth in front of us. He seems intense. I am totally rapt by the shot. "It's going to be a beautiful shot," I tell him. "If we get it!" Woody says. "We did a lot of this kind of shot in *Hannah*, but the actors were very good." It's the first time we've talked to each other spontaneously, and not about the weather.

Take 14: Grandpa is still not fast enough climbing the stairs.

Take 15: OK, but not great. Red is all red from pushing the dolly. Woody is silent, looking at the ground, hand on his face, searching, motionless. "You want to try something else?" Tom asks him. "No. Just thinking," Woody answers. "Let's try one more time."

Take 16: During the take, Woody shakes his head no. It's good for Dickie, though. It's 8:00 P.M. Woody goes to Mom and Pop and talks with them in a very low voice. Then he says, "Real fast" to Grandpa, and we go on.

Take 17: "That was perfect for me," Woody says, turning to Dickie. But Jimmy Sabat thinks Ruthie missed her lines at the end. Woody listens to the sound track. Ruthie swallowed the "out" of "ovaries out." Woody asks Jimmy to rerecord the line immediately, and we go on.

Take 18: "No good, Kay." Again poor Grandpa, who is definitely tired.

Take 19: "We're dead. Let's go again," Woody says. Grandpa is off. Pop, too, this time.

With the producers off discussing penalties, and each crew member thinking about his part of the job, Woody looks lonesome and exhausted. His nephew's girlfriend is still watching. Grandpa asks for a glass of water. "Let's try one more and then quit," Woody says.

Take 20: OK. But not great.
(Takes 10, 14, 15, 16, 17, and 20 are printed.)

We wrap at 8:30 P.M.

Now it's the race to the dailies. But "Catastrophe!" Jeffrey has lost his book with the addresses and phone numbers of all his friends, the stars. Larry and I watch Woody leave.

We arrive late. Woody has started. Jeffrey dares to enter; I sneak in behind him. The dailies are not very good. The camera movement between Roger and Sally on one side of the roof, and Porfirio and Irene at the door, doesn't work. And Irene and Porfirio are not that great in the scene either. The "sky" in the wide shot of the roller-skating rink looks fake, though the rink looks beautiful. Just as the screening ends, Bob Greenhut enters. "I'm here. You can start rolling," he jokes. "You just arrived for the worst dailies I ever saw," Woody tells him. The atmosphere is a little tense. "Fletcher, you should go home now," Woody says to Andrew. We leave, too.

It's a bad end for the week. It looks like Roger is going to have to leave his bathtub in Paris, and Manulis will be coming back, too.

Monday, January 27, 1986   *Thirteenth Week*

"Manes is a crook," Ed says. "Even though it's painful for me to say it about a friend of mine." He asks Governor Cuomo to act. But Cuomo thinks it's premature. "I am the mayor," Ed adds, "and whatever happens in my administration, good or bad, I take responsibility for." (Daily News and New York Times)

More from Uranus: A fifteenth moon, a tenth ring, and a magnetic angle are discovered. And Miranda appears to be a "bizarre hybrid of the geology of Mercury and Mars and some of the large moons of Jupiter and Saturn." (New York Times)

In Jerusalem, Talmuds mix with Gospels according to St. John, priest collars with yarmulkes, and nuns with the Yeshiva boys, in an unusual experiment in Jewish-Christian understanding. (New York Times)

Bears trounce Patriots, 46–10, in the Super Bowl.
"Kid Dynamite" wins his seventeenth KO.
And two more are gone:

The Singing Cowboy of "Oklahoma!," actor-singer Gordon MacRae, died of cancer at sixty-four.

The last surviving Oklahoma Blue Devil, vocalist and drummer Ernie W. Williams, died at eighty-one.

9:00 A.M. We're back in Astoria, but we're not going to re-shoot the roller rink. Woody will not use the long shot; the closer ones should be enough for the sequence. But Jackhammer at his window is back in. And Roger will definitely have to come out of his bathtub for a while; he's being contacted in Paris to see if he can come back for a day this week.

10:15 A.M. We are in Grandpa and Grandma's bedroom, look-ing toward the dining room, where Mom and Pop continue argu-ing about the cultured-pearl letter.

Shot 26: Grandpa is lacing Grandma into her corset upstairs. Mom and Pop are back to the cultured-pearl letter. Rereading the letter, Pop discovers that Mom hasn't typed what he dictated but has been improvising! The two argue about Pop's business sense. Little Joe comes in and ask for fifteen cents to buy a Masked Avenger ring. Mom and Pop turn their anger on him. "What do you think I am, made of money?" Pop says. "Concentrate more on your schoolwork and less on the radio," says Mom. Rabbi Baumel says Little Joe plays hooky, she tells Pop, and Pop starts yelling at Little Joe. *(30 seconds.)*

Take 1: Very good. Mom says her line: "The man doesn't know the first thing about business" to one of the chairs at the dining-room table, and the effect is very funny.

Take 2: Good again. Dickie asks for one more. "We're going to do a couple more," Woody answers. And to Pop: "Start walking on action."

Take 3: OK. Woody makes little adjustments. To Pop: "Exag-gerate on 'cultured pearl.'" To Mom: "When you turn, really talk to the chair."

Take 4: Woody cuts; the actors are not into it.

Take 5: Dickie cuts. The camera movement is no good.

Take 6: Mom flubs a line. "I'm sorry!" she says. "It's OK, let's continue," Woody tells her. She puts her head in her hands. Her anger at having messed up a line and her anger at Pop seem to meld.

Take 7: Very good. But "Mom's hair was squealing," Jimmy Sabat says.

Take 8: Good again. Now Woody works on intonations.

Take 9: Dickie cuts. The boom dipped into the frame. "Up, up, up, up, up, . . . you're out!" Dickie tells Louis.

Take 10: Good. "Finished," Woody says.

(Takes 1, 2, 6, 7, 8, and 10 are printed.)

The next shot is the following scene. Woody, script in hand, looks for another angle and Carlo follows. From the kitchen? "Too flat," Carlo says. Woody goes back to the living room. The camera setting is decided quickly, as though Woody doesn't want to lose the thread, the feeling of the scene. Woody lets Carlo work.

11:00 A.M. "Kid Dynamite" is supposed to pay us a visit this afternoon. The tango teacher is back and is taking Bea to a corner of the stage to practice the lindy. Bea listens to it on the radio in a following scene (sequence 32). Abe goes off with them to watch his sister-in-law dancing. Hammer wears a Chicago Bears T-shirt today! The roller-skating rink is being dismantled on stage F, and the snowman is still on the table in the carpenter shop; somebody has put a plastic bag on his erect penis.

12:00 noon. A blocking session with Grandma, Little Joe, Aunt Ceil, Mom, Pop, and Cousin Ruthie. Grandma calls Woody "dear," but Woody is not very warm with her. He rushes her a little, as if she irritates him. He has her go down the stairs looking for her teeth ("Where are my teeth? I can't find my teeth anymore!"). He asks her to do it quickly, without looking at the stairs! (Grandma's bad legs make walking hard for her.) Because she's not fast enough, Woody has her go to the kitchen, which is closer. Now the camera movement doesn't work anymore. The dolly is dropped and the shot simplified. Everything will happen on the stairs, at the doorway, and in the kitchen in the back. Carlo goes to work.

12:50 P.M. Shot 27: While Pop is yelling at Little Joe, Grandma, her bosom finally laced into her corset, comes from upstairs, looking for her teeth. "Where did you put them, Mama?" Ceil asks from the kitchen. "In a glass of water! Where do you think?" Grandma answers, annoyed. Mom announces that Little Joe has been using Grandma's teeth to play hockey with his friends. It sets Pop off again. Little Joe responds by asking for a Masked Avenger ring. Mom advises him to take back deposit bottles. And finally Ruthie, still listening to the Waldbaums' party line, announces that Mrs. Waldbaum's cousin is pregnant, and that they're not sure who the father is. Mom suspects it is Adelman the druggist. "He should drop dead," she concludes. *(30 seconds.)*

Take 1: Carlo cuts. There is a shadow on Pop. Anyway, Ruthie was too slow reacting. Woody goes to talk to her. He takes the Pepsi bottle from the table (it was too obvious in the shot) and puts it at Ruthie's feet.

Take 2: Woody cuts: "We're dead!" Grandma missed her cue . . .

Take 3: Again. Grandma didn't hear Ceil. "Give her the 'Mama!'" Woody says to Ceil.

Take 4: Very good. Woody goes to each of the actors. He asks Grandma to come down two stairs before starting to talk.

Take 5: "Let's do it again." Woody is half satisfied.

Take 6: Woody cuts. Ceil is too late.

Take 7: Good. Ruthie is much faster, but Ceil could do better, and Mom should come a little more to the right for the framing.

Take 8: The pace is not perfect. "Let's do it again."

Take 9: Dickie cuts. There's a problem with the camera movement.

Take 10: Ruthie flubs her lines. Anyway, Mom was not on the right mark.

Take 11: Good. "One more and we're finished," Woody says, and to Grandma: "Don't be so angry."

Take 12: Very good.

(Takes 4, 7, 8, 11, and 12 are printed.) Completed at 1:20 P.M. We break for lunch.

3:15 P.M. Shots 24 through 33 form a long establishing sequence where all the members of the family and the neighbors (the Waldbaums and the Communists) are introduced in a succession of events that characterize both them and the atmosphere in Little Joe's house. Now it's Bea's turn.

Shot 29: Bea has a new hat, and she's showing it off. "It looks like something you feed the cat," Pop says. Mom comes to her defense, but Bea doesn't look impressed, and goes to the yard to show the hat to Ceil. *(10 seconds.)*

This shot is the beginning of the scene where she shows her hat to Abe and Ceil through the window (29A), a shot we did the second week in Rockaway.

Take 1: There's a problem with the zoom. It should be finished by the time Mom crosses the frame.

Take 2: Good, but it could be better.

Take 3: OK. Woody asks Bea to continue primping as she leaves. Bea is a little moody today, but she's still good.

Take 4: Good. "One more and . . ." Woody asks the actors to exaggerate again, Bea in her primping, Pop in the way he's chewing, and Mom in the way she slaps him.

Take 5: "Madonna!" Richie is right next to Carlo and screams, "Rollin'!" in Carlo's ears, and Carlo doesn't like it. The take is fine, though. But Woody wants one more. He asks Bea to finish her lines in front of the mirror, before leaving.

Take 6: "Right on!" Dickie says.

(Takes 2, 3, 4, 5, and 6 are printed.)

Woody goes to the kitchen with Kay and Tom, and sits at the table, rereading the script: "I'm trying to figure out what we can handle."

The actors and the crew settle in the living room. We all wait, talking quietly. The mixture of the two groups and all the equipment makes for a nice, but curious image. Santo passes through. He seems a little irritated by all of us having taken over his set (with no respect!). He checks a few things, moves some fragile vases to safety, then leaves, not wanting to see more.

3:35 P.M. Rehearsal. We are in the kitchen. Grandpa sits at the table. Abe, Ceil, and Bea are standing. Woody is in the middle of them all, script in hand. Carlo, Tom, and Mom watch. As always, the blocking session starts out vague: "You know. . . . You could do this." Woody watches the players going through the action, asks them to just say their lines, no acting, and follows them with his hands framing the scene, makes a few corrections. Bea goes from the sink to the refrigerator. Abe comes in from the yard where he has just seen Doris, the Communist's daughter, and Ceil follows him. Bea starts to dance and Grandpa says his lines. The problem is that Grandpa's lines are quite long. Is he going to make it? "Yes," he says. Now where should the radio be? On the refrigerator? Bea suggests that the radio be on very low at the beginning of the scene, and that when the lindy hop comes on, she goes to turn it up. "We could do that. It's possible," Woody says. "It's possible, though I don't know how to do it." And he's silent for a while.

At the beginning, it is a shock to see this big director who has done fourteen movies, and more than a few good ones, hesitating, taking advice from actors, and saying out loud, "I don't know how to do it." And then, after seeing him doing it again and again, one begins to have an idea of what all this means. Woody gets all the elements together, the script in his hand, the set lighted, the actors ready, and stands silently in the middle of everything, letting himself be taken by the atmosphere, by the sound of a voice, by a face, by an angle, by a line of the script. He knows what he wants, but at this point, he prefers to let the elements lead him and be ready to act when the inspiration strikes. And since each of the elements—the lines, the casting, the decor—has been intensely prepared, the magic, most of the time, works itself out. And though it is impossible to see what is happening in his head, it's fascinating to witness the process.

4:15 P.M. Carlo is working. Grandpa tells me he was an extra in *Stardust Memories* and had a small part in *Annie Hall*. He was the deaf husband of Woody's aunt. In the end, the scene was cut! Grandpa considers Woody a genius: "Always thinking!" And his favorite Allen film is *Bananas*.

5:00 P.M. Shot 32: In the kitchen, Grandpa is having tea and eating cake. Bea can't decide whether she should go to the Catskills or on a cruise. "The men are younger in the mountains, but they're richer on a cruise," she explains. Grandpa gives his opinion: "At this point, I'll settle for anything!" Abe comes back from the yard, where the action was—the Waldbaums complaining about Ruthie ("Stop listening . . ."), Mom and Pop reacting ("Let them take her ovaries out!") and the Communist chasing his son ("I'll kill you!") "She's a pretty girl, next door—the Communist—what a build! And they believe in free love . . ." Abe says. "Go back to your fish, you're happier with your flounder," Ceil tells him. "That's why I married you!" he tells her. The lindy starts on the radio, and Bea dances for the family. *(30 seconds.)*

Grandpa had a short monologue at the end while Bea was dancing, complaining about the life she's leading: "Beauty parlor six times a week, dance lessons . . . and she still can't trap a victim. . . ." But Woody, not wanting to take any risks, cut it.

First rehearsal: Grandpa says, "At that point . . ." Woody: "No. 'At *this* point'. . . And don't look at her."

Second rehearsal: Grandpa says "that" again. Woody reminds him, "'At *this* point.' It's very important." He talks to him like he's a child, and poor Grandpa looks upset. It's a little embarrassing. "And not so angry," Woody tells him.

Take 1: Grandpa misses his cue. It's a pity because he really has a great look. But it appears this is going to be difficult.

Take 2: "Eat the food, enjoy yourself," Woody says to Grandpa just before "action." But Dickie cuts; the camera is no good.

Take 3: Good. Grandpa did it. He said "I'll accept anything" instead of "I'll settle for anything," but it works. "Perfect," Woody tells him. But Bea was a little late on her cue.

Take 4: Just before "Action!" Woody repeats the line to Grandpa. And . . . he flubs it! Poor Grandpa wants to crawl into the woodwork. Woody makes no comment.

Take 5: Grandpa did it. Beautifully. The first really good take.

Take 6: Good, but some trouble with the zoom. "Jimmy Mazzola! A little coffee for Pop," Dickie screams, taking good care of Grandpa.

Take 7: Good. Woody asks Abe to emphasize the "you" of "That's why I married you." Then Woody argues with Bea because she wants to listen to the lindy-hop music before the take to get a good rhythm, and he doesn't think it's necessary.

Take 8: Woody adds the following dialogue at the end of the scene:

Bea: "How do you like it, Abe?"

Abe: "Take the gas pipe!"

Take 9: A problem with reflections on Abe's glasses. But still good. And Grandpa is excellent now, "At this point . . ."

Take 10: Very good. But Abe thinks he can do better with his "That's why I married you." His "Take the gas pipe" was perfect, though.

Take 11: Poor Grandpa is getting tired now. He misses his cue because he has a mouth full of cake. And maybe Woody overdid it by repeating, "At this point . . ." before "Action!"

Take 12: "A lot of energy, guys," Woody says before "Action!" The take is very good.

(Takes 5, 6, 7, 8, 9, 10, and 12 are printed.)

We wrap at 5:45 P.M.

Tuesday, January 28, 1986

Marcos invokes the spirit of his assassinated opponent Benigno Aquino as his secret supporter, and accuses Corazon Aquino of planning to decree martial law. (New York Times)

Ed blasted on "crook" line. But "has no worry about public confidence." (Daily News)

And 65 percent of Americans approve of Ron. No president in the history of the United States has shown such stability; Roosevelt and Eisenhower had only 60 percent approval ratings. (New York Times)

9:00 A.M. A series of reshoots today, including the difficult shot from last Friday, with all the family introduced one after the other (sequence 24), the hospital room, Jackhammer at his window, and the singer. Woody thought the second singer looked too modern, and has now cast actress-singer Kitty Carlisle Hart, widow of Broadway playwright and director Moss Hart, and the Marx Brothers' leading lady in *A Night at the Opera*. Originally, Woody wanted somebody like Barbara Cook.

But first we'll do a shot in Little Joe's house, where Pop complains to Mom about the noise her family is making (sequence 33). Carlo is lighting the set.

Grandma waits on the porch. Since she has trouble walking, she prefers to stay near the set. "Kid Dynamite" didn't come yesterday because he met a girl, Brian tells me. And Jimmy Mazzola shows Grandma's teeth to Woody before putting them in Little Joe's desk, where Mom will discover them. Even with all this reshooting, Woody is in a good mood and much more relaxed. I get a nice hello smile.

10:10 A.M. Shot 33: While Bea is giving a lindy-hop demonstration, Pop is eager to get back to business; there's another letter for Mom to type. But Mom wants to see Bea dance. Pop is furious. He starts complaining about Mom's family living here: "Your parents, your sister, her husband, their kid, your unmarried sister. . . !" "We all need to band together," Mom explains. "They're doing the banding, I am doing the supporting!" Pop replies. "What does Daddy do for work?" asks Little Joe. "That's none of your business," Pop tells him, looking uncomfortable. But Little Joe presses. "He's a big butter-and-egg man," Mom tells him, and while looking in Little Joe's desk, she finds Grandma's teeth. "Ma, I found your teeth!" Little Joe asks for a Masked Avenger ring. "Forget the Masked Avenger ring, and pay more attention to your schoolwork," Pop says, cuffing his head on principle. *(39 seconds.)*

Take 1: Not great. "We're going to do it different ways, but don't start fighting too early," Woody tells Mom and Pop.

Take 2: A little better. "Do your line while you find the teeth, so we don't lose time," Woody tells Mom.

Take 3: Dickie cuts. Pop was blocked by the dining-room chandelier when he started his lines.

Take 4: There's a little problem with Mom's exit. It would be better if she exited the frame more to the right.

Take 5: Good. But let's go again.

Take 6: Dickie cuts. Pop's arm passed too much in front of the camera.

Take 7: OK. Woody to Pop: "You should react more to Little Joe. You can hit him, really."

Take 8: Little Joe muffs his line.

Take 9: Pop really hit Little Joe: "It helps." "Good, but keep it lower," Woody tells him.

Take 10: The best one, but Pop is not satisfied; he thinks he can do better.

Take 11: Little Joe misses his line again. The boy is starting to tire of being hit, though Pop is not as strong as Rabbi Baumel.

Take 12: Now it's Pop's turn to mangle a line.

Take 13: Very good. "One more and . . ."

Take 14: Good. But Woody asks Mom to really wave Grandma's teeth around, and play up the line: "Ma, I found your teeth!"

Take 15: Just before "Action!" Woody tells everyone, "Fast!" Good. The teeth bit is funny, but Mom "flips out the frame" according to Dickie.

Take 16: "Good, Wood. Right on!" Dickie yells.

(Takes 2, 5, 7, 10, 14, 15, and 16 are printed.) Completed at 10:45 A.M.

Pop hugs Little Joe. Since the Rabbi Baumel scene, where Little Joe broke down and Pop cheered him up, a nice relationship has developed between them, and Pop is the one with whom Little Joe is the most natural.

Now Carlo goes back to work to prepare the reshoot of last Friday night's difficult scene (shot 24).

11:15 A.M. In the rooms downstairs, Abe plays chess with Woody, Pop and Mom rehearse their lines in Mom's room, and Ceil reads the *Daily News*. And on the King Cole roof, an artist is painting a lighthouse on a cliff. Bea will see it when she's abandoned by Manulis at Breezy Point. With a little fog, the lighthouse will look real.

Kitty Carlisle Hart is alone upstairs in her room. Angela introduces me. Kitty speaks fluent French; she was raised in France and Switzerland. She is elegant, and has a completely different look, certainly slimmer, from the previous singers. Last Friday, she received a phone call asking her if she wanted to be in a Woody Allen movie. Yesterday, she recorded the two songs, and here she is. She met Woody once at a dinner party and he told her how much he admired her husband. But she doesn't know him very well, and she hasn't seen him yet this morning. She tells me that she sang at Astoria in the forties for the boys in the army (like Sally), and that she is involved in the refurbishment of the studio. There is a picture of her in the studio pamphlet with Donald Manes.

11:30 A.M. "Everyone will have to duck down," Dickie says, because of the reflections in the windows.

Shot R24: Same action: It starts on Mom and Pop arguing about the cultured-pearl letter. Pop goes to get a cigarette, Grandma calls down for Grandpa, and Ceil joins Ruthie to find out more about Mrs. Waldbaum's ovaries. But the pace is much quicker. Since Grandpa cannot walk fast and talk at the same time, Woody gives his line, "And this one listens to the party line!" to Pop. Woody asks Grandpa to hurry as best as he can, "And remember, you just say, 'Coming, I'm coming!'"

Take 1: OK for the camera, but Mom stumbled on a word. Woody hides his annoyance.

Take 2: "We're dead!" Grandma was late calling Grandpa. ("Nathan! . . . Nathan!")

Take 3: All the action was much faster. But Grandpa overdid it: He left before the camera was on him.

Take 4: Very good. The first one.

Take 5: Good, but Ceil should come a bit later.

Take 6: Pop became much too angry. It's a pity, because he started great.

One of the PAs tells us that the space shuttle has blown up. Seven are dead. We continue.

Take 7: There are problems with the camera movement, and anyway, the scene needs more energy.

Take 8: We're dead again. Grandma forgot to call Grandpa. Too bad. The take was going well to that point.

Take 9: Good, but Mom hesitated on a word. It's worth printing, though. Woody gives a little gesture of despair.

Take 10: Cut. Poor Mom, for the second time. She rarely misses her lines, and on this scene! "That's all right," Woody tells her.

Take 11: Cut. Somebody dropped a pen.

Take 12: There was a problem with the timing between Pop and Grandpa. Not a very good take.

Take 13: Cut. Trouble with the sound!

Take 14: No good. Grandpa was right on time, but Pop was a little late.

Take 15: Same as 14. Woody looks desperate.

Take 16: Good for Woody, but Dickie is not satisfied.

Take 17: Woody cuts because Mom is too late.

Take 18: Right on.

(Takes 4, 5, 9, and 18 are printed.) Completed at 12:40 P.M. We move upstairs to stage F. But first, we go to hear the news.

1:00 P.M. In the teamsters' room the TV is on, and everybody is gathered, shocked. Bobby Greenhut, Barbara, Brian, Ezra, the Hebrew tutor, Little Joe, Patti, the nurse, Dickie. The network is replaying the tape of the explosion. The power of this image of death before your eyes—and it's not fiction. Silence. All the faces are solemn. "It's the worst thing that's happened to America since Kennedy's death," Jane tells me.

But life goes on. The boys are moving the equipment upstairs. We break for lunch at 1:25 P.M.

In the commissary, Dustin Hoffman's stand-in, wearing a black shirt and red headband, is having lunch with Isabelle Adjani's stand-in, who is almost as pretty as the original.

3:00 P.M. We're back on the set. I'm pals with Grandpa now. He's exhausted from this morning's work, getting out of his armchair and walking up the stairs eighteen times. But he manages. He has decided to call me Terry.

The Hebrew tutor tells me he wants to be an actor, and is going to do a play Off-Off-Broadway soon. He teaches only to make a living.

3:15 P.M. Shot R154: The hospital room.

Mom and Myla are back in their beds, the nurse standing off to the side. The family has gathered by Mom's bed, but all on one side now; the first time, Grandpa and Grandma were at the foot of it. The dolly is a little longer, too. Same action.

(2 takes and 2 prints.) Completed at 3:20 P.M.

We move to the broadcast studio for Kitty. It has been re-painted in brighter colors, and looks prettier. Carlo starts to work. Ruthie tries a few mime steps; she studied with Marcel Marceau for a year in New York. Abe takes Angela to a corner. "Where are you going?" Mom asks. "Leave me alone!" Abe replies.

Grandpa talked to Grandma about me, and we start to socialize. This is her first movie. She used to act in the theater. Her son was a theatrical producer. He brought her to New York a few years ago from Boston. Woody interviewed her once two years ago, but the film was canceled. Then she lost her son last March. She was alone in New York (her other son lives in San Francisco) and feeling desperate, when Woody called her back. He remembered her! Working on this movie was a great help. She considers Woody America's Sholem Aleichem, whose stories were the basis for *A Fiddler on the Roof.*

Grandma is a sweet, sensitive, intelligent woman, and every-body on the set likes her. I still have one problem with her, though. Every now and then, she uses Yiddish expressions and references that are lost on me. At the end of our conversation, Grandma notices my dilemma. "Are you Jewish?" she asks me. No. A Gentile! She seems a little disappointed; such a nice man!

3:45 P.M. A very elegant Kitty is under the spotlight. She calls to the Salad Sisters, "Fern, darling." Carlo goes to introduce him-self. A first rehearsal starts. Woody arrives in the middle of it, and listens. At the end, he goes to say hello to Kitty, and thanks her for having accepted. Then he stands to the side while Carlo works to make the lighting even more flattering. Woody doesn't seem much at ease with Kitty, though he's very polite. He gives her a little smile now and then, but he keeps his distance. He goes to relax by talking with Brian, and poor Kitty is alone in front of her mike. So Woody makes the effort, and goes to chat with her. Brian takes a picture of the two. Typically, Kitty smiles, and Woody bends his head to one side, taking on the Zelig look.

4:30 P.M. Shot RR149: Kitty sings "They're Either Too Young or Too Old." It finishes on a close-up of her.

She sings along to her voice in playback. There are a few problems with synchronization; it will be important for the close-up. A professional, Kitty knows right away when she is out of sync.

(4 takes and 3 prints.) Completed at 4:45 P.M.

Kitty goes to change for the next song.

4:55 P.M. Kitty is back in a beautiful red dress.

Shot RRA107: Now she sings "I'll Be Seeing You," while the camera moves back for a wider shot.

It is totally different than with the two other singers. It is certainly less comic, but, Woody is right, it's more of a *clin d'oeil* to the period, more in the spirit of the movie. And having been an actress and a singer at the time, Kitty might actually have sung the songs.

The melancholy returns. The boys are listening and watching. Kitty definitely has class, and a certain fragile, nostalgic look. And as the takes go on, it works even better. These sorts of nuances for a basically simple shot are partly what gives Woody's work its quality. He is able to take enough distance with the scene to see if it works, how it works, why it works. I am sure it is both conscious and unconscious with him, but it is that kind of perfectionism and lack of self-indulgence that makes him a great artist.

(4 takes and 3 prints.)

6:00 P.M. We're back on stage G to shoot Jackhammer at his window. The roller rink is half destroyed. Santo and Carlo talk about the fog scene, where Bea and Manulis get lost at Breezy Point, which will be shot on this stage. But the conversation is not without complications. First, Santo has not seen Antonioni's *Identificazione di una Donna*, the fog scene in which was Woody's inspiration. It was also shot in a studio, Carlo explains, not bigger but taller, so the lights on the ceilings didn't interfere with the fog. The second difficulty is that Carlo's English is far from perfect, and Santo has to know precisely what Carlo needs.

6:30 P.M. Jackhammer is waiting in his kitchen, and Carlo is lighting. Woody was pleased with neither the lighting nor the framing of this scene.

Shot R18: It's the same long shot through the window of Mr. Jackhammer having breakfast. The camera is set up off-center, with different lighting and framing.

(3 takes and 3 prints.)

We wrap at 6:35 P.M.

Wednesday, January 29, 1986

More shuttle news. It exploded seventy-four seconds after lift-off. Six astronauts and high school teacher Christa McAuliffe died. It was the worst disaster in U.S. space history.

Manes steps down.

"I am going to do anything I can to steal everything I can from everybody," Ed says. He's talking about New York's aggressive efforts to take film production from Hollywood. (Variety)

And two more leave us:

"Best-selling author/founder of Scientology/friend to millions" L. Ron Hubbard died of a stroke at seventy-four.

Actress Lilli Palmer died of cancer at seventy-one.

9:00 A.M. It's the same old routine—Woody plays chess with Abe, Jane is on the telephone, most of the family is in the hands of the Salad Sisters, and Carlo and the boys are lighting the shot. Cliff reads Dorothy Parker's autobiography not too far from the set, in case he is needed. And Louis is doing brisk Wednesday business. I buy a card but with no great hope, just out of habit. For the past two days now, Bea has been eating and eating; she's always hanging around the crew's food. Near the King Cole roof, the artist is finishing the lighthouse on the cliff. First, he drills holes for the window and the beam; a flashing light will be put behind it. The lighthouse model will be put in the back of the set, and with a little fog, "everybody is going to believe it," he tells me.

10:00 A.M. "Give me Ceil, Abe, Ruthie, and Mom," Tom says. The bodies have names now. After a little more than a week together, a true bonding has developed between the family and the crew, and within the family itself. We all like each other. Abe "flirts" with Angela. Cousin Ruthie listens to Grandpa and Grandma tell stories from the old country. Mom and Ceil are always together. And Pop likes to hang around with the boys, or chat with Nicole or Myla.

We're having a general rehearsal. It's Yom Kippur, and the Communist neighbor is eating, working, and listening to his radio. It is the scene just before the one in which Abe breaks down the fence (shot in Rockaway the second week). The family is in the living room, scandalized (sequence 76). Woody is behind the camera for an informal blocking session, putting the actors in different spots. To Ruthie: "I'm pretty sure you're going to walk." To Tom: "I also want a couple of relatives here." And to Carlo, after a few rehearsals: "It looks better." It's funny the way Woody seems to take a certain pleasure saying things like, "We could," "Maybe," "If it works," "I am not sure," while he is blocking.

The blocking is set. Carlo needs half an hour for the adjustments, and Jimmy Sabat, complaining again that the actors move around too much, sets his mikes.

11:00 A.M. Shot 76: It's Yom Kippur. The family, all dressed up, sits in the living room, "doing nothing," exasperated. A radio is blaring out.

Ceil: "It's terrible. They have no respect."

Abe: "They should be thrown out of the neighborhood."

Mom: "It's a disgrace."

Abe: "And my nerves on edge because I'm so hungry."

The cause of this uproar is the Communist neighbor; he's eating, working, and listening to his radio very loud on Yom Kippur. And, as Ceil says: "They're Jewish, but they don't believe in God. Just Stalin." The tension grows. Ruthie thought one could at least turn on the radio, but Abe is positive. "For twenty-four hours, you're supposed to do nothing. You can't turn on a light switch— nothing—you're supposed to just sit, and fast, and pray, and atone for your sins." Abe is beside himself, mostly, as he honestly said before, because he's so hungry. Mom spurs him on. Abe decides to go and "talk" to the Communist. *(57 seconds.)*

The scene is funny, the actors and the lines perfect. You have the feeling that at this point Abe hates Yom Kippur as much as the Communist. The problem, as always, is getting the exact blocking, the actors saying their lines at the right moment, and standing at the right spot, so the image will be nice and the pace correct.

Take 1: Cut. Mom stumbled on a word.

Take 2: "It's not going to work," Woody says of the kitchen.

Ruthie now sits next to Grandma, instead of across from her. While Carlo and Jimmy make their adjustments, Woody goes to flirt with Bea.

Take 3: Dickie cuts just before "Action!" He's spotted a piece of tape.

Take 4: Woody cuts. Again the problem is in the kitchen. Grandma and Ruthie should be talking more quietly.

Take 5: Dickie cuts in the middle of the take because of problems with Mom's entrance into the frame. But the acting was good, Woody tells the cast.

Woody glares at me. What did I do? Maybe I'm too close?

Take 6: Cut. Little Joe already had the yarmulke on, and Mom is supposed to do that!

Take 7: Cut. Ruthie was not on time. Bea is not happy because she has nothing to do, except stand there.

Take 8: First completed take. It looked OK, but Woody is not satisfied. "More energy," he tells Ruthie.

Take 9: The first good one. During the take, Woody was saying the words to himself.

Take 10: Dickie cuts. He again has a problem with Mom when she goes to the hallway. It goes from a wide shot to a nice close one of her putting the yarmulke on Little Joe in front of the mirror. But the transition is difficult because she passes so close to the camera.

Take 11: Very good. The first to be printed. Woody now asks Abe to become "really angry."

Take 12: Woody cuts. Mom was a little late because her bracelet opened and fell off. "Try to finish your lines before getting to Little Joe," Woody says, always accelerating the pace.

Take 13: The timing looks perfect. Woody goes to each actor.

Take 14: Cut. Abe's timing is not good, and Ceil missed her cue. Woody becomes tense.

Take 15: Very good. "One more and . . ."

Take 16: Cut. Ruthie said her lines as though she were reciting them.

Take 17: "Right on!"

(Takes 11, 13, 15, and 17 are printed.) Completed at 12:10 P.M.

1:00 P.M. Shot 78: Ceil, Mom, and Pop are in the living room. Abe is at the Communists'. Ceil is worried. "He's been there two hours." "Meanwhile, the radio is still on," Pop remarks. "Better

be careful," Mom says, "the daughter believes in free love!" Pop
asks for more information. Mom tells him what happened to Mrs.
Silverman. *(15 seconds.)*

A very short scene with no big camera movement and no problems with the actors.

(2 takes and 2 prints.)

We break for lunch at 1:15 P.M.

2:30 P.M. After winning $1,600 in the Super Bowl pool Mon-
day, Louis wins first prize today ($300) with the cards. No com-
ment!

Woody comes to the set with a guest this afternoon, a woman
in her late forties with red hair and wearing a red skirt, red boots,
and a black sweater with a red tie around it. Joffe's other daughter,
the one who got beaned with the lollipop, is visiting with her boyfriend, too. We're doing a wild track of Mom telling Mrs. Silverman's story, how she had the stroke after seeing Doris kiss the
black guy.

Mom has a really wonderful voice—nasal, energetic, spontaneous, with a very peculiar way of pronouncing certain words,
"A big LonG KiSS . . ." "You knoaw Missis, Zilverman— she
likes to knoaw what's goaing on." It seems the lines were written
just for her. Different versions are done, slow and fast. Then
there's one with "a black man," another one with "a colored
man," and one with "a shvartza."

As soon as that is completed, Woody works on the next shot,
where Abe finally comes back from the Communists' (sequence
83). Woody does rough blocking as usual, but now with authority—"camera here," running from one side of the room to the
other, going through Abe's action. Carlo is astonished. Woody's
behavior seems not at all natural. It looks like he is doing it for the
"Woman in Red." Suddenly he disappears with her into his room.

3:15 P.M. Woody is playing chess with Abe while the Woman
in Red interviews him in his room. Ceil, Mom, Pop, Jeffrey, and
Bill have gathered at the Salad Sisters'. Bea is also here but is
definitely moody today. Could she be jealous of the Woman in
Red? Fern is reading her mail in the other corner. In the room
next door, Werner, Cousin Ruthie, and her real mother listen to
Grandma; Grandpa is taking a nap in an adjoining room, and
Dickie is watching TV with the teamsters.

When you ask how many weeks are left, you get several answers. Ezra says two, Tom says three, and it's not the kind of question you ask Woody.

4:00 P.M. Everybody is back on the set. There are two new guests. One is a teenage boy with a punk haircut, dressed in black tie and black patent-leather shoes. The other is a Japanese woman who is a writer for *The New York Times*. Woody introduces the Woman in Red to Carlo and to the other guests. I withdraw, embarrassed. Maybe I'm paranoid, but one of the boys says to me, "Did you see? He never introduced you to Carlo the first day!" The boys seems aware of the situation, and become almost overly nice to me. I am one of them now, and that makes the situation even more awkward for me.

5:00 P.M. Shot 83: The family is still waiting. After hearing Mrs. Silverman's story, Ceil is on edge. The door opens. It's Abe. "It's about time!" Ceil says. But the radio is still on, and Abe's behavior is strange, relaxed. They start to question him. What did he do for two hours? "Talked . . . or should I say, listened," Abe says. And he ate! Then he starts to talk funny: "I should atone for my sins? What are my sins? Who did I bother? . . ." Everybody is stunned. He has no guilt anymore! "The only sin is the exploitation of the workers by the bosses." Pop understands now, but Mom would like to know if the daughter "got a hold on him." Abe goes on: "The problem is not between man and some imaginary super being . . ." When he sits down, Ceil notices some red on his cheek. He tells her it's cherry pie. *(44 seconds.)*
Once again, the lines are great and seem to have been created for Abe; he's perfect. Bea is playing solitaire in the dining room and is getting tired of being an extra.
Take 1: Woody cuts. Abe was too late slamming the door.
Take 2: Dickie cuts. Problems with the dolly while following Abe.
Take 3: Good, even very good for Dickie and Woody. But Jimmy could do better with the sound. Woody is not overjoyed.
Take 4: OK. But Dickie could do better this time.
Take 5: Dickie cuts very quickly.
Take 6: First really good one. Woody asks Abe to now be more aggressive and defensive when he does his speech.
Take 7: Good. Woody goes to Bea in the back and shows her

how to play solitaire. Carlo takes the opportunity to adjust some lights.

Take 8: Abe starts jovially and finishes his speech with passion in his voice. "Don't be too angry, but firm, definite, convinced," Woody tells him.

Take 9: Cut. Abe muffed a line.

Take 10: Woody cuts. Abe's entrance was no good.

Take 11: Cut. Abe has said "the exploitation of the bosses by the workers."(!)

Take 12: Dickie cuts quickly. He wants to be better situated on the dolly. Woody goes to the Woman in Red.

Take 13: Good. "Let's go again." But Abe is getting warm. The Salad Sisters take care of him. Ezra, who always arrives on the set when we are on overtime, discusses the schedule with Tom. Woody goes to flirt with Bea, showing her card tricks. The writer for the *Times* and the teenage boy get tired of being pushed aside, and leave. We go on.

Take 14: Good. Woody goes to Abe with the script, and checks the lines with him.

Take 15: Cut. Abe missed one word.

Take 16: After Abe answers Ceil's question about the red on his cheek ("It's cherry pie") he improvises on the Communist's "literature." It goes on for a few seconds.

Take 17: Very good. But this time, Abe doesn't improvise.

Take 18: Good. The pace is much faster. But "Let's go again," Woody says.

Take 19: Abe is really angry this time.

(Takes 6, 7, 13, 14, 16, and 17 are printed.)

"It's a wrap," at 6:00 P.M.

Something went wrong today. Maybe he's getting tired of seeing me. I got more than a few of those strange looks, the "What are you doing here?", "Who are you?" kind.

What did I do? "What are my sins?"; "Who did I bother?"

Thursday, January 30, 1986

A NATION PRAYS AND ASKS WHY? (Daily News)
And actor Leif Erickson dies of cancer at seventy-four.

9:15 A.M. We're back on the King Cole roof, waiting for Roger. He has just landed in a Concorde from Paris and is on his way to the studio in a limousine. All this to spend a few hours on the roof with Sally! Jimmy Mazzola is spraying the roof. Frankie complains that it smells like fish, but Abe isn't around. Jimmy Sabat swears that he's given up gambling; he's lost too much. If he continues to read the *Racing News* every day, he tells me, it's only to help out friends. And Kay is singing "Let's All Sing Like the Birdies Sing."

The news is we'll be reshooting the hospital scene (third time), and certainly the two songs (fourth time), but still with Kitty.

Nobody knows the reasons for the hospital reshoot, but for the song scene, we'll have a new background.

10:15 A.M. Everybody is here—Porfirio, Irene, Roger, in surprisingly good shape, Sally, and Woody. Sally has a fever. She gives me a nice smile, as usual. Woody gives me a nice smile, too. The scene has been broken into three shots—first, Roger, Sally, and the lightning; second, their reaction when they hear the voices on the stairway; and third, the arrival of Irene and Porfirio. Mom and Ceil, in curlers, and Abe, in jeans, are here to watch the beautiful people.

Shot R68B: Same action as last time. Roger and Sally are at the door, trying to open it. The lightning flashes. Sally goes to the edge of the roof and screams. Roger joins her. Then they hear voices behind the door.

Take 1: Good. No comments for Roger, but Woody goes to talk to Sally.

Take 2: Good again. Woody asks Sally to be even more frightened by the lightning.

Take 3: Cut. A spark from the lightning machine fell onto the roof.

Take 4: Cut. Frankie's boom was visible, and Sally lost one of her artificial nails.

Take 5: "Knock all over the door with your hands," Woody tells Sally before the take. But he cuts. Sally missed a line: "Sorry, Woody!"

Take 6: Cut. Another spark.

Take 7: Another one!

There's something wrong with the machine. Al, the effects specialist, and Jimmy Mazzola work on it. Silence on the set. Woody stands in front of Sally, as usual, hands in pockets, whistling, looking at her. It's a nice image.

Take 8: Sally loses another nail, but the take was still good. "One more and . . ."

Take 9: Good again. But Sally asks for one more. "Right away."

Take 10: Very good.

The intensity with which Woody watches Sally acting is fascinating, as if he lives every minute of her performance.

(Takes 1, 2, 8, 9, and 10 are printed.)

A quick wild track of Sally's lines. "Lightning! We'll get electrocuted!'' and we move to the reaction shot. Woody explains to the actors how it will be edited, while the boys quickly set up the camera.

Now Roger and I say ''tu'' to each other. Roger loves the Concorde; this was his first trip on it. He left Paris not too early this morning, and hopes to be back tonight or tomorrow morning at the latest. Everything is, of course, divine in Paris. The director, Walter LeMoli, is stunning, the people at Le Theatre de Bobigny are charming. And Jean Louis Barrault and Madeleine Renaud have asked him to play *Solo* (the play that was written for him) for the Samuel Beckett eightieth birthday, for three weeks this April at Le Theatre du Rond-Point on the Champs-Elysées. Roger just hopes Woody will not need him for the reshoot.

10:55 A.M. Shot R68C: It's Roger and Sally's reaction to the appearance of Porfirio and Irene.

Woody directs them as the scene is shot: ''Anguish . . . You can't believe it! . . . You want to get out of here. . . . But now you listen. . . .'' Roger is not used to being directed like that; he starts to get creative. ''Don't make any faces. Look at me,'' Woody tells him.

(4 takes and 2 prints.) Completed at 11:00 A.M.

It's finished for Roger. He runs to catch the 1:00 P.M. Concorde. He'll be in Paris tonight by 10:00 P.M. Woody tells him he will not need him in April for the reshoot, so he'll be able to stay in France.

11:15 A.M. Carlo sets up for Irene and Porfirio's appearance and reaction shot. Sally, already back in her extra-large clothes, comes with Baby Dylan to say good-bye. Woody immediately takes the baby in his arms, and starts making faces. But Baby Dylan ignores him, fascinated by the neon Camel sign. Woody tries again, kissing her soft neck. Baby Dylan fusses; she wants to watch the neon in peace. Woody gives up, and takes her for a look at the sign.

11:20 A.M. Sally and Baby Dylan are gone, and we go back to work.

Shot R68D: Porfirio and Irene come through the door, and discover Roger and Sally.

The main difference from the earlier takes is that they finish their lines on the staircase. And as they enter, Irene sees Roger at once, saying only, "Roger!" Same problem with the blocking. Irene is much bigger than Porfirio. It's a funny effect, though, when the Playboy of the Western World hides behind Irene upon seeing Roger.

(11 takes and 7 prints.) Completed at 11:30 A.M.

Finished with the King Cole roof. We go back to Little Joe's house.

12:00 noon. We're all waiting in Little Joe's living room. Dickie sleeps on the sofa, a cup of coffee in his hand; he looks mummified, like Mrs. Silverman. Nicole reads Somerset Maugham's *Of Human Bondage,* and Jimmy Mazzola complains that he was told only one hour ago that he'll have to produce a dinner for five for the next scene. Jimmy had to discuss the menu with Santo, send one of his boys to do the shopping, and then do the cooking!

12:40 P.M. Abe and Ceil are already in nightgowns. The menu is chicken, mashed potatoes, noodles, and carrots. Santo finishes setting the table. Woody serves Grandpa some carrots, and Carlo adjusts the lights.

Shot 85: The family is having dinner, but it's time for Abe's favorite radio show, *Bill Kern's Favorite Sports Legends.* While the family eats, Abe, totally involved in Kirby Kyle's story, stands by the radio. The family gets noisy, and Abe asks for silence. The family quiets down.

Abe wonders if he could take his plate with him and eat as he listens. "You could if you want to," Woody says. First, the family doesn't quiet down enough when Abe asks them to. Woody asks him to say it sooner, and he tells Mom to move more quickly so she won't hide Abe's enthralled face too long.

(5 takes and 2 prints.)

We move directly to the next shot.

Shot 89: The dinner is over. The family is gone. But Abe is still by the radio, totally involved.

(1 take and 1 print.)

We break for lunch at 1:00 P.M.

2:00 P.M. Barbara is exhausted. Angela is sick today, and Drew is on vacation, so Barbara has to do the job of three. She tells me that Little Joe knows everybody on the *Ishtar* set now; he spends half his time with them. I ask him if he has seen Isabelle Adjani. "Oh, no. I just know Dustin, Warren, and Elaine," Little Joe tells me.

3:15 P.M. Carlo is still working in the kitchen for the next shot. We're reshooting the Dowdy Housewife listening to the Phyliss and Paul soap opera while cleaning her kitchen (sequence 11). But the dowdy housewife has become Mom.

Tom is getting a haircut from Romaine. Bobby Greenhut is helping Woody solve a chess problem. Nicole has abandoned Somerset Maugham to learn how to knit; the first sweater will be for her.

3:30 P.M. Before shooting, Jimmy Mazzola shows Woody the cake for Mom and Pop's anniversary (sequence 103). Woody would like more decoration, and there is another problem—Mom is supposed to bite the head off the little male character. Before, the little characters were made of sugar; now they're made of hard plastic.

Shot R11: Mom is in the kitchen, cleaning the table, while listening to her favorite radio show—the Phyliss and Paul soap opera.

Woody and Mom first listen to the playback. He gives her a few hints about where to move and on which word. But he doesn't want to restrict her. "You do what you feel like." Between each take, Jimmy Mazzola and Jimmy Frederick put the leftovers back on the plates—pieces of eggs, banana peels mixed in the gravy with bits of bread, and so forth. "After he says, 'Say yes!', look real thoughtful," Woody says. Mom suggests throwing the banana peels in the garbage can.

(5 takes and 5 prints.)

Woody goes straight to Carlo to talk about the next shot, where Aunt Ceil listens to her favorite show, *The Famous Ventriloquist* (sequence 96). "The problem is, we've looked this way so many times," Woody says in the hallway.

5:30 P.M. Carlo's ready now. First rehearsal. Abe and Ceil run through their lines. Woody is behind the camera. He wants Mom and Ruthie in the shot, but they're not ready. Jeffrey and the Salad Sisters need at least half an hour to prepare them. "Forget Mom, but we need Ruthie. And let's use Grandma instead of

Mom." But Grandma isn't ready either. So we wait for Ruthie and Mom, and Woody goes back to his chess.

6:15 P.M. Shot 96: Cousin Ruthie plays cards with Little Joe on the carpet, Mom knits, and Ceil sews while the famous ventriloquist performs on the radio. Ceil bursts into laughter at every joke. Abe comes down the stairs, the newspaper in his hands. He seems irritated. Ceil continues to laugh. "He's a ventriloquist on the radio. How do you know he is not moving his lips?" Abe angrily asks. "Who cares? Leave me alone!" Ceil answers him, as she continues laughing. *(45 seconds.)*

Take 1: Woody cuts. He wants the playback of the radio show to start later.

Take 2: Cut. Again too soon with the playback. There's a misunderstanding with the gambling department.

Take 3: Cut. Frankie messed up again. There's a little tension; everybody is tired.

Take 4: Abe started in too soon. The playback should be higher so he can hear his cue. Frankie will then lower its volume so Jimmy can record clean.

Take 5: Woody ends up cueing Abe. "You're really annoyed," he tells him before the take. And to Ceil: "Really disgusted . . . 'Get out!'" Ceil's laugh is great. Woody laughs. She's even better than Herbie Hanson's paid laughers.

Take 6: Woody laughs again during the take. In the middle of the take, Ceil sees Woody laughing. He acts out a bigger laugh, and she starts hers. Very good. "One more and . . ."

Take 7: Very good again.

(Takes 6 and 7 are printed.)

We wrap at 6:40 P.M.
Woody is still laughing.

Friday January 31, 1986

Manes is ducking scandal. Ed says: "He is faking the severity of the illness." In fact, Ed's sick of Manes: "My role is to get him out." (Daily News)

Furor over convent in Auschwitz: Jewish groups call nuns' site an affront to the memory of the millions dead. (New York Times)

Good review for Herb Gardner's The Goodbye People. *The film is set at Coney Island with Pop in the role of Michael Silverman.* (New York Times)

8:50 A.M. We are upstairs on stage G to reshoot the hospital scene.

Shot RR154: Same action, but no more dollying. The camera starts on the nurse and Myla (Mom's roommate), then pans with the nurse to Mom in bed, surrounded by the family.

(3 takes and 2 prints.)

We move back downstairs to Little Joe's house. Ken shows Woody a few stills of young men. Woody picks one within two seconds; Cousin Ruthie has a boyfriend now.

10:00 A.M. Angela is tense this morning. Abe proposes practicing some chiropractics on her. They start at it. We watch. Angela seems to relax and says Abe is very soft and soothing. Abe gets a little warm; he's sweating. It doesn't look too chiropractic from here.

Grandpa tells me he speaks French, but Grandma denies it. Grandma is right. At the end of the hall, Mom and Pop, arm in arm, are going to the set. The Mazzola brothers won first and second place in the cards this morning.

10:45 A.M. We're back in for Mom and Pop's wedding anniversary. There will be a voice over, but Jimmy suggests recording the sound, just in case. Woody OK's the idea.

Shot C102: The family is gathered around the dining-room table, laughing and drinking. Pop gives Mom a large box. It's a new coat with a fur collar. Mom kisses Pop. Everybody is having a good time. *(28 seconds.)*

No big directing, and, once the blocking of each actor has been set, no big problem.

(3 takes and 2 prints.)

Shot C102A: The camera pans in close-up across the faces, laughing and cheering. At the end, Mom kisses Pop again.

(4 takes and 2 prints.)

Woody quickly decides the camera setting for the following shot, where Bea gets ready for her date with Manulis (sequence 49). The camera will be looking toward the kitchen and hallway. Carlo needs at least an hour and a half. Woody and the actors go back to their rooms.

Jimmy Mazzola is going to have to eat the twenty-five little sugar characters he had specially made for the cake. In the end, Mom didn't bite the head off. The cake wasn't even in the frame!

12:15 P.M. The snowman's penis has been bent down, and the plastic bag is gone. He looks a little sad and lonely in the carpenter shop. Jimmy Frederick and Danny come back from shopping for the family's dinner, and the family hangs around the Salad Sisters' quarters.

The nurse tells us about Meryl Streep's stand-in in *Heartburn*, who met Dustin Hoffman one day in the elevator. He suddenly asked her what she was doing right now, and took her straight to a producer for a part she would be perfect for. But it was too late. The part had already been cast!

We break for lunch at 12:55 P.M.

A sign on Bea's door says: DON'T DISTURB. I'M SLEEPING. THANKS. DIANNE X X X.

2:15 P.M. Manulis makes a strong entrance as he arrives at the Salad Sisters' for makeup. Everybody is impressed; Mom stares at him and Pop shakes his hand firmly. It's the first time they've seen him. "Fifteen-minute warning," screams Richie in the hall.

2:45 P.M. Everbody is back. We're shooting Bea getting ready for her date with Manulis while the family, having finished dinner, continues its everyday routine. "Can I see the dialogue?" asks Woody. Tom calls for silence. Abe complains to Jimmy Mazzola because every day they give him the same newspaper. He knows it by heart now. Tom asks for one in Hebrew. And Woody threatens to hit Little Joe if he doesn't quiet down.

"I just want to do one line at a time," Woody says, "just the mechanics." The actors begin. Woody is next to them, script in hand. For each line, he describes the action, and he changes it right away if it doesn't sound good after the actor does it. Woody moves slowly, little touch by little touch. Ruthie is in the frame. Bea enters through the hallway door, just behind Ruthie. After each decision is made, Woody goes back to consult the script. There are absolutely no indications of directing in the script. But between the lines, there is a meaning from which he starts to find the appropriate action on the set. Now Bea is coming through the other door. Little Joe goes from the refrigerator to the stairs, and finally out of frame. Now it is Pop, instead of Abe, who sits at the kitchen table with the newspaper.

3:00 P.M. First rehearsal: "Real slowly," Woody asks. Some of the linking in the action of the actors seems to work, but it's still not polished. Abe is not in the shot anymore. "Let's try again."

Second rehearsal: There is a problem with Pop's exit from the kitchen, and Bea's entrance. "Let's do it again from the start."

Third rehearsal: Woody has Bea come in, go out to the dining room, then come in again. She says almost a third of her lines out of frame, from the dining room, instead of staying in the kitchen as if she were only there to deliver them. It seems to work, basically. But there is a final problem between Bea's entrance and exit and Little Joe's. "Let's try it at a better speed. Just to see what happens."

Fourth rehearsal: Woody tells Bea exactly when she should come in (after Little Joe comes in), and go out. "Let's try again from the start."

Fifth rehearsal: "It's very good. It's going to be great. When we get it!" Then some directions for each one:

To Pop: "Get up motivated, looking for your cigarettes."

To Mom: "Really hit Little Joe. But pass in front of the camera quickly."

To Bea: "A little excited at the beginning. And more and more at the end."

Sixth rehearsal: "I've got it screwed up. This side of the screen is empty!"

3:15 P.M. As with the first establishing scene of the family, which we've shot twice (scene 24), this is a very difficult and long shot, a full minute. It's hard getting the blocking and the pacing just right. It's even more difficult since the camera doesn't move much. The good pacing must be achieved only through what goes on within the frame, without the help of camera movement.

Seventh rehearsal: Bea is good. But Woody is not satisfied yet. "There're one too many things in it. It's too busy."

Eighth rehearsal: "We're fine. Now I got it." Pop stays in the kitchen. Bea uses the same door, the one to the dining room, to come in and out. And Little Joe comes in and out only once.

3:30 P.M. Woody asks Carlo what he thinks of Manulis's coming in at the end of the scene. "Yes," answers Carlo hesitantly, "but no street!" At first, Woody doesn't get it. Then he realizes and laughs. The camera is set in the direction of the front door, and if it opens . . . Woody goes to each actor to remind him of the details, and finishes by telling everybody, "It's not as confused as it seems!" But Carlo has to make some adjustments. We all stay in the living room, keeping our voices low to let Carlo work. Outside, on the porch, Barbara is entertaining the SAG representative; he seems to enjoy her conversation.

4:20 P.M. Shot 49: The kitchen. Dinner is over. Mom is putting things in order, Pop reads the paper, and Aunt Ceil tenderizes the meat (she cleaned the fish this afternoon). The radio is on. Bea, dancing to the music, dashes in and out, asking for her red belt, all excited. Pop asks what's happening. Mom tells him that Mr. Manulis has finally asked Bea out. "What'd he do? Go blind?" Pop jokes. Cousin Ruthie, still at the phone, informs everybody that Mrs. Waldbaum found a purse in the subway, but she hasn't decided if she is going to give it back. Bea gives some more details on Manulis: "He is so handsome!" She met him in the Catskills. "He dances, he rides horseback, he's some tennis player." Pop asks what he does for a living. "His firm imports coffee." Little Joe asks Pop what he does for a living. Pop asks Little Joe to go get his cigarettes. Then he suggests to Bea that maybe it's time she compromised. "I don't know the meaning of that word," Bea answers. But the bell rings. Manulis! Bea panics. She asks Ceil to open the door. But Ceil's hands smell of fish and meat, so Mom goes. (1 minute, 2 seconds.)

Before the take, Woody dances to show Bea how he wants it.

Take 1: Cut. Bea flubbed a line. Anyway, at the beginning, Bea was hogging the frame. She has a difficult blocking; she has to be at very precise spots and she almost never stops speaking.

Take 2: Dickie cuts. Camera no good.

Take 3: Dickie cuts again. The first time Bea came in, she took one step; the second time, she took two. Woody asks her not to stop at the door, but go directly to the second mark.

Take 4: Woody cuts. Little Joe was too late.

Take 5: Not bad! The first one completed. Ceil goes a little out of frame when she is pounding the meat, and Mom should show more of her back at the beginning. "Be more panicked after the bell," Woody tells Bea. Ruthie must also be at a precise spot when she appears in the door frame to deliver her line.

Take 6: Cut. Ruthie missed her line.

Take 7: Cut. Ruthie again. The camera is reloaded.

It looks like Ceil is having fun with the meat, her cigarette in her mouth. "This is going to be our last shot tonight," Tom says to Woody. "OK," Woody answers.

Take 8: Cut. Ruthie again. And Mom and Little Joe's blockings were off; Mom hid Little Joe. "That's not right."

Take 9: Dickie cuts. "Louis! You're way in . . ."

Take 10: Cut. Ruthie missed her cue. "More animated. Your voices sound dead," Woody tells Mom and Pop. And to Bea, "Keep it alive!" He starts dancing in front of her. Bea doesn't find it funny anymore.

Take 11: Bea is good, very good. But she moves on and off her marks too much, Carlo and Ray complain. And a bad shadow falls on her. Bea says she can do it.

Take 12: Good all the way.

Take 13: Dickie cuts. Ceil's cigarette fell on the floor and she went out of frame to get it. As was the case in *Stardust Memories,* Ceil never stops smoking in this film.

Take 14: Very good all the way again.

Take 15: Good again. But Jimmy Sabat could do better.

Take 16: Dickie cuts. Louis's boom again. The gambling department is taking it a little too easy. Too many wins this week!

Take 17: Good. Woody to Bea: "You've got one or two more for me?" Bea says yes. Woody asks her to go faster and do less dancing.

Take 18: Very good. The shot has been tightened, and the pace is much better.

Take 19: Woody cuts. Bea's arrival was not good.

Take 20: Woody cuts. Ruthie was not fast enough.

Take 21: Cut. Bea left too early, and Pop was a little late.

Take 22: Just before "Action!" Woody yells, "Real fast!" Very good.

(Takes 5, 12, 14, 17, 18, and 22 are printed.) Completed at 5:25 P.M.

Carlo and Woody decide on the camera setting for Manulis's arrival, to be shot first thing Monday morning. The camera will be in the hallway in a corner, using the opening door to hide the outside so there will be "No street!"

5:45 P.M. Stage G. Before wrapping, Carlo and Woody come to see the set for the Breezy Point fog scene. We start those scenes Monday. Santo is here, and the set is almost finished. One road is curving, another one at a diagonal. There is sand, reeds, rocks, and in the background, the artist's lighthouse on the cliff. But there's already a problem. The dialogue inside the moving car is rather long, and the road is rather short. The car could turn around, or Woody says he can shorten the dialogue. Everything looks OK otherwise.

We wrap. 6:00 P.M.

Woody speeds to the dailies, and Jeffrey races behind with Larry.

In the van back to Manhattan, the driver asks me if Woody's chauffeur is also his bodyguard.

Monday, February 3, 1986   *Fourteenth Week*

"Enough is enough," Ed says. He won't deliver a State of the City Address. And, "I'd seize Marcos's pad," he adds, in reference to the million-dollar tax question. (New York Times and Daily News)

Fourteen are dead in two days in Haiti. "Baby Doc" invokes a state of siege and, helped by his Tontons Macoutes, stays "firm as a monkey's tail." (New York Times)

"Shining Path" Peruvian rebels kill twelve people in an Andean village. More than six thousand Peruvians have died since the rebels first started their guerrilla war in May 1980. (New York Times)

South African President P. W. Botha proposes to free Nelson Mandela in exchange for Andrei Sakharov and Anatoly Shcharansky. But the U.S. and the Soviets have already agreed on exchanging Shcharansky for a few spies. (New York Times)

Swedish diplomat Alva Myrdal, Nobel Peace Prize winner for her efforts to promote disarmament, died this weekend.

His name is Kebawah Duli Yang Maha Mulia Paduka Seri Baginda Sultan Hassanal Bolkiah Mui'zzaddin Waddaulah. At thirty-nine, he is the sultan and absolute ruler of Brunei, one of the newest (independent from a British protectorate in 1984), smallest (221,000 people living on 2,226 square miles), and wealthiest (average income $18,000) nations. The sultan lives in a $400 million palace with 1,788 rooms, its own mosque, a heliport, and parking for eight hundred vehicles, with several dozen spaces *reserved for his sports cars. He is prime minister, finance minister, and interior minister. Two of his brothers run the foreign ministry and the ministry of culture, youth, and sports. Their father, former Sultan Omar Ali Saifuddin, is minister of defense and head of the armed forces. Brunei's richness comes from petroleum found in 1929, and gas in 1965.* (New York Times)

9:00 A.M. We are going to shoot Manulis's arrival. The wall behind the staircase has been taken out (an advantage of a studio) to give more space for the camera and Carlo. Grandpa and Grandma are ready to be "deposited" into the armchairs in the background, but Manulis is still in the hands of the Salad Sisters. And Bea has asked for a ten-minute warning to get into her dress.

Jimmy Mazzola is tired today; the weekend was too short. His wife is in California visiting some family, and he's going to join her at the end of the shooting; they'll rent a house on the beach. Liz has cut her red hair; it looks fresh, like a just-mown lawn. Drew is back from her one-week vacation in Mexico with a nice tan.

10:00 A.M. Everybody is back. Grandpa is in a bad mood today, but Grandma is smiling as always, and gives me a warm hello. Abe likes Manulis; he thinks the guy is funny. Bea is cold and complains to Jimmy Sabat, who had the heat turned off because it was too noisy.

A first rehearsal. Bea asks if she should sit or stand when the bell rings. Woody doesn't care. She doesn't care. Carlo wants her to sit. While the last adjustments are made, Pop chats with Manulis. Bea complains about the cold again. And Ceil starts kneading the meat. She looks a little tired of it, though, as does the meat, but it's better than cleaning Abe's fish.

10:30 A.M. Shot 50: The bell rings. Bea panics. Mom goes to open the door, and Manulis appears, laughing, friendly, relaxed. Mom is impressed. Pop joins them. They shake hands. Pop notices Manulis's firm handshake. Manulis hates it when someone "puts a dead paw in your hand," he explains. Bea comes in; Manulis calls her "Sugar" and they leave. Mom asks Pop what he thinks. "What'd she do? Fall into a vat of perfume?" Mom says that when they were younger, "Bea used to be considered the pretty one." "Some contest!" Pop answers. Mom is getting tired of Pop's jokes.

"You're lucky I love you, you old douche bag!" Pop tells her, hugging her. *(50 seconds.)*

Manulis is very relaxed. He is aware of the effect he is having on everybody. But Manulis is by nature relaxed; it's just part of his easygoing nature.

Take 1: Woody cuts. Mom said, "Comin', Comin'!" Woody wants, "I'm comin'. I'm comin'!"

Take 2: OK. Woody asks Manulis to be more exuberant. Manulis gives us a demonstration, and everyone starts laughing, Woody being the first. Then Woody asks Grandpa to hold his paper higher.

Take 3: Woody still laughs at Manulis. Dickie thinks Mom and Pop should come in a little later, and Woody asks Abe to make a move with the checkers; he is playing with Little Joe in the living room. He asks Manulis to add even more energy.

Take 4: Good. Woody asks Manulis to be even more boisterous, and to "keep that laugh going."

Take 5: Cut. For the camera.

Take 6: Good. "One more and we are finished." Manulis gives me a wink; the man is having a great time.

Take 7: Good. But not perfect for Dickie.

Take 8: OK. Woody to Manulis: "Just do what you were doing, but be more aware of Little Joe and Abe."

Take 9: Manulis improvises; he snaps Pop's suspenders! Woody likes it. "Not too many gestures. But it's great, and your laugh is good."

Take 10: "OK. One more and we . . ." To Manulis: "Not too much hands. But it was a very good take. Don't forget the laughing." Manulis doesn't seem at all tired of it.

Take 11: Good. But Manulis doesn't laugh so much. Woody insists again: "Do the movements as you feel them. But laugh!"

Take 12: Woody cuts. Manulis was not on his mark. "Take your time. We've got enough good takes," Woody tells him.

Take 13: Woody cuts again. Manulis is getting tired now. "Give her some more time," Woody tells him, referring to Mom.

Take 14: Woody cuts: "I'm sorry. Tell her your name."

Take 15: Good. But Dickie is not so happy.

Take 16: "Sidney Manulis!" he almost screams. But Woody cuts. Manulis said, "Is Tess ready?" instead of "Bea." He's sweating a little. Fern dabs it away.

Take 17: Good. "But maybe not enough laugh."

Take 18: Good. Manulis paid more attention to Bea this time. "Finished!"

(Takes 2, 4, 8, 9, 17, and 18 are printed.) Completed at 11:05 A.M. We move to stage G.

11:15 A.M. The set for Breezy Point is finished, but Carlo needs two hours of preparation. The only lighting will be twelve lights hanging from the ceiling; three more have to be hung. For the interiors of the car, stronger lights have to be put behind the speedometer and the radio, which will light Bea and Manulis's faces.

The floor is being wetted down, too, and the car is sprayed with a mat finish so there will be no reflection from the studio lights. Jimmy Mazzola tests the fog: no smell today. Dry ice is put in front of the smoking-machine nozzle so the smoke, keeping its density, stays on the ground for the two or three minutes needed for the shot. For the moment, the fog seems to crawl across the floor. It looks beautiful, reminiscent of Francis Ford Coppola's *Rumble Fish.*

Carlo hasn't had any news from Antonioni for a while. But now the Taviani brothers have asked him to work with them. They are doing a story about immigrants, *Good Morning, Babylon,* some of which they are shooting in America.

12:15 P.M. The family is being kept on hold in case we have a problem with the fog; they will be sent home at around 3:00 P.M. if everything goes well. Bea has gone to flirt with Woody while he plays chess with Abe. Grandma brings Romaine the loksham kugel she cooked especially for her this weekend. Little Joe comes back from the *Ishtar* set. "It's too early," he tells me. "Nothing is happening. Warren and Dustin are still in their rooms."

We break for lunch at 1:00 P.M.

The commissary is busy today. The head of the studio, George Kaufman, is having a small party here in the middle of the room. Louis and Frankie share a table and exchange some comments with the pretty waitress. Jimmy Sabat has gone to place some bets for his friends. The teamsters are at another table. Bobby Greenhut, Ezra, and Tim talk about the schedule (one, two more weeks?).

Barbara has taken the science tutor out to lunch. And Little Joe goes from table to table, entertaining everybody.

Just as I am leaving, Little Joe, who is in the middle of a conversation, asks me to wait for him; he wants to talk to me! We go back to the set together. Little Joe wants to know exactly what my job on the set is. Then he tells me that Penelope, the Woman in Red who visited last Thursday, is also writing a book on Woody.

2:35 P.M. The fog is in. It's beautiful, but you can't see more than three feet. We're all wearing white masks. Woody appears in the fog. He looks disgusted, but pauses to laugh at us. Then he checks the camera, and puts on a mask himself.

Shot 52: A long shot of Manulis's eight-cylinder Buick appearing in the fog. The car approaches. We can see only the headlights. *(10 seconds.)*

Since the road is wet, visibility is nil, and the car is traveling toward the camera, it's Jimmy Mazzola who drives Bea. With his moustache, and in Manulis's hat, he's not recognizable. Jimmy likes that. He asks Woody if he wants the windshield wipers on; sometimes it's necessary in the fog. "Don't get creative, Jim. Just drive the car," Tom tells him.

(6 takes and 2 prints.) Completed at 2:50 P.M.

The next shot is the dialogue inside. The boys begin to set up the camera.

3:15 P.M. Times Square and the King Cole roof are being destroyed. The huge letters and cigarette package from the Camel billboard are being stored and will be sold after the reshoot. It's all quiet at the Salad Sisters' place; the family has been sent home. And in the hall next to stage G, Warren (in white bathrobe and tennis shoes) is going to the *Ishtar* set. "What's all this smoke?" he complains. (Jimmy Mazzola overdid it again: The stuff is invading the whole studio!)

4:00 P.M. Shot 52A: Inside the car. Bea and Manulis are driving in the fog. Bea is "still a little tipsy from the beer," though she had only one; "Alcohol affects me strongly," she says. Manulis feels fine, though he had ten. And Manulis loves the fog. "It's very romantic," Bea agrees. "You're a romantic, Sidney," "You want to hit me in the stomach?" Manulis asks Bea. Bea is a little surprised. "Why?" "To see how tight it is," Manulis says. But the engine starts coughing, then stops. Out of gas! In the middle of Breezy Point. "Just like in the movies," Bea remarks. "We're stuck here . . ." Manulis says. "What's a girl to do?" Bea says, a little anxious, but still interested. *(43 seconds.)*

The camera is just in front of the Buick, facing the windshield. Jimmy Mazzola and Jimmy Frederick are just behind the car, using a piece of lumber and a camera box to shake the vehicle, giving the illusion of motion. Bea and Manulis's faces, seen in close-up through the window, are lighted by the speedometer and the radio. Woody and Kay are wearing earphones; we can't hear anything. Woody goes to the car between takes to give the actors a few directions.

(6 takes and 4 prints.)

Woody takes his script and walks through the fog, followed by Carlo. A long shot of the car stopped in the fog is decided on. Then we will go back to the front of the car for the end of the scene. "I think we should do them in order," Woody tells Tom. They decide to do only one more shot tonight, and wait to see the dailies tomorrow morning to check the look of the fog.

5:30 P.M. Shot 53: The car is stalled on the roadside in the fog. The radio plays "La Cumparsita." Manulis, the diehard romantic, hearing the sound of the waves, surrounded by fog, suddenly "finds it awfully hard to resist the urge to kiss" Bea, and makes his move. Bea resists at the outset; it's their first date. But she "must admit the setting is romantic." They are ready to go at it when "La Cumparsita" is interrupted by a special bulletin. A "mysterious object has been reported in the sky over New Jersey. . . . Scientists say it could be extraterrestrial. . . . Police and militia are heading toward Wilson's Glen, where the object is reported landing. . . ." *(20 seconds.)*

Same as the previous shot. Woody has his earphones on; we can't hear the dialogue.

(7 takes and 3 prints.)

A wild track is done.

And "It's a wrap" at 6:10 P.M.

Woody and Carlo will look at the dailies tomorrow at 7:40 A.M. before coming to the studio.

Tuesday, February 4, 1986

The pope visits Mother Teresa's home for the dying in Calcutta. Eighty-six are still alive. The daily report is written on a black-board: two admissions, no releases, and four dead. (New York Times)

Problems with servicing the shuttle have been reported in past several months. A twelve-member panel is named in an inquiry. (New York Times)

Aliens in U.S. will face AIDS testing. (New York Times)

The beautiful people mobbed the Sutton theater last night for a screening of Hannah and Her Sisters. *Mick Jagger, Goldie Hawn, Glenn Close, and Carly Simon loved it. (Daily News)*

The "Dynamite Kid" becomes "B'klyn's Birdman of Boxing." (New York Post)

And Augusto Ruschi, who dedicated his life to studying the flora and fauna of the vanishing Atlantic Coast rain forests, was dying as a result of having touched poisonous Dendrobates toads in the Amazon in 1975. President José Sarney, moved by an appeal to him by Brazilian poet Affonso Romano de Sant'Anna, contacted Raoni, the chief of the four-thousand-strong Txucarramae. A Brazilian air-force plane flew to the Xingu, five hundred miles northwest of Brasilia, to collect herbs, as well as Sapaim, a shaman from the nearby Caimura tribe. Raoni and Sapaim met Ruschi in Rio de Janeiro. They started to smoke ten-inch hallucinogenic herbal "cigars," and exhaled over the patient while chanting in their own language. Raoni then massaged Mr. Ruschi's body, and appeared to extract a green, strong-smelling pasty substance that he identified as the toad poison. While blowing smoke, the Indian chief rubbed it between his palms, and it disappeared. Finally, the patient took an herbal bath. The ritual was repeated for three days, and last Saturday Mr. Ruschi was pronounced cured. (New York Times)

9:00 A.M. Two bits of good news this morning. The screening yesterday for the beautiful people was a big success. "It's going to be a disaster!" Woody had told Carlo beforehand. And the fog looked good in the dailies this morning. So we continue happily.

Shot 53A: A front shot of Bea and Manulis seen through the

windshield. The first special bulletin has just ended. Bea's nervousness gives Manulis courage ("I'll take care of you, babe"), and his "romanticism" returns; he makes another move. Bea seems just about ready now, when there's another interruption on the radio. *(38 seconds.)*

It's the same tight framing as yesterday's front shot. Woody, earphones and protective mask on, is at the edge of the frame on Bea's side, watching the actors' faces. Jeffrey Mazzola uses a fan to move the fog. And once again, we can't hear anything.

(7 takes and 4 prints.)

10:00 A.M. The doors of the studio are opened to get rid of the fog so the next shot can be prepared. It's Bea and Manulis listening to the invasion of New Jersey by Martians (sequence 53C). A long, slow, curving shot (over a minute) will accompany the lengthy broadcast scene, with Bea and Manulis's faces in close-up behind the windshield. Because of the lack of light and surplus of fog, the camera has to be quite close (less than a foot from the window) so the scene can be kept in focus. Manulis's eight-cylinder Buick has a long hood, and the boys have to strip it down, removing the fenders, the hood, and the top part of the engine so the track can be set. It will take two hours, and then another two hours to put everything back together for the next shot.

It's a craftman's job and a challenge. The boys like that. The semicircular track is put on stands on either side. It has to be solid enough to hold the weight of Dickie and Mickey. The camera is put directly on the dolly (no tripod, no head) so it's low enough. Black cloth covers the track at both ends so, when filming from the front and the end of it, the camera will not pick up the metal structure.

Carlo doesn't like using many accessories like video cameras to check the image, or the Louma crane for the camera movements. Maybe the Louma would be good for very special shots, like the one in Hitchcock's 1937 *Young and Innocent*, where he started with a wide shot of a ballroom, and ended on a close-up of the drummer's winking eye, or the famous opening shot of Orson Welles's 1958 *Touch of Evil*. But not for Woody's movies, and especially not for this one. Carlo feels that when you use a lot of high-tech gadgets, you lose something and the result doesn't come from within anymore.

Another thing Carlo likes about working with Woody is that

they do everything on the spot, spontaneously, with the feeling of the moment. It's impossible to plan what's going to happen.

Like Kirby Kyle, Carlo has heart.

12:00 noon. Dickie and Mickey are on the dolly. Wax is applied to the piece of plastic under the camera so it can pan smoothly. Dickie sits on a little camera box, and Mickey lies under the lens. They are covered by black cloth to prevent reflections in the window. Red is ready to slowly push the dolly. He must arrive at the other end of the track exactly one minute and thirty seconds after he has started. He puts a page of the script in front of him, on the box Dickie is sitting on, so he can check at which spot he should be on each word.

The actors are inside the car. There are problems with the black drapes covering the track at the ends. They show on camera. Reeds are brought instead, and put in front of the track. Is there going to be a problem for continuity with the following shot? "Ma, no!" Carlo answers.

Shot 53C: Bea and Manulis listen, stunned, to Don Richards, broadcasting from Wilson's Glen. ". . . events are simply astonishing. . . . An alien spacecraft. . . . It has landed. . . . The doors are opening. . . . Someone is emerging from the aircraft. . . . Long tentacles. . . . Horrible-looking creature. . . . It's sending out beams of hot light. . . . It's carrying fire. . . . The crowd is running. . . ." *(1 minute, 36 seconds.)*

Manulis is so big that he completely hides Bea when the camera arrives on his side; he has to be careful to lean a bit back. Woody moves with the dolly. For the first minute, the actors just listen to the broadcast on the playback.

(4 takes and 3 prints.) Completed at 12:30 P.M.

The boys put the car back together before lunch. And the following shot, the car lurching away (sequence 54), is prepared.

It's snowing outside, and the snowman is being readied just in case. Baby Dylan and Sally come to have lunch with Woody.

We break for lunch at 1:00 P.M.

2:45 P.M. Jimmy Mazzola is making heavy fog so the car will disappear quickly when it lurches away. But first we'll do a wild track. "We don't need more smoke for the wild track," Tom says. Woody goes to sit in the backseat of Manulis's Buick.

Shot 54: Back to a long shot of the car in the fog, seen from behind. It's just after the long broadcast. The two are really concerned now, especially Manulis. "Maybe we should get to a phone," Bea suggests. Manulis starts the car. There's gas now! The car pulls away and disappears. Manulis is driving fast. He's growing more and more nervous. Then there is a big noise. They've hit something and are stuck. *(12 seconds.)*

(2 takes and 2 prints.)

In the next shot, Bea and Manulis are dumbstruck. The camera is set in the interior, on the backseat.

3:30 P.M. Bobby Greenhut is in a wonderful mood today so he comes to kid the boys some. To Red: "Fifteen minutes to get a screwdriver!" And for Dickie: "He used to hand-hold the camera.

Now we have to fix it for him. Too much food and drugs!" The boys continue to work.

4:15 P.M. Shot 55: The car is stopped, leaning to one side. It's stuck in the sand (the camera is inside, looking at the actors from behind). Manulis is panicked—"C'mon, we better make a run for it"—while Bea is more in control. Manulis dashes out. He runs to the front of the car: "Horrible tentacles! . . . The Martians are coming! . . . Our lives are over! . . ." "Pull yourself together, Sidney," Bea says. She gets out of the car. But Sidney has disappeared in the fog. *(25 seconds.)*

Woody is next to Dickie in the backseat. Again Woody asks Manulis to exaggerate.

(6 takes and 4 prints.)

Woody quickly decides the next shot, where the couple get lost in the fog. Carlo asks Santo to fill the background with reeds; all the equipment back there has to be moved. Woody disappears to his room.

5:00 P.M. The *Vogue* writer has been more or less dismissed as Santo's driver because he was doing too much sleeping on the set. He has been replaced by Gil, a PA who worked on location at the start of the shooting. Gil also worked on *Heartburn*. He tells me how everybody, even Nicholson, had a crush on Meryl Streep because she was so good and charming. The only one who was not enamored of her was Jimmy Sabat, though they have known each other for a long time and were good friends before. In one scene, she asked him to use two stationary mikes because the movement of the boom was distracting her. "Now that she's a star . . ." Jimmy told me.

6:00 P.M. Shot 56: Manulis disappears in the fog. Bea is standing next to the car, and can't see anything. "Sidney! . . ." Manulis is not too far, but she can't find him. "They're probably up there in the sky. . . ." he says. "Where are you? . . ." But suddenly, nothing. Bea starts walking. "Sidney! . . . Where are you? . . ." *(31 seconds.)*

The action is not too difficult; Woody asks only for more exaggeration from Manulis. The trick is getting a perfect blocking: Manulis disappears, the camera pans, and Bea starts walking.

(3 takes and 2 prints.) Completed at 6:15 P.M.

A wild track of Manulis, "Help! . . . Help! . . ." and we're done with him for the rest of the movie. The great Manulis disappears in the fog.

Now a point of view of Bea in the fog, with the lighthouse in the back. I have to leave for a meeting in town. I try to depart discreetly, but the boys notice.

Ray: "Where are you going?"

Ken: "What do you think you're doing?"

Hammer: "You know that now he shows up at nine A.M. when the call is at eight A.M.!"

In the hall by the production offices, Bob Greenhut is playing football with Bea and Andrew, and Woody is playing chess with Ezra. Woody wandered quite close to me today. After *Hannah's* good reception, the temperature is getting back to normal. It's about time. . . .

Wednesday, February 5, 1986

On Monday, there was a bomb blast on the Champs-Elysées in Paris: eight wounded, three seriously. On Tuesday, one exploded in a crowded bookstore in the Latin Quarter: four wounded. (New York Times)

Twenty-one rebels and seven army soldiers have died in fighting in Colombia. (New York Times)

Oil prices plunge.

And Charles Manson loses his sixth bid for parole. Mr. Manson told the panel that if he was released, he might go to Libya, Iran, or "join the revolution down south somewhere, and try to save my life on the planet earth." (New York Times)

9:50 A.M. Hammer is right: I'm coming in later and later. Yesterday after I left, they filmed the point of view of Bea walking in the fog (sequence 56A).

Shot 56B: Bea is walking in the fog, calling for "Sidney!" An engine is heard starting. Sidney, in his panic, has forgotten her. Bea continues walking, but she can't see her own nose. She passes the rocks and reeds. Suddenly, there's the sound of water. She looks down and sees she's walking into the ocean. *(45 seconds.)*

The ocean is a little pool. Rocks and reeds have been placed in Bea's path. We can't see two feet ahead.

(3 takes and 2 prints.)

One wild track for Jimmy. And the fog sequence is over. Just one last pickup shot.

Shot 53B: A close-up of the radio, to be inserted just when the second special bulletin occurs.

Dickie holds the camera, sitting in the backseat. Woody doesn't come back to "direct" the shot. Carlo checks the framing, and the scene is completed in one take.

"Breezy Point" is over. Stage G will now become Polly Phelps's Pennsylvania field.

11:00 A.M. The future reshoots include Bill Kern telling the Kirby Kyle story (Woody didn't like the studio at the New School), Kitty singing "I'll Be Seeing You" and "They're Either Too Young or Too Old" (the second time for Kitty, but the fourth for the sequence—the studio again), the Dowdy Housewife who has become Mom will be shot for the third time (Mom can do better), and finally the searchlights in Rockaway, the third time. Will we do these reshoots before the end of next week, or during the scheduled reshoots in April? It depends whether Woody thinks he'll need these sequences for his first cut or if he can wait.

We are back in Little Joe's house to shoot Bea returning in the middle of the night, exhausted, after Sidney has abandoned her in Breezy Point. Carlo is lighting, and with all the family back, the Salad Sisters' headquarters is hopping again. Cousin Ruthie, Walkman on, rehearses "South American Way," while Aunt Ceil gets into makeup. Uncle Abe has his hair fixed as Angela entertains him, and Grandpa is listening to Grandma telling more tales from the old country. Fred (Robert Joy), Bea's new date, is here, too. Bea neglects him, and poor Fred feels a little awkward in the middle of our family. He played Madonna's boyfriend in Susan Seidelman's *Desperately Seeking Susan.*

Yesterday, there was a crew screening of Robert Mandel's *F/X.* Tom, Ken, Patti, Jimmy Mazzola, who can be seen passing by in the opening sequence, and a few others worked on the movie. The film's production manager, Michael Peyser, and the production designer, Mel Bourne (Tim's father), have also collaborated with Woody. The boys thought the film was OK.

12:00 noon. Shot 57: The hallway. It's the middle of the night; Mom appears in her nightgown and opens the door. It's Bea, looking pitiful. "You forgot your key? Did you have a nice time?" Mom asks. *(9 seconds.)*

Pop had put his pajamas on, but now he is not in the scene. So he stays with us to watch. From behind the camera, Woody arranges Bea. "Pull up your shirt." The shoes are lost. "Hold them in your hands." Then he tries it without the jacket. The bag and the hat are removed, and the jacket ends up draped over her shoulder.

Take 1: "Don't knock at the door," Woody tells Bea. "Sorry," she says, "I got creative."

Take 2: Bea comes in a bit too far.

Take 3: Now Mom has stood back "a pinch" too much, Dickie says. Otherwise, it's good for Woody.

Take 4: Very good. Bea looks really desperate. "We should try to find you something to say," Woody tells Bea. She answers: "It was all right!" "Let's try," Woody says.

Take 5: Very funny, thanks to Bea!

(Takes 3, 4, and 5 are printed.) Completed at 2:05 P.M.

12:30 P.M. Carlo and the boys are working on the next shot, Fred's arrival during the family dinner. The sink and parts of the kitchen wall have to be taken out so there will be more room for the camera. And Jimmy Mazzola is getting the dinner ready: chopped liver, huge pickles, gefilte fish in jellied broth and in liquid broth, and holy bread for the Sabbath.

Now that the big Times Square transparency has been rolled and stored, the crew is building the new broadcast studio for Kitty, so we can relinquish the stage upstairs, which is the doing of Ezra, no doubt.

As soon as we finish the film, Richie is going to work on *Ishtar*; they have four more weeks. He has just read the script, and tells me it's very funny. And Nicole has convinced Myla to take up knitting. Now they don't talk to each other anymore; they silently knit and knit and knit.

We break for lunch at 1:00 P.M.

Little Joe is having lunch with Cousin Ruthie and the Hebrew tutor at the commissary. But, as usual, Little Joe leaves them to work the room. Everybody knows him by now, and nobody pays him much attention. I am granted a few words: "Is the food good?" I ask him for news on Warren and Dustin. "You see," he replies, "Warren and I, we get along fine. But with Dustin, we didn't have an opportunity to really talk."

A little later, Dustin arrives at the commissary, but Little Joe has already gone back to the set. Dustin has a lively, intelligent face. He's wearing his black shirt and red headband again.

2:30 P.M. I'm sitting at the kitchen table with Nicole and Myla, and in front of me is Drew with her hair piled up. I am Pop's stand-in and Drew is Grandpa's. In the middle of it all, seven or eight of the boys are bustling around with ladders, pins, nails, and hammers. Carlo has a way of watching you without seeing you: looking at your nose, your mouth, your ears, your hands. Ray puts the light meter on your cheek, on your forehead, under your nose. It's a game of light and shadows. You can feel the heat of the bulbs. Nicole and Myla are silent, motionless, professional. But they're not wasting any time; they're studying my sweater to see how it's made.

3:20 P.M. The menu is changed. Instead of fish, the family is having stuffed cabbage with sliced carrots and pickles, and hot soup for the first course. Woody seats his guests. He asks for a cutting board so Ceil can cut the cabbage. "You got it!" Jimmy Mazzola answers. The seating arrangements are revised. Abe and Mom will be standing. Then Woody has the actors run through their lines.

Fred is still a little overwhelmed by the family. Ceil tries to put him at ease: "How about a piece of meat?"

3:45 P.M. While Carlo makes the final adjustments, everybody waits in the half-lit, disordered living room. Woody speaks to Brian. Little Joe and Cousin Ruthie entertain Fred, who seems to relax a little. Mom, who is pregnant, sits in Jimmy Sabat's chair behind his sound equipment, rubbing her belly. Romaine and Jeffrey work on Bea's hat. And Grandma is not feeling so well; the fish at lunch wasn't too good.

Shot 113: It's dinnertime in the kitchen. Everybody has gathered around the table. Ceil is chopping the cabbage, and Abe gives his opinion on current events: "The war is good for business. Production is up." "For my business, it's the same," Pop says. "What is your business, Dad?" Little Joe asks. Pop bites his tongue. Grandpa comes to the rescue: "He's a big butter-and-egg man." Everybody nods. Then the bell rings. "Another poor victim," Bea's new date. Bea dashes in. "He's lovely. . . . He works in my office. . . . He was engaged, but his fiancée died in a car crash . . . so he's obviously marriage-minded," and she rushes to open the door. Grandpa prays it's the good one, and Abe thinks "he has to be 4F," since "all the men are in the army." Bea comes back with Fred. Everybody stares at him. Fred is extremely well groomed, and refined. Mom offers him some food. Abe points out he brought "some fresh sea bass," but Fred is not hungry. There's an awkward silence. Bea says they're going to the ballet. "Yes, *Afternoon of a Faun* . . . it makes me cry," Fred says. More staring. Finally the couple leaves. As soon as the door closes, Mom asks Pop his opinion. "If you ask me, he looks a little effeminate." "Whatever he is, he's 4F," Abe concludes. *(1 minute, 24 seconds.)*

Take 1: Cut. Grandpa didn't make it: "He's a big . . ." And Abe knocked over a Pepsi bottle.

Take 2: Cut. Grandpa made it. But nobody was expecting it, and they all stopped talking, as though to let him talk.

Take 3: Cut. The family was talking too much, and not fast enough.

Take 4: First completed take. But Mom is so pregnant, she blocks the entire left side of the frame. And when Fred comes in, everybody is supposed to be quiet and not too friendly.

Take 5: Dickie cuts. Anyway, Grandpa and Abe were a little late with their lines.

Take 6: Woody sits just behind Grandpa. First good one. "Be louder," Woody tells Little Joe.

Take 7: "Good, Wood!"

Take 8: Cut. Little Joe missed his line.

Take 9: Dickie cuts. Louis's mike was casting a shadow.

Take 10: Cut. Grandma was leaning in the whole time, waiting for Ceil to give her some cabbage, and Abe was not lively enough. The overall action was a little confused. Abe starts to argue: "You see, this is not our fault. It can easily be explained by technical difficulties. . . ."

Take 11: Abe flubs a line: "Shit, fuck . . ." Everybody laughs.

Take 12: Cut. Little Joe said his line "What is your business . . ." to Grandpa. Woody asks the actors to continue the conversation until Fred exits. When Fred says that *Afternoon of a Faun* makes him cry, there should be a silence. And they should wait for the door to slam shut before talking about Fred.

There are problems with the gambling department. The actors are moving around everywhere, and another boom is needed, but there's no space for it. "There should be a solution," Woody says. The camera will start lower at Bea's entrance, so a portion of the ceiling will not be in the frame, and Frankie can sneak his boom in. The changes are made.

4:35 P.M. Take 13: Cut. Abe was a little late. And when Grandpa says his line, there should be approval from everybody.

Take 14: Cut. Grandpa said "egg and butter" instead of "butter and egg."

Take 15: The first really good one. "Maybe waiting for the door was a little long?" Woody says. Bea tells him she messed up; she can be quicker. "A lot quicker?" Woody asks.

Jimmy Mazzola has to clear the plates between the takes. And the cabbage is getting ridiculously small. Ceil doesn't have anything to chop anymore.

Take 16: Cut. A problem with a light. Good otherwise, except Little Joe: "More curious—'What's your business?'" and the approval after Grandpa's line needs to be more obvious.

Take 17: Cut. Pop should be more violent at the beginning when Little Joe eats with his hands, and Abe quicker.

Take 18: Very good. "Stay out of the frame until they both leave," Woody tells Mom. "One more and we . . ."

Take 19: "Don't forget, right on!" Woody tells Little Joe, and to all, "A lot of energy!" But cut. Pop muffed a line.

Take 20: Cut. To Little Joe: "Come on. You're late!"

Take 21: Cut. Pop again.

Take 22: Good. But Grandma could do better, and Little Joe got creative. After the couple left, he said, "Strange to go to the ballet," and Woody doesn't like it. Everybody should definitely not be so friendly to Fred. And after ". . . it makes me cry," Woody asks for "a couple of seconds and a half of silence."

Take 23: Very good. "Finished!"

(Takes 15, 18, and 23 are printed.) Completed at 5:15 P.M.

The next shot will be in the living room, the camera seeing everything: the hallway, the dining room, the kitchen, and Grandpa and Grandma's bedroom. It will take an hour and a half to light.

6:00 P.M. The snowman's penis has been cut in half, and someone has nailed it to his belly. Jeffrey is scandalized because *Purple Rose* has received only one Oscar nomination. If she hadn't chosen this profession, Myla says she would have been a midwife.

Dennis Kear is one of the stand-ins who has been with us since we arrived at Astoria. He has been Woody's stand-in since *The*

Front (1976). But he's never had a part, even as an extra. Though he doesn't have the same features, he's about the same size as Woody, and about the same complexion; when he puts the black glasses on, he has the same look. Dennis would like to be an actor, but is working in computers for the time being.

Grandpa tells me about the only film where he had the lead. It was called *Stigma* and was made ten years ago. The subject was venereal disease. The movie did beautifully in Europe. There were lines in front of the theaters. But it didn't do well here in America, and it didn't help his career.

7:15 P.M. Overtime has started, and Ezra is on the set. But Carlo is ready and everybody is back in. Woody checks the camera as the actors read their lines.

Woody: "The movement's very good."

Carlo: "Yes!"

Woody: "What? Now you're going to light it?"

Carlo (laughing): "Ma, no!"

Just a few minutes of adjustments are needed. Woody takes Pop to a corner and rehearses with him. Pop tries different tones and speeds of delivery. Woody selects what he likes. "Perfect!" And we go.

Shot 114: It's after dinner. Bea is at the ballet with Fred. And the routine is back: Mom knits, the radio is on, and Pop has just thought up a new scheme—engraving. "I could make a few dollars. And let me tell you the beauty part. When you engrave gold rings and lockets, what you cut out falls down on your table, and it accumulates. . . . Gold dust!" Mom is not convinced, and prefers discussing the baby's name. "If it's a girl, I thought we could name her Lola." "Lola! What do you want her to be? A stripper?" Mom wants "an 'L' name, after Uncle Louie." "An 'L' name after your Uncle Louie? How about Louse?" Pop jokes. *(40 seconds.)*

I bet with Ezra. He says five takes because the actors are good. I say ten takes because of Woody.

Take 1: Good. "Let's go again."

Take 2: Little problems with Pop's lines at the end, but still OK.

Take 3: OK. But Woody has the feeling that when Pop stepped over the dolly track, he changed his pace. Dickie is not aware of it, but Woody wants to check through the camera. Now Ezra tells me I might be right.

Take 4: "No good!" for Dickie.

Take 5: Cut. Pop missed a line.

Take 6: Good. Woody asks Pop to lower his level, but keep the same intensity.

Take 7: Very good. It looks more fluid.

Take 8: Woody cuts. He suddenly has doubts about the radio. Is it OK for the period? We are much later in the film. And Santo is not here. "If there's any doubt, we should stop," Ezra says.

(Takes 2, 6, and 7 are printed.)

We'll continue tomorrow morning. "Don't touch anything, guys! Live set!" Jimmy Mazzola yells.

"It's a wrap!" at 7:55 P.M.

Thursday, February 6, 1986

The Filipinos wind up an intense campaign. The vote is tomorrow. A statement by the Catholic prelate gives a virtual endorsement to Aquino over Marcos. "I shout to you, danger, danger, danger— we face danger!" Marcos says. (New York Times)

There is a third bombing in Paris, in another bookstore. Nine are wounded, three badly. (New York Times)

Baby Doc is said to be seeking asylum. Three European contries rebuff him. But he denies the whole thing. (New York Times)

"The Purple Rose of Cairo" is nominated for best screenplay.

There is a new sandwich at the Stage Delicatessen: sliced turkey, pastrami, roast beef, Swiss cheese, cole slaw, and Russian dressing. It is called the Mike Tyson Triple Decker, and costs $10.25. "The only other boxer we have a sandwich named for is Muhammad Ali," says Joe Greenwald, the owner of the Stage. After he knocks out Ferguson on the sixteenth, Tyson plans to eat two of his sandwiches in one sitting. (New York Times)

8:40 A.M. The radio was OK for the "engraving scheme" scene (sequence 114). Three more takes are done, the last two printed, and at 9:00 A.M. we move to the next shots, the radio giving bad news on the war, and the warden calling for a blackout (sequence 116). The scene in between, Little Joe in his bedroom, hearing the radio downstairs (sequence 115), will be done when we move upstairs. The camera is back in the living room, the sofa is out, and we'll have to wait almost two hours for lighting.

10:00 A.M. The shooting is supposed to be completed at the end
of next week (Friday the fourteenth). The only shot left, the submarine appearance, will be done by the second unit the week after,
on Staten Island. A fifteen-foot model has been sent out from California. It will be put in water next to a miniature pier. The optical
effects will be done later by Greenberg Associates.

Hannah is opening tomorrow nationwide, at more than four
hundred theaters. It's the first time a Woody Allen movie has
opened this widely; usually they start playing only Los Angeles and New York and then the rest of the country. But Orion
believes in the film. Tonight, at the Sutton, Woody is giving a
crew screening.

11:30 A.M. Carlo's ready, and everybody's back. Woody rereads the script, and listens to the playback of the news broadcast.
The actors run through their lines. The blocking is decided. But
Woody wants a change. In the script, when there was news, Ceil
turned the dial for music, the warden was heard from the street,
then more bad news on the radio. Woody wants to put all the
news at the beginning. While Jimmy Sabat works on it and Carlo
makes a few last adjustments, we wait on the spot.

I'm just behind the camera and next to Woody, our elbows
nearly touching. Juliet Taylor comes in and talks to him about
Hannah. He's anxious to see how it's going to work outside New
York and Los Angeles—in Oklahoma, for instance. "People will go
to see it twice in New York and Los Angeles," Juliet says. "A lot
of people have already seen it for free," Woody answers. "The
other day at the restaurant, a waiter came to me and said, 'You
were great in *Hannah*!'" "He must be a very important waiter,"
Ezra concludes.

Now Brian comes in. We are still crammed between the dolly
track and the wall. I give Brian the article on Tyson's triple decker.
He reads it, and gives it to Woody. Woody reads it, and gives it
back to Brian, who gives it back to me.

Finally, Ray comes to me. I become a little tense, but Woody
doesn't seem to disapprove. We talk about the *Purple Rose* nomination. Ray, like me, thinks *Purple Rose* is wonderful, and we both
like the script of this one a lot. I have the feeling Woody is listening, but maybe not; we're talking very quietly. Ray tells me that
Carlo had wanted a contrast between the warm colors of the family
scenes and the coldness of the broadcast studios. But seeing the

first dailies, Woody didn't like it. This explains some of the re-shoot.

All this happens in a less-than-one-square-foot space and Woody hasn't given me any hello or sign in three or four days.

11:50 A.M. Woody is at the camera. We rehearse. "Mechanically, it's fine. The problem is I couldn't follow everybody!" He's losing Abe's body and Mom's head. Mom's armchair is elevated a bit; now her feet don't touch the ground anymore. But Mom looks comfortable, again caressing her pregnant belly. There's a last-minute change; after the blackout, Pop doesn't shut off the last light, Ceil does it. And instead of saying, "The news is so depressing," Ceil says, "Oh, God, another air-raid drill."

Shot 116: A family evening. Grandma and Grandpa are in nightgowns in their bedroom in the back. Abe and Pop play cards in the dining room, Mom knits, and Ceil listens to the radio. The news is bad. Americans are retreating on two fronts, Japanese and German. Ceil turns the dial to find some music, but the bad news is everywhere. Mom asks Pop what he thinks: "You think Hitler's gonna win?" Pop wonders "about the wisdom of bringing new life into this world." Then the warden is heard from the street: "C'mon . . . Lights out . . . Blackout . . ." Ceil is really depressed. "Between the Communists and the Nazis, give me those Reds," Abe states, still a little under Doris's influence. "Stick to your fish," Ceil tells him. They switch the lights off one after the other. And Pop concludes, "You know what W. C. Fields said. To settle a war, the leaders of the countries involved should meet in a stadium and fight it out with socks filled with horse manure." *(1 minute, 4 seconds.)*

Take 1: There's a problem with shutting off the lights. Ray cuts the power while the actors fake it. And Ceil doesn't do the last one at the right moment. There's bad synchronization.

Take 2: Very good. "One more . . ."

Take 3: Right on again. But Louis is afraid he cast a shadow with his boom.

Take 4: Good. Dickie thinks that Ceil's light went off too early. But Carlo says it's OK.

(Takes 2, 3, and 4 are printed.) Completed at 12:25 P.M.

Bea stays to watch Carlo and Woody setting up the next shot. The next sequence, Little Joe spying on Bea and Fred in the kitchen, will be done in two shots. First, Little Joe going down the stairs, then, Bea and Fred in the kitchen. The boys start to work. We break for lunch at 1:00 P.M.

Dustin is again having lunch at the commissary. Talking to some others on the *Ishtar* crew at another table, he says loudly, "Storaro is doing a good job. But the director . . ."

The King Cole roof is being dismantled. The snowman, still in the carpenter shop, continues to suffer the persecution of evildoers. More screws in his belly, and somebody has put a dirty coffee cup on his half-size penis! On stage G, the gray drapes for the fog are being replaced by black drapes for the night in the Pennsylvania field.

2:30 P.M. We're back on the set. The camera is on the staircase, looking up. The wall has been pushed back, and Bobby Ward and his "Moes" are working on the dolly track.

Jack Rollins is visiting today, and making phone calls in the production office; with his oversize cigar, he looks like a producer. Fred is, in the real world, not at all "effeminate." And Little Joe is a little lost; Barbara is neglecting him. He is much quieter and nicer in such moments. Tomorrow is his birthday, and today is Pop's.

3:30 P.M. Shot 119: Little Joe, awakened by the radio, walks down the stairs to spy on Bea, who puts out cookies and milk for Fred. *(25 seconds.)*

Fred is supposed to be at the table, but he is out of frame. Bea again gets creative and starts rearranging the milk and cookies on the table. "Don't worry about that," Woody tells her. Then Woody works on her blocking. She goes in and out of the frame. No dialogue.

(2 takes and 2 prints.) Completed at 3:40 P.M.

Fred and Bea's love duet is set up very quickly. The camera looks from the opposite angle to the kitchen, with the hallway in the background. Woody dashes out, followed by Bea. But Bea comes back to ask Tom if she could come in a little later tomorrow morning.

4:55 P.M. Ready. Bea comes in with Fred and Woody. Woody sits at the kitchen table and has the two of them go through their lines. Motionless, he stares at them. They are both excellent. Woody asks Carlo if they could sit closer, so when Bea enters the frame with the cookies and milk, the camera can zoom in. And he doesn't want to rehearse, but the gambling department needs at least one. So, "Let's rehearse without performing it."

5:15 P.M. Shot 119A: The radio plays low in the background. Bea sits at the kitchen table next to Fred. She pours the milk and offers him some cookies. Fred seems a little tense. She had a wonderful night, Bea tells him. But Fred thinks he should go. "I have to drive back to the Bronx." Bea gets closer. "Fred . . . you must know I have a little crush on you." But Fred starts to sob. "What is it? Is it still your fiancée?" Bea asks, moved by such sensitivity. "Every time I hear that song on the radio," Fred says, "my memory goes back to Leonard. . . ." Bea is stunned. "You never said your fiancée's name was Leonard." "How could I?" Poor Fred answers, desperate. Bea begins to realize he might not be the one. *(1 minute, 50 seconds.)*

Take 1: Bea doesn't lean in enough and is out of frame when she pours the milk. And there are too many pauses between the lines.

Take 2: Good. But Woody wants Fred to really cry. Fern is called to put some liquid in his hands, something he can rub in his eyes. Fred suggests he cry for real.

Take 3: The liquid worked, but Fred was really crying, too. Woody tells him the liquid is enough. But the take could have been better. Bea waited too long to react at the end. And Dickie didn't see the tears very well on camera. Fern adds more liquid. "Don't think about crying. Just think about playing the scene," Woody tells Fred.

Take 4: Good. Fred is perfect. And Dickie saw the tears. Woody asks Bea to toast with the glasses of milk.

Take 5: Dickie cuts. "Louis! Up—up—up—"

Take 6: Very good. Woody lets the scene run at the end, instead of cutting immediately, as usual. He seems satisfied. "We can stop or do another one. How do you feel, guys?" Fred asks for one more. Woody asks him to add a few sobs at the end, and to wring his hands more. "And be more polite and less abrupt when you want to leave."

Take 7: Good. But Fred would like one more again. "If you don't mind?" he asks Bea. "I love it!" she says.

Take 8: Very good. "Happy?" Woody asks the actors. Fred looks happy, and Bea loved it.

(Takes 2, 3, 4, 6, 7, and 8 are printed.)

The air-raid warden is brought in for a wild track: "Blackout . . . Lights out . . ."

We wrap at 5:50 P.M.

Friday, February 7, 1986

Vice-President Bush stands by his attack on New York Governor Mario Cuomo, but concedes that it was harsh. Last month,

Cuomo said that ethnic prejudice lay behind assertions some peo-
ple have made that he, as an Italian-American, would have a hard
time being elected President. And he added that he was tempted to
run just to show that a person of his heritage could win. A few
days later, Bush responded by accusing Cuomo of "divisiveness,"
adding, "he's telling us to ignore the millions of blacks, Jews,
Irish, Italians, Latins and Poles who shattered the bonds of dis-
crimination, and built this great land." (New York Times)

Hannah and Her Sisters *opens today. "It's a masterpiece.*
'Hannah' is Woody's greatest triumph," says Rex Reed *of the*
New York Post. *"Hurrah for 'Hannah.' Woody's latest—and*
greatest—is really 'Manhattan' with a heart," says Kathleen Car-
roll *in the* Daily News.

The crew screening was held yesterday evening and the room
was packed. Everybody was there—Jack Rollins, Jane, the Salad
Sisters with their men, the gambling department with their ladies,
and all the rest. The screening was, of course, a success. At the
end, Carlo came to see how people liked it. But Woody didn't
come.

It was strange to see Bea on-screen flirting (again!) with
Woody; Mom trying to reason with him when he thought he had
cancer; Woody asking for Max's sperm; Sally, very different, but
very touching; and a glimpse of Andrew (with long hair), Lark,
Daisy, and even little Moses. But the film was a bit of a surprise
for everyone. Only about 20 percent of the script and the original
shooting made it in. The rest was from the reshoot. And the result
is entirely different from the original concept and script. Originally, Max had more scenes, including one in an art gallery, and
there were more scenes with Woody and Hannah together. Michael Caine and Barbara Hershey made love in a boat, and that was
cut. At another point, Barbara Hershey was coming with her fiancé
for dinner in Hannah's apartment; Michael Caine tried to kiss her
and she accidentally stabbed him in the hand with scissors. The
very beautiful scene where Hannah, in bed with Michael Caine,
tells him she, too, is fragile was not in the original script.

9:00 A.M. A door has closed on Little Joe's fingers. He is proud
and courageous, and doesn't complain, but there's panic for a while
there.

It's snowing heavily, so we're going to shoot the snowman. He's already at the location.

9:30 A.M. In front of the school entrance, two blocks away from the studio, the snowman looks in better shape than in the carpenter shop, dressed in a black jacket, scarf, and a felt hat. The penis is not on at the moment. A car stops. Three tourists from India come up and ask if they can take a picture of themselves with the snowman (Woody is not here yet). It seems it's the first time they've seen one.

Woody arrives. The real school principal comes out to shake hands with him (Does he know about the penis?). For the moment, Santo is holding the carrot that plays that part.

Shot D102: Little Joe and Andrew are touching up the snowman. A couple passes by. Andrew pulls out the big carrot, and puts it in place. The school principal, a woman, comes out. The two kids make a run for it. *(15 seconds.)*
Take 1: Good.
Take 2: Cut. Andrew cannot find the hole for the carrot.
Take 3: Cut again! The spot has been marked, but the hole is not big enough. Jimmy Mazzola widens the hole with a knife. He also gives Andrew a new carrot. The first one was getting a bit ragged after going from hand to hand . . .
Take 4: Good.
(Takes 1 and 4 are printed.)

In the van back to the studio and Little Joe's house: "This guy is too lucky. We haven't had a snowstorm like that since 1968. And one week before the end of the shooting," Jimmy Mazzola says.

11:30 A.M. Back in Little Joe's house to celebrate New Year's Eve with the family (sequence 182). Woody has the grandparents in their nightgowns, and asks Abe to take off his tie. It's decided that they won't have the champagne called for in the script, but coffee and ginger ale. Woody, Bea, and Little Joe are whistling today.
Shot 182: The family's 1944 New Year's Eve. Everybody cheers and kisses. Mom is holding the baby. "I'm a little scared for the future," she says. But Pop is optimistic today. "What are you scared about? . . . Don't worry so much!" Bea comes from upstairs with Little Joe. She has awakened him for the New Year: "God! I wish this war would be over. There are no single men around. . . ." But Ceil thinks Bea is going to meet him this year. "I have a feeling in my bones." Abe proposes having some fish. And the festivities continue. *(52 seconds.)*
First, a few rehearsals. A doll is standing in for the baby, who will be brought at the last minute. "More festive, folks. There's a lethargy. It looks grim!" Woody says after the first rehearsal. "Bea should start from higher on the steps," Dickie says. "Then there's a long time before my line," Bea answers. "Then fill the time. 'Happy New Year!'" Woody tells her. The baby is brought in by the real mother, and given to Mom. The mother stays with us, just in case. The baby has dark curly hair, and is very quiet.
Take 1: Cut. Bad start.

Take 2: "No good!" for Dickie. A problem with reflections.

Take 3: Good. The baby is a real pro, smiling at everybody, even Abe!

Take 4: Woody cuts: "We don't get enough of the background at the beginning."

Dickie: "I got three seconds."

Woody: "Not enough,"

Dickie: "OK. I'll give you four."

Take 5: It looks very good. But Louis and Kay think the camera wasn't on Mom when she said her line. Dickie has doubts about that.

Take 6: Dickie cuts: "No good!" This time, Kay and Louis are obviously right.

Take 7: Very good. Abe is great, offering his red snapper. Woody laughs.

The baby is given back to her mother. Mom congratulates her on her daughter's behavior. They go. And we wait for another baby.

12:25 P.M. Guess who the other baby is? Baby Dylan herself. Sally, back in her baggy clothes, brings her proudly. It's Baby Dylan's first movie role, and Sally is excited. Mom takes Baby Dylan in her arms. Woody, for once, doesn't rush over to make some faces for her. We go on.

Take 8: Good, but Little Joe was a little out of frame at the end. Baby Dylan is a little tense and looking everywhere, not used to being in front of the camera. Sally hides in the corner just next to me. You should see her face.

Take 9: "Quick. Baby's frightened. Looking for Mama," Dickie remarks before the take. It's good again. But just after it finishes, Baby can't take the tension any longer, and starts crying. Woody hurries over to quiet her down. Sally stays in her corner, in agony.

Take 10: Baby Dylan started to cry at the end, but it's still good.

(Takes 5, 7, 8, 9, and 10 are printed.)

Mom apologizes to Sally. Woody takes Baby Dylan to his room.

We break for lunch at 12:50 P.M.

2:15 P.M. Carlo is lighting the kitchen for the sequence of the family listening to the Polly Phelps story. Baby Dylan is on

Woody's sofa with Sally, watching him play chess. Mom and Ceil are chatting in their room, while Abe reads the paper next to them. The rest of us are finishing Pop and Little Joe's birthday cake at the Salad Sisters'.

3:00 P.M. Shot 165: The family members have forgotten their own interests and listen in the kitchen to the Polly Phelps broadcast. Grandma sits in a chair in the dining room.

Grandma is given a shirt and needle and thread so she can sew. Woody checks through the camera. He complains because Bea has checked it just before, and has gotten makeup on the eyepiece.

Take 1: "I don't think Ceil should smoke. And Little Joe should eat," Woody says just before the take. But it's no good. Bea, who has to enter the frame, didn't hear Dickie's cue.

Take 2: Woody cuts. Grandma, carried away by her sewing, was singing.

Take 3: Cut again. "Just sew," Woody says to Grandma. This time, she was running the thread through her mouth. It's important, because at the beginning of the shot she is prominent in the foreground.

Take 4: Good. "One more . . ."

Take 5: Good.

(Takes 4 and 5 are printed.) Completed at 3:10 P.M.

The shot is finished. Everybody moves, except Grandma, who stays in her chair and continues to sew.

3:30 P.M. Bea picks the cards. And I lose! The snowman is melting in the lobby, returning to his earlier disheveled state. And the well where Polly Phelps will fall is being built on stage G. The radio truck has already arrived. The atmosphere is mellow. *Hannah* is a big success, we're on schedule, and we should finish by next Friday at the latest.

4:00 P.M. While Carlo makes final adjustments on the members of the family in the kitchen, Woody waits in the living room. Whistling, he types a few words on Pop's typewriter, then takes a few dollar bills from his pocket and paces, playing with the bills. Finally, he goes to Andrew.

Shot 170: The camera pans on the family's attentive faces silently listening to Polly's story. *(30 seconds.)*

Woody is in the kitchen with them, staring at each face, as Dickie tells him which one he is on.

Take 1: Cut. Dickie lost Abe at the end.

Take 2: Good. Now a faster version.

Take 3: Dickie is not convinced it's good. Carlo: "No good. No emotion" (because of the faster pan). Woody: "Let's do another one slow."

Take 4: Good. Pop adds a nice move toward Little Joe.

(Takes 2, 3, and 4 are printed.)

Woody asks Little Joe to go sit on Pop's knees. "And you could hug him, and be nice to him," Woody says to Pop.

Little Joe: "What? Him, being nice to me?"

Woody: "That's science fiction."

Carlo needs ten minutes to make some changes. The shot is now only of Pop, Little Joe, Ceil, and Mom. So the others are free. Ezra, Jimmy Mazzola, Tom, and Jimmy Davis sit around the dining-room table and discuss next week's schedule. Before leaving, Grandma asks if she could take a cushion from the sofa for her back. But Richie refuses her without pity. "It's a set dressing."

4:55 P.M. Shot 173: Ceil, Mom, and Pop with Little Joe on his knees, stunned, as they learn of Polly's death. The camera moves closer to Pop and Little Joe.

Take 1: Good. One more with a little variation. Dickie will announce when he is in close-up so Mom can caress Little Joe's head.

Take 2: Good.

(The 2 are printed.)

"It's a wrap" at 5:00 P.M.

Monday, February 10, 1986   *Fifteenth Week*

Haiti's Baby Doc flees to France with his wife, Michelle, in a U.S. Air Force jet. (New York Times)

In the Philippine election, Aquino is ahead. Marcos hints at invalidating the vote. (New York Times)

Train collision in western Canada. Up to forty are dead and eighty injured. (New York Times)

Achille Lauro seajack epilogue: Mrs. Marilyn Klinghoffer dies of cancer. (Daily News)

A clean house or sex? Women who try to do it all face chronic fatigue. (Daily News)

After Rome, Paris, and New York, Jean-Luc Godard's Hail Mary *continues to create an uproar, now in Rio de Janeiro.* (New York Times)

And British actor Brian Aherne dies of heart failure at eighty-three. He made his acting debut at age eight in England, in a pantomime show with Noël Coward. He made his Broadway debut in The Barretts of Wimpole Street *in 1931, opposite Katherine Cornell. He made his American film debut in Rouben Mamoulian's* Song of Songs, *opposite Marlene Dietrich, in 1933. He married, then divorced, Joan Fontaine. In the last years of his life, Mr. Aherne moved with the seasons among his three homes, summer in Switzerland, fall in New York, and winter in Florida.*

9:00 A.M. Barbara went back to Philly this weekend, and lost her voice yelling at her daughter. Richie has a new haircut, almost punk. Cliff shaved his beard, but kept a small moustache. And the tango teacher is back with us to practice the conga with Bea.

Carlo is setting the scene where Pop explains his bagel scheme to Mom, Bea dances the Conga, Ruthie listens to the Waldbaums' party line, Grandma looks for her teeth, and Abe brings eels (sequence 162).

10:00 A.M. Shot 162: The radio is on. While Mom tries to do the laundry, Pop tries to talk to her about an idea he "just came up with that I think is going to make us rich." Mom thinks the cab is fine, but Pop doesn't want to "drive a hack my whole life." He explains his plan to Mom. "Pay attention. . . . While Jewish families up North always have the pleasure on Sunday morning of bagels and lox, what about the Southern families? Now . . . if Marty [Greenbaum] and I package bagels and lox, and ship them, kept fresh, don't ask me how yet, so that Jewish families can enjoy their breakfast. . . . What do you think?" Mom finds it "idiotic," and doesn't "have the strength to tell why." Ruthie announces that "Mrs. Waldbaum's cousin may be made a judge, but he has to pay somebody off," and, off-camera, Ceil tells everyone that "Abe brought home eels!" *(46 seconds.)*

First rehearsal. Woody is at the camera. He asks Pop not to be so angry, and to try to stretch his lines so the camera will be able to stay on him until Ruthie arrives. Then he asks the grandparents to look for the teeth in the background.

Woody (to Grandma): "Don't look at the camera!"

Grandma: "When do I say my lines?"

Woody: "Nothing. Not yet!"

A second rehearsal is held for Dickie. Ceil is with us in the grandparents' bedroom in the back. Bea is also here, watching. They are not in the scene but Ceil has to say her off-camera line. And she forgets. "Oh, shit!" Woody: "It's OK."

10:15 A.M. Take 1: Cut. Mom almost tripped on Louis's cable, thanks to her huge laundry basket.

Take 2: Good. Ceil is not perfect, but a wild track will be done anyway.

Take 3: "Right on!" The gambling department can do better with the sound, though.

Take 4: Good. Woody asks Pop to be more enthusiastic about his idea at the beginning and to start to talk earlier, while he's walking to the kitchen door.

Take 5: Dickie cuts. Either Pop was late, or the camera was too early. Bea goes back to her dressing room, tired of watching.

Take 6: Good. "One more . . ."

Take 7: Dickie cuts. Pop should yell at Mom when she's in the kitchen; his quiet delivery makes it seem that she's close by.

Take 8: OK. But Pop can do better, and Ruthie overdid it.

Take 9: Cut. Pop didn't get his lines "Marty and . . ."

Take 10: Good.

(Takes 4, 6, and 10 are printed.) Completed at 10:35 A.M.

Woody rereads the script. He wants to see how much of the next scene he can get into a single shot. Then he looks for the camera angle, moving stealthily from one place to another, switching from the camera's point of view to the blocking—Bea dancing the conga, Abe with his eels (Woody mimes holding the slithery beasts), Grandma looking for her teeth—so Carlo can get an idea of what's going to happen. First Woody considers doing the scene in the kitchen. But Carlo feels the room is too small for so much action. Woody resets everything to the living room. He decides to cut before the grandparents' lines. Carlo doesn't like the idea, but to leave them in is too risky; if there are problems with the grandparents, the first part of the scene will be lost as well.

11:30 A.M. The snow covering the snowman in the lobby has melted completely. Somebody has broken his nose, but he still wears his jacket and scarf; the carrot/penis has been removed.

Shot 162A: Ruthie hangs up the phone. Waldbaum has just yelled his standard complaint, "Stop listening to . . ." from the yard. The radio plays a conga. Bea turns it up, and starts to dance; she has just learned it from her dance teacher. She encourages Ruthie to join her. Abe appears with the eels, and scares Bea, teasing her. Now Ceil has joined the dance, and with the radio blasting the conga music, the three women dance around the table. *(31 seconds.)*

Woody starts with an informal rehearsal. He realizes that the baby can't stay in the room with the music. "Pop should take her out," he decides, "and Ceil should come here, bringing or taking something, I don't know what." Ruthie hangs up; Bea starts to dance; Abe appears with the eels. Woody asks them to try it from the beginning. But, "What am I supposed to do?" Ruthie asks. "That's a good question," Woody replies. It's decided that Ruthie will join Bea just after Abe scares her with the eels. "That's the general idea," Woody says, turning to Carlo.

Now it's a rehearsal with Carlo at the camera: "You look like a creep," Woody graciously tells Bea, who takes it without comment. Ceil's joining Bea and Ruthie in the conga was not in the original plan, and it has a spontaneous, realistic look to it. Carlo needs ten minutes for adjustments.

12:00 noon. Dickie wants a rehearsal. Woody tells Bea, "Don't start to dance right away. You should adjust the radio." And at the beginning, she should dance for Pop. Jimmy Mazzola is in the kitchen, gloves on, preparing the eels; they look calm today.

Take 1: Woody lets the scene run. Very good. Bea goes back to sipping her Diet Pepsi.

Take 2: Dickie cuts. Abe was not on his mark. But the eels were perfect. Bea complains.

Woody: "What's the matter?"

Bea: "It smells so bad!"

Woody: "It's just fish." And he turns to Abe: "When you enter the frame, don't run."

Take 3: Dickie cuts. "Louis . . ." Jimmy Mazzola comes up next to us with his gloves on. Bea is right; it stinks.

Take 4: Good. "Two good ones. One more and . . ."

Take 5: Good.

(Takes 1, 4, and 5 are printed.) Completed at 12:20 P.M.

The setting of the following shot has already been decided, so

Woody dashes out. But Tom calls to him, "Woody, we'll work on this shot until one P.M., and then break for lunch." Woody yells "OK!" from the porch. "The most cooperative man on the set!" Brian mutters to me.

We break for lunch at 1:00 P.M.

Baby Dylan is here (that's why Woody was in such a hurry). Grandma and Pop are playing with her. But the only thing Baby Dylan likes to do is tear out Little Joe's red hair. And Little Joe lets her. Tonight, Woody will look at Baby Dylan's dailies; Sally is very anxious.

2:30 P.M. Carlo, too, had lunch with Baby Dylan. He likes her, but finds her a bit rambunctious. He prefers eating with grown-ups.

Shot 162B: In the middle of the turmoil, Grandma comes in. "Where are my teeth?" Grandpa is just behind her. "A woman can't keep track of her own teeth. Look at me. I'm eighty-three, I got all my teeth." "Quiet, Nathan!" *(12 seconds.)*

First rehearsal: "Wait a minute! I have to say my line," Grandma complains to Grandpa, who is a little too eager to start acting. As usual, Woody is a little awkward around them, and treats them a little roughly. "No big moves," he tells Grandma, who has a tendency to be somewhat theatrical. He asks them to pick up the pace, which is dangerous for Grandma, given her bad legs. And they have to finish on the right marks. "We've got the action fine," Woody says. "Let's go."

Take 1: No good. Grandpa misses his start. Woody just sits.

Take 2: Grandpa doesn't finish on his mark. Mom and Ceil have come to watch.

Take 3: Grandpa hesitates on his last line, "my own teeth." "Let's keep going!" Woody says.

Take 4: Good. And Woody was complaining . . .

Take 5: Good. But Dickie can do better.

Take 6: A problem with Grandma's blocking at the end, and Grandpa could improve. "Turn around and look at Papa," Dickie says to Grandma.

Take 7: Grandpa again.

Take 8: Good. But Woody thinks that Grandma paused too long at the end.

Take 9: "No good," Dickie says. Grandma was in the wrong position.

Take 10: Cut. Grandma was too late with her lines and Grandpa followed her too closely.

Take 11: Good.

(Takes 4, 5, 8, and 11 are printed.) Completed at 3:10 P.M.

Now we are ready for the big ending, when the family's choreography reaches its pinnacle to the strains of the conga, and stops when the music is interrupted by the broadcast from the Pennsylvania field. Woody settles on a camera angle and the movement, a dolly following the action.

4:00 P.M. It's the last week, and the atmosphere is relaxed but wistful. Soon we will lose our family; after fourteen weeks, ten hours a day, everybody had come to feel a part of it. And each will be going on to other projects. There will, of course, be the reshoot in April, but it will not be the same. Richie is going to *Ishtar;* the company left the studio Friday and is on location in Manhattan. Mom is going back to her home in California. Pop is going to Los Angeles, too, but with his real wife, Jill Eikenberry, and their two kids. Pop and Jill are doing a TV series, *L.A. Law,* together and have to shoot the pilot soon. A lot of the crew will go on to James Toback's *Pick-Up Artist,* starring Molly Ringwald. The film is being produced by Warren Beatty, and the director of photography is Gordon Willis. So far, those set to join that production include Brian, Tom, Dickie, Kay, and Bobby Ward with his "Moes." The shooting should start at the end of May, just after Woody's reshoot. Nicole and Myla have no projects for the moment. They have given up knitting, and are back to crosswords and their books. Dennis takes it easy, reading his computer magazines.

4:30 P.M. Shot 162C: The radio is still on loud, the women are dancing around the table, and Grandpa and Grandma are arguing and looking for the teeth. Suddenly Mom runs down the stairs, furiously chasing Little Joe. "Look what he did!" she yells. Pop catches him. "See what he did with his chemistry set. He dyed my fur coat!" Mom says. Pop is incredulous. Mom: "I'm going to hit him." "No. I'm going to hit him," Pop says, pulling the belt from his trousers. But Little Joe escapes, and runs into the kitchen. Pop races after him. They run one lap—kitchen, hallway, living room, dining room—as the conga line continues. "Who cares! Who cares! Everybody take the gas pipe," Abe screams. After the second lap, Pop catches Little Joe, and starts hitting him. But the radio conga is interrupted by a special bulletin from Pennsylvania. Polly Phelps, an eight-year-old girl, is still trapped in a well after seven hours. The family pauses, Pop stops hitting Little Joe, and they listen. *(1 minute, 5 seconds.)*

"You guys are looking for teeth. But don't start yet!" Woody tells the grandparents. After having told everyone their blocking, Woody goes behind the camera: "I want to see a rough rehearsal."

First rehearsal: Little Joe runs too fast. It could be dangerous, and Pop is really unable to catch him. And the women dancing the conga are too late.

Second rehearsal: The family is caught up in the action. They're unstoppable. Woody whistles once, twice. "It's going to work just fine," he tells them. "I panned because I was chicken," he says to Carlo, adding that he still wants a dolly for the scene.

5:00 P.M. All the adjustments have been made. Since the camera movement and the blocking are so complicated, Dickie wants to rehearse. Woody asks Little Joe not to scream when Pop hits him with the belt. "But it hurts!" Little Joe says. "Take it like a man," Bea tells him. Woody checks with Jimmy to make sure Mom's line "He dyed my fur coat" will be heard in all the commotion. It's Kay who makes the Polly Phelps announcement, reading it from the script.

Take 1: Dickie cuts. He had a bad start.

Take 2: Cut again. Frankie's boom got into the frame. And there was too much dancing. The women should move around the table faster.

Take 3: Good. "Everybody freeze!" Dickie yells at the end. Woody checks the last image.

Take 4: Woody cuts. Mom has said, "with my chemistry coat . . ."

Take 5: Good. Woody asks that when the special announcement is heard, the actors stop their various bits of business one at a time.

Take 6: "Right on!"

(Takes 3, 5, and 6 are printed.) Completed at 5:30 P.M.

Woody dashes out.

Tom (to Bob Greenhut): "We're on schedule, and could, even if we wrap now, finish on Wednesday evening with the house, and go onto stage G for Polly Phelps on Thursday morning."

Bobby: "Let's use this half an hour to set the next shot. I hate to lose it."

Always greedy, these producers.

We wrap at 6:00 P.M.

Tuesday, February 11, 1986

The Tylenol lunacy strikes again in Yonkers. A twenty-three-year-old woman dies after taking a couple of capsules. (New York Times)

Because of the "almost mystical aura" surrounding the release of Hannah and Her Sisters, *Orion plans an unusual push. "We're selling it more as an entertainment rather than as the latest in the Woody Allen series."* (Variety)

And suburbs are a magnet to homosexuals. In some quarters, gays are becoming as familiar at the local bank and hardware store as their heterosexual neighbors across the street. Many are reacting to a fear of AIDS, a New Jersey professor of sociology asserts. "A number of men say they are tired of hearing about funerals, tired of hearing about someone who has died."

"Our next-door neighbors refer to us as 'the boys,'" says Michael, a thirty-eight-year-old coordinator for a television network, who lives with Bill, forty-five, a lawyer for a governmental agency. "It took me a number of years to realize that straight people were just as good as gay people, and I lament that," he adds.

Margaret, a thirty-eight-year-old psychotherapist, and Nancy, a thirty-five-year-old computer consultant, live in Jersey City with Cory, the two-year-old child Margaret conceived through artificial insemination. They want to move to the suburbs, where they can have what they call a "Mom and Mom lifestyle" and where little Cory can ride his bike. They wonder, though, whether two women whose "hobbies are politics and foreign films" can find happiness in the kind of town where most people are "puttering around the house and fixing things up." Margaret talks about "being a den mother," and Nancy aspires to be a "Little League coach." Their message is: "Family structure in this country has changed so much that a couple like us is not going to be considered aberrant in the suburbs." (New York Times)

9:00 A.M. It's snowing heavily. Ten inches are expected this afternoon. We're back in the family house, as Mom, in her night-gown, listens to the Phyliss and Paul soap opera and cleans the table. This is the third reshoot for the scene and the second for Mom. Woody wants a faster version, and Mom can do even better than she did last time. Jimmy Mazzola and Jimmy Frederick are setting the table with half-eaten fried eggs, pieces of bread mixed with banana peels, and still-smoldering cigarette butts. Since Jimmy Sabat is stuck in the snow (he lives on Long Island), the gambling department has recruited Liz to operate the boom.

Shot RR11 is identical to the previous version. For the most part, Mom will be able to improvise, but two or three specific actions are required to match some of the lines in the soap opera, like throwing the banana peel in the garbage can when Paul asks Phyliss to say yes, and to spit in the can because the cigarette butt is smoking while Paul is talking about the French Riviera.

Take 1: "Keep it disgusting," Woody tells Mom before she starts, "and don't forget the banana!" But he cuts quickly. Mom didn't start from the beginning.

Take 2: "The first dishes were OK, but you can do better with the banana."

Take 3: Woody cuts. "You're much too late." And the smoke in the garbage can is not obvious enough. Jimmy Mazzola suggests getting a smoke machine to put in the can for denser smoke. How long will it take? Two minutes. Woody gives his OK.

Since it's snowing, Woody wants to reshoot the snowman. The dailies were good, but you can always do better.

Jimmy is back, but his system isn't working perfectly. And now the cigarette in the can is creating enough smoke on its own. Woody considers putting the whole ashtray into the can; that way there will be plenty of smoke. But Jimmy disagrees; he likes to do things right. Woody looks at him with an intrigued smile.

Take 4: Good. But Dickie didn't see enough smoke. "Now that we have a couple of good ones, one more, really exaggerated," Woody tells Mom.

Take 5: Mom went a little too fast, though Woody seems satisfied. He whistles "Tea for Two," and does a few tap-dance steps.

Take 6: "I missed the banana!" Mom says. Woody wants to stop here, but Mom talks him out of it; she is not happy with her performance; she can do better. We go on.

Take 7: No good. "Right after the banana, you stay still. You're caught up."

Take 8: Very good.

(Takes 2, 3, 4, 5, 6, and 8 are printed.) Completed at 9:30 A.M.

We're finished with the first floor of the house and move upstairs. The first shot is in the bathroom, where Grandpa is struggling with Grandma's corset. The camera will be in the hallway; Carlo goes to work.

10:30 A.M. Ruthie's boyfriend is lonesome, wandering in the lobby. He was here yesterday, too, and is a little tired of waiting, and Ruthie ignores him. Jimmy Sabat finally arrives. It was terrible out there on Long Island, he says—cars all over the road, you couldn't see three feet ahead. The King Cole roof looks terrible, too, like a tornado has swept through. The boys are destroying it, showing no respect.

There's a dilemma for the snowman scene. When we first shot the sequence, Woody picked, at the last minute, one of the passerby extras to play the principal. But they didn't know that in the production office, and this morning they called the extra they thought was the principal (who, in fact, had ended up as a passerby). So now there are two passersby and no principal!

Myla has been dressed to play one of the passersby (her second role in the movie after the hospital scene). Dennis is being dressed, too. He will be the second passerby (his first role in a Woody Allen movie after ten years as Woody's stand-in!).

Someone who must be extremely delighted by this change of schedule is Andrew. This morning, he went to school, and then was summoned to be with us on the set.

Another reshoot is planned for this afternoon—Mom, Pop, and Little Joe learning of Polly's death.

Grandpa is now entertaining Ruthie's boyfriend. These American women—either they run after men, like Bea, or they change men every minute, like Sally, or they just ignore them entirely, like Ruthie!

10:45 A.M. Shot 25: The bathroom. "Suck in . . . suck in!" Grandpa screams, trying to lace Grandma into her corset. "Pull harder, Nathan!" "The woman is in her seventies, and her bosom is still growing!" Grandpa complains. *(15 seconds.)*

Grandma has to take her teeth out, and also do the scene in underwear. It's a little embarrassing, but Grandma is a good sport about it.

Take 1: Very good. The image of this woman with her huge

bosom, being laced into her corset by this skinny man, is quite funny. Everyone is laughing. But in reality it is still a little awkward, and Woody becomes gentler with them.

Take 2: "On 'action,' pull for a few seconds before talking," Woody tells Grandpa. It works well. Grandpa is having fun, but Grandma isn't enjoying it so much.

Take 3: Cut. Grandpa flubbed a line.

Take 4: "Right on."

(Takes 1, 2, and 4 are printed.) Completed at 10:50 A.M.

We move to Little Joe's room for a new scene Woody has written, a scene playing off the Rienzi episode, where he showed the kids some of his inventions. This scene was not in the script and has been written during the shooting. Ruthie and her boyfriend are kissing in her bedroom, with music from the radio in the background, when suddenly they hear Little Joe's voice (he has Rienzi's microphone).

After explaining the scene to Carlo, Woody stands silently, looking at the ground, hands in pockets, little fingers out, thinking. Carlo stands next to him, silent, too; he rereads the pages of the script, then waits, looking around. The boys quietly move the equipment inside the room. Woody sits on the bed, head bent, his hands between his crossed legs, going back into his shell, focused inward. It lasts five minutes. But the inspiration is not there, and Woody decides to do another scene before this one. Tom suggests Abe and Ceil listening to Sally's *Gay White Way* radio gossip show. Woody agrees, and we move to Abe and Ceil's room. This scene was not in the original script either.

11:05 A.M. We're all in Abe and Ceil's room. Woody rereads the script, and asks for the radio Little Joe brought back from the repair shop. "We could put them in bed, for once," Woody says. He starts to walk through the action for Carlo. The radio is on, Ceil is in bed eating chocolate, Abe sits on the edge, undressing, then we hear static and Abe stands up and hits the radio. Woody and Carlo decide to put the camera at the door. Woody dashes out.

11:45 A.M. Ruthie wanted to rehearse the scene with her boyfriend, she tells me, but he refused, so that's why she's ignoring him. But her real mother tells her that he refused because she was embarrassing him.

Kay has a friend, a professor at U.C. Berkeley, who organizes seminars on various topics, inviting personalities from different fields to talk. The next colloquium scheduled is "The Immortality of the Soul." After seeing *Hannah*, the professor phoned Kay to see if Woody would be interested. "Absolutely not!" Woody answers after hearing the topic of the symposium.

Nicole is standing-in in Abe and Ceil's bed, and Dickie is sleeping in Bea's bed. On Bea's night table, there's a glimpse of her literary tastes—*The Rest of My Life with You*, by Faith Baldwin; *In Search of a Husband*, by Harris; and *The Constant Nymph* by Margaret Kennedy.

12:30 P.M. Shot 144A: The radio is on, playing Sally's *Gay White Way*. Ceil is already in bed, eating chocolates. Abe is undressing, pulling off his socks. Ceil muses about the beautiful people and the beautiful places Sally is describing. Abe is not impressed; the whole subject irritates him. The radio gets staticky. Abe goes to it, starts hitting it, and succeeds in breaking it. *(47 seconds.)*

For the second time, Tom asks Abe to sit on the bed so Woody can check the framing. "Sure," Abe calmly replies. Then he screams, imitating Tom's big voice: "Don't fall apart!" The little hall is very crowded, so Carlo retires to the bathroom with me, grumbling amidst Grandma's hanging stockings.

Take 1: Ceil misses her start.

Take 2: Very good. The way Ceil eats the chocolates is great. She really likes them.

Take 3: Abe is sweating. Since Fern cannot get to him, Brian dries his forehead with a Kleenex. A touching scene! The take is again very good.

(Takes 2 and 3 are printed.) It's 12:35 P.M.

We break for lunch at 1:00 P.M.

Patti is going to practice Shiatsu on Hammer during lunchtime. It's a Japanese pressure massage, she tells me.

In the van on the way to the snowman location with Chopin's *Nocturnes*, and Little Joe, Cliff, Richie, Kay, Dickie, Carlo, Bill, Brian, Andrew, Liz, Dennis, and the principal. We're crammed in because "the fucking other van is fucking gone to fucking take the fucking teamsters to their fucking lunch," Danny explains.

3:00 P.M. School is out. The snowman, without carrot, is already in place and attracting attention. He's being protected by two bodyguards, Richie and Doug, so the kids won't hurt him. Drew has twisted her knee during a fall in the snow. Tim takes her back to the studio in his little van. Jimmy Mazzola says he'll go take care of her as soon as the shot is completed.

Shot RD102: Same action, but the camera starts wider, and zooms in closer at the end.

Take 1: No good. The principal seems to know ahead of time that the carrot is in. Andrew is accomplished at placing the carrot now.

Take 2: Camera cuts.

Take 3: The carrot falls out.

Take 4: The carrot falls again. Woody goes to talk to the principal.

Take 5: Surprise. After the kids run away, the principal takes the carrot as before, but this time looks around, and starts biting into it. Everybody laughs. Brian bets me five hundred dollars that this take will not be in the movie. "Too risky for his reputation," he says. Woody goes back to the principal.

Take 6: Same thing, but the principal keeps the carrot in her mouth. Woody is having fun. What's next?

Take 7: She does the same, but stays longer before going back in. "No good." Woody goes back to her.

Take 8: Good. A kid from the crowd has thrown a snowball into the frame at the end of the take. But Woody doesn't mind.

(Takes 1, 5, 6, and 8 are printed.) It's 3:25 P.M.

4:30 P.M. Drew is at the Salad Sisters', a sack of ice on her knee. She's feeling better. Jimmy has taken good care of her, and now he stays to entertain her; obviously a holistic healer, he believes in the importance of the psychological part of the treatment. Tim is also here. He's taking off his shirt to show Drew the scrape on his back. A few other boys pass by to see how she is doing. Drew, you see, had to take her trousers off.

In the rooms next door, Santo is being entertained by Barbara, and Woody plays chess with Abe. The latest news is that we'll pass our last hours together Friday night doing the searchlights in Rockaway.

5:30 P.M. We're almost ready to shoot Ruthie pantomiming in front of her mirror. The room being small, Mom and Ceil come to watch with me from the balcony; we see the scene through the window. Mom and Ceil are getting along well. For the last two weeks, they've been hanging around together all the time. Wanting to be nice, I compliment Ceil on her scene with the chocolates. "You were great in bed this morning." "Thank you, darling," she answers. And the two ladies burst into laughter, amused by my poor English! Then we talk about their roles and acting in general. Mom would like to do more comedy, but she's not sure she knows how to be funny, while Ceil would like to be serious and is afraid of being too funny. "Are you crazy?" Mom says. "There is nothing better than getting a big laugh." But Ceil is a romantic. She sticks to her idea. She wants to move people, to make them cry.

Shot 95: Ruthie, all dressed up, sings and dances in front of her mirror a la Carmen Miranda, to "South American Way," which plays on the radio. Pop and Abe come to watch, and join in at the end. *(1 minute, 30 seconds.)*

His job finished, Carlo comes out to the balcony. After two hours of lighting, Carlo needs to relax, staying near the set, though. He cracks a few "Italian" jokes that the ladies appreciate. Ray joins us, too. The balcony is the place today.

Take 1: Very good. "Hold your positions, kids!" Dickie screams. Woody checks the last framing: "That's perfect." Then to Ruthie: "Maybe, at the end . . ." But Ruthie already knows; she can do even better.

Take 2: Dickie cuts. There was a problem with the camera movement.

Take 3: Cut. Ruthie lost one of her earrings.

Take 4: Good. Woody asks Ruthie if she could dance as well with the music much lower. "Yes," she answers.

Take 5: "Perfect," but Dickie thinks he saw somebody pass by in the background. But who? Nobody was back there. Woody: "Let's do one more."

Take 6: Good.

(Takes 1, 4, and 6 are printed.) It's 6:30 P.M.

Now we go back downstairs to reshoot Little Joe and his parents learning of Polly's death.

7:00 P.M. Shot R173: Ceil, Mom, Pop, and Little Joe on Pop's knees, are stunned and sad as they learn of Polly's death.

The parents were doing too much in the previous takes. "Just think about it. Don't do any particular thing." Kay reads the lines for the newscaster.

Take 1: Woody cuts. "We've got the same thing. Just listen," Woody says to Pop.

Take 2: Woody is not satisfied: "Maybe you should hold Little Joe more. But emotionless."

Take 3: "That's better. Let's do one more."

Take 4: It's OK. "We can try one more. I don't know what else to do." Woody says. Then, "Will it help you guys to talk?" Pop says yes.

Take 5: "That was good. One more and we're finished."

Take 6: Good.

(Takes 3, 4, 5, and 6 are printed.)

We wrap at 7:10 P.M.

Wednesday, February 12, 1986

Evelio Javier, a leading Marcos foe, is chased across a town square and killed by gunmen. (New York Times)

Anatoly Shcharansky is freed in a prisoner trade after eight years in prisons and labor camps. (New York Times)

Lech Walesa resists. Charges are dropped, though he hasn't retracted his statement mentioning his doubts over the government's claim of victory in parliamentary elections. (New York Times)

Donald Manes resigns as Queens borough president and county Democratic leader. (New York Times)

Officials say the fatal tampering with Tylenol is an isolated case. (New York Times)

And Sidney Stone dies at eighty-three of heart failure. He spent years in vaudeville and burlesque, and appeared on Broadway in such productions as Three Men on a Horse *and* Damn Yankees. *More recently, he was in* Sugar Babies. *He gained national prominence as Milton Berle's commercial announcer, the one who regularly used the pitch line "Tell ya what I'm gonna do!"*

9:00 A.M. Last day with the family. We're going to film Ruthie and her boyfriend this morning. Finally, instead of flirting on the bed, they are going to do it in the kitchen, as Bea and Fred did.

Carlo is finishing the lighting. In the living room, Jane flirts with Bill on the sofa, Nicole just next to them, concentrates on her knitting.

9:30 A.M. Shot A134: Ruthie, back from school, comes into the kitchen with her boyfriend. He sits at the table, a little shy. Ruthie, making eyes at him, turns on the radio, takes the bottle of milk from the refrigerator, and joins him. Then, closing her eyes, she offers him her lips when Little Joe's voice comes out of the radio: "Take your hands off her, you little creep. Take your books and get out!" Panicked, the boyfriend flees. *(30 seconds.)*

Woody starts to change Little Joe's lines, writing the new ones on a little piece of paper. Then Ruthie has to change into a more colorful jacket. Cousin Ruthie is a little mischievous after her success yesterday in the "South American Way" number. But Woody likes her. Several rehearsals are done. Woody directs them verbally, saying Little Joe's lines ("You little creep!"). He cues the actors. It's hesitant, slow at the beginning. "You're too calm," Woody tells them. Then the scene starts to come alive. "That's the idea. Next is pictures."

Take 1: Woody cuts. There was no milk in the pitcher. "Jimmy Mazzola!"

Take 2: Woody cuts. Ruthie forgot to go to the radio. But he forgot to cue her, she replies.

Take 3: OK. Woody hasn't stopped directing them verbally, and screams Little Joe's lines: "You little creep! . . . Get out! . . . Yes, you!"

Take 4: Good. "Better float," Dickie says. But Carlo, watching from the sidelines, doesn't think Ruthie reacted strongly enough: "No feeling!"

Take 5: Dickie cuts. He sees the soundstage in the background when the door opens; the actors shouldn't open it so wide.

Take 6: Good.

(Takes 4 and 6 are printed.) Completed at 9:55 A.M.

A wild track of Little Joe. Woody sits at the kitchen table to write more lines for him. Then he directs Little Joe by saying the line just beforehand. "Don't hit me! . . . Don't touch my dial!" "That's OK," Woody says when it's finished. "We're going to work on that for a while and see if it works." And he gives the sheet of paper to Kay.

11:00 A.M. "Catastrophe!" in the living room. Nicole's V-neck sweater is too small. Everybody has a suggestion. Frankie thinks she should leave the side open so we can see something, Angela likes it the way it is, and Dennis doesn't care. Carlo is working upstairs on the last big scene for the family, in which Mom has her first labor pains.

We're all feeling nostalgic, Mom and Pop, Abe and Ceil, and me, sitting in Mom's room, telling sad stories. When Ceil's baby was four months old, he fell on his head. She had to take him to the hospital for X rays, on the horrible sort of machine Woody used in *Hannah*. And Abe tells about the time he cut his thumb with a big knife that his parents had forbidden him to touch. But "I had to have a bagel!" he says.

12:00 noon. Carlo and the boys are working hard. It's a tough shot to light because the camera sees everything—all the rooms on the second floor, and down the stairs to the first floor.

Ken wants to travel through Europe this summer, and asks me the best way to do it. "Take the train," Dickie says. "They're fantastic. They fly, seats are great, and food's excellent. You eat like at home!" The tone of the conversation has been set; we're going to talk about food. Dickie reminds Kay of the film they did together in Michigan in 1964. Does she remember that night when they had those beautiful shrimps and chicken? Kay can't recall it!

Shot 153: Ceil and Abe are in their bedroom, and Mom and Pop are in theirs next door. The four of them talk from one room to the other. "Jimson's Coffee is having a slogan contest," Ceil announces, ". . . and you can win a refrigerator." "Fraud," says Abe. But everyone eventually gets into the slogan-writing spirit. Mom comes up with "Good to the last drop" but Pop informs her that Maxwell House is using it. Suddenly, Mom starts screaming. The baby is coming. The others accompany her to the stairs. *(45 seconds.)*

"Is this the way it happens?" Woody asks. Tom has his own ideas, and thinks there are always false alarms before the real one. But Pop thinks it can also happen on the first alert. Woody listens and learns while the two of them continue to argue.

Tom: "It doesn't happen suddenly like that."

Pop: "But in the old times . . ."

To allow the camera to easily pan back and forth from one bedroom to the other, Mom and Pop are put in Bea's room. (Nothing has been filmed there up to now.)

Take 1: Cut. Jimmy is picking up a clock on the sound track.

Take 2: Good. But Woody has a feeling Dickie was a little late.

Take 3: A very good one.

Take 4: Woody adds a line for Abe: "I knew if you ate codfish, it would induce it." But the arguing starts again. Which fish? Dickie has more ideas on the subject, but Woody has the last word; it will be halibut. The take is good. But Dickie needs another one.

Take 5: Woody cuts. Mom didn't hear Ceil's cue.

Take 6: Very good.

(Takes 3 and 6 are printed.)

A wild track for Abe: "I knew if you ate . . ." One with halibut, and one with codfish.

And we break for lunch at 1:30 P.M.

3:00 P.M. Behind the debris of the King Cole roof, in the middle of what was Times Square, the luminous backdrop that was used once for the Crooner has been brought from upstairs. Colorful neon lettering has been added: WELL HOUSE COFFEE. GOOD TO THE LAST DROP. Since neon is so expensive, the "Max" of Maxwell has been dropped.

Carlo has had a nice lunch and is in a great mood, doing his Italian number. Ray had a funeral to attend and Hammer has taken over; now he really has to work! Tom is working with Brian on organizing the Toback movie. Santo has been approached to do the Toback movie, but he's already committed himself to his good pal Ulu Grosbard's next project. He'll never work on the West Coast, Santo tells me; it has to do with his "emotional affiliation."

At the Salad Sisters', it's party time. Jane is getting a punk haircut, and Bea is taking pictures of everybody with her Polaroid: Jane, Ezra, even me!

4:00 P.M. Kitty, elegant as ever, is back with us. Woody is much more cheerful with her, taking her hands in his, and apologizing for having had to ask her back. Carlo follows, and kisses her hand. Pop, Mom, and Ceil came to watch the beautiful woman sing. Abe is here, too. He has brought his camera with its mile-long lens.

Same song, same singer, same nostalgia. Kitty starts with "I'll Be Seeing You." In the middle of the take, Bea, Andrew, Jane with her new haircut, and Little Joe in pajamas (for his next scene) join us. Almost everybody is on the set now. It's nice to see all their faces together; it would be a good ending for the book, or the movie. But the song is over, and Kitty goes to change for the next number.

4:30 P.M. Today is Ash Wednesday, and there is a rumor that a priest is coming to the set. We will have to line up, the priest will do his duty, and Woody will watch. We're told Woody is still thinking about converting to Catholicism, but since that rumor is being spread by Jimmy Sabat, who is Catholic, we don't have a lot of faith in it.

Kitty comes back, all in green. Now she sings "They're Either Too Young or Too Old." No problems. When it's over, Brian takes another picture, Woody with his usual expression, Kitty smiling. Then Kitty leaves us.

Ezra: "Do you think we're done with that scene?"
Woody: "I hope!"
Ezra: "Next time, we could put her in front of the Camel sign."

Woody (miming the action): "With smoke going out of her mouth while she sings . . ."

6:00 P.M. We're back in the house for the scene of Little Joe in his bed.

Shot 115: The camera starts on the staircase, tilts up, and pans to Little Joe in bed, listening to the radio from the living room announcing the bad news.

"Do you want to drive it?" Dickie asks Woody. Woody changes the framing a little, then explains to Dickie and Red what scenes come just before and just after, so they can get a good feeling for the movement. There will be two versions. The first is a simple pan from the staircase to Little Joe. The second will have the camera dollying in on Little Joe.

(5 takes and 4 prints.)

We move next door to Bea's room.

7:00 P.M. Jimmy Mazzola really overdid it this time. Woody had suggested that in a shot where Bea listens to the radio, Abe should be in the background eating fish. Jimmy has procured six platters with five different sorts of fish on each. The smell is all over the house. Jimmy tells us he was tired of Woody always saying, "That's all you've got?" What's worse, we're not even shooting the scene tonight, so the fish will have to be kept in the commissary refrigerator. Abe has gone home and isn't even here to appreciate it.

7:15 P.M. Ready for the leg scene. Bea has nice legs, so the boys hang around, just in case a light needs to be changed.

Shot 150: Close-up of Bea's leg as she paints on her stockings. Zoom back for a wide shot. *(27 seconds.)*

Woody lies on Bea's bed, reading one of her screen-romance magazines, affecting a blasé indifference. Bea gets ready. With or without shoes? Without, Woody says. Between each take, Fern "redresses" the leg. For the second take, Woody asks her to show a little of the white at the top of her leg. She doesn't think it will be very attractive, but she does it for Woody . . .

(3 takes and 3 prints.)

And on this sexy note, we wrap at 7:35 P.M.

Thursday, February 13, 1986

The U.S. Secretary of Interior ousts Lee Iacocca as chairman of the Statue of Liberty advisory commission. (New York Times)

Ed seeks to rescind a law giving Manes a pension at age fifty-five. (New York Times)

And Frank Herbert dies at sixty-five of cancer. His novel Dune *has been translated into fourteen languages, and has sold more than twelve million copies since it was published in 1965.* Dune *was rejected by twenty publishers before one accepted it.*

9:00 A.M. The Pennsylvania field on stage G. The set is very simple. The sand of Breezy Point has been spread out, and straw has been scattered over it. In the middle of the stage, a rough well made of several pieces of wood has been excavated (the stage is equipped with trapdoors). Cars are parked around the well, including a period well-digging truck, a fire truck, a white Cadillac ambulance, two police cars, a radio truck, and cars belonging to onlookers; there are about seventeen cars all together.

The scene will be lighted only by the car headlights, and a few other lights simulating them. Since the batteries won't be able to hold up for long, Jimmy Mazzola and Ray are putting all the headlights on AC, using dimmers.

Dickie is not the only one recuperating this morning. Louis sleeps on Kay's stool, and Frankie lies on a bale of hay.

10:00 A.M. Little Joe's house is empty, in the dark, and in disorder. It looks like a house after a good weekend. Near the production offices, Mom's dressing room is now occupied by the Midget, and Little Joe's by Jockey Jack Williams. And in the Zukor theater, fifty extras are waiting. It's the usual bunch—old couples, teenagers, a 1943-vintage priest, four tall firemen, six cops, six news photographers, two ambulance attendants, the mayor's wife, and the sheriff's wife.

10:30 A.M. We may not shoot the searchlights tomorrow night in Rockaway: Blizzard conditions are expected in the evening. We'll go there in the afternoon, though, because Woody has decided that Manulis should take Bea to an amusement park funhouse instead of the roller-skating rink—he is not pleased with how that turned out.

Jimmy Mazzola and Ray are going mad. There are not enough dimmers, and the bulbs of the old cars' headlights are popping one after the other, unable to withstand the additional power.

The Polly Phelps Newsman (Ivan Kronenfeld—he was on the King Cole roof the other day), Fireman Reilly (Frank O'Brien), Jockey Jack Williams (Michael Venezia), and the Midget (Pepi Hermines) are wandering around on the set, a little bored and ready for action. Jockey Jack Williams is a real jockey, and missed a race today to be in the movie (Jimmy Sabat tells me he's "good enough"). And the Midget is obviously a real one. He's a tall midget, though, almost the jockey's size, and has come with a short midget.

11:30 A.M. The additional dimmers and bulbs have arrived. The boys work hard, but Jimmy Mazzola tells me he doesn't have as many men as he needs. It's a slow process.

12:40 P.M. They are still working on the headlights. Woody comes to the set to see what's happening. He's with the man to be interviewed in the field. John Doumanian (the Polly Phelps Man) has been in several of Woody's movies. He was a coke addict at Paul Simon's mellow party in *Annie Hall*, a Porsche owner in *Manhattan*, an Armenian fan in *Stardust Memories*, and a Greek waiter in *Zelig*. In real life, he manages rock-'n'-roll bands and produces records. He's in the movies just for fun.

When Woody arrives on the set the way he is now, it is rather like the arrival of a king's court. There are the favorites (Sally and Bea), the dauphins (Andrew and Baby Dylan), the prime minister (Carlo), the Secretary of State (Jane), the courtiers (Jeffrey and Brian), all the ministers (Tom, Santo, Jimmy Sabat, and the Salad Sisters), and the chronicler (the Frenchman). It's a very cosmopolitan kingdom.

12:50 P.M. We're ready for the first shot.

Shot 163: "It has been seven hours," the Newsman says, "and still emergency workers have not been able to contact or free eight-year-old Polly Phelps. Volunteers to go down into the well are limited by the narrow size . . ." The Newsman is with Jockey Jack Williams, who failed in his attempt to descend into it. *(26 seconds.)*

Woody chooses the setup, a long, establishing traveling shot, starting from the Newsman in close-up, and finishing as a wide shot, including background action. Woody rides the camera, stopping every foot to check the framing and the position of the extras. He plays with the car headlights. "They should stay together, but move from one spot to the other," Woody tells Tom of the background extras. Once the blocking is set, the shot is up to Dickie to get a good float, and Tom to keep the extras moving as planned. Carlo checks Woody's blocking, and makes a few adjustments.

At first, the background is not lively enough; they have yet to get into the mood. Woody puts Jockey Jack Williams a little behind the Newsman, and he has him join the Newsman after a while. Then he has the jockey stand directly next to the Newsman.

A little problem with a few of the headlights. Some of them are still burning out. But we make it.

(9 takes and 3 prints.)

"I think we're OK on this shot," Woody says to Tom. But Ezra has already started worrying. It's 2:00 P.M., we've done one shot (at least eight are needed for the sequence), and we break for lunch.

At the commissary, the Priest has invited Jockey Jack Williams and Fireman Reilly to his table. Jeffrey Mazzola is having trouble with the kitchen. They are tired of Abe's fish, which are taking up too much room in their refrigerator (and they don't yet know that we're not going to shoot the scene today).

3:10 P.M. Woody is eating chocolate and discussing the next shot with Carlo, the Newsman doing the interview. It will be a simple dolly-in on the two men. Tom asks Woody if he can release Jockey Jack Williams because he has a race tomorrow. But first we need a wild track from him.

3:30 P.M. The Astonishing Tonino was in town yesterday, and gave Ken a call. Tonino lives in New Jersey, and wants to know when he'll be needed to perform his stunt in the milk can.

There's uncertainty about tomorrow. We still have the eight shots of this sequence, one scene with Abe and the fish in Little Joe's house, Manulis and Bea in Rockaway, and the searchlights. Bob Greenhut, who, in the tradition of all the great producers, doesn't have any heart, wants to work late tonight, finish tomorrow morning, do the scene in Little Joe's house just after, rush to

Rockaway before nightfall to shoot Bea and Manulis in the funhouse, and finish with the searchlights in the evening. That way, only the second unit will be required for the submarine on Tuesday, and the film will be finished. The boys like overtime for the money, but they like to take it easy, too!

4:00 P.M. Shot 164: "Shouldn't the well have been boarded up?" the Newsman asks the Polly Phelps Man. "Yes . . . I can't understand it. . . . We'll do it tomorrow. . . ." the Man answers. "Tomorrow . . ." the Newsman begins, talking now to his listeners. *(12 seconds.)*

There is another "photographer," a man in his fifties, accompanied by his spouse. He has an Instamatic, and never stops taking pictures of Woody. Woody has noticed, and it's beginning to get on his nerves.

Woody asks that someone bring the Polly Phelps Man coffee during the Newsman's broadcast. Other than that small adjustment, the shot is easy and quickly done.

(5 takes and 3 prints.) Completed at 4:10 P.M.

"Visitors are banned from the set," Tom says. The photographer and his wife have to go. He should have been more careful. He was coming too close, and using a flash on his camera. He thought he could get away with it because he's a friend of Jimmy Mazzola!

5:00 P.M. The rumor that Bob Greenhut's scenario will be put into action is more and more persistent. We'll be here till 11:00 P.M. Then we'll come back tomorrow, and work until the movie is finished. There's supposed to be a meeting going on now in Woody's room with all the big shots—Bob Greenhut, Ezra, and Tom.

5:30 P.M. The meeting is over and everybody is back. The producers don't exactly look relaxed or overjoyed. With Ezra, it's normal, though he hasn't had a face that long since the day in Rye Playland when we were waiting for the sun to go. Bob Greenhut doesn't look too great either.

Woody looks the same as always, and goes back to work as if nothing has happened. He doesn't seem to have lost his concentration, and is immediately ready to ignore everything going on around him. At this moment, you sense an incredible stubbornness, power, and energy coming from that little man. And it's all the more powerful since he stays very low-key, soft and quiet. "After checking everything, I think we're in pretty good shape," he tells Carlo.

Shot 163A: A dolly near the well. Everybody bustles about as Fireman Reilly yells, "Can you hear me? . . . Polly! . . ." But Polly doesn't answer.

Again, Woody rides the camera and checks the framing at each foot. He moves some people. Carlo checks it: "Very good!" Carlo asks only two things: to pan quicker at the end, and to wait a beat before starting the dolly. "You'll cut it later if you want." Woody OK's it. During the take, Jimmy Mazzola and his men, from out of frame, add some camera-bulb flashes to the image.

(4 takes and 2 prints.) Completed at 5:40 P.M.

Everybody stays silently in position. Rereading his script, Woody walks among the extras, looking for the right angle. It seems like time has stopped, with all the lights on and everybody frozen. Woody passes close to them, followed by Carlo. The Priest, the Midget, and the Newsman are brought in. "The question is . . ." Woody begins, can the Midget go down the well easily? It's quite narrow. Jimmy Mazzola assures him there will be no problem. So the next shot will be of the Midget getting lowered into the well. "We're getting pretty far in the scene with this shot. We're doing pretty good," Woody tells Tom before going back to his room. The Midget stays with us so Jimmy Mazzola and he can practice the descent while Carlo works.

6:15 P.M. Bob Greenhut is talking with Jockey Jack Williams, trying to get some tips out of him. Jimmy Sabat stays beside them, feigning a lack of interest. The Midget is watching Jimmy Mazzola preparing the rope and the huge well drill, which will lower him into the well. He doesn't look very enthusiastic about the whole thing. Jimmy has joined Bob Greenhut and the jockey now. "You see, I don't bet anymore but . . ." he says, taking his marked-up track paper from his back pocket.

6:40 P.M. Shot 167: "Fireman Reilly has suggested a volunteer midget be lowered into the well. . . . That is what is transpiring at the moment," the Newsman announces to his listeners. But suddenly, "I'm stuck! . . . I'm stuck!" the Midget yells. "This is just terrible," the Newsman begins. But the Midget is finally unstuck, then lowered the rest of the way in. *(1 minute, 35 seconds.)*

Ceil, who is visiting, asks Brian to take a picture of her imitating Woody.

"Comfortable?" Jimmy Mazzola asks the Midget hanging at the end of the rope. Woody watches. It looks OK in rehearsal, but Jimmy is not satisfied. There is not enough slack in the rope. He climbs up the well-digging machine.

The image is quite funny. And when the Midget screams in his high voice, "I'm stuck!" it's hard not to laugh, even though Polly is still trapped down there. Most of the directing once again involves the blocking and camera movement; after having checked both of them, Woody gives the camera to Dickie. Between takes, Fireman Reilly and the Midget exchange their impressions on the lowering.

(6 takes and 3 prints.)

Woody rereads his script by one of the car's headlights. He

goes to Tom to tell him how many shots are left. Ezra's ears prick up. Woody wants to shoot the scenes in order: "If not, we'll get confused."

7:45 P.M. Shot 167A: A different angle of the crowd watching the lowering of the Midget.
(3 takes and 2 prints.)

8:15 P.M. Now that the family is gone, the Salad Sisters are getting bored in their room. So they settle into a corner of the soundstage, chatting with the Polly Phelps Man. He asks them about the stars they have worked with. They talk about Liza Minnelli and Dudley Moore in *Arthur*, until they see me with my pen and pad in hand, and abruptly stop. They don't want to jeopardize a future job.

8:45 P.M. Shot 169: The Midget is bringing Polly up with him. The Newsman crosses through the crowd, making his way to the well. "She's out! . . . They have her out! . . ." he screams into his microphone. "The prayers of an entire nation are with her . . ." *(10 seconds.)*
Woody needs seven rehearsals to decide on the blocking of the scene. It's an important shot, and the audience won't actually see Polly come out. Woody has to build as much tension and uncertainty as possible. He has the Newsman walk (the camera dollying to his left) in front of the crowd. Woody positions a few extras in the foreground so the Newsman will pass between two groups. He asks him to push some of them aside. Until now, the people around the Newsman have not been moving; they were only trying to see over the heads. Woody has them move, too. He runs through the different blockings.
(5 takes and 5 prints.) Completed at 9:00 P.M.

9:15 P.M. Woody sits on the fender of the fire truck, his script in hand, head bent forward, thinking. Tom stands next to him and waits in silence. Carlo sits on the running board. The difficulty is that Woody has to consider the kind of shot he wants to do, what he will need to make it work, and which parts should be done tonight so all the extras won't be needed tomorrow. After more than thirteen hours of work, with everybody around and waiting, it must be difficult to think about all these things at once.

9:45 P.M. A last shot has been chosen. It's after Polly's death, when everybody goes back home. Tomorrow, the Priest, Polly's mom (Yolanda Childress) and pop, the Midget, Fireman Reilly, and half of the background extras will come back. Since Carlo shouldn't take long to set the shot, the extras wait in the hall just outside the stage.

Not a lot of pretty girls among the extras today. There is Marie, eighty years old (she was one of the churchgoers in *Hannah*), and André, who is just a little younger. Marie is happy because she recognized Jane from a show they did together when Jane was working at NBC. Marie and André have been here since 7:00 this morning. They like it because they're making a lot of money, but they wouldn't mind going home about now. The atmosphere in the crowded hall is cheerful, though. The Priest, his rosary and Bible in hand, is very popular, but maybe "a little effeminate," as Pop would say. "He's a very nice man," Marie tells me.

The boys would like to go home, too. To cheer us up, Dickie tells us about "a little joint" on the way back to town where we could stop and have a bite; they're open late, and the "food's excellent!"

10:15 P.M. Shot 174: Polly's dead. With the sound of Polly's mom sobbing in the background, and the soft voice of the Priest comforting her between prayers, everyone starts home in silence. The shot finishes on the door of the radio truck being closed by the technician. *(20 seconds.)*

"I want editorial approval for this day!" Ezra tells me, seeing me writing in my corner. After three and a half months, Ezra can't get used to the idea of me snooping around like this. He thinks Woody is crazy for letting me do it!

Woody is working on the blocking. One after the other, the headlights will go out. Though not quite naturalistic, it's a nice idea. Dickie takes over the camera. "Nice shot," he says. But he is getting a reflection of "the producer and the Frenchman."

(3 takes and 2 prints.)

"Leave your pistols at the door!" Jimmy Mazzola screams to the cops before they go. Sandwiches have been brought, but everybody is in too much of a hurry to get home.

We wrap at 10:35 P.M.

Back to Manhattan in Jeffrey's car with Judy and the Polly Phelps Man. Woody does impersonations of Fred Astaire, I learn, as well as excerpts from *West Side Story*.

Friday, February 14, 1986

More poison Tylenol capsules are found. A second bottle is discovered, leading to a nationwide warning. (New York Times)

France wants the U.S. to provide a home for Baby Doc. But the U.S. is not hot to do it. (New York Times)

Hannah and Her Sisters is hot in Manhattan; it's number one for the first week.

A Jersey woman has hit the lottery jackpot for the second time. She made $3.9 million last October, and $1.4 million yesterday. (New York Times)

And a new rule forcing high school coaches to remain seated at all times during the game creates an uproar across the country. In Yonkers, Coach John Volpe considered showing up at games in a wheelchair. When his Marist High School War Eagles took the court, Coach Ron Bell had a seat belt bolted to his metal chair. In Indiana, an outraged coach had himself tied up to his chair with heavy rope, and another one intends to show up nailed inside a plywood box with only his head protruding. (New York Times)

9:30 A.M. Late call today for our last day. We're back to the Pennsylvania field for Polly's rescue, hopeless since she died yesterday. Except for the grandparents, the family is back this morning, and Mom and Ceil, with curlers in their hair, have come to watch the events. The two midgets are back, too; they were heard speaking German to each other this morning in their room!

For the last day, the game is twenty dollars a card. Bob Greenhut takes one. If he wins, he'll donate the money to the reshoot fund, he says.

10:45 A.M. Polly's parents wait on the side with the Priest while Carlo works. Polly's Mom has already started sobbing.

Shot 171: The camera starts on Polly's parents, her mother sobbing and her father holding her, then passes the glaring headlights to finish on the Priest praying. *(25 seconds.)*

Polly's Mom doesn't need any liquid for the crying; she's a real "paid mourner."

"Sometimes it's very good, sometimes it's strange," Woody says to Carlo, giving him back the camera. Carlo checks it and likes it, and Dickie takes over.

(3 takes and 2 prints.) Completed at 11:15 P.M.

Woody wants to reshoot the establishing shot (number 163), with the well-drilling machine more obvious.

12:00 noon. Shot R163: Same as 163. It starts on a close-up of the Newsman talking to his audience, then the camera dollies left to the crowd, the headlights, and the drill. Since the jockey isn't here any longer, the camera moves on before the Newsman starts talking about him.

(2 takes and 2 prints.)

Before deciding to stop, Woody checks with Carlo to see if they have enough. He tells him how the sequences will be edited, reminding him of the shots and their angles, the intercutting with the listeners. They decide to move on.

Tom announces the plans. First we'll do a few wild tracks in the field (the Newsman), and in the house (Little Joe and Mom). Then we move to Rockaway to shoot the new funhouse scene (Manulis and Bea) before nightfall. We finish the day with the searchlights, and Tuesday we're back in the studio to finish the house scenes.

1:00 P.M. We are in the hall next to the production offices. Mom is depressed because she didn't have a chance to say good-bye to everybody. Woody passes by, giving no sign. But just before entering his room, he stops, wets his fingers, and wipes them across his eyebrows, without giving us a glance, but totally aware of us.

For our last day together, the gambling department does me a favor. I win second prize—three hundred dollars!

In the bus to Rockaway are some pretty girls and Manulis in a big sheepskin jacket. He didn't know he would be coming back until two days ago, he tells me.

2:30 P.M. We're back in Murphy's bar on Beach Ninety-sixth Street, just next to the Needlemans' residence. The caterer is setting up, the jukebox is on, and Bea is a having a drink with the teamsters. Jane, Andrew, and the Salad Sisters are having beer and Irish coffee. It's a nice atmosphere. Woody and Carlo have gone to look at the funhouse location next door.

Lunch with Angela, Cliff, Patti, and Manulis. Angela shows us Abe's farewell gift, heart-shaped red earrings. Manulis tells us that he lifts weights, and that he has a brother even taller and stronger than he; if Bea only knew. One day, the two brothers were at Disney World on the magic train, and they started fighting. The train went off the track!

3:00 P.M. The rumor is we won't shoot. Woody didn't like the funhouse. But we're all proceeding as if everything's on schedule.

3:30 P.M. We're not shooting the funhouse. The place looked depressing and was in need of a paint job.

Dickie gives me a lift to Beach 115th Street in his leather-interior turbo Thunderbird. Dickie lives in New Jersey, two hours from town. He has to wake up at 4:30 every morning to beat the traffic and arrive on time. This is why he recuperates on the set so much.

The first person we meet on 115th Street is Frankie, Jimmy Mazzola's friend. He was just passing by, saw a couple of trailers, and wondered what film it was.

4:00 P.M. Waiting for the night. Morton Nussbaum's chiropractic center has its modern facade back, and Little Joe's house looks almost as real as the one in the studio. In the luncheonette at the corner of Rockaway Boulevard and Beach 116th Street, a middle-aged man asks the boss, "Are they shooting *Hannah and Her Sisters?*"

Inside the wardrobe trailer, everybody is getting ready for a cold night. Tom comes in, talking into his walkie-talkie: "Ken, I just saw Carlo and Woody driving away. Where are they going?" Ken doesn't know!

5:30 P.M. Next Tuesday afternoon, instead of the funhouse, we'll shoot in a bowling alley in Manhattan. Woody has just seen it and likes it.

Carlo has started setting up the camera. The boys are taking the snow off the houses on the other side of the street. Woody is in the back of his station wagon, Jane at his side, making phone calls. Bea has gone back home with Fern; there's no big makeup session for the searchlights. Mom and Pop are in their trailer. And Andrew is with Drew.

6:30 P.M. It's dark, but we're waiting for more searchlights. It is not clear if they're coming from Pennsylvania or from Ohio. But they're stuck on the road, maybe by the blizzard. It has started snowing.

Woody's films have at least one "white room" scene. They're named after the sequence in *Zelig* where Dr. Eudora Fletcher/Mia Farrow has her sessions with Woody in the country house. It was shot and shot again, almost twenty times. In *Broadway Danny Rose*, there were two "white room" scenes, the one with Woody and Tina Vitale/Mia Farrow in the reeds, and the one in the abandoned factory. For this film, it looks like we're going to have one, these damned searchlights.

7:00 P.M. Mom and Pop are on the porch. In the dark, with all the lights, the snow looks beautiful. It has been decided that we will do the shots with the two searchlights we already have. Then we'll wait till 8:00 P.M. for the ones from Ohio. A wide shot of the street and the sky without the searchlights is also done. If the lights don't work tonight, this blank image will be given to the lab so searchlights can be superimposed onto it.

7:30 P.M. Mom, Pop, Carlo, and I are waiting inside Little Joe's house. It's much smaller and really depressing. So we dream about sunny beaches, and Carlo's little house in Sardegna, where you can jump from the window into the Mediterranean.

7:45 P.M. The Ohio searchlights have arrived! Though it's still snowing, everything is set and we shoot quickly. At 8:00 P.M., we wrap.

Tuesday, February 18, 1986   Sixteenth Week

On Saturday, the Philippine bishop endorsed the protests against vote fraud. Ten more opposition activists were reported slain.
   On Sunday, Marcos was declared victor. Aquino said she won.
   On Monday, Ron called the vote suspect and sent Philip Habib

to meet separately with Corazon Aquino and Marcos. (New York Times)

The death toll from South Africa riots this weekend is fourteen. More than one hundred have died since January 1, 1986. (New York Times)

Tamil rebels kill fifty-five Sri Lankan soldiers. (New York Times)

Fourteen are dead and forty injured in a fire in Rio de Janeiro. (New York Times)

The FBI is assigning high priority to the Tylenol inquiry.

Another knockout for Tyson (18-0) against Jesse Ferguson. "I try to catch him on the tip of his nose because I try to punch the bone into his brain," the "Dynamite Kid" says. (New York Times)

"I think the sense of humor is one of the most important weapons by which you defend yourself. I think the moment I would have lost it, the moment when I would have been unable to look at what's happening a little bit from the side, I would have failed, simply," Anatoly Shcharansky says. (New York Times)

Paul Stewart dies at seventy-seven of a heart attack. He appeared in nearly five thousand radio shows during the thirties, and produced the War of the Worlds *broadcast for Orson Welles's Mercury Theater.*

9:30 A.M. We're back in Little Joe's house in the Astoria Studios, in the kitchen, waiting for the fish; Jeffrey Mazzola has gone to get them from the commissary. Only Bea, Ruthie, Abe, and Little Joe are back this morning; we have to shoot a few pickup shots of them listening to the radio.

The fish have arrived, and their smell quickly spreads over the set. Bea and Little Joe complain, and Abe doesn't look very enthusiastic about eating week-old fish at 9:00 in the morning.

Shot A102A: The camera pans from Abe at the kitchen table eating fish, with Little Joe having milk and cookies behind him, to Bea standing next to the refrigerator and listening to the radio. *(15 seconds.)*

Bea, who needs to know about her motivation, asks if it will be a romantic song. "We don't know yet," Woody answers. Abe takes bites of the big fish, chews but doesn't swallow; a bucket is put under the table so he can spit it out between takes.

(3 takes and 2 prints.) Completed at 9:45 A.M.

A few wild tracks are done for Little Joe's other scenes. "Hey,

Dad! Got fifteen cents?" "But I want my Masked Avenger ring!" and a scream that leaves all of us petrified. Then we move to the grandparents' bedroom for an insert of Bea's hand turning the radio dial.

10:15 A.M. Shot A102B: Bea's hand turning the radio on. *(5 seconds.)*
(3 takes and 3 prints.)
We move upstairs to Little Joe's room.

11:30 A.M. It's a strange atmosphere today. It's the last day with a complete crew. The shots are short, with no dialogue, not very interesting, and not requiring much work. With only half of the family, it's not like before. So the boys take it easy and talk about what they're going to do over the break before the next job. "You've been here so long, you deserve credit on the movie," Ray tells me.

Shot A102C: The camera moves from Ruthie on her bed reading *Screen Romance* to Bea and Little Joe playing checkers on his bed. *(18 seconds.)*

Woody checks with Kay to see if he can put the *Life* magazine with Sanford on the cover on the bed. And "You take your dolly on my pan," Dickie tells Red.

(2 takes and 2 prints.) Completed at 12:00 noon.

We're finished at the studio and move to town for the bowling alley.

1:00 P.M. The Beacon Lanes on Amsterdam and Seventy-sixth Street is a nice ten-lane bowling alley, all in wood, with a bar in the back. A few posters have been put here and there.

BUTTERFINGERS ARE RICH IN ENERGY

COCA-COLA IS A SIGN OF GOOD TASTE

LIME COLA: NOT TWICE AS MUCH BUT TWICE AS GOOD

Baby Dylan is here. She's eating Woody's glasses while he rubs her belly with his nose. Sally has come, too; but Andrew is sick today. Manulis is back with us, always jovial.

We break for lunch at 1:30 P.M.

2:30 P.M. We're back at Beacon Lanes. The owner, a woman, keeps an anxious eye on Cliff, his brush and bucket in hand, and the boys who are changing the chandeliers and the bulbs. Ceil is here; she lives just next door. Manulis has his bowling shoes on, and is very successful with the pretty extras. The boys, always considerate, introduce me to some of them. And when the women ask about my accent, "He's from Brooklyn," the boys answer for me.

A chandelier falls and breaks. The owner rushes to look, but it's one of ours. "This isn't a Toback movie. That's your next job!" Jimmy Davis tells the boys.

4:00 P.M. Jimmy Mazzola gives Bea a bowling demonstration. Woody watches. Bea tries and, though the ball is a little heavy for her, she makes a good score. She jumps with joy, but Woody doesn't seem impressed. Tom decides to show us how it should be done, but fails to convince.

There are wiring problems. The wires are old and not strong enough to take the power needed for our lights.

4:30 P.M. Shot A51C: It starts on a wide shot of the bowling alleys with balls returning, then moves right to Manulis in action, Bea watching. *(21 seconds.)*

The bowling balls roll back, returning, in the foreground. The Mazzola brothers are sending them back, from just outside the frame, so there is less of a gap between them. In the background, extras are bowling, too. The difficulties come only from the speed of the balls, from getting the right pace so the image looks good. *(8 takes and 5 prints.)*

5:30 P.M. After seeing the dailies, Woody wants to reshoot the Polly Phelps sequence. It will be done during the April reshoot.

Shot A51D: It follows a ball returning, to reveal the couple. It's Bea's turn, and Manulis stands closely behind her, "coaching" her. Bea rolls the ball and makes a strike. She goes back to her seat, as Manulis looks on, stunned. *(18 seconds.)*

Woody asks Bea to go to her seat as soon as she releases the ball, not waiting around for the result, leaving Manulis alone. Then he asks her to throw the ball with both hands, legs apart, the ball between her legs. It's very funny, with Bea's face scrunched into her short-sighted look.

(6 takes and 5 prints.) Completed at 6:00 P.M.

Woody would like to do another shot. But the wires are burning, and we've booked the bowling alley only until 5:30 P.M. The Beacon Lanes customers have started arriving.

We wrap at 6:10 P.M.
Before leaving, Bea gives Manulis a big long kiss. Obviously, after Woody, he is her favorite.

Wednesday, February 19, 1986

Rainstorms strike the West Coast. Thousands are evacuated in the face of floods and mud slides. (New York Times)

Bishop Desmond Tutu defuses a confrontation near Johannesburg between police and black protesters. (New York Times)

Robert De Niro, Gregory Hines, Karen Allen, and Mandy Patinkin, among others, came to bowl at the Madison Square Garden Bowling Center in a benefit for the Second Stage theater yesterday. Diane Keaton came to watch, but didn't bowl. (Daily News)

And Anatoly Shcharansky speaks about his cellmates: Arkady Tsurko, a Jewish Leningrad teenager jailed for advocating the tenets of Western European Communists; Ints Tsalitis, a Latvian who received a six-year sentence for obtaining three thousand signatures for a nuclear-free zone in the Baltic States; a Roman Catholic priest sentenced for teaching religion to children; Vasif Melano, sentenced to seven years for protesting the exile of Andrei Sakharov; an Armenian jailed for promoting a referendum on whether their republic should remain Soviet; and two Russian Orthodox priests, Gleb Yakunin and Dmitri Dudko.

The man who became his best friend in the prison of Christopol in the Tatar Republic was a Russian Orthodox activist, Vladimir Poresh, an expert in eighteenth-century French literature sentenced for conducting religious seminars. Poresh had anti-Jewish feelings. "For him, Passover was a terrible holiday. . . . But when I translated for him the text of the Haggadah, he was so surprised when he read and saw that there is absolutely nothing contradicting his religion. What I got from him is concentration on some inner things. He was constantly studying himself from a religious point of view. I was controlling myself rationally, and he was trying to control himself spiritually. I think this exchange of experience, not even by words, but when you sit together, was useful for both of us." (New York Times)

8:30 A.M. Breezy Point is lovely today, with a temperature in the fifties and a low sky. We're having lox and bagels at the Surf Club and, though it's only second unit, everybody is here—Santo, Cliff, Jeffrey, and Judy, his assistant, who has become a blonde.

We're in 1901, to shoot Guglielmo Marconi flying his box kite, and receiving the first wireless message from across the Atlantic. Marconi's assistant is played by Jimmy Mazzola, and Marconi himself by Jimmy's friend, a 260-pound man with a laugh like Manulis's.

9:30 A.M. We're on the beach, waiting for the wind, which we need so Marconi can fly his kite. But there is absolutely none! The camera is set for a very long shot (300mm lens). We wait.

Jimmy Mazzola, in costume, starts his four-wheel drive, his friend Marconi at his side, and is going to show us how he can pop a wheelie, but he gets stuck in the sand. Everybody applauds, but Jimmy is not amused. We all push, except Woody; the truck just gets more and more stuck. The only way out is to take shovels and dig.

Woody is back in his huge gray parka. Santo wears a real Basque beret, and with his beard looks like a French monk. The wind has started up a little. Should we wait longer here, and risk losing the light for the submarine shot on Staten Island, or should we go to the submarine now and come back here later if we have time?

For the moment, we stay. Cliff has to paint Marconi's kite because it's white and doesn't show up very well against the sky. He gets into the four-wheel drive, which has been freed. Jimmy Mazzola puts it in first, and—comic relief—gets stuck again!

10:30 A.M. We don't shoot. A long shot of the coast has been taken for a test, and we move to Staten Island. Jimmy Mazzola, resigned, gives his costume back to Jeffrey, and Marconi is also disappointed; he came all the way from Pennsylvania this morning to be in the movie!

Because the forecast was good, overcast and not too cold, the company had briefly considered shooting the Tonino sequence this week. But the days being too short, we'll do it in April.

11:30 A.M. Staten Island. The fourteen-foot model Nazi submarine was used as a Japanese one in Steven Spielberg's 1941. The company wanted Das Boot, but it's still in Germany, and the customs problem are too complicated. Greenberg Associates is here, along with the owners of the model and their team, and some impressive equipment—two four-wheel drives, a small rowboat, two scuba divers, and ten tall men equipped with yellow-and-orange parkas, huge waist boots, and walkie-talkies. The submarine is equipped with an air-compression system that makes it submerge. Then, when the air is released, it surfaces. It is attached by cables at each end, and the four-wheel drive pulls it forward.

The submarine is going to be photographed emerging from the water as it goes forward. Because of its scale, it will be filmed at eighty-two frames per second, so the waves will look real. And this image will be superimposed on the one we shot at Coney Island. But first we have to wait for the tide to come in. The two scuba divers are in the water around the fourteen-foot model, testing the air compressor.

12:30 P.M. We're still waiting for the water. There is also a slight problem getting the submarine to surface upright as it moves forward. It loses its equilibrium, and comes up at an angle.

The camera is being set close to the water, directly on the ground. Sandwiches and hot soup are brought for the crew.

1:00 P.M. It has started to rain lightly, and it's cold. The U-boat definitely doesn't work. "It worked very well in California," the owner tells Sandy. Now it's lying on its side on the sand. They have decided to cut a hole in the middle so the water can go through and stabilize it. But they don't have a pair of cutting pliers. "Jimmy Mazzola!"

Some people from the neighborhood have come to watch, and are wondering why fifty people are shooting a Nazi U-boat model on a deserted Staten Island beach in the rain. The owner has trouble cutting the hole and everybody has suggestions. Carlo thinks they need a keel (for a submarine?). People are taking pictures.

2:00 P.M. It's still raining lightly, and it's getting darker and darker. The submarine is back in the water. The scuba divers, too, though they are not very excited about the prospect after lunch. Woody sits in the director's chair, and waits philosophically, looking at the water and listening to the waves.

Another test is done. "Catastrophe!" It's even worse than before. "It's a pity," Ezra says, "it's such a beautiful day!"

2:45 P.M. We decide to shoot anyway. A wide shot of the submarine surfacing without moving forward. Then a close-up of the boat totally emerged, with the big swastika. But it's not over. First, the submarine resists, it will not surface. Five of the guys put the rowboat in the water and help the scuba divers. Carlo starts to get nervous, Woody goes to walk alone on the beach, and Dickie, lying next to the camera, with the rain and the water almost surrounding him, is sleeping; Jane is impressed.

Finally, we get the shot, and at 4:00 P.M., "It's a wrap!"

Friday, February 21, 1986

"I'm so angry that I figuratively would like to kill somebody," Ed states as the Parking Violations Bureau scandal grows. (New York Times)

The submarine looked surprisingly good. The crew went back to Breezy Point to shoot Marconi, without Woody. There was, however, no visibility, only fog. So they shot the beach, and came back home.

D IARY: RESHOOT

Friday, April 25, 1986

"Even the Frenchman is back," Woody told Jane this morning.
"But he knows your name," she assures me. Almost everybody is
back, even Baby Dylan, Moses, and Andrew, though there are a
few remarkable absences. Tom, in preproduction on the Toback
movie, has been replaced by his second, Ken. Jimmy Mazzola, also
on another film, has now become Joe Badalluco, which sounds as
good when you scream it. The gambling department is in Florida.
Louis is now a beautiful blonde, and Jimmy Sabat has been replaced by the blonde's brother. The Salad Sisters have split up;
Romaine is here, but Fern is in North Carolina.

Carlo went to Italy to see Antonioni, who is very sick, and
won't be doing his film. So Carlo is going to do a Herbert Ross
comedy starring Michael J. Fox this summer, before coming back,
like everybody else, to the next Woody project in September. As
for now, we only know that it is going to be a small production,
with two or three main characters, and no children. Mia is in it.
And Woody? He hasn't decided yet. It is said that Woody has
ideas, treatments, and even scripts, for his next twelve films.

On the huge stage G where the King Cole roof and Little Joe's
house were, several new sets have been built, among them three
broadcast studios, much more glamorous than the ones in the first

shooting, and a bathroom. The first floor of Little Joe's house has been pushed into a corner and, between huge black drapes, Polly Phelps's Pennsylvania field has been rebuilt in another corner of the stage. The hospital room has been brought from upstairs and repainted. Woody asked Santo for a very specific color: "Like refried beans."

There are about forty new pages of script; half of them are new scenes, and the other half rewritten ones. The big and sad news is that the entire opening sequence with the Astonishing Tonino is out. It was decided that it would be too unlikely at this time of the year to get the needed three cloudy days in a row. The other big sequence out is the whole *Herbie Hanson Show*.

Woody doesn't want to show me the rough cut. "Even the producers didn't see it," Jane told me. Since he has written a new voice over and totally changed the order of the scenes, it is difficult to follow what's happening anymore. But the numbers of the new scenes for this reshoot give a rough idea of where in the story they should be.

Scene X105: *The Radio Playhouse of the Air,* a very popular radio show that specializes in "bringing the home audience tense and moving dramas—even classics." A director is rehearsing Anton Chekhov's *The Three Sisters*. The producer, his assistant at his side, watches from the booth, as Sally, his girlfriend, plays Irina. She's awful. The director stops her.

Director: "No, no, Sally. This is a climactic moment!"

Sally: "I came to a climax."

Director (referring to the Tuzenback character): "He's pouring out his heart."

Sally: "So let him pour, I'm not stopping him . . ."

Tuzenback can't take it anymore, and starts complaining about her. But Sally hangs on.

In the booth, the assistant tries to tell the producer that Sally might not be the ideal choice for the role. But the producer disagrees: "Listen to her. She was born to do classics."

The director stops the rehearsal. The other actors leave. "I've sent for the sponsor," the director whispers to Tuzenback, "Maybe we can override the producer and get rid of her." Then he goes back to talk to Sally alone. He asks her why she wants to be an actress. "I want to be on radio. I'll do anything on radio, act, give the weather report—I can sing—dance—I'm a wonderful dancer." The director mentions that there is no point dancing on

radio. Sally knows, "'cause they can't see you . . ." The director tries again.

Director: "Sally, do you understand this play?"

Sally: "It's about illusions."

Director: "Good."

Sally: "Now I have to ask you a question."

Director: "Yes?"

Sally: "What are illusions?"

The situation looks hopeless. And "when the sponsor arrived, it made no difference because as it turned out he was also sleeping with Sally."*

* voice over

The scene is done in seven shots. Woody is using several actors from the previous shooting. Two of the actors in the Chekhov drama are the Effects Actor from the sound-effects studio (sequence 45), and the Pretty Girl of the *Nick Norris—Private Detective* show (sequence 42), playing Olga. The assistant to the producer is Mr. Rydell from the Tonino sequence.

We move to another studio, all black-and-white, to shoot scene X106. It's Sally's big day. She is finally going to make it on the air with her debut as Irina. Olga says her line, "It's exactly a year ago today since father died. . . ." Sally, using her fingers to follow the lines, gets ready. She's about to begin when she is pushed aside by a man:

"We interrupt this program to bring you a special bulletin. The Japanese have bombed Pearl Harbor . . . enormous casualties to the United States. . . . We bring you a special report on the enemy attack and a statement from the President of the United States."

All the actors go to the booth to find out more. Sally is not very happy.

The scene is filmed in one shot. These two scenes will replace *The Herbie Hanson Show.*

Monday, April 28, 1986

The first hours of the morning are spent completing the parts of scene X106 not finished Friday afternoon (Sally interrupted by the Pearl Harbor announcement).

Then we do some pickup shots:

Scene X103: An old actor playing Macbeth: "Tomorrow, and tomorrow, and tomorrow . . ."

The scene is filmed in two shots. The first one is of a technician in the booth, and the second is of the old actor saying the monologue. He gets about halfway through. This is one in a series of pickup shots for *The Radio Playhouse of the Air* show, and is done in the same black-and-white colored studio as the Pearl Harbor scene.

We stay in the same studio to shoot another scene (number X104) for *Radio Playhouse,* the famous Broadway Star "who suffered from something called mike fright. She was a great actress before thousands of people, but froze up when she was in front of a microphone. They had to put a lampshade and light bulb on the mike."

The famous Broadway Star is played by the second singer (the good one) who sang "I'll Be Seeing You" and "They're Either Too Young or Too Old." A show is in progress. Woody has given the actors lines, but there will be a voice over. A lampshade is put on the mike; the image is very funny.

Bill Kern is next, to tell the Kirby Kyle story (scene R84). We shoot in the opposite corner of the same studio. There have been a few changes in the lines, but the scene is basically the same.

We are in Sally's bathroom now (scene A144), where she's doing voice exercises in front of her mirror. Sally arrives in pajamas. Woody gives her a sampling of faces, and it is quite funny. Sally even tries "I hear the cannon roar," from the elocution class.

Sally also records a wild track for her *Gay White Way* show, using her "femme fatale" voice and talking about the Latin dancer, Greer Garson and Walter Pidgeon's latest film, and Max Gordon's next play; Abe and Ceil will hear this part in their bedroom.

The last shot of the day is a reshoot of the Reba Man (R48) but with a different actor and different lines. The Reba Man is played by Nick Norris, the little fellow, and the dialogue is shorter:

Reba: "Who dat comin' in de back doah?"

Man: "It's only me, Reba—Mr. Pennwhistle."

Reba: "Well, come in and take a load off your feet. You look like an unmade bed."

It is as funny as the first version, but Nick Norris seems to prefer his previous part.

Tomorrow we're reshooting Polly Phelps. Two scenes from the first version will be used, and before leaving, Carlo and Ray check them on a Moviola so they'll be able to match the lighting.

Tonight, dailies with Carlo and Santo. Woody has already seen them. Carlo, who saw the rough cut, tells me that the Needlemans now open the film. The dailies are excellent; the studio looks much nicer and Sally is very funny.

Tuesday, April 29, 1986

The Pennsylvania field. Everybody is back: Polly Phelps's parents, the Priest, the Newsman, the Polly Phelps Man, the Midget, Fireman Reilly, even Jockey Jack Williams.

Five shots are going to be redone:

Shot R163A: A second establishing shot of the scene, just after the Newsman has introduced it.

Shot R164: "Should not the wells have been boarded up?"

Shot R167: The lowering of the Midget into the well. "I'm stuck!"

Shot R169: "She's out. . . . The prayers of an entire nation are with her. . . ."

Shot R174: The end, when everyone goes back home.

And there will also be a few pickup shots of the Priest praying, and Polly's Mom sobbing.

Thanks to his rough cut, Woody knows now exactly what comes before and after, so he stages each shot very precisely. The main reason we are reshooting these Polly Phelps scenes is to improve the lighting.

There is a little problem with the Priest, who doesn't know his "Hail Mary." He was raised Protestant, and gave up on religion altogether, he admits, while in high school. And it isn't easy finding a Catholic on the set who knows it by heart. Santo will be the man; the Priest goes to a corner to learn it.

The Hebrew tutor is now one of the news photographers around the well. And Baby Dylan comes to visit. She's getting a little fat; it's time for her to start to walk. Sally tells me that Baby Dylan has been chosen for the family's New Year's Eve scene. "She was so much better than the other one. I had no other choice," Woody said.

Wednesday, April 30, 1986

Bea's real father is dying. He has been very ill for a year. First her mother called to say that she should come, and she was ready to go. But the doctor called back, saying he was better. We are going to try to finish all her scenes in three days so she can go to him Friday evening. He is in Baton Rouge.

We are back in Little Joe's house with the full family, Nicole, Myla, and Dennis.

First, we will reshoot the entire Yom Kippur sequence:

Shot R76: The family is exasperated by the Communist's radio blasting away on the holy day; Abe decides to go and talk to him.

Shot R78: Abe has been gone two hours, and the radio is still blasting. Mom starts telling the family what happened to Mrs. Silverman.

Shot R83: Abe returns.

The only scene that is really rewritten is R83. The others are reshot so the lighting will match. For Abe's return from the Communists' house, Woody has rewritten the end. Last time, after his speech on "the exploitation of the masses by the bosses," Abe improvised on the subject and Ceil noticed the red on his cheek. Now, Abe starts into his speech again:

Abe: "Religion is the opium of the masses."

Ceil: "God'll punish you."

Abe: "Don't be . . ."

And Abe goes on, until . . . he starts to feel chest pains, and has difficulty breathing. The family begins to panic. "Maybe it's indigestion. What'd you eat over there?" Abe then confesses that he only ate "a couple of pork chops, some clams, and chocolate pudding . . . and I had some French fries."

Twenty takes will be necessary to get the scene.

It's 7:00 P.M. when we go to scene 162. Woody is exhausted, but we're trying to do all the scenes with Bea before Friday night.

Shot R162: Mom chases Little Joe, her dyed fur coat in her hand: "I'll kill him!" Pop catches him; he escapes; Pop races after him.

Shot R162A: Grandma searches for her teeth in the living room.

Shot R162B: Bea dances the conga with Ruthie; Ceil joins in.

The camera movement of R162 has been simplified. Grandpa doesn't follow Grandma anymore in R162A, and the blocking of R162B is a little different. In fact, Woody has cut the scene of Pop chasing Little Joe. He reshoots the beginning and will use the ending (when Pop catches Little Joe, starts to hit him, then is stopped by the Polly Phelps broadcast), shortening the chase. R162A and R162B will be edited in between.

The family seems happy to be back together. Abe continues to "flirt" with Angela, Pop shows me pictures of the blue 1950s MG he bought while he was in California doing his TV pilot, and Grandpa isn't so sure about the pope's visit to the Rome synagogue yesterday.

We wrap at 8:45 P.M.

Thursday, May 1, 1986

We're back for the hospital scene, for the fourth time, but Woody has written dialogue for it now, and has added Sy to Mom's bedside.

Scene X154: All the family gathers around Mom's bed, along with Sy. Bea introduces Sy to Mom, then they leave with Little Joe to take him on a tour of Manhattan. "Sy has a new car." As soon as they leave, Grandma complains about Sy being married. "Why is she wasting her time with him?"

Ceil: "He's supposed to be getting out of it, but you know how tight some women hold on."

Abe: "Oh, tell me about it."

Then Mom and Pop discuss the baby's name:

Mom: "Are you sure you want to call the baby 'Ellen'?"

Pop: "Why not? It'll be in memory of your cousin Eddie."

Mom: "In memory? He's not dead yet."

Pop: "He should be."

The "refried beans" color of the hospital room is darker than before. Woody directs the scene just next to Ruthie, at the edge of the frame, making faces during the takes to encourage the actors.

We move back to Little Joe's house for several shots introducing each member of the family. Woody has cut all the introductory shots (scene 24 to 33), where he linked the actions of the family members. He will use only portions of those scenes, but with a new voice over, and additional shots introducing the family more succinctly.

Shot R26: Mom is knitting in the sitting room when Pop comes in.

Pop: "Are you telling me that the Atlantic is a greater ocean than the Pacific?"

Mom: "No, have it your way. The Pacific is greater."

Woody tries different tones: Sometimes Pop does it angrily, other times more low-key. In some takes, he leaves the room at the end, and in others he stays.

Shot R26A: Same blocking. Pop comes in:

Pop: "Tess, where are my cigarettes?"

Mom: "They're wherever you left them."

Pop: "Oh, good. I thought I lost them."

Woody will choose one shot or the other.

We move to Abe and Ceil's introduction scene:

Shot R27: Ceil is in the kitchen.

Abe (offscreen): "I'm home! I have a nice bluefish."

Ceil: "Wonderful. He brings home free fish, and I have to clean them. The story of my life. Sad but true. Other women get flowers. I get fish."

Abe (entering): "If you're not happy, take the gas pipe."

Ceil: "That's his answer to everything!"

Abe: "You know what you should do?"

Ceil: "Yes?"

Abe: "Take the gas pipe."

Ceil: "Cute."

It's very funny. In the script, the scene was much shorter.

Abe (offscreen): "I'm home! I brought fish."

Ceil: "Oh, wonderful. He gets free fish and I have to clean them."

Abe (entering): "You don't like it? Take the gas pipe."

Ceil: "That's his answer to everything: Take the gas pipe . . ."

Ruthie's introduction now:

Shot R29: Ruthie sits at the phone, listening to the Waldbaums' party line.

Ruthie: "Mrs. Waldbaum's having her ovaries out."

Ceil (coming in): "Both or one?"

Ceil's line is added on the set.

And finally Bea's introduction:

Shot R29A: The family is at the kitchen table, having dinner. Bea comes in, a sheet of paper in hand.

Bea: "I've made a list of attributes that I must have in any man I take seriously. He must be tall, attractive, kind, a good sense of humor, a good provider, willing to travel, have children, a good dancer, a nondrinker, Jewish, intelligent, and faithful."

Three endings to the scene are considered, with Pop cracking different jokes:

"Too bad Moses is dead, although I don't know if he was a dancer."

Or, "Intelligent and faithful. Isn't that a contradiction?"

Or, "Gee, too bad I'm married."

Woody decides to shoot only the first two jokes, and asks the family to react to Bea's list and Pop's joke. "I don't know if Moses was a good dancer, but he could swim," Abe comments.

Friday, May 2, 1986

It's 8:30 A.M. Bea's father has died. She's in her room, crying. As soon as her agent, Sam Cohn, opened the door, she understood. She had three more scenes left and was supposed to leave tonight.

There is a great sadness on the set, and an uncertainty about the future of the shooting. The whole schedule will have to be changed.

Santo has to hurry to finish the flappers' set, and the Masked Avenger gets an urgent phone call to come to the studio (these two shots had been scheduled for Monday).

We begin with the last of the family's scenes, without Bea. Monday we will have very little to do, and Tuesday we're scheduled to go to the beach.

Scene 179X: The family prepares for New Year's Eve, listening to the broadcast from the King Cole Room. Mom and Ceil get a little nostalgic hearing about all the beautiful people drinking champagne. "Don't you want to hit the hot spots and drink champagne from my slipper?" Ceil asks Abe. But Abe isn't too enthusiastic, "Besides," he adds, "only creeps and crazy people go out on New Year's Eve." "Then you should definitely go out, Abe," Ceil says. Then she tells everybody that Roger and Irene are going to be at the King Cole Room tonight; they said so on their talk show. "Do you think they're happier than us?" Pop asks Mom. "How many times do I have to answer this question?" Mom replies.

It's a completely new scene to be edited, just before Monica Charles sings. Another choice for Mom's final line, when she answers Pop's question about their happiness, is shot: "Is that a trick question?"

Next is scene A26: The end of *The Masked Avenger* show. The Avenger has caught the crook. "I hope you'll enjoy making license plates—you'll have to do it for the next twenty years." The announcer closes the show—"Be sure and tune in tomorrow for another adventure of the Masked Avenger when he flies over the city rooftops and we all hear his cry . . ." And the Masked Avenger chimes in, "Beware, Evildoers, wherever you are."

A new scene is added to introduce the Masked Avenger. At last, he has his show! The mayor from the Tonino sequence is now the crook.

The last shot of the day is a pickup of two flappers listening to a love song (40A), to be edited with the Victrola man's shots.

On Monday, we'll reshoot the Chekhov show with the Pearl Harbor announcement; Woody didn't like the man who read the bulletin.

Monday, May 5, 1986

We start by reshooting the Chekhov performance. The new Pearl Harbor man is quite different. The first one was young, had a real character face (large glasses and strong features), and read the bulletin quickly and in a panicked voice. And though he has had small parts in previous Woody Allen movies (*Zelig*, *Stardust Memories*, *Broadway Danny Rose*, and *The Purple Rose of Cairo*), he is in real life a lawyer who wants to be an actor. The new Pearl Harbor man is much older, handsome, and reads the bulletin slowly and dispassionately. He is a professional actor and was an actual radio actor and announcer.

Woody has also improved Sally's part. While all the actors rush to the booth to learn more, ignoring her, she emphasizes her annoyance: "Did you see how he pushed me? There was no need to push! Who's Pearl Harbor, anyway?"

The new announcer tells us that at the time, people had actually never heard of Pearl Harbor.

The next shot is a new version of the sound-effects studio (scene R45):

Effects Actor: "Quick, the building is on fire!"

Effects Actress: "Out the door, it's our only hope!"

Effects Actor: "Hurry, before it explodes, we've got to make that train!"

And the Sound-Effects Man blows the train whistle.

For this third reshoot of the sound-effects studio, Woody chooses a short version, even shorter than the second one, and goes back to "the building on fire" from the original script.

It is the same Sound-Effects Man and tiny Effects Actress, but the former Herbie Hanson is the new Effects Actor.

The last shot of the day is a reaction shot of a family to Uncle Walt's faux pas (scene 69B). A mother is feeding her two children in the kitchen while they listen to Uncle Walt singing the "Uncle Walt Squirrel Rangers' Club Song." The show ends, and Uncle Walt, who thinks he's off the air, remarks, "That ought to hold the little bastards." The mother drops a plate of spaghetti.

Woody again directs the players verbally during the take. Woody wants her to really drop the plate of spaghetti, and does it himself to show her how. The kids are shocked!

We wrap at 3:00 P.M., and tomorrow, since it's supposed to be overcast by afternoon, the call is for 1:00 P.M. on the beach. For Wednesday, three different call sheets are prepared. By the end of the day tomorrow, we'll decide which schedule to follow.

The funeral of Bea's father was this morning.

Tuesday, May 6, 1986

Baby Dylan has taken Woody's limo to Coney Island with her mom. Lunch is being served on the beach by a caterer called "The Next Supper." There's a beautiful sun; the boys are shirtless, and the women have put on shorts. But Woody sticks to his corduroy trousers and those shoes. He and I exchange a few words about the weather.

But there is big news. Since Bea won't be back before Thursday at the earliest, and since we don't have enough scenes to keep busy until then, Woody has come up with an entirely new sequence over the weekend. Yesterday at noon he told the production office that it involves Sally, a gangster, and a killing. Woody wants a nightclub for the killing, a car on a road, and a house in New Jersey. Rocco, the gangster, was contacted yesterday, and the contract signed this morning. Woody polished the script last night: six pages, mostly dialogue. Jane typed it this morning and is distributing it now. The nightclub will be the El Morocco, and the interior of the Jersey house will have to be built so we can start to film the sequence on Thursday. So the new schedule is: Wednesday, Rocco and Sally inside the car; Thursday, the killing in the nightclub and the Jersey house scene; and Friday, we're back to Little Joe's house for the last shots.

Today, we start with a close-up of Little Joe, with the binoculars, seeing the submarine surface (scene R137B). It's still sunny and a large screen is set up to block the sun and make the day look cloudy.

Then Woody takes the kids to a corner of the beach parking lot to record some wild tracks for the scene on the roof where they see Miss Gordon:

"Oh, I'm dying. I need a cold shower!"

"My heart! I can't take it, my heart!"

"Oh, I'm on fire! I'm on fire!"

"Oh, God! Somebody call the fire department!"

Woody repeats each sentence before each kid does it. He wrote the new lines on a yellow pad, half an hour ago on the beach.

Then we go back for three scenes with the kids on the beach.

Shot B26: The gang discusses the different Masked Avenger rings: the compass, the decoder, and the secret-compartment ring.

The discussion is a new scene that will follow the *Masked Avenger* studio sequence.

Shot C26: The kids run away down the beach.

Shot R37: The gang arrives on the beach to count the money they've made for "the new state in Palestine."

Woody has rewritten the dialogue, but the blocking is exactly the same. Nick thinks they should maybe leave some for Palestine. "Don't worry about Palestine. It's way over in Egypt," Little Joe tells him. But Nick still think they're committing a sin. "What if the rabbi finds out?" "He's not gonna find out. And even if he does, I can handle the rabbi," Little Joe answers confidently.

This scene will come, of course, just before the slapping in Rabbi Baumel's office.

Wednesday, May 7, 1986

Italian actress Monica Vitti (the star of Antonioni's *L'Avventura*) is on the set visiting Carlo. She's in town with Alberto Sordi for an Italian comedy film festival.

Scene B106: Inside the car driving into the night, just after Rocco (Danny Aiello) has killed Mr. Davis. Sally is still in shock. Rocco makes her understand he has to get rid of her. "It's nothing personal. It's just bad luck you were a witness."

Sally: "My whole life I have had bad luck."

Rocco: "Me, too."

Sally: "Where are you from?"

Rocco: "Brooklyn."

Sally: "Me, too."

Rocco: "Where 'bouts?"

Sally: "Canarsie."

Rocco: "Me, too. Eighty-fifth Street."

Sally: "I was Eighty-sixth Street."

Things seems to look better now. Sally used to eat at Joey's Clam House, and Joey and Rocco are practically brothers. Sally's father owns White's Garage. "White's Garage? You know how many times I robbed that place? Jesus. What a funny coincidence. I don't meet anybody from the old neighborhood in years. I finally do, and I gotta kill her." Sally swears she won't squeal, but Rocco is sorry; he can't take the chance. Since he doesn't have a gun, they're going to stop at his mother's to get one. "You'll love her. Maybe she remembers you."

The dialogue is broken into two shots as they drive into the night. In reality, the car is in the middle of the Pennsylvania field. The car is being rocked with the same system used on Manulis's Buick—two boys shaking the back with a beam and a box. On either side of the vehicle, on two dolly tracks, the boys are pushing lights back and forth for the passing streetlamps. Carlo cues them himself.

Thursday, May 8, 1986

We're at El Morocco on Fifty-fourth Street, between First and Second. The "World's Most Famous Nightclub," which "provides exquisite atmosphere, elegant food, and superb service" is a replica of the 1920s original. But it's not like the old times. The zebra-skin chairs are plastic, the plants and flowers, which used to be changed daily, are plastic, too. And though there are plenty of pictures of the beautiful people who used to frequent the place, the clientele today is said not to be so beautiful—mostly businessmen with their mistresses.

We're here to film the killing.

Shot A106: The nightclub is empty. The owner, Mr. Davis, is at one of the tables counting money. Rocco enters, coming down the stairs, ready to do away with Mr. Davis.

Shot A106A: A closer shot of Mr. Davis already dead, seen from Rocco's point of view. Davis is under the table, one of his hands sticking out.

Shot A106B: The shooting. Rocco takes aim at Davis and fires.

Shot A106D: Sally comes down the stairs, and screams, "You killed Mr. Davis!" Rocco aims at her, but the gun doesn't work. She makes a run for it, but Rocco catches her. She screams as Rocco drags her out.

Shot A106C: A close-up of Sally, horrified. "You killed him! Oh, God. You killed Mr. Davis!"

Rocco asks Woody if he should grin after killing Mr. Davis. Rocco wonders if they do that; he's never killed anybody. Woody doesn't think so. So Rocco suggests smelling the flower in his lapel. Woody OK's it.

When Rocco grabs Sally, she screams, high-pitched and loud. Like the rest of us, she and Rocco end the scene giggling; her squeal is both funny and unbearable. And after each take, Rocco apologizes for having grabbed her so roughly. The actors are enjoying themselves.

We finish the sequence at about 1:00 P.M. Before leaving, a hungry Woody asks Drew for some crackers, "the dullest one."

At around 3:00, everybody is back at Astoria. Rocco's mom's New Jersey house is ready: a short hallway, a kitchen, a small dining area, and a living room. As always, it's been constructed with an incredible attention to detail: the homemade pasta hanging to dry, the peppers, the picture of the Madonna. Santo designed it Tuesday afternoon, the boys started building it Wednesday morning (five carpenters, five scenic artists, and five set designers), and it was ready at noon today.

Scene F106: Mama (Gina DeAngelis) is taking good care of Sally, feeding her pasta and peppers. "Sure, I remember you when you had little pigtails and braces on your teeth. You were the cutest little thing in the neighborhood." Then to Rocco, handing him a pistol: "You need bullets, too?"

Sally begs for mercy. She says she won't talk, that she knows a lot about people on Broadway, and she never tells.

Mama: "What do you do?"

Sally: "I been everything. Coat-check girl, cigarette girl, I modeled. I want to get into radio. That's my dream. It was my dream."

Rocco: "She sings, Mama."

Mama: "That's nice."

Sally: "And I can act and I'd just do anything to be in radio. I'd be glad to give the weather report or interview people . . . I think I'm a natural . . . I'm a great dancer."

Mama: "You can't dance on radio!"

Sally: "I know, 'cuz they can't see you."

Mama takes Rocco aside. She doesn't think the girl is going to give him trouble, "She's [pointing to her head] not too fast up here." Besides, it's late, Rocco needs to rest. Rocco likes the girl, too, and feels sorry for her: "She wants to get into radio so badly. I think a lot of men take advantage of her, she's so pretty." They agree not to bump her off, and "Maybe Cousin Angelo can help her," Mama says. "He knows people in radio. Even a small part. They owe him a favor."

"And so that's how Sally wound up playing Chekhov . . ."*

Gina DeAngelis was also the mama in the party scene in *Broadway Danny Rose*. She is a nice, colorful woman. When Woody called her two days ago about being in the movie, she refused because she'd just gotten out of the hospital. But Woody insisted, saying he really needed her, and she finally agreed. Woody is giving her a lot of attention, encouraging her. She's nervous and misses her lines sometimes, but she's very good in the part.

Mama: "I've got to get it straight."
Woody: "You have it all right."
Mama: "It's no good."
Woody: "It's good."

The scene, done in two shots, is long. At 7:00, we have to stop because Rocco has to get to the theater for the play he's in. We'll finish in the morning.

Friday, May 9, 1986

Bea is back with us. She has brought her mother with her.

We finish the Rocco scene first, then move to Little Joe's house. Woody had wanted to reshoot the hospital scene today, too, but the production office has been unable to contact Sy.

Scene R32: Bea turns up the radio, and starts dancing the lindy. As she does, she ponders which is better for finding men— the mountains or a cruise. "I met my husband at a mountain resort so I'd advise you to go on a cruise," Mom tells her. Pop appreciates the joke! But he asks Mom to get back to the subject, the cultured pearls. Mom is fed up with Pop's business schemes. "You don't have a business head . . ." "Forget it," Pop answers, furious, "I'll stay my whole life at the job I do."

* voice over

(L to R:) Mama (Gina DeAngelis); Sally (Mia Farrow); Baby Dylan

Mom: "There's nothing wrong with it."

Little Joe: "What do you do, Dad?"

Pop: "That's none of your business."

But, Little Joe insists, all the other kids know what their fathers do. Pop tells him to do his homework. Little Joe asks for fifteen cents for a Masked Avenger ring. Mom tells him to pay more attention to his schoolwork and less to the radio. Little Joe answers that she always listens to the radio herself.

Mom: "It's different. Our lives are ruined already, but you still have a chance to grow up and be somebody."

Pop: "You think I want you working at my job?"

Little Joe: "I don't even know what your job is."

And the exchange goes on, Mom finally telling Little Joe that Pop "is a big butter-and-egg man."

Pop: "What do you mean our lives are ruined already?"

Mom: "I didn't mean *ruined* ruined. . . . We're poor but happy—but definitely poor."

Then Abe comes in and closes the conversation: "Isn't this a beautiful bass? Who wants to join me?"

This new scene, done in two shots, is the conclusion of the sequence introducing the characters. Woody has taken the ideas and dialogues from the previous version, and has created a different scene, one that emphasizes the mystery about Pop's job, and plays up Little Joe's asking for the Masked Avenger ring.

The last shot is 179Y: It's New Year's Eve. Bea plays solitaire at the dining-room table while Monica Charles sings on the radio. Pop passes by: "No date tonight?" Bea shrugs. "It's OK. We're all together," Pop says.

There is one scene left (R113): Bea gets ready for her date with Fred, painting on her nylons and talking with Mom about the right man. Bea thinks Fred is the one. Mom fears Bea is going to be disappointed again; she's too demanding, she looks for perfection too much. Mom thinks one has to compromise. "I compromised with Martin. I wanted someone tall, and handsome and rich." The conversation goes on like this, about love, marriage, how they got married in the old country. Bea seems to really like Fred. "Well, we'll say a prayer for you. Maybe this time next year you'll look like me," Mom says, patting her pregnant belly.

But the scene is very long, almost four pages of dialogue; it will be shot Monday morning.

I have to go back to work on the manuscript. A second and last farewell to everybody.

APPENDIX: CONTINUITY CREDITS

Continuity

More than a summary of the story, what follows is a chronological ordering of the scenes as they appear in the final script (on the left side of the page), and a chronology of the shots from the first days of editing on the right.

The numbers correspond to the ones in the diary; those of the first shooting. None of the scenes from the reshoot are included. The sequences marked CUT don't appear in the final film.

SCRIPT	SHOOTING
1 We are in the 1920s on a gray November morning, as Carleton Foxx of WPGT gives us, live from the Jersey Shore, thanks to the miracle of radio, a description of the event: the weather, the crowd, the WPGT band playing.	(not filmed)

2   (People listen to their radios   CUT   2   Wide shot of a Firehouse.
as Carleton Foxx (offscreen)   Firemen and a man listen to the
introduces the spectacle.)   radio. Cars pass by.

   The World's Greatest Escape   2A   Closer shot of the fire-
Artist, the man known as "The   house. The firemen have left.
Cat with Nine Lives," the man
who defies science and   2B   Wide shot of a Chinese
challenges death, The   couple steam-ironing. The man
Astonishing Tonino, is going to   turns up radio.
perform. He will be chained,
and put in a sealed milk can that   2C   Dolly right/zoom in on an
will be hurled into the icy   old couple listening to the radio
waters of the Atlantic. And   with earphones.
Tonino will escape!
                                           2D   Wide shot of a rich couple
                                          having tea. Dolly/zoom in with
                                          the maid, as she wheels the cart
                                          out, to the radio.

                                           2E   Wide shot of a family at
                                          the kitchen table. Dolly right as
                                          the little boy goes to tune the
                                          radio.

                                           2F   Long shot of a black man at
                                          the kitchen table. His wife
                                          serves him.

                                           2G   A pan around a beauty
                                          parlor with five patrons and the
                                          attendants.

                                           2H   Zoom back from a parrot
                                          to reveal a rich woman in a
                                          bathtub. Her maid crosses.

3   (Back on the Jersey Shore.)   (not filmed)
The crowd is excited. They're
pushing each other and Carleton
Foxx. Someone spills hot soup
on the mayor, and the mayor
does a little dance. But Carleton
Foxx continues his broadcast.
He has a few words with Mr.
Rydell, the promoter of the

stunt. Then tries to reach
Carmella Tonino, the wife of the
escape artist, who is sitting next
to City Councilman Arthur
O'Donnell. But someone kicks
out a wire, breaking the
connection! The technicians
work feverishly and Carleton
Foxx interviews Carmella
Tonino, who speaks only Italian.
The broadcast is restored.

4   (Shots of still-rapt listeners.)   (not filmed)
  Carlton Foxx continues to
describe what's happening. Now
City Councilman Arthur
O'Donnell has spilled some hot
soup on himself, and here comes
Tonino!

5   The Astonishing Tonino   CUT 5 (two cameras)
arrives with his entourage.   1. High angle. Long shot of
  Doctor Max Kachaturian, the   Tonino between two lifeguards
leading osteopath from Zagreb,   running on the pier toward the
who is not licensed in the   camera.
United States, checks Tonino.   2. Front medium shot
  Tonino is put into the   following Tonino.
straightjacket. He kisses his
wife. Then she goes to pray
with the family priest.
  Carleton Foxx tries to get
some technical information from
one of the noted scientists
present, but gets only an answer
in Italian.

6   (Listeners rapt.)   (not filmed)
  The can is being hauled over
the water. Carleton describes
Carmella Tonino's dress.

7   The can is dropped into the
sea. Carleton Foxx continues his
broadcast; the can is in the
water. Everybody is anxious.
Suddenly, a puff of smoke.

8   The listeners hear static.
They start hitting their radios.
Carleton Foxx's voice fades in
and out.

CUT   8   Medium long shot of the
Chinese laundry man hitting the
radio.

8A   Pan from the old man to
the old lady as they react to
static.

8B   Wide shot of the young
rich couple as the man hits the
radio and turns it off.

8C   Medium shot of the little
boy banging the radio. The little
girl joins him.

8D   Long shot of the black
couple. The woman covers her
ears, the man exits.

9   The technicians are repairing
the cable. It starts to rain. The
can is still in the water, and it's
pouring now!

(not filmed)

9X   Listeners getting more and
more static. Carleton Foxx's
voice is heard from time to
time: "I understand we're
experiencing some little
technical difficulties . . . . Bear
with us. . . ."

(not filmed)

9Y   The milk can has risen. But
it's empty; no Tonino! The
mayor's wife has fainted. Now
they have spilled hot soup on

(not filmed)

her, too. Carmella Tonino
leaves, waving her hands,
resigned. The band continues to
play.

A10 (Joe's voice over: "Of
course, it was a little primitive
back then . . . . But by the time
I was born and growing up in
Rockaway, there was nothing to
compare with radio. . . ."
    Establishing views of
Rockaway.

RA10 High angle. Long shot
of the beach. Zoom out to reveal
Beach 115th Street.

RA10A Long shot of the right
side of Beach 115th Street
(opposite angle). Pan left and
zoom in to Rockaway
Boulevard.

RA10B Pan from a long shot
of the ocean to a close-up of
Little Joe watching the horizon.

RA10X Long shot of Little Joe
standing in front of the
Rockaway bathhouse.

10 In Little Joe's house, Little   CUT
Joe and his friends (Dave, Nick,
Burt, Andrew, and the
Communist's Son) listen, totally
rapt, to a horror story on the
radio.

10 Slow pan on the faces of
the six kids as they listen,
enthralled.

11 In her kitchen, a dowdy
housewife listens to the Phyliss
and Paul soap opera.

RR11 Wide shot of Mom
cleaning the kitchen table as she
listens.

12 A crooner sings "All or
Nothing At All" in a radio
studio.

R12 Close-up of the control
console. Boom up to a medium
shot of the Crooner through the
booth window.

13 Young girls listen,
swooning to the Crooner's song
on a malt shop's radio. Cousin
Ruthie is among them.

R13 Medium shot of the
waitress turning up the radio.
Pan with her as she leaves, then
onto Ruthie and girlfriends at

the counter, swooning to the
song.

R13A   Medium shot of boys
looking disgusted. Dolly right to
a close shot of the girls' bottoms
and feet moving to the song.

14   (omit)

15   At a street corner, in front
of a newsstand, men have
gathered to listen to a ball game
on the radio. It's the end of the
game. "The Yankees lose!" One
of the men has grabbed one of
the others while listening, and
without realizing it, is
strangling him.

CUT   15   Tilt down the building to a
long shot of four men around a
table.

15A   Close shot of the meat
shop. Pan right to the four men.

16   A cultured family listens to
a string quartet on the radio.

CUT   16   Dolly/zoom back and pan
from a close shot of the radio
revealing the cultured family.

17   The string quartet is
playing in a studio.

CUT   17   Wide shot of the string
quartet.

18   Mr. and Mrs. Jackhammer,
two real character types, eat
sausages in their kitchen while
listening to a broadcast of
*Breakfast with Irene and
Roger*, Broadway's most
sophisticated couple.

CUT   R18   Long/wide shot of Mr.
Jackhammer through his
window.

18A   Wide shot of the
Jackhammers eating.
Dolly/zoom in closer.

19   Jackhammer's fantasy. He
and his wife are at Sardi's, with
all the beautiful people. Max
Harris comes to tell them about
his production of the new
Eugene O'Neill play about lost
souls.

CUT   19   The party seen in reflection
in a mirror. Pan left and dolly
into the party. Pan right to Max
Harris. The Jackhammers
approach. Zoom in closer.

20 Little Joe and his pals listening to *The Masked Avenger* show, and to the announcer hawking the Masked Avenger ring.

20 Dolly right in a wide long shot following the kids going to school. Cars pass by.

21 (The announcer reminds the kids of the Masked Avenger whistle ring.)
Classroom. The teacher is writing on the blackboard. Whistles are heard. She turns around, annoyed. We see Little Joe and his pals.

21 Medium shot of the teacher writing on the blackboard. Whistles. She turns abruptly.

21A Wide shot of the classroom. The kids blow their whistle rings, then put on innocent faces.

21B Wide shot of the classroom. The teacher enters the frame and walks down the aisle. The kids blow their rings as she passes. She stops and turns. Zoom in on her as she walks back down the row.

22 (The announcer reminds his young listeners of the Masked Avenger magnifying-glass ring.)
Hebrew class. Rabbi Baumel lectures the kids about the funds they will have to collect to help promote a Zionist state in Palestine. He explains its importance.
But Little Phil is on fire. Little Joe has burned his shirt, using the sun and the Masked Avenger magnifying-glass ring.

22 Wide shot of the kids. Pan to Rabbi Baumel lecturing.

22A Medium close-up of the rabbi, then pan to the kids as he goes on with the lecture.

22B From behind the kids, low angle of the rabbi as he approaches in the aisle, continuing his lecture, until Phil catches on fire.

22C Medium long shot of the left side of the classroom, kids listening, Little Joe in the middle.

22D Wide shot of the entire classroom listening.

22E Medium close-up of Little Joe and Little Phil, as Joe focuses the magnifying ring on Phil's shirt.

22F Wider shot of Phil and Little Joe as Phil's shirt starts burning. Rabbi Baumel runs in and grabs Joe.

23 Establishing shot of Little Joe's house in Rockaway.

23 Tilt down from a lamppost to Little Joe's house.

24 Introduction of the family. Cousin Ruthie is at the phone listening to the Waldbaums' party line. Pop dictates to Mom a business letter about cultured pearls he wants to sell. Mom doesn't think it's a good letter. Grandma calls for Gandpa, who was reading his paper. He leaves mumbling. Cousin Ruthie announces that Mrs. Waldbaum is going to have her ovaries out. Aunt Ceil sympathizes.

R24 Master shot of Mom and Pop in the dining room. Dolly in, following Mom exiting to the kitchen. Pan right as she comes back, hold on Mom and Pop closer. Dolly/pan left with Pop going to the living room, hold on Grandpa sitting in armchair reading the paper. He stands up. Pan with him to the hallway. Hold on Ruthie at the phone. Ceil enters from the right.

25 Grandpa tries to lace Grandma's huge bosom into her corset. "Suck in! Suck in!"

25 Wide shot of Grandpa and Grandma working at it in the bathroom.

26 Pop rereads the letter. But Mom hasn't typed what he dictated. Mom and Pop argue. Little Joe asks for fifteen cents to buy a Masked Avenger ring. The parents turn their anger on him.

26 Master shot of Mom and Pop in the dining room. Little Joe crosses. Zoom in on Pop.

27 Grandma appears in the living room, looking for her teeth. Mom says Little Joe was playing hockey with them. Little Joe again asks for a

27 Medium shot of Grandma walking down the stairs. Pan right, following her, and zoom back as Grandma exits, revealing Ruthie on the phone and Ceil in

Masked Avenger ring. Ruthie announces that Mrs. Waldbaum's cousin is pregnant, and they don't know who the father is. Mom is sure it's Adelman the druggist: "He should drop dead!"

the kitchen in the background. Mom, then Pop, appear in the kitchen. Mom approaches and joins Ruthie by the phone.

28   Uncle Abe arrives in the backyard with a huge sack of fresh fish from Sheepshead Bay. "Ceil, I've got fish!" He drops them on the ground. Ceil appears and starts complaining about cleaning them.

28   Dolly/zoom back with Abe as he enters the yard and dumps fish on the ground.

28A   Pan/zoom back with Ceil as she exits the house and joins Abe in the yard.

29   Inside, Bea shows off her new hat. She goes to the yard to show it to Ceil and Abe. Seeing all the fish, she wonders who needs so many. Abe: "You don't like it? Take the gas pipe!"

29   Medium close-up of Bea primping with her hat in the mirror. Zoom back as she leaves, revealing Pop in the kitchen in the background. Mom crosses.

29A   Medium close-up of Bea at the window. Dolly/zoom back, revealing Abe and Ceil in the yard with the fish.

30   Waldbaum appears, screaming from his yard, "Stop listening to our party line!" Mom and Pop appear at the door and start arguing with him. Mrs. Waldbaum joins in and says she can hear Ruthie's breathing. Ceil tries to calm the Waldbaums by offering them some of Abe's fish.

30   Pan back and forth between Little Joe's parents and the Walldbaums as they argue. Pan left to Ceil at the end as she offers the fish.

31   In the other yard, the Communist is chasing his son, who has put a firecracker up the

31   Wide shot of the Communist's yard. Dolly/zoom in on the Communist chasing

cat's behind, and Doris, his
pretty daughter who believes in
free love, appears. "Dad, we
were discussing Trotsky!"

his son to a close shot of Doris
coming out the door.

32   Inside. Bea, listening to the
radio, wonders where to go to
get a man. Abe comes in,
talking about Doris—"What a
build!" Ceil follows and tells
him to stick to his fish. Bea
starts dancing to the lindy,
which plays on the radio.
Grandpa complains about the
life Bea is leading.

32   Medium shot of Bea
standing next to the radio. Pan
left with her as she goes to the
sink. Pan right as Abe and Ceil
enter. Pan back to Bea dancing
the lindy.

33   Pop wants to dictate
another letter. Mom prefers
watching Bea dance. Pop
complains about the noise
Mom's family makes, and the
way he supports them all. Little
Joe asks him what he does for a
living. Pop is embarrassed.
"He's a big butter-and-egg
man," Mom says.

33   Medium shot of Pop in
dining room. Pan left as he joins
Mom. Then dolly/zoom back
and pan right with them as they
walk into the living room,
revealing Little Joe at his desk.

34   Kids going to school.

34   Tilt down from a roller
coaster to a long shot of Little
Joe walking in the street. Pan
right with him until he exits
around the corner.

34A   Same as 34 but closer.

35   Classroom. Show and Tell.
Little Evelyn has brought a
ship-in-a-bottle her brother
made. Little Arnold has brought
a contraceptive he found in his
parents' night table. And Little
Ross has brought the new
Masked Avenger ring with the
secret compartment.

35   Master shot of the
classroom as each kid goes to the
front for Show and Tell.
Dolly/zoom in on Little Ross.

35A   Medium shot of the
classroom, the kids listening.
Zoom in on Little Joe.

36   Little Joe and his pals are in the street collecting funds for the new state in Palestine.

36   Wide shot of Little Joe and Nick asking passersby on Beach 116th Street for money. Pan left with Little Joe around the corner on Rockaway Boulevard as he goes on.

37   On the beach. They're counting how much they've made. People have given pennies! Do they have enough to each buy a ring? They wonder if they're committing a sin. Andrew thinks he just saw Epstein, who will surely tell the rabbi!

37   Dolly right with Little Joe, Nick, and Andrew as they walk by the water and stop to count the money.

38   Mom, Pop, and Little Joe in Rabbi Baumel's office. Rabbi Baumel's heart is full of grief, it swells with anguish. Mom says Little Joe listens to the radio too much. Rabbi Baumel thinks radio tends to induce bad values, lazy habits. "You speak the truth, my faithful Indian companion," Little Joe tells him. The rabbi hits Little Joe. Mom hits Little Joe. Pop hits Little Joe.

A38   Wide establishing shot of the Hebrew school.

38   Wide long shot of the rabbi behind his desk, Little Joe and his parents standing next to him. Dolly in to a closer shot while the rabbi talks.

38A   Close-up of the Rabbi for the beginning of his lines.

[History of radio]

39   Marconi is flying his box kite on the beach and gets the first wireless message from across the Atlantic.

CUT   39   Long shot of the coastline
39A   Pan across the foggy beach to the ocean.

40   A man with a Victrola plays a record into a microphone.

CUT   40   Long shot of the man at the radio control.

40A   Dolly/zoom in with the man as he goes to put a record on the Victrola, turning the speaker to the mike.

41   An amateur radio station: the Cooper family in their garage. Mrs. Cooper is the announcer and piano player, Mr. Cooper is the technician, and Eunice Cooper, the daughter, sings.

CUT   41   Start on a window. Pan left to Mrs. Cooper at the piano, introducing the show. Dolly/zoom back to reveal Eunice behind the mike and her dad in the background. Hold on her as she sings. Zoom in on her at the end with her mom still in the background.

A42   A broadcast tower. The creation of the first network.

A42   Medium long shot of the radio station. Tilt up to the top of the tower.

42   The *Nick Norris—Private Detective* radio show. Two men, a huge one and a tiny one, and a pretty girl. The Pretty Girl comes for help. The Tiny Man (Nick Norris) answers with a loud voice that they're going to help her. "Shall I warm up the car, boss?" the Big Man says, in a high Oriental voice.

CUT   42   Close-up of the announcer opening the show. Dolly back, revealing the three actors in a wide front shot.

42A   Same as above but zoom back to a medium shot of the actors.

43   Jessica Dragonette sings "Italian Street Song."

CUT   43   Close shot of Jessica Dragonette singing. Dolly/zoom back to a wide shot, revealing the orchestra.

43A   Medium close-up of Jessica Dragonette.

44   (omit)

45   Sound-effects studio. A sound-effects man, an actor, and

CUT   R45   Wide shot of the two actors and the Sound-Effects an actress. "The building is on fire!" Effects . . . "I hear hoofbeats." Effects . . . "It's Johnny. He's armed!" The cavalry arrives. Effects . . .

Man. Pan and zoom in to the Sound-Effects Man at the end.

R45A   Same as R45 (shorter version).

46   The *Whiz Kids* radio show. All the kids are arrogantly smart. "What are the moons of Saturn?" "Now who wrote the lines . . ." But the most arrogant of them all is Sanford.

CUT   R46   Side angle of the five kids with the Whiz Master in the background. Dolly left and pan right to a front shot of the four kids.

47   *Amateur Talent Hunt* radio show. The emcee introduces the talents: the singing housewife, the dancing dentist, and the telephone operator who imitates a monkey.
   (Alternate version:) The singing housewife, the woman from Bayonne who does dialects, the dentist who plays the harmonica, the gentleman of many sounds (like the Hawaiian guitar), and the telephone operator who talks like a monkey.

CUT   47   Wide shot behind the audience to the emcee, the contestants, and the band on the stage.

47A   Wide shot of the contestants and the emcee. Dolly in on two contestants as the emcee introduces them. They perform. Dolly back for the monkey lady.

47B   Same but alternate version.

48   *Reba, the Maid* radio show. A single actor plays Reba the maid and her playboy boss.

CUT   48   Close-up of the announcer introducing the show. Dolly/zoom back, revealing the Reba Man. At the end, he approaches to talk directly to the camera.

49   Little Joe's House. Bea is getting ready for a hot date. Mr. Manulis has finally asked her out! Pop thinks Manulis must have gone blind. Ruthie, still at

49   Medium shot of Bea coming in. Zoom back to a master shot of the kitchen; Pop reads the paper, Mom cleans, and Ceil kneads meat. Ruthie is

the phone, announces that Mrs. Waldbaum found a purse in the subway and doesn't know yet if she'll return it. The bell rings; Bea panics.

50   Manulis appears. Everyone is impressed. He and Bea leave.

51   The date. They skate, they eat clams, and cotton candy, they drink beer.

52   They are driving in the fog. Bea is a little tipsy from the beer. Manulis finds the fog romantic. But the car starts coughing. They're out of gas, in the middle of Breezy Point!

on the phone in the background, telling about the Waldbaums. Little Joe and Bea go in and out.

50   Medium shot of Bea in the kitchen. Pan right with Mom to the hallway. Manulis appears. Pop joins them, then Bea. Manulis and Bea exit on the right to the outside. Mom and Pop exit on the left, back to the kitchen.

A51   High/wide shot of the roller-skating rink.

A51A   Pan left with Manulis skating. He picks up Bea.

A51B   Dolly back and pan right with Manulis and Bea skating together.

A51C   Wide shot of the bowling lanes. Pan right to Manulis bowling. Bea watches.

A51D   Pan right, with ball returning, to Bea, who takes one. Dolly/zoom back as she rolls it, Manulis behind.

51   Zoom back and pan left with the waiter to a wide shot of the restaurant. Zoom in closer to Bea and Manulis eating an drinking.

52   Exterior. Front shot of the car approaching in the fog. Headlights.

52A   Front angle. Close shot of Bea and Manulis behind the windshield, driving in the fog.

53   The radio plays "La Cumparsita." Manulis starts to make his move. It's getting hard for him "to resist the urge to kiss Bea." Bea admits the setting is romantic.

But an announcer interrupts the music on the radio for a special bulletin. A mysterious object has been reported in the skies of New Jersey. It could be extraterrestrial.

The music resumes. Bea is worried, but Manulis assures her he will take care of her. And he goes back to making his move. Bea is apparently ready to give in, when there is another interruption on the radio. It's Don Richards, live from Wilson's Glen. The spacecraft has landed. He describes what he sees. "Horrible creatures, with long tentacles, sending beams of hot light . . . killing people—" And he's cut off. Bea and Manulis start to panic. They decide to get to a phone.

54   Manulis starts the car. (There's gas now!) and starts driving into the fog. Manulis wants to get away from Jersey and go to a less populated area.

55   They hit something. The car is stuck. Manulis thinks they'd better make a run for it.

53   High/wide rear angle of the car stopped in the fog, out of gas.

53A   Front angle, close shot of Bea and Manulis. First special bulletin.

53B   Insert close-up radio.

53C   Dolly around the car. The announcer reports the landing of Martians. They listen.

54   High/wide rear angle of the car as it lurches and drives away in the fog.

55   Interior of the car, from behind the actors. Manulis jumps out of the car, goes in front of it, then disappears. Bea gets out, too.

56 Manulis exits the car, and starts really to panic, "Horrible tentacles . . . The Martians are coming . . . Our lives are over . . ." He disappears in the fog. The radio goes on about the Martians. Bea is more self-controlled. She gets out of the car and starts walking in the fog, calling, "Sidney!" She hears the sound of a car pulling off; in his panic, Sidney has abandoned her. She continues to walk in the fog, and ends up walking into the ocean.

56 Medium shot of Manulis in the fog. Pan right, then dolly with Bea as she walks into the fog.

56A Bea's POV as she walks into the fog.

56B Dolly/zoom back with Bea as she walks in the fog. Tilt down to her feet as she walks into the water.

57 Mom and Pop in pajamas open the door, late that night, to a totally disheveled Bea; "Did you have a nice time?"

57 High angle. Medium shot of the hallway as Mom opens the door.

58 The *Breakfast with Irene and Roger* radio show.

The show is on; Roger and Irene are having their breakfast. At Lindy's Roger ran into Walter Winchell, who said he'll try to be at the Stork Club tonight. Irene has a lot to say about the latest Moss Hart play, which is just divine, but she'll talk about it tomorrow morning. The announcer closes the show. Everybody in the studio congratulates the couple, but Roger and Irene start insulting each other and fighting, throwing things at each other. The others separate them. Irene disappears upstairs.

They were like that earlier

58 Medium shot of Roger and Irene's portrait. Pan right past the technicians. Pan/dolly right along the bar with the maid. The pan continues to reveal Roger and Irene at their breakfast table. Zoom in to a closer shot of the two.

58A Medium close-up of the announcer closing the show. Dolly/zoom back to a wide shot, revealing Roger and Irene. They fight. Pan left with Irene at the end as she goes up the stairs. Hold on the stage manager.

this morning, the stage manager
comments. He wonders what
happened at the nightclub last
night.

59   Exterior. Last night. Roger
and Irene enter the King Cole
Room.

(not filmed)

60   Interior King Cole Room.
Everybody is here tonight.
Hemingway is at the bar. Roger
and Irene seem perfectly at
home, saying hello to everyone.
Irene chats for a moment with
Margaret. Sally the cigarette
girl appears and Roger dashes to
her. Buying Camels, he asks her
why she doesn't return his calls.
Sally is tired of doing it in hotel
rooms, in the back seats of cars,
in stalled elevators; she thinks
he's going to lose his respect for
her. But the table is ready, and
Irene calls Roger.
   Roger and Irene sit at their
table. Gail joins them. Roger
realizes he paid for the cigarettes
but forgot to get them!

60   Wide establishing shot of
the nightclub. Zoom in to Roger
and Irene as they come in. Pan
left as they follow the maître d',
who leads them to the table.

60A   Dolly back and pan right
with Roger and Irene crossing.
Irene meets Margaret. Pan left,
losing her and following Roger,
who joins Sally. Zoom in closer
on the two.

60B   Orchestra playing.

60C   Medium shot of Roger
and Irene sitting at their table.
Gail joins them, then Roger
exits.

61   Roger stands next to Sally.
He's in love with her, he says.
Sally wants him to marry her
then. But Roger can't, the
show's ratings are too high.
Sally wants to be on radio.
Roger is working on it, he says.
Sally insists on the fact, saying
she's a natural talent. She
leaves.

61   Wide shot of Sally
approaching. Pan right with her
to a close shot. She stops by the
mirrored column. Roger appears
behind her on the left of the
frame.

62   The Latin band plays "Tico Tico."

62   Wide long shot of the stage. Dolly/zoom in and pan left from the band to the singer.

62A   Tilt up from the singer's feet to her face.

63   Roger goes back to the table. Tom and Jessica have joined them. Tom is happy because Jed Harris loved his new farce, *The Christmas in the Congo*. Roger sees Dick Rodgers, and decides to go and ask him if he would come on the show.

63   Medium shot of Irene, Gail, Tom, and Jessica at the table. Roger joins them, then exits.

64   Roger is back with Sally. He's aflame with longing. He says he's talked to the head of the agency about Sally. Sally becomes more sensitive. By now, Roger is really exploding with desire. There must be a place. Sally thinks of something, and goes. Roger follows her.

64   Wide shot of the orchestra and the dancers. Pan right to a close-up of Roger and Sally next to the mirrored column. Pan right with them at the end as they leave.

65   It's really fun at Irene's table. Another couple arrives, Brenda and Porfirio, the Playboy of the Western World. Irene takes a cigarette, and starts to light it, but Porfirio takes the lighter from her hand, and lights her cigarette with a hundred-dollar bill.

65   Wide shot of the room. Dolly/zoom in and pan left with Brenda and Porfirio as they cross and join Irene's table. Zoom in closer as Porfirio lights the hundred-dollar bill.

66   Roger and Sally arrive on the King Cole roof. The music from downstairs can be heard. With all the lights of the city, it's beautiful. Roger feels much

66   Medium shot of Roger and Sally as they come through the door. Dolly right and zoom back as they walk in, revealing the roof.

better, and makes his move.
Sally would like to talk a little
more about the head of the
agency, but . . .

67   They're having more and
more fun at Irene's table.
Porfirio is really irresistible.
Now he's making his favorite
cocktail, the champagne martini,
and offers it to Irene. The tango
music starts. Porfirio persuades
Irene to come and dance.

68   On the roof, they're
already finished. Sally thinks
maybe it helped that she had the
hiccups. But Roger is now
anxious to go back downstairs.
He goes to the door. It's locked
from the inside! They're stuck.
Sally panics: She's going to lose
her job. Lightning strikes
nearby. Sally screams. Roger
asks her to shut up.
    Suddenly, voices are heard
behind the door: "If you've
never made love under the stars
before, you're in for an
experience," a male voice says.
The door opens. It's Irene and
Porfirio. ("True story? I don't
know . . . There were many
others. . . .")*

*voice over

66A   Medium shot of the two
as they embrace. Dolly in and
pan right with them as they go
to the edge of the roof, and
begin . . .

67   Medium long shot of
Irene's table. Pan left with
Porfirio and Irene as they go to
the dance floor.

67A   Close shot of Porfirio and
Irene, following them as they
dance the tango.

68   Medium shot of Roger
zipping up his trousers. Pan
right with him as he goes to the
door; hold on Sally under the
water tank fixing her stockings,
the Camel sign in the
background.

68A   Medium long shot of
Sally. Dolly back with her as
she joins Roger at the door.
Zoom back as Roger goes to the
edge of the roof. Sally follows,
then as Roger disappears behind
the stairwell, Sally goes back to
the door. Zoom in to medium
shot of her.

R68B   Medium shot of Roger
and Sally trying to open the
door. Lightning. Pan right with
Sally to the edge of the roof.
She screams. Roger joins her.
They react to the voices behind
the door.

R68C   Medium shot of Roger
and Sally reacting to Porfirio
and Irene's arrival.

R68D   Medium shot of Irene
and Porfirio as they come
through the door, and react to
Roger and Sally.

69   The *Uncle Walt* radio
show.
   It's the end of the show.
Uncle Walt advises his young
listeners to be nice and eat their
cereal. Then he sings the "Uncle
Walt Squirrel Rangers' Club
Song." "That ought to hold the
little bastards," he says at the
end, but he's still on the air.

CUT   69   (two cameras)
   1. Dolly/zoom back from the
technicians in the booth to a
long shot of Uncle Walt at the
piano, singing.
   2. Close-up of Uncle Walt
with the technicians in the
background.

70   (Another story concerning
Mr. Needleman and his wife,
who live in Little Joe's
neighborhood.) One evening,
the Needlemans leave their
modest home to go to a movie.

R70   Night. Wide shot of the
Needlemans' residence. They
come out of the house, down the
stairs, and exit on the left.
Zoom in as a car pulls up to the
front of the house. The
headlights go out.

71   Two burglars arrive on the
Needlemans' street, try a few
houses, and finally get into the
Needlemans'.

(*see* R70)

72   Inside. The Burglars are in
the middle of the robbery when
the phone rings. They hesitate.
It rings on. One of them picks it
up.

72   Inside. The Burglars enter
with flashlights. Master shot of
the two, lighting each other
with the flashlights, answering
the phone, turning on the radio,
guessing each tune, and
winning.

73   The *Guess That Tune*
studio. "You, Mr. Needleman,
have been chosen from the
telephone book to 'Guess that
Tune'!" Fanfare, applause.

73   (two cameras)
   1. Wide shot behind the
audience of the emcee and the
band on the stage.
   2. Medium shot.

72   The Burglars are stunned.

72   The Burglars.

73   Radio show. The band plays the first melody.

73   Radio show.

72   The Burglar on the phone knows the tune. He turns the radio on to hear it better— "Dancing in the Dark."

72   The Burglars.

73   The radio show. "That's right!" Second melody.

73   Radio show.

72   "Chinatown, My Chinatown," the Burglar correctly announces.

72   The Burglars.

73   The radio show. "That's correct!" Third and last one.

73   Radio show.

72   The second Burglar knows it—"The Sailor's Hornpipe."

72   The Burglars.

73   Radio show. "You won the jackpot!"

73   Radio show.

74   Later that night, the Needlemans, returning from the movie, find their house robbed.

74   Wide shot of the interior. The light comes on. The living room is in disorder, the window opened.

75   But the next morning a truck full of gifts arrives.

75   Medium shot of the Needlemans at their balcony, stunned. Zoom back to reveal the gifts, the truck, and the delivery men.

76   It's Yom Kippur, and the Communist neighbor's radio is blasting away. He's working and eating, but he's Jewish! In Little Joe's house, everyone is shocked. Abe's nerves are on edge, mostly, he admits, because

76   Wide shot of Abe and Ceil in the living room. Pan left with Mom crossing to the hallway, where she puts on Little Joe's yarmulke. Ruthie and Grandma are seen in the background in the kitchen. Pan right with

he's so hungry. He reminds
Ruthie what you're supposed to
do: "nothing, just sit, and pray,
and atone for your sins."
Encouraged by the rest of the
family, he decides to go and talk
to the Communist.

Mom, back to the living room.
Dolly in with Abe as he goes to
the window to look at the
Communists' house. Mom
enters on the right of the frame,
Ruthie on the left. Abe exits.

76A   Abe's POV. Long shot of
the Communists' yard. The
father hammers and the mother
hangs laundry.

76B   Another angle of the
Communists' yard. Close front
shot of the kid throwing a ball.
Dolly right and zoom back,
revealing Doris bringing her
father a sandwich.

77   The backyard. Abe appears.
beside himself, and dashes to the
Communist's yard, asking him
to turn off his radio. They
argue, then the Communist
suggests Abe come in and talk
about it.

77   High/wide long shot. Abe
comes through the door. Pan
with him as he crosses the yard
and goes to the Communist.

78   Two hours later, inside
Little Joe's house. Ceil is
worried. Abe is not back yet,
and the radio is still blaring.
Mom mentions that the
daughter believes in free love.
Then she tells what happened to
Mrs. Silverman.

78   Medium close-up of Ceil.
Pan right to medium shot of
Mom and Pop.

79   One evening, Mrs.
Silverman heard a car in the
street. She opened her door for
a look, sipping her cup of cocoa.

79   Mrs. Silverman's front
door. Her shadow appears. She
opens the door. Zoom in to
closer shot.

80   It's Doris, the Communist's
daughter, accompanied by a tall
black man. He takes her to the

R80   Mrs. Silverman's POV.
Long wide shot of Doris kissing
the black man.

door, and gives her "a big long kiss."

81 An ambulance arrives in the street.

81 Front/long shot of the ambulance appearing at the corner. Pan right with it as it approaches.

82 Mrs. Silverman, seeing the kiss, has had a stroke, and is put in the ambulance. She is mummified, still holding her cup of cocoa.

82 Dolly back with the attendants as they carry the mummified Mrs. Silverman to the ambulance.

83 We're back in the house. Ceil is impressed. But Abe comes back. And the radio is still on! What happened? For one thing, Abe ate. Then he starts talking peculiarly, with no guilt, and begins a speech on the exploitation of the workers by the bosses.

83 Master shot of Ceil, Mom, and Pop. Pan left to pick up Abe entering kitchen. Dolly right with him as he enters. Pan with him as he sits in the armchair.

84 *Bill Kern's Favorite Sports Legends*, Abe's favorite radio show. Today, Bill Kern is going to talk about Kirby Kyle, the baseball player who had heart.

84 Wide shot of Bill Kern telling the story.
84A Same as 84 but in close-up.

85 Abe listening to the radio, fascinated.

85 Wide shot of the family having dinner in the kitchen, with Abe standing next to the radio, rapt.

86 Baseball field. Kirby on the mound, throwing the ball.

86 Front medium shot of Kirby pitching to the camera.
86A High/wide shot of Kirby pitching and the batter swinging.

87 Kirby in the woods with his dog, hunting. His rifle goes off.

87 Dolly/long shot of Kirby running with his gun and dog

across the field. Then hold. He exits on the right of the frame.

88   Baseball field. Kirby throwing the ball with one leg, but with heart.

88   Front shot of Kirby pitching with one leg.

89   Kirby is back hunting. Another accident.

89   Close shot of Abe by the radio, totally rapt. The family is gone.

90   Baseball field. Kirby throwing the ball with one leg, one arm, but with heart.

90   Front shot of Kirby pitching with one leg and one arm.

91   Another accident.

91   Medium long shot of Kirby aiming his gun. Pan right to the ducks in the lake.

92   Baseball field. Kirby throwing the ball; he has one leg, one arm, and is blind, but also has instinct, instinct and heart.

92   Front shot of Kirby on the mound with one leg, one arm, and black glasses.

A93   Bill Kern in the studio. The following year, Kirby was run over by a truck. The following season, he won eighteen games in the big league in the sky.

A93   Bill Kern in the studio (end of 84).

93   (omit)

93   (omit)

94   *Future Stars of Tomorrow,* Ruthie's favorite radio show. A youngster singing.

94   Medium close-up of the little girl singing, "Let's All Sing Like the Birdies Sing."

95   Ruthie pantomimes a song in front of her mirror.

95   Dolly right around Ruthie singing and dancing "South American Way" in front of her mirror. Hold at the end as Abe and Pop join in.

96   *The Famous Ventriloquist,*
Ceil's favorite radio show. Ceil
listens to it at the radio,
laughing out loud at every joke.
Abe: "He's a ventriloquist on
radio. How do you know he's
not moving his lips?"

96   Wide shot of Mom and Ceil
sitting in the living room, Ceil
laughing. Abe comes down the
stairs, irritated, his paper in his
hand, and interrupts.

97   *Thomas Abercrombie,*
Mom and Pop's favorite radio
show. The World's Famous
Counselor on Affairs of the
Human Heart, and his Court of
Human Emotions. Abercrombie
counsels a couple who fight over
the husband's mother.

97   Close-up of the host
introducing the show. Pan right
to a front shot of Abercrombie
and the couple.

97A   Medium close-up of
Abercrombie. Pan left to a
medium close-up of the couple.

98   Little Joe imagines his
parents on Abercrombie's show.
They complain about each
other. Abercrombie thinks they
deserve each other. So they
gang up on him.

98   Medium close-up of
Abercrombie. Pan left to a
medium close-up of Mom and
Pop.

99   The only time Little Joe
met a radio star. His parents
have taken him to the zoo.

99   Medium long shot of an
elephant. Pan right to Little Joe
with Mom and Pop, watching
Sanford and his parents cross.
Dolly back for a shot of the six.

100   Sanford the Whiz Kid is
here with his parents.

(*see* 99)

101   Pop starts talking with
them. They answer coolly but
politely at first, then they
abruptly depart, snubbing them.

101   Medium front shot of
Little Joe and his parents, over
Sanford and his parents'
shoulder.

101A   Pickup shot of Little Joe
and his parents leaving.

101B   Medium front shot of
Sanford and his parents over

Little Joe and his parents'
shoulders.

101C   Pickup shot for Sanford's
last line.

A102   Bea always listened to
music. And to this day, there
are songs that remind Little Joe,
the minute he hears them of
people and events from the past.

RA102   Wide shot of Bea
sitting on the porch steps,
listening to the radio. Little Joe
and his gang run inside, then
run out with food.

A102A   Medium shot of Little
Joe drinking milk and Abe
eating fish. Pan right to Bea
standing next to the radio.

A102B   Bea's hand turning the
radio on.

A102C   Medium shot of Ruthie
sitting on her bed, reading
Screen Romance. Pan left to Bea
and Little Joe playing Chinese
checkers on Little Joe's bed.

B102   Little Evelyn (whom
Little Joe had a crush on but
who didn't like him) and Little
Linda, the pretty girl (who liked
him but whom he didn't like).
That was when he found out
what life was all about.

B102   Dolly right, following
Little Joe running along side
bathhouses. He runs down the
stairs. Pan left as he goes to kiss
Little Evelyn under the pilings.

B102A   Closer shot of Little Joe
kissing Little Evelyn. She
pushes him. Pan left to Little
Linda as she looks on sadly. Pan
back to Little Evelyn, who now
lets Little Joe kiss her.

C102   His parents' anniversary,
the only time he saw them kiss.
And his mom did something
that taught him about their
relationship: She took the man

C102   Wide shot of the family
around the dining room table.
Pop gives Mom a box. Mom
opens it. Dolly/zoom in on the
two as they kiss.

off the anniversary cake, and bit his head off.

D102   The day Little Joe and Andrew got into trouble for building a snowman with a penis.

E102   The time Mr. Zipsky had his nervous breakdown, and ran down the street in his underwear, wielding a meat cleaver.

F102   The day Bea took Little Joe with her date Chester to Radio City Music Hall.

C102A   Profile close-up of Ceil, Abe, and Ruthie. Dolly left to a profile close-up of Mom, Pop, and Little Joe.

RD102   Wide shot of Little Joe and Andrew finishing the snowman. Andrew puts in the carrot/penis. Zoom in. The principal comes out. They run away.

RE102   Zipsky comes out of his house. Pan left with him as he runs down Beach 115th Street. Zoom in as he runs back and forth on Rockaway Boulevard.

F102   Bea, Chester, and Little Joe come through the door. Pan right with them and Dolly/zoom back, revealing the Grand Foyer.

F102A   High wide shot as they walk through the Grand Foyer to the staircase. Pan left as they cross, climbing the stairs. They exit the frame. Zoom in on the chandelier.

F102B   Pan left with them as they arrive at the top of the stairs. Then pan right with them as they cross the mezzanine.

F102G   Long/front shot as they approach. Dolly back with them in medium shot and pan left as they cross the balcony. Hold on the balcony with the chandelier in the background. Little Joe comes back to look.

F102J   Front shot of them as they enter the theater and take seats.

G102   On a New York street, a man is giving tickets for the *Herbie Hanson* radio broadcast to reluctant pedestrians. He has success with only the weirdest ones.

(not filmed)

103   *The Herbie Hanson Show.* Backstage. The ratings are terrible. The producer thinks it is the script, and the head writer thinks that it is Herbie Hanson who is not funny. But the producer has had an idea. He gets four paid laughers, and one of them is Sally the cigarette girl. They give a demonstration of their talent.

CUT   103   Silhouette of the adman behind the closed door.

103A   Medium shot of the adman, and producer, and the gag writer.

103B   Medium shot of the two female paid laughers. Pan right to male laugher and Sally as they laugh.

103C   Wide shot of the producer and the adman as they watch the paid laughers.

104   Inside the theater. The audience rushes into their seats: "A casting nightmare."

CUT   (filmed but not used)

105   (omit)

106   The announcer reads the commercial for the Associated Life Insurance Company. ". . .and remember, life is short, but death is forever!" Then he introduces Herbie Hanson. Herbie starts his monologue. After the first joke, only the paid laughers laugh.

CUT   R106   (two cameras)
   1. Medium shot of the announcer introducing the show and Herbie. Pan right to Herbie's entrance. Hold on him for two jokes.
   2. Wide/long shot behind the audience. Same action.

After the second, same thing. He starts his third joke and Sally starts to laugh before he finishes. Herbie is annoyed— "That's not funny"—but Sally goes on, and the three other laughers join in. Now the audience starts to laugh at the paid laughers. The paid laughers like it and go on. The audience laughs even more, and Herbie gives up.

Then, one after the other the paid laughers stand up and give demonstrations of their laughs. The audience applauds each of them. Herbie begins to panic. The orchestra starts to play. Everybody quiets down.

Herbie is ready to start again, when he is pushed by a man running out from backstage. There's an interruption of the show for a special bulletin. In response to the Japanese bombing of Pearl Harbor, President Roosevelt has declared a state of war.

At the end of the message, the show goes on. Herbie is ready to start again, but the audience is rushing out.

R106A
1. Medium shot of Herbie cracking jokes.
2. Medium close-up of Herbie.

R106B
1. Medium shot of Herbie reacting to the paid laughers.
2. Medium close-up of Herbie.

R106C
1. Medium shot of Herbie pushed aside by the Pearl Harbor man, who reads the special bulletin. The audience leaves.
2. Wide/front shot from behind the audience.

R106D
1. Medium shot past Herbie to the audience for the first and second joke.
2. Wide shot of the audience. Same.

R106E
1. Closer shot of the four paid laughers.
2. Wide shot of the audience.

R106F
1. Close shot of the paid laughers as the audience leaves.
2. Wide shot of the audience.

A107   Radio studio. A singer sings "I'll Be Seeing You."

CUT   X107   Medium shot of the singer.

107   (on the song until 110)
A girl and a soldier kiss good-bye.

CUT   R107   Grand Central. Dolly/zoom back wide, revealing Sally and Charlie the soldier. Zoom in as they kiss.

108   Posters in an ice cream parlor: LOOSE LIPS . . . and DON'T LET THIS SHADOW FALL ON THEM.

108   Medium long shot of Ruthie and her girlfriends admiring the waitress in her WAC uniform.

R108   Pan from the flag to the teacher. Zoom back wide, revealing from behind the kids pledging allegiance to the flag.

109   Mrs. Riley in her Victory garden, growing vegetables in pots, smiling proudly and giving the V sign.

CUT   A109   Grand Central. Wide shot of Sally with Tom the sailor. Zoom in as they kiss.

109   Front shot of Mrs. Riley in front of her Victory garden. Zoom in as she points at the vegetables.

110   Cub Scouts collecting scrap iron.

CUT   A110   Grand Central. Wide shot of Sally with the marine. Zoom in as they kiss, then Sally speaks to the camera.

110   Dolly right with the kids to the container, where they drop the scrap iron.

111   Manhattan. A small crowd has gathered around a man with a microphone. It's a street interview. Mr. and Mrs. Globus, Mr. Brooks, and the Bigot give their opinions of the declaration of war.

CUT   111   Dolly/zoom back from the kiosk, revealing the group gathered around the newsman and his microphone.

112   Little Joe and his pals collect tin foil.
    Then the kids listen to the radio, to a message from the Masked Avenger, "Be on the lookout for enemy planes . . ."

112   Front shot of a housewife giving tin foil to Little Joe and his pals. Dolly back and pan right as they run down the stairs and on to the next house.

113 Little Joe's house. The
family is having dinner. Mom is
pregnant. Abe thinks the war is
good for business; production is
up, he says. Little Joe asks Pop
what his business is. He's a big
butter-and-egg man, Grandpa
answers. The bell rings. Bea has
a new date; he's lovely, very
sensitive, his fiancée died in a
car crash. Grandpa prays that
he'll be the one for her. And
Abe thinks he has to be 4F, since
all the men are in the army.

Fred appears. He's taking Bea
to the ballet, *Afternoon of a
Faun*. It makes him cry, he
explains.

Once they leave, everybody
has an opinion. Pop finds him a
little effeminate, and Abe thinks
that whatever he is, he's 4F.

CUT 113 Wide shot of the family
having dinner in the kitchen.
Pan and zoom in with Bea as she
crosses to go to open the door.
She returns with Fred. Hold on
them.

114 A little later, in the living
room, Pop is explaining a new
scheme to Mom—engraving.
Mom doesn't seem impressed,
and changes the subject to the
name they should give to the
baby.

114 Begin with a master shot,
then pan right with Pop crossing
the dining room to join Mom,
who is sitting in the living
room.

115 Little Joe is awake in his
bed, listening to the radio
downstairs.

115 High angle down the
stairs. Tilt up and pan left to
Little Joe's bedroom. Dolly in to
Little Joe listening.

116 Living room. The family
is listening to the news on the
radio. The news everywhere is
bad. The air-raid warden calls
from the street for a blackout.

116 Medium shot of Ceil at
the radio. Dolly right to reveal
Pop and Abe playing cards in
the dining room, then to Mom
sitting in the living room,

The family starts switching off
the lights.

117   Mom and Pop go outside
and look at the searchlights in
the sky. It's beautiful.

118   A little later, Little Joe is
awakened by music on the
radio. He sneaks out of his bed.

119   Little Joe spies on Fred
and Bea. Fred wants to go. Bea
tells him she thinks she has a
crush on him. Fred begins to
sob. It's the song on the radio,
which reminds him of his late
fiancée, Leonard. The awful
truth is dawning on Bea.

120   Exterior studio.

121   The *Biff Baxter, G-Man*
radio show is on. Biff Baxter is
beating the Nazis and the Japs,
both. The show ends. Biff
breaks down. Everybody tries to
cheer him up. But Biff is still
worried. What if his plan
doesn't work?

122   Draft physical. Biff Baxter
panics; his papers show he has

knitting. The warden is heard.
They stand up and switch the
lights off. Dolly left with Mom
and Pop crossing.

R117   Mom and Pop coming
out of the house, lighted by the
searchlights.

RR117   Mom and Pop's POV
of the searchlights.

(*see* 119)

119   Looking up the stairway
as Little Joe comes down. Pan
left and dolly right to kitchen.
Bea enters the frame to get
cookies, then exits.

119A   Master shot of Bea and
Fred at the kitchen table. Zoom
in as Bea moves closer to Fred.

120   Wide shot of the building
entrance. Tilt up to the top.

121   Medium shot through the
booth window of the three
actors from behind. Zoom back
for a wide shot, revealing the
announcer and the effects man.

121A   Medium front shot of
the effects man. Pan left to the
actors and the announcer. Zoom
in at the end on Biff and the
producer.

122   Master shot of men lined
up. Pan to Biff talking to the

asthma and every other
affliction. But the sergeant is a
tough guy. The doctor
announces that Biff is 4F—flat
feet. Biff screams with joy.

123   The *Biff Baxter* radio
show is on. Biff is beating the
Nazi.

124   Little Joe and his pals are
on the roof with binoculars to
spot Axis planes. Dave expresses
doubts about the fact they can
get over here so easily. But the
Masked Avenger said they
could! Suddenly Little Joe spots
something interesting.

125   Their POV. Miss Gordon
undressing by the window.

*124   The kids are all excited.
She's going to take a shower.
They make comments, but she
disappears from the window.

*Because of difficulties during
shooting, the shot numbers here
were changed.

sergeant. Dolly/zoom in as he
goes to the doctor.

123   Medium shot of the
effects man. Pan left to Biff and
the German.

124   Close-up of the cornice.
Boom up and dolly back,
revealing the five kids from
behind.

124A   Low wide angle. Front
shot of the kids at the edge of
the roof.

124B   Close-up of Nick. Pan
right to a close-up of Little Joe
as he spots something.

125   Kids' POV. Miss Gordon
undresses and disappears.

125A   Kids' POV. Miss Gordon
reappears wrapped in a towel.
The towel falls. She dances,
nude. But after a while, she
notices that she's being watched,
and closes the curtain.

125B   Close-up of Dave
reacting to Miss Gordon.

125C   Close-up of Burt's
reaction.

125D   Close-up of Andrew's
reaction.

126   (omit)

126   Front shot of the five kids.

127   Disappointed, they look to another window, and spot Mrs. Goldstein cooking.

124   But Nick spots something interesting:

128   Their POV: A man is at a short-wave radio. It's Mr. Rienzi.

128   Pan left to right on a medium close-up of the kids' faces.

128A   Kids' POV: Rienzi seen through his window with his short-wave radio.

124   He's surely a spy, and with a name like that, he must work for Mussolini!

129/130/131 (omit)

132   Another of the kids' POV. Miss Gordon is back at the window, completely naked, dancing in front of her mirror.

124   The kids are going crazy. They can't believe it! They're making comments . . .

133   The school hallway. The kids discuss sneaking into Rienzi's apartment after school today, "for our country."

CUT   133   Low angle of Rienzi's hallway. The kids sneak around the corner, approach, and exit to the left.

133A   Close shot of the kids coming through the door. Pan left with them and zoom back to reveal Rienzi's apartment.

R133B   Medium shot of Rienzi coming through the door. Pan left with him as he joins the kids.

A134   Wide shot of the kitchen with Ruthie and her boyfriend. They sit and start to kiss but Little Joe's voice comes out of the radio. The boyfriend leaves.

134   Classroom. With Little Joe and his pals among the others. Principal Peter announces that their regular teacher has the flu, and introduces the substitute teacher, Miss Gordon! The kids are stunned. Little Joe almost screams. Miss Gordon asks him to come to the blackboard. He starts dancing the way she did by the window. Miss Gordon is stunned.

134   Wide shot of the classroom. Pandemonium. Little Joe tells everyone that the principal is coming. They quiet down.

134A   Wide shot from behind the classroom of the principal as he enters the room.

134B   Wide shot of the classroom reacting to the principal. Then to Miss Gordon. Zoom in to Little Joe, Burt, and Andrew.

134C   Close-up of Little Joe and Andrew's reaction.

134D   Close-up of Burt's reaction.

134E   Close-up of Nick's reaction.

134F   Close-up of Dave's reaction.

134G   Another group of kids react to the principal.

134H   Medium shot of the principal. Pan right and zoom in to Miss Gordon coming through the door. Pan left as she joins the principal. The principal exits. Hold on Miss Gordon as she writes her name on the blackboard.

134J   Medium close-up of Miss Gordon writing at the board, then turning and asking Little Joe to come up.

134K   Medium shot of Little Joe. Dolly back and pan left with him as he goes to Miss Gordon. He dances.

134L   Close-up of Nick's reaction to Little Joe's dancing.

134M   Close-up of Little Joe's reaction to Miss Gordon's arrival.

135/136   (omit)

137   The kids are on the beach, talking about Miss Gordon and women in general; Rita Hayworth, Betty Grable, Dana Andrews . . . Then the kids go home, leaving Little Joe, who wants to be alone.

137   Long shot. Dolly left with the kids as they walk by the ocean. Hold.

137A   Front shot of Little Joe. Dolly with him as he walks alone by the water.

138   Looking at the sea, Little Joe is dreaming of Miss Gordon, when he sees a German U-boat surface! He faints.

138   The submarine emerging.

139   Sally begins to tell her story, talking to the camera.

CUT   139   Wide shot of Sally, dressed as an usher, taking tickets from theater patrons. Dolly/zoom in to a medium shot of her as she talks to the camera.

140   Adult-education class.
Sally takes a course to improve
her elocution. "Hark! I hear the
cannon roar . . ."

141   Exterior studio.

142   Sally sings the laxative
commercial, "Get Regular with
Re-Lax." The director, the
adman, and the writer argue
about her interpretation. The
sponsor likes her, but his wife
doesn't.

140   Wide shot of the adult-
education classroom from
behind.

140A   Wide front shot of the
classroom. Dolly/zoom in to the
terrible man.

140B   Close-up of a man
repeating the quotation.

140C   Close-up of an old lady.

140D   Close-up of the man
with the French accent.

140E   Close-up of the
housewife with the green hat.

140F   Medium close-up of
Sally.

141   Tilt down from the top of
the RCA building to the
entrance.

142   Medium shot through the
booth window of the band
playing. Dolly right to Sally
singing. Pan right to the
director, the writer, and the
adman inside the booth, behind
the console.

142A   Medium close-up of
Sally and the whistler, the
director, and others in the
background.

142B   Medium close-up of
adman Bill. Pan right to the
sponsor and his wife, Doris.

A143   Tilt down from the
Sardi's sign to Sally approaching
in the street. Dolly back with
her.

143   Sally sings for the USO.

R143   Long shot. Dolly right, past the crowd from behind, to Sally singing onstage.

R143A   Close-up of a poster. Dolly left and zoom in to Sally singing. Zoom back to a front shot of her.

144   *The Gay White Way* radio show. Sally has her own show now, a Hedda Hopper–style gossip show.

144   Studio columns. Dolly in and pan right, revealing the announcer. Pan left and zoom in to Sally.

144A   Pan right from the radio to Abe and Ceil on the bed. Pan left, with Abe going to the radio and hitting it.

145   Little Joe in a radio-repair shop retrieving a big radio.

(not filmed)

146   Little Joe, the huge radio in his arms, walking down the street.
   He goes along the highway, stops a cab, and gets in.

146   Long shot of Little Joe exiting the repair shop, the huge radio in his arm.

146A   Long shot of Little Joe with the radio on the highway. A cab stops. Little Joe gets inside.

147   The driver is Pop. He says he's just helping a friend.

147   Close shot of Little Joe shoving the radio into the cab. He discovers that the driver is Pop.

147A   Close-up of Pop. He says he's helping a friend.

148   The cab pulls away.

148   Close-up of the rear of the cab. Long shot as it drives away.

149   The same radio personality singing "They're Either Too Young or Too Old."

X149   Medium close-up of the singer.

150 (Over the song:) Bea is in her room painting nylons on her legs.

150 Close-up of Bea's leg as she paints on her nylons. Zoom back as she primps.

151 (Over the song:) Ruthie staring moon-eyed at a sailor.

151 Medium shot of the sailor and a girl kissing. Zoom back to reveal Ruthie swooning.

152 (omit)

153 Little Joe's house. Ceil tries to come up with a coffee slogan so she can win a refrigerator. Abe thinks the whole thing is a fraud. Mom and Pop join in the slogan writing. Suddenly, Mom begins to go into labor.

153 Medium shot of Abe and Ceil in their room. Pan left to Mom and Pop in their room. Mom goes into labor. Dolly/zoom back with them as they cross the hallway. Pan left and tilt down as they go down the stairs.

154 The whole family at the hospital visiting Mom, who has just given birth to Little Joe's little sister.

RR154 Pan right with the nurse to the whole family around Mom's bed.

155 Stock footage of Times Square.

156 Exhibition Hall. Bea and her new boyfriend Sy take Little Joe for a tour of Manhattan.

156 Tilt down from THE WINGS OVER AMERICA poster to a close shot of Sy and Little Joe behind a cannon. Dolly left and zoom back to a profile of Bea, Sy, and Little Joe.

157 At the arcade, the distorting mirrors.

157 Horn and Hardart Automat. Dolly/pan right along the food dispensers to the mirror, revealing Bea, Sy, and Little Joe in reflection.

158   At the Tango Palace. Bea
dances with Sy. Little Joe
watches.

158   Medium shot of the band
playing. Pan left and zoom back
to a wide shot of the dancers.

158A   Pan right from a sailor,
past Little Joe, to a medium shot
of Bea and Sy dancing—dolly
left with them, then lose them,
and pan left on to a medium
shot of Little Joe watching.

159   In the street, they're
offered free tickets to a radio
broadcast.

(not filmed)

160   *The Silver Dollar Jackpot.*
Bea is a contestant. She chooses
fish for her category. She
identifies all six of them, and
wins the jackpot.

160   (two cameras)
  1. Long shot from behind the
audience to the stage with the
band and the emcee. Bea comes
onstage. Applause and fanfare.
  2. High/wide angle.

160A
  1. Medium shot of the emcee
and Bea. A man enters with the
fish.
  2. Medium close-up of the
three actors.

160B   Wide shot of the
audience reacting, laughing, and
applauding.

160C   Medium close-up of the
emcee and Bea.

160D   Long shot of the band,
the emcee, and Bea for the final
fanfare.

160E   Wide shot of the
audience. Zoom in to Sy and
Little Joe, laughing and
applauding.

161 Bea, Sy, and Little Joe exiting Macy's where Bea bought Little Joe a chemistry set. Sy tells Bea that in one week, he will be free from his wife and children.

162 Little Joe's house. Pop is explaining a new scheme to Mom: He wants to ship bagels and lox to Jewish families in the South who cannot get them for their Sunday breakfast. Mom finds the idea idiotic, and doesn't have the strength to tell him why.

162X Abe has brought a sack of eels. Ceil wonders if eels are kosher. Bea starts to dance the conga, which has just started on the radio.

162Y Mr. Waldbaum complains from his yard about Ruthie. Ruthie hangs up and joins Bea in the conga. Grandma is looking for her teeth again. Grandpa complains she can't keep track of them. Mom appears, screaming, chasing Little Joe; he dyed the fur coat Pop gave her for their anniversary, using his chemistry set. Now Pop is chasing Little Joe through the house, while the conga plays. Abe suggests that everybody take the gas pipe.

Pop catches Little Joe and starts hitting him. But the conga is interrupted for a special bulletin. In a Pennsylvania field,

161 Master shot of Bea, Sy, and Little Joe exiting Macy's. Dolly back with them.

162 Medium shot of Pop in the dining room. Pan right with him to the kitchen door. Mom emerges from the kitchen. Hold on medium close-up of Pop. Pan left with him to the living room; Ruthie is at the phone in the background.

162X Medium shot of Ceil at the window. Pan right to Abe in the yard with the eels. Dolly/zoom in to Mr. Waldbaum complaining from his window.

162A Medium shot of Ruthie in the hallway hanging up the phone. Pan right, revealing Bea dancing the conga in the dining room. Abe appears with eels. Ruthie joins Bea to dance the conga around the table.

162B Pan left from the kitchen to the living room with Grandma looking for her teeth. Grandpa follows.

162C Master shot of Mom coming down the stairs chasing Little Joe. Pan right with her from the hallway to the dining room. Pop catches Little Joe, but Little Joe escapes. Pop chases him. Dolly left to pick them up eight-year-old Polly Phelps has fallen into a well. She has been trapped for seven hours. Pop stops hitting Little Joe, and all the family listens.

163   The Pennsylvania field, in the night. Car headlights. The Newsman stands next to the jockey, who failed in his try to descend into the well. Fireman Reilly calls into the well to Polly. No answer.

164   The Newsman is interviewing a man: "Shouldn't the well be boarded up?"

A165   Polly's family. Her mom sobs in her pop's arms.

165   Little Joe's family, now totally rapt, gathered around the radio.

166   Other listeners are the Communists, the Waldbaums, and so forth. On the radio, the Newsman gives details about Polly's life: her dog, Cleo . . .

running through the kitchen. Dolly right with them as they start another lap. Pan left to find them in the hallway, then pan right as Pop catches Little Joe and starts hitting him. The special bulletin is heard. Zoom in on them as Pop stops hitting Little Joe.

R163   Medium close-up of the Newsman. Dolly left to a long shot of the glaring lights, the cars, and the crowd.

163A   Dolly left in a medium shot along the well as Fireman Reilly calls for Polly.

164   Medium shot of the Newscaster interviewing the Polly Phelps Man. Dolly/zoom in on them.

(not filmed)

165   Wide/long shot of the family listening in the kitchen. Slow dolly in to a closer shot.

166   Dolly back to a wide shot of the Communist family listening.

166A   Medium shot of Mr. Waldbaum turning up the radio as Mrs. Waldbaum crosses.

166B   Medium long shot of Mrs. Needleman. Pan to the radio, then pan to Mr. Needleman listening.

166C Dolly/zoom back to a wide shot of the rich couple listening.

167 The Pennsylvania field. The Priest is with the little girl's parents. Fireman Reilly has suggested lowering a midget. They're doing it now. But the Midget gets stuck! Finally, they succeed in lowering him.

167 Medium close-up of the Newsman. Dolly/pan left past the crowd to Fireman Reilly lowering the Midget.

167A Master shot. Pan left on the crowd watching.

168 Various listeners, totally rapt.
The Newsman announces the Midget has found her, and the two of them are being pulled from the well.

168A Wide shot of a pub with the patrons listening.

168B Close shot of a newsstand man in his kiosk.

168C Medium shot of a woman sitting alone in a snack bar.

168D Zoom back from the parrot to a wide shot of the rich woman in her bathtub.

169 The Pennsylvania field. She's out; everybody is pushing to see. The Priest is praying.

169 Dolly left with the Newscaster walking through the crowd.

170 Little Joe's family. The Newsman announces Polly's death.

170 Pan right in close-up on the family's stunned faces.

171 Pennsylvania field. Polly's family, sobbing.

171 Medium close-up of Polly's parents sobbing. Dolly left past the flashing lights to the Priest praying.

172 Other listeners, also stunned.

172A Pan in close-up from Doris and her brother to their parents.

172B Medium close-up of the Waldbaums, stunned.

172C   Medium close-up of the pub's patrons gathered at the bar, stunned.

172D   Close shot of the rich family with the butler, stunned.

173   Mom and Pop hold Little Joe warmly.

R173   Ceil, Mom, Pop, and Little Joe, stunned. Zoom in on Pop and Little Joe.

174   The Pennsylvania field. It is over. Everybody is going home.

174   Long shot of the crowd going home. Dolly and pan left to a close shot of the rear of the radio truck as the doors close. Lights go out.

175   The King Cole Room. It's New Year's Eve. The band leader introduces Monica Charles. She sings.

A175   (two cameras)
   1. Wide establishing shot. The band plays and the band leader makes the introduction.
   2. Medium close-up of band leader.
175
   1. Wide shot of Monica Charles singing.
   2. Medium close-up

176   Sally, now a radio personality, arrives with her date, the Masked Avenger.

176   Wide shot of Sally coming in with the Avenger. Dolly/zoom back as they join the table of radio personalities.

177   Irene is being interviewed on the stage. She wishes that 1944 will bring peace and our boys home.

177   (two cameras)
   1. Wide shot of Irene on stage.
   2. Medium close-up.

178   Sally joins a table of radio personalities. We recognize the Reba Man, Bill Kern, Herbie

178   Dolly right in medium close-up along the radio personalities' table.

Hanson. They all laugh and
drink. Sally suggests going to
the roof. There is a beautiful
view from there, she says.

179   The band plays onstage.

179A   (two cameras)
1. Pan left to Sally and the
Avenger. Tilt up as they stand
to go to the roof.
2. Wide shot. Pan from the
dancers to the band playing.

180   Sally and her group arrive
on the roof with bottles and
glasses. Looking at all the lights
of the city, they become
nostalgic. What is 1944 going to
be like? And what are they
going to become? All those
people in their homes, listening
to them. Are future generations
going to remember them?

180   The group comes through
the door. Zoom back and dolly
right with Sally and the
Avenger as they go to the edge
of the roof.

180B   Medium shot of Irene
with the announcer of her show.
Dolly left and pan right with
Roger crossing and joining Biff
Baxter under the water tank.

180C   Medium close-up of
Sally, the Avenger, and Max.

181   Downstairs, in the King
Cole Room, it's midnight.
Everybody cheers, and the band
plays "Auld Lang Syne."

181   (two cameras)
1. Pan from the crowd, past
the dancers to the band onstage.
2. Wide shot.

182   Little Joe's house. The
family celebrates, too. Bea has
awakened Little Joe. She hopes
the war will be over soon, so the
men can come back. Ceil feels
"in her bones" that Bea is going
to meet her man this year.
Mom is a little anxious about
the future, but Pop is optimistic.
Abe suggests having red
snapper; it's very good with
champagne.

182   Master shot of the family
celebrating in the dining room.
Pan left to Bea and Little Joe
coming down the stairs. Pan
back with them as they join the
others.

183   On the King Cole roof, everyone cheers the arrival of the New Year. Sally dances with the Avenger, who yells his signature phrase, "Beware, Evildoers, wherever you are!" Sally laughs. They dance on.

183   Pan left to right on the group celebrating. It starts snowing. Pan right with the group as they go through the door. Then after the Avenger has given his warning and closed the door, pan left to the empty roof.

Credits

A Jack Rollins and Charles H. Joffe Production

RADIO DAYS

Associate Producers   Ezra Swerdlow, Gail Sicilia

Musical Supervision   Dick Hyman

Casting   Juliet Taylor

Costume Designer   Jeffrey Kurland

Editor   Susan E. Morse, A.C.E.

Production Designer   Santo Loquasto

Director of Photography   Carlo Di Palma, A.I.C.

Executive Producers   Jack Rollins, Charles H. Joffe

Produced by   Robert Greenhut

Written and Directed by   Woody Allen

Production Manager   Thomas Reilly

First Assistant Director   Ezra Swerdlow

Second Assistant Director   Ken Ornstein

Production Coordinator   Helen Robin

Script Supervisor   Kay Chapin

Assistant to Mr. Allen   Jane Read Martin

Production Associate   Joseph Hartwick

Assistant Production Manager   Timothy M. Bourne

Art Director		Speed Hopkins

Assistant Art Directors		W. Steven Graham, Dan Davis, Tom Warren, Michael Smith, Randall Drake, Steve Saklad

Art Department Research		Glenn Lloyd

Set Decorators		Carol Joffe, Les Bloom

Set Dresser		Dave Weinman

Property Master		James Mazzola

Master Scenic Artist		James Sorice

Standby Scenic Artist		Cliff Schorr

Construction Coordinator		Ron Petagna

Chief Construction Grip		Arne Olsen

Camera Operator		Dick Mingalone

Assistant Cameraperson		Michael Green

Second Assistant Cameraperson		Jay Levy

Camera Trainee		Liz Dubelman

Still Photographer		Brian Hamill

Key Grip		Bob Ward

Dolly Grip		Ronald Burke

Gaffer		Ray Quinlan

Best Boy		Jim Manzione

Production Sound Mixer		James Sabat

Boom Operator		Louis Sabat

Sound Recordist		Frank Graziadei

Rerecording Mixer		Lee Dichter, Sound One Corp.

Musicians Coordinator		Joe Malin

Music Recording Engineer		Roy B. Yokelson

Assistant Engineer		Diane Andolsek

Music Recording Supervisors		Walt Levinsky, Sam Parkins

Makeup Design	Fern Buchner
Hair Design	Romaine Greene
Assistant Costume Designer	Judiana Makovsky
Men's Wardrobe Supervisor	Bill Christians
Women's Wardrobe Supervisor	Patricia Eiben
Costume Assistants	Alvin Perry, Lauren Gibson, Deborah Lancaster, Jessica Fasman
Supervising Sound Editor	Bob Hein
Sound Editor	Michael Moyse
Assistant Film Editors	Martin Levenstein, Jon Neuburger
Assistant Sound Editors	Frank Kern, Barbara Minor
Apprentice Sound Editor	Amy Briamonte
Projectionist	Carl Turnquest, Jr.
Assistant Production Coordinator	Amy Herman
Production Auditor	Peter Lombardi
DGA Trainee	Judy Ferguson
Casting Associate	Ellen Lewis
Additional Casting	Todd M. Thaler
Transportation Captain	Harold "Whitey" McEvoy
Studio Manager	Steve Rose
Vocal Coach for Ms. Farrow and Ms. Keaton	Janet Frank
Location Scouts	Richard Baratta, Nicholas Bernstein, James Davis, Barbara Heller, Tom Paolucci, Gilbert S. Williams
Production Staff	Claudette Didul, Judie Fixler, Barbara Green, Doug Ornstein, Richard Patrick, Tracy Robin, Drew Rosenberg, Larry Rudolph, Angela Salgado, Scott Schaffer, Jay Scherick, Jordan Thaler
Color by	DuArt Film Laboratories, Inc.
Prints by	DeLuxe ®

Optical Effects   R/Greenberg Associates

Titles   The Optical House, N.Y

Negative Matching   J. G. Films, Inc.

LENSES AND PANAFLEX ® CAMERAS BY PANAVISION ®

CAST (*in order of appearance*)

Mike Starr, Paul Herman   *Burglars*

Don Pardo   Guess That Tune *Host*

Martin Rosenblatt   *Mr. Needleman*

Helen Miller   *Mrs. Needleman*

Danielle Ferland   *Child Star*

Julie Kavner   *Mother*

Julie Kurnitz   *Irene*

David Warrilow   *Roger*

Wallace Shawn   *Masked Avenger*

Michael Murray   *Avenger Crook*

William Flanagan   *Avenger Announcer*

Seth Green   *Joe*

Michael Tucker   *Father*

Josh Mostel   *Abe*

Renee Lippin   *Ceil*

William Magerman   *Grandpa*

Leah Carrey   *Grandma*

Joy Newman   *Ruthie*

Hy Anzell   *Mr. Waldbaum*

Judith Malina   *Mrs. Waldbaum*

Dianne Wiest   *Bea*

Fletcher Farrow Previn   *Andrew*

Oliver Block   *Nick*

Maurice Toueg   *Dave*

Sal Tuminello   *Burt*

Rebecca Nickels   *Evelyn Goorwitz*

Mindy Morgenstern   *Show and Tell Teacher*

David Mosberg   *Arnold*

Ross Morgenstern   *Ross*

Kenneth Mars   *Rabbi Baumel*

Andrew Clark   *Sidney Manulis*

Mia Farrow   *Sally White*

Lee Erwin   *Roller Rink Organist*

Roger Hammer   *Richard*

Terry Lee Swarts, Margaret Thomson   *Nightclub Customers*

Tito Puente   *Latin Bandleader*

Denise Dummont   *Latin Singer*

Dimitri Vassilopoulos   *Porfirio*

Larry David   *Communist Neighbor*

Rebecca Schaeffer   *Communist's Daughter*

Belle Berger   *Mrs. Silverman*

Guy Le Bow   *Bill Kern*

Brian Mannain   *Kirby Kyle*

Stan Burns   *Ventriloquist*

Todd Field   *Crooner*

Peter Lombard   *Abercrombie Host*

Martin Sherman   *Mr. Abercrombie*

Crystal Field, Maurice Shrog   *Abercrombie Couple*

Marc Colner   *Whiz Kid*

Robert Bennett   *Teacher with Carrot*

Joel Eidelsberg   *Mr. Zipsky*

Danny Aiello   *Rocco*

Peter Castellotti   *Mr. Davis*

Gina DeAngelis   *Rocco's Mother*

Shelley Delaney   *Chekhov Actress*

Dwight Weist   *Pearl Harbor Announcer*

Ken Levinsky, Ray Marchica   *USO Musicians*

Jeff Daniels   *Biff Baxter*

J. R. Horne   *Biff Announcer*

Kuno Spunholz   *German*

Henry Yuk   *Japanese*

Sydney A. Blake   *Miss Gordon*

Kitty Carlisle Hart   *Radio Singer*

Robert Joy   *Fred*

Henry Cowen   *Principal*

Philip Shultz   *Whistler*

Mercedes Ruehl, Bruce Jarchow   *Admen*

Greg Gerard   *Songwriter*

David Cale   *Director*

Ira Wheeler   *Sponsor*

Hannah Rabinowitz   *Sponsor's Wife*

Edward S. Kotkin   *Diction Teacher*

Ruby Payne, Jaqui Safra   *Diction Students*

Paul Berman   Gay White Way *Announcer*

Richard Portnow   *Sy*

Tony Roberts   Silver Dollar *Emcee*

Barbara Gallo, Jane Jarvis, Liz Vochecowizc   *Dance Palace Musicians*

Ivan Kronenfeld   *On-the-Spot Newsman*

Frank O'Brien   *Fireman*

Yolanda Childress   *Polly's Mother*

Artie Butler   *New Year's Singer*

Diane Keaton   *New Year's Singer*

Gregg Almquist, Jackson Beck, Wendell Craig, W. H. Macy, Ken Roberts, Norman Rose, Robert Tate, Kenneth Walsh   *Radio Voices*

"The Flight of the Bumblebee"
by N. A. Rimsky-Korsakov
Performed by Harry James
Courtesy of CBS Records

"Dancing in the Dark"
by Arthur Schwartz and Howard
Dietz

"Chinatown, My Chinatown"
by William Jerome and Jean
Schwartz

"Let's All Sing Like the Birdies
Sing"
by Roger Hargreaves, Stanley J.
Damerell, and Tolchard Evans

"I Double Dare You"
by Jimmy Eaton and Terry Shand
Performed by Larry Clinton
Courtesy of RCA Records

"You're Getting to Be a Habit with
Me"
by Harry Warren and Al Dubin

"September Song"
by Kurt Weill and Maxwell
Anderson

"Body and Soul"
by John W. Green, Edward
Heyman, Robert Sour, and Frank
Eyton Performed by Benny
Goodman Courtesy of RCA
Records

"In the Mood"
by Joe Garland
Performed by Glenn Miller
Courtesy of RCA Records

Radio Show Themes
by Dick Hyman

"Carioca"
by Vincent Youmans, Gus Kahn,
and Edward Eliscu

"Tico, Tico"
by Zequinha Abreu, Aloysio
Oliveira,
and Erwin Drake

"La Cumparsita"
by Matos Rodriguez
Performed by the Castilians
Courtesy of MCA Records

"Frenesi"
by A. Dominguez
Performed by Artie Shaw
Courtesy of RCA Records

"All or Nothing At All"
by Jack Lawrence and Arthur
Altman

"The Donkey Serenade"
by Herbert Stothart, Rudolf Friml,
Bob Wright, and Chet Forrest
Performed by Allan Jones
Courtesy of RCA Records

"South American Way"
by Al Dubin and Jimmy McHugh
Performed by Carmen Miranda
Courtesy of MCA Records

"Mairzy Doats"
by Milton Drake, Al Hoffman,
and Jerry Livingston
Performed by The Merry Macs
Courtesy of MCA Records

"If You Are But a Dream"
by Moe Jaffe, Jack Fulton, and Nat
Bonx
Performed by Frank Sinatra
Courtesy of CBS Records

"Begin the Beguine"
by Cole Porter

"Opus One"
by Sy Oliver
Performed by Tommy Dorsey
Courtesy of RCA Records

"You and I"
by Meredith Willson
Performed by Tommy Dorsey
Courtesy of RCA Records

"Paper Doll"
by Johnny S. Black
Performed by the Mills Brothers
Courtesy of MCA Records

"Pistol Packin' Mama"
by Al Dexter
Performed by Bing Crosby and
The Andrews Sisters
Courtesy of MCA Records

"If I Didn't Care"
by Jack Lawrence
Performed by The Ink Spots
Courtesy of MCA Records

"Schloff mein Kind"
Performed by Emil Decameron
Courtesy of Vanguard Recording
Society, Inc.

"I Don't Want to Walk Without
You"
by Jule Styne and Frank Loesser

"Remember Pearl Harbor"
by Sammy Kaye and Don Reid
Performed by Sammy Kaye
Courtesy of RCA Records

"Babalu"
by Margarita Lecuona and S. K.
Russell
Performed by Xavier Cugat
Courtesy of PolyGram Records

"They're Either Too Young or Too
Old"
By Arthur Schwartz and Frank
Loesser

"That Old Feeling"
by Lew Brown and Sammy Fain
Performed by Guy Lombardo
Courtesy of RCA Records

"Re-Lax Jingle"
by Dick Hyman

"Lullaby of Broadway"
by Al Dubin and Harry Warren
Performed by Richard Himber
Courtesy of RCA Records

"American Patrol"
by F. W. Meacham
Performed by Glenn Miller
Courtesy of RCA Records

"Take the 'A' Train"
by Billy Strayhorn
Performed by Duke Ellington
Courtesy of RCA Records

"(There'll Be Blue Birds Over)
The White Cliffs of Dover"
by Walter Kent and Nat Burton
Performed by Glenn Miller
Courtesy of RCA Records

"Goodbye"
by Gordon Jenkins
Performed by Benny Goodman
Courtesy of RCA Records

"I'm Gettin' Sentimental over
You"
by Ned Washington and George
Bassman
Performed by Tommy Dorsey
Courtesy of RCA Records

"You'll Never Know"
by Harry Warren and Mack
Gordon

"One, Two, Three, Kick"
by Xavier Cugat and Al Stillman
Performed by Xavier Cugat
Courtesy of RCA Records

"Just One of Those Things"
by Cole Porter

"You'd Be So Nice to Come Home
to"
by Cole Porter

"Night and Day"
by Cole Porter

The Producers Wish to Thank the Following for Their Assistance:

The Mayor's Office of Film, Theatre, and Broadcasting

Albert G. Ruben Insurance Co., Inc.	Antique Wireless Association, Inc.
On Location Education, Inc.	Lee Lighting America Ltd.
St. Regis-Sheraton Hotel	General Camera Corp.
Pepsi-Cola Company	Sessums and Slagle
Donald Saddler	Paul Huntley, Ltd.

Filmed at Kaufman Astoria Studios in New York

EPILOGUE

DECEMBER 18, 1986, at Astoria Studios in Queens. While press
screenings have already begun for *Radio Days*, Woody is finishing
the shooting of his next film. He started in October and should be
done by the first week of January. A week of reshoots is planned
for the end of January—the same week *Radio Days* will be released in New York.

A big house has been built in the middle of the sound stage,
and Mia Farrow, Dianne Wiest, and Sam Shepard are working on a
scene.

Because several of the actors in this film have other engage-
ments, Woody is shooting the film in continuity, and though he
doesn't like it, editing it as he goes. For these reasons, he is also
reshooting instantly.

Now we are reshooting a scene with Mia Farrow and Sam Shepard. The scene is not easy, and Sam has trouble with some of
the dialogue as well as with the blocking. He asks to have some
of his lines cut, and suggests changes in the blocking. Woody listens, observes, and agrees most of the time. It is this openness of
mind that, one year later, still amazes me: the total lack of self-
indulgence, the readiness to change, to adapt to a new situation or
the needs of an actor. Maybe it is this mixture of confidence in his
talent, linked with perpetual seeking, that makes Woody a true
artist.

The day goes on in the same atmosphere of complicity and quiet intensity as the previous shooting had. All the faces are the same, including the grips, the electricians, and the teamsters, and it is as if the shooting of *Radio Days* were simply continuing.

However, for me, the journey must now end. It has been a great experience, full of surprises and discoveries that I have tried to share in writing this book. Perhaps the biggest surprise of all came last June, when I saw the final premix print of *Radio Days*. As I was watching the movie, beyond living with Bea's problems, Abe's fish, Roger's needs, and Sally's ingenuity, I experienced something I had totally missed while reading the script and witnessing the shooting: I was deeply moved.

As *Hannah and Her Sisters* (Woody Allen Fall Project 1984) is competing for the Oscars, *Radio Days* (W.A.F.P. '85) will be released, and the shooting of W.A.F.P. '86 will be ending. But, as usual, Woody is farther ahead: Everybody has been informed that shooting of the next film will start in August (W.A.S.P. '87), when it is not too cold outside.

New York
December 1986